[handwritten inscription]

Christmas. 1905.

Mr.. Mrs. Fitzhugh.

Brigham Young

Brigham Young

By

M. R. Werner

Author of "Barnum"

Illustrated

New York

Harcourt, Brace and Company

COPYRIGHT, 1925, BY
HARCOURT, BRACE AND COMPANY, INC.

Copyright, 1924, 1925, by
The Curtis Publishing Company

First edition, June, 1925

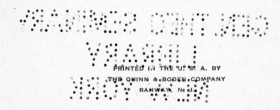

To
WILLIAM L. O'BRIEN

PREFACE

It is impossible to write the life of Brigham Young without also writing the history of Mormonism, and it is impossible to write the history of Mormonism without writing the life of Joseph Smith, Jr., its author and proprietor. This book attempts to carry out the three tasks together, but I do not claim that I have written a complete history of Mormonism up to the present day. It has been my aim to write that history as it was affected by the personality of Brigham Young, and as it affected his personality. But one cannot write about Brigham Young without explaining Joseph Smith. However, I am primarily interested in Brigham Young, because it is my conviction that without Brigham Young the Mormons would never have been important after the first few years of their institutional life, but without the Mormons Brigham Young might have been a great man. He was the sturdy character among the leaders of the Mormon movement, and it is due to his personality rather than to any other factor that Mormonism developed into a widespread creed and an extraordinary economic organization. That personality was an exceptional compound of unbounded religious enthusiasm and practical economic and political ability. On the celebration of his birthday in Utah many years after his death a rhetorical anniversary orator said: "He was a Vermont Pericles, an American Cromwell, a Western Columbus." A more temperate admirer, Lincoln's Secretary of State, William H. Seward, is credited with the remark that America had never produced a greater statesman than Brigham Young. Brigham Young himself put the matter more simply when he said to his people in the course of a sermon: "I am a Yankee; I guess things, and very frequently I guess right."

It is necessary to recall the importance of the Mormon movement in American affairs during the span of Brigham Young's life, from June, 1801, until August, 1877. Its political and economic significance, as well as its influence on social life, cannot be overestimated. The two permanent issues of the government from 1830, when Mormonism was founded, until 1877, when

Brigham Young died, were slavery and Mormonism. Other issues came, were solved, or solved themselves, but it seemed to the politicians of the period that slavery and Mormonism would be with them forever, and therefore they did not find it necessary to do anything about them until acute circumstances compelled hasty action. During the first fifty years of the nineteenth century there was almost as much worry throughout the United States about Mormonism as there was about slavery. At the organization of the Republican Party Brigham Young and his Mormons occupied the attention of the platform framers, and in the campaign processions of General John C. Frémont there was a large banner reading: "The Abolishment of Slavery and Polygamy; the Twin Relics of Barbarism." By 1840, ten years after the organization of the Church, Mormonism had become a national issue and had aroused international interest. Even those who wrote rabidly against them admitted in their prefaces that it was important to fathom the depths of rascality of this people. They had to admit Mormons were peculiar and extraordinary, much as they wished to make them out only criminal and profane. From 1840 until the death of Brigham Young Mormonism continued to arouse the perplexity of the nation and the curiosity of various peoples in the world. Even to-day statements about the Mormons are found occasionally in the newspapers, when some one contends that they are, or are not, practising polygamy, or that they do, or do not, dominate politics.

The story of the Mormons in the history of the United States is a great drama, and it is one of the few stories of that stature in our past. With that fatal inevitability which constitutes tragedy, the elements of Mormon philosophy and economics were, in the circumstances of the United States of the period, sure to produce opposition and persecution. And the Mormons could no more have changed these elements of their philosophy and economics than they could have changed the color of their eyes. Their struggle was not, as their contemporaries tried to make out, a simple conflict of right and wrong, but a more intricate clash of personalities and ambitions. From the beginning when, through their prophet, Joseph Smith, Jr., the Mormons claimed direct communion with God, other people who did not dare to aspire to such distinction, defamed the characters of their leaders, and drove the followers from their homes, until the end, when, at the age of seventy-one, Brigham Young was arrested for lascivious cohabitation, the story of Brigham Young and the Mormons is one long series of struggles against men and nature. Even to-day the story retains elements of mild tragedy. It may be said by some that the Mormons have triumphed over their environment, for the Census Bureau now credits them with more than 400,000 members, and the Church is immensely wealthy, but polygamy, one of the distinctive spiritual fruits of their new revelation, is against the law of the land, and the same spirit of skepticism which is beginning to doubt the virgin birth of Christ is beginning, among the younger generation of Utah, to question the visions of Joseph Smith, Jr.

Viscount Amberly in a study of Mormonism summed up its past achievements admirably:

"In a nation remarkable for its toleration of every creed, it has excited the most implacable hatred, calling down upon itself a sanguinary persecution, from which it has emerged stronger than before. In an unexplored and barren region, it has founded a flourishing colony which is likely before long to take its place as a State of the American Union. In the midst of a Democratic Republic, it has erected a Theocratic despotism. Among believers, accustomed from infancy to think that all revelation had closed with the last book of the New Testament, it has procured the acceptance of a new revelation as equal in authority to the Bible, and has established the persuasion that men are still inspired, as they were of old, to communicate the will of God to mankind. Among races accustomed for centuries to look with abhorrence upon the practice of polygamy, it has implanted in its followers the firm conviction that to be the husband of many wives is an act of the highest virtue."

It is my purpose to show how these things happened. It is not my intention to expose Mormonism. My conviction is that Mormonism is a perfect example of religion carried to its illogical conclusions, and that is what makes it more fascinating than most of the dissenting sects in the religious history of the United States. All other sects were amazed by its effrontery and outraged by its acts only because the Mormon leaders were men with literal minds; they determined to puzzle out exactly what the Bible meant in everything it said and to act upon what other churchgoers were content merely to repeat. And the Mormon minds were so literal and so untrained that they could not understand the persecution which was visited upon them by the Christians of other denominations and by the exponents of other economic and political beliefs. This persecution bewildered, baffled, and enraged them. To take the Bible seriously was both their crime and their misfortune, and it was too bad for their comfort that there was not a little cynicism in their fanaticism.

Neither do I intend to accept the Mormon theology. Gibbon has pointed out the necessary attitude: "The theologian may indulge the pleasing task of describing Religion as she descended from Heaven, arrayed in her native purity. A more melancholy duty is imposed on the historian. He must discover the inevitable mixture of error and corruption which she contracted in a long residence upon earth, among a weak and degenerate race of beings." My attitude towards the religious emotions and experiences recorded by Joseph Smith, Brigham Young, and the men around them is based on the advice of William James: "The only sound plan, if we are ourselves outside the pale of such emotions, is to observe as well as we are able those who feel them, and to record faithfully what we observe."

Mormon and anti-Mormon literature is frequently unreliable. Most anti-Mormon writers, and some Mormon writers, like the inhabitants of that mythical South Sea Island where people live by taking in each other's washing, live by quoting each other. Personal religious predilections have led men and women to pervert facts for the comfort of their own souls. It is now possible, however, to write of the Mormons in the proper perspective. They have a history and some attendant traditions, as well as appropriate legends and martyrs; and their present condition, though it is one of material prosperity and placid growth, seems to indicate that never again will they be extraordinary enough to add to that background.

Polygamy has been abolished, and with it has disappeared the most fruitful source of opposition to Mormonism. Almost every outraged woman who visited Utah from 1860 to 1880 wrote a book on the horrors of having half a husband and dedicated it "To the Suffering Women of Utah." The books invariably combine disturbed equanimity and unintelligent inaccuracy, and pretend to reveal secrets which no good Mormon wished to keep. As history they are useless and as entertainment ineffective, but they seemed to satisfy a need at the time; there were so many of them, and they went into so many editions. People bought them, and, if they knew nothing about Mormonism, believed them. And so the Mormon became to the minds of men, women, and children in the eastern states a sort of leering, horned beast, who would steal your wife, marry your daughter, and baptize your baby while you were not looking.

The sex interest in polygamy, so far as Brigham Young is concerned, is still widespread. The first question men ask concerning him is, "How many wives did he have?" Brigham Young, in the course of one of his sermons, had something vigorous and interesting to say about this curiosity:

"We say, give us the truth; but when strangers come to see me their first reflection is, 'I would like to ask him a question if I dare.' What is it? It is all about wives. My conscience! what a generation of gentlemen and ladies we have! Why the mind of a pure Saint and Christian is above such things. If it is necessary to take a wife, take one; if it is necessary to have a husband, have one. If it is necessary to have two wives, take them. If it is right, reasonable and proper and the Lord permits a man to take half a dozen wives, take them; but if the Lord says let them alone, let them alone. . . .

"But, instead of such principles as these occupying people's minds now-a-days, it is, 'How many wives have you, Mr. Young? Oh, I do want to ask Mr. Young how many wives he has.' Ladies who come into my office very frequently say, 'I wonder if it would hurt his feelings if I were to ask him how many wives he has?' Let me say to all creation that I would as lief they should ask me that question as any other; but I would rather see them anxious to learn about the Gospel. Having wives is a secondary consideration; it is within the pale of duty, and consequently, it is all right. But to preach the Gospel, save the children of men, build up the kingdom of God, produce righteousness in the midst of the people; govern and control ourselves and our families and all we have influence over; make us of one heart and one mind; to clear the world from wickedness—this fighting and slaying, this mischievous spirit now [1871] so general, and to subdue and drive it from the face of the earth, and to usher in and establish the reign of universal peace, is our business, no matter how many wives a man has got, that makes no difference here or there. I want to say, and I wish to publish it, that I would as soon be asked how many wives I have got as any other question, just as soon; but I would rather see something else in their minds, instead of all the time thinking, 'How many wives have you;' or 'I wonder whom he slept with last night.' I can tell those who are curious on this point. I slept with all that slept, and we slept on one universal bed—the bosom of our mother earth, and we slept together. 'Did you have anybody in bed with you?' 'Yes.' 'Who was it?' It was my wife, it was not your wife, nor your daughter nor sister, unless she was my wife and that too legally. I can say that to all creation, and every honest man can say the same; but it is not all who are professed Christians who can say it, and I am sorry to say it, not all professed 'Mormons' can say this." [1]

There was much more to Brigham Young than his family life, and, while due attention will be paid to that in its proper place, it is my aim to tell the rest of his story, which has been hidden by the skirts of his wives since his death, and which was beclouded by partisan animosity during his lifetime. What Gibbon prefaces as his intention with regard to Constantine, I have tried to adopt as my principle with regard to Brigham Young: "By the impartial union of those defects which are confessed by his warmest admirers, and of those virtues which are acknowledged by his most implacable enemies, we might hope to delineate a just portrait of that extraordinary man, which the truth and candor of history should adopt without a blush." Since those things for which his unthinking admirers often praise a man most are sometimes his most obvious defects, and since those defects for which his most implacable enemies blame him with the greatest fervor are just as often his most important characteristics, there is not much chance of doing a man injustice so long as the materials of adulation and hate are available. In the case of Brigham Young we are fortunate in possessing a full library of Mormon propaganda and anti-Mormon polemic.

But the nineteen volumes of the sermons delivered by Brigham Young and his principal associates in Salt Lake City, which were printed for the edification of the Saints abroad, are the most valuable source of material. The *Journal of Discourses by Brigham Young, President of the Church of Jesus Christ of Latter-day Saints, His Two Counsellors, The Twelve Apostles and Others,* as the books were called, are stenographic reprints of most of the sermons delivered in Utah. In these the whole life of the man and the Church is vividly portrayed. I have checked this direct testimony with every other available source of material, and it is on the whole accurate, for, given freedom of speech, almost any man usually succeeds in giving himself away.

My thanks are due to Elizabeth Hall Dietz for valuable assistance.

M. R. W.

[1] *Journal of Discourses,* vol. 14, pp. 160, 162.

Table of Contents

List of Illustrations

xvi   LIST OF ILLUSTRATIONS

BRIGHAM YOUNG

Chapter I

IN THE BULRUSHES

I

THE early life of the Mormon Moses is shrouded in the commonplace. Behind the bare facts of his first thirty years one can imagine the stirrings of ambition, but there is little indication in the events of his youth and early manhood of the preëminence he was later to display.

Brigham Young was born on June 1, 1801, in Whitingham, Windham County, Vermont. On that day, some of his disciples said later, the heavens were heard to resound slightly, and towards evening a star is said to have twinkled more irregularly than usual, indicating thereby that God was manifesting particular interest in this one of his many children.

Whitingham, Vermont, was not proud in later years of the only man from town who was heard of throughout the world. A writer of Whitingham history, in discussing the connection between Whitingham and Brigham Young, wrote: "We deem it of little consequence in what locality he was born; it is sufficiently humiliating that Whitingham was his birthplace." Upon the occasion of the centennial celebration of the town in 1880 a native poet in the course of a lengthy historical poem recited these lines, which won the admiration of his audience for his wit and poetic ingenuity:

> "What hath she done in all these years,
> Old Whitingham, 'mid smiles and tears?
> Raised her Goodnows and her Starrs,
> Merchants and bankers, (bulls and bears),
> Reared the mayor of a city,
> And Brigham Young. Lord, what a pity!
> Pity! not for our good mayor,
> But for that Mormon old soothsayer. . . .

3

I said one Brigham Young she'd raised,
But soon she set him flying,
Too many wives would set us crazed,
One at a time is better."

Brigham Young was no more proud of his New England birth-place than it was of him. In a sermon addressed to his people many years later he said: "We are surrounded with circumstances that control us to a certain degree. My father and mother moved into the State of Vermont, and it happened that I was born there. I cannot help that. They might have stayed in Massachusetts, close to Boston. If they had, I should have been born there, and I could not have helped that. . . . I have no power to control such circumstances."

Brigham Young could have claimed credit as a son of the American Revolution. His father, John Young, enlisted in that war when he was a boy and served throughout the fighting, taking part in four engagements under George Washington. After the War he walked home, a distance of one hundred miles, carrying with him a cannon ball, which is still preserved in Utah. Brigham's grandfather, Joseph Young, was a physician and surgeon in the French and Indian War. After the Revolution John Young returned to his birthplace, Hopkinton, Massachusetts, where he took up farming. He married Nabby Howe, a girl from the neighborhood, and Brigham was their ninth child.

When Brigham was three years old, the family moved to Sherburn in New York, and thereafter wandered about in the western part of New York State to different farms, from which they found great difficulty supporting themselves. It has been recorded that the Young family was the poorest family that ever came to Whitingham, Vermont, and that at the time of Brigham's birth John Young did not own a cow, a horse, or any land, but gained a poor living as a basket maker. They settled on new land in western New York, and at an early age Brigham helped his father to clear the ground. Brigham Young said later that he spent eleven and a half days in school. In the Tabernacle he once remarked reminiscently to his followers: "In my youthful days, instead of going to school, I had to chop logs, to sow and plant, to plow in the midst of roots barefooted, and if I had on a pair of pants that would cover me I did pretty well." The family poverty made thrift a necessity, and it is therefore not surprising

that in later years it became in Brigham Young's mind the greatest
of the virtues. He once said in a sermon: "If my mother and
her grandmother got one silk dress, and they lived to a hundred
years, it was all that they wanted. I think my grandmother's
silk dress came down to her children. She put her silk dress on
when I went to see her. It was, I think, her wedding dress, and
she had been married some seventy years." As a result of this
early influence, Brigham Young found it incomprehensible that
his wives and his children, and the Mormon women in general,
should want fine clothes in abundance, and he never tired of
preaching against extravagance in his family and in his congregation. From the pulpit he once told his people how clothes were
obtained in his father's family: "The uncle of Brother Merrell,
who now sits in the congregation, made me the first hat that my
father ever bought for me; and I was then about eleven years of
age. I did not go bareheaded previous to that time, neither did I
call on my father to buy me a five-dollar hat every few months, as
some of my boys do. My sisters would make me what was called
a Jo Johnson cap for winter, and in summer I wore a straw hat
which I frequently braided for myself. I learned to make bread,
wash the dishes, milk the cows, and make butter; and can make
butter, and can beat the most of the women in this community
at housekeeping. Those are about all the advantages I gained in
my youth. I know how to economize, for my father had to do
it." Brigham grew up to be one of those boys, instinctively
capable with their hands, who can take apart a clock to fix it
rather than to see what makes it go round, who can mend a
chair without breaking it, and who, at an early age, are seen on
farms efficiently helping their fathers to build hen-houses and
pig pens.

Brigham's mother died when he was fourteen years old, and
his discipline and direction in his youth were largely under the
control of his father. Brigham once summed up his father's
disciplinary method: "It used to be a word and a blow, with him,
but the blow came first." John Young was apparently a stern
moralist, for his son once said that when he was a boy he was
not allowed to walk more than half-an-hour on Sunday, and it
was to be understood that that half-hour was merely for exercise and not for pleasure. The effect of this stern morality
was to turn Brigham Young towards innocent pleasure rather
than away from it. "The proper and necessary gambols of

youth having been denied to me," he once told his congregation, "makes me want active exercise and amusement now. I had not a chance to dance, when I was young, and never heard the enchanting tones of the violin, until I was eleven years of age; and then I thought I was on the highway to hell, if I suffered myself to linger and listen to it. I shall not subject my little children to such a course of unnatural training, but they shall go to the dance, study music, read novels, and do anything else that will tend to expand their frames, add fire to their spirits, improve their minds, and make them feel free and untrammeled in body and mind." This attitude of Brigham Young's caused him to encourage dancing and theatricals among the Mormons, and he built at Salt Lake City the first theater of any importance in the western United States.

John Young, although he was stern, was not thoroughly unpleasant about it, if we can believe Heber Kimball, Brigham's best friend during his early life, and later his right-hand man in the Church of Jesus Christ of Latter-day Saints. In a sermon one Sunday at Salt Lake City Heber Kimball became enthusiastic about Brigham's father: "I cannot refer to any man of my acquaintance in my life," he said, "as being so much like God as was Brother Brigham's father. He was one of the liveliest and most cheerful men I ever saw, and one of the best of men. He used to come and see me and my wife Vilate almost every day, and would sit and talk with us, and sing, and pray, and jump, and do anything that was good to make us lively and happy, and we loved him. I loved him as well as I did my own father, and a great deal better, I believe. Thus you see that I am not partial in my feelings. If I see a tree bring forth better fruit than the tree I was brought forth from, I will like that tree the best." And then he quoted Christ to the effect, "Who is my mother, or my brethren?"

In spite of this strict home training, Brigham Young admitted to his people that he was not entirely uncontaminated as a boy. "When I went into the world," he once said, "I was addicted to swearing, through hearing others. I gave way to it, but it was easily overcome when my judgment and will decided to overcome it." However, the habit sometimes took hold of him again in later life when he was in the pulpit.

In his early years Brigham Young showed that independence of the thought, morals, and customs of his environment which was so characteristic of him in later life. When he was a young man, his father urged him to sign a temperance pledge. " 'No, sir,' said I, 'if I sign the temperance pledge I feel that I am bound, and I wish to do just right, without being bound to do it; I want my liberty;' and I have conceived from my youth up that I could have my liberty and independence just as much in doing right as I could in doing wrong. . . . Am I not a free man, have not I the power to choose, is not my volition as free as the air I breathe? Certainly it is, just as much in doing right as in doing wrong; consequently I wish to act upon my own volition, and do what I ought to do. I have lived a temperate life; I feel as though I could run through a troop and leap over a wall!"

When he was twenty-three years old, Brigham Young married for the first time. The girl was Miriam Works, the daughter of Asa and Jerusha Works, of Aurelius, Cayuga County, New York, where Brigham had wandered in the course of his traveling occupations. For eighteen years during his youth and his manhood he lived in Aurelius, where, in the typical Yankee manner, he followed the manifold occupations of joiner, house painter, and glazier. Before this he had done odd jobs on farms and had set type on Ball's Arithmetic, but after his marriage he settled down to the permanent business of painter, glazier, and carpenter, and he said in after years that he had "done many a hard day's work for six bits a day." Brigham Young was never ashamed of his early occupations, and at times he was proud of them. When he was Governor of the Territory of Utah, he received a letter from an Englishman, addressed, "To His Excellency, Brigham Young, Governor of Utah, Indian Agent for the Territory, and President of the Church of Jesus Christ of Latter-day Saints." Next time he met the gentleman, Brigham Young said, "I see you have given me my titles." "Yes, Governor, I think they are all there," the writer answered. "No, sir," said Governor Young, "they are not; you have left out a most important one, the first I was ever honestly entitled to in my life, and which I have done nothing to be cashiered of since." "You mean the Generalship, Governor; beg pardon, allow me to add it, sir." "No, no matter now, Squire, but next time you shall put it in by itself, without the others. It will read then right sprucely: 'For His Excellency, Brigham Young, Painter and Glazier.'" He was compelled to leave the painting business, so he said later, on account of the prevalent practice of adulteration: "Because I had either to be dishonest or quit; and I quit." In order to support his wife and two daughters, Brigham Young supplemented his other trades by working on farms during harvest from sunrise to sunset for seventy-five cents a day. In winter he chopped wood for eighteen cents a cord and was compelled to take his pay in corn at seventy-five cents a bushel. In the spring of 1829 he removed to Mendon, Monroe County, New York, where his father lived, and it was there a year later that Brigham Young first saw a copy of the Book of Mormon.

II

During his youth and adolescence Brigham Young showed less interest in religion than most of his neighbors, friends, and family. With that independence of custom, which he maintained vigorously throughout life, he refused to be stampeded into faith, although he was geographically located in its very maelstrom. Mendon, New York, was about fifteen miles southeast of Rochester, and the entire surrounding country was one of the most fertile fields for the revival preachers in the United States of that period. The rest of Brigham's family had been influenced sufficiently by their environment to become earnest Methodists, but he, during his youth, held himself aloof from all religious sects because he could not find one that satisfied his own ideas of God and His Heaven, or one that seemed sufficiently reasonable or attractive to change those ideas. He believed fervently in a god, in a heaven and in a hell, but he refused steadfastly to accept any one else's interpretation of them. His father was devout, and he urged Brigham to accept the family creed. John Young had named one of his sons Lorenzo Dow Young, after the famous evangelist of the time, and two of Brigham's other brothers took an intense interest in religion. Brigham Young once said that his brother Joseph "was solemn and praying all the time," and that he had not seen Joseph smile for a period of four years or laugh for two years. His brother Phineas had become an active Methodist, preaching and seeing visions, and he once practised healing by laying hands on a young woman.

But in spite of his independence of institutional religion, God and his emissaries had a great interest in Brigham Young when he was a boy, if we can believe the evidence of his brother,

Lorenzo Dow Young. In 1816, when he was nine years old and his brother Brigham was fifteen, Lorenzo dreamed a dream, which he recorded in detail more than fifty years later: "I thought I stood in an open, clear space of ground, and saw a plain, fine road, leading, at an angle of forty-five degrees, into the air, as far as I could see. I heard a noise like a carriage in rapid motion, at what seemed the upper end of the road. In a moment it came in sight. It was drawn by a pair of beautiful white horses. The carriage and harness appeared brilliant with gold. The horses traveled with the speed of the wind. It was made manifest to me that the Saviour was in the carriage, and that it was driven by His servant. The carriage stopped near me, and the Saviour inquired where my brother Brigham was. After informing Him, He further inquired about my other brothers, and our father. After I had answered His inquiries, He stated that He wanted us all, but He especially wanted my brother Brigham. The team then turned right about, and returned on the road it had come." It was at this time that young Brigham considered that if he had a pair of pants that would cover him he was doing pretty well, and he would have been surprised to learn that the Saviour was looking for him.

When he was young, Brigham went to hear Lorenzo Dow, who had a great reputation as a hortatory preacher throughout the backwoods and the cities of this country, and whose fame had even spread to parts of England. Many years later Brigham Young told his own congregation about this experience in his youth:

"He was esteemed a very great man by the religious folks. I, although young in years and lacking experience, had thought a great many times that I would like to hear some man who could tell me something, when he opened the Bible, about the Son of God, the will of God, what the ancients did and received, saw and heard and knew pertaining to God and heaven. So I went to hear Lorenzo Dow. He stood up some of the time; he was in this position and in that position, and talked two or three hours, and when he got through I asked myself, 'What have you learned from Lorenzo Dow?' and my answer was, 'Nothing, nothing but morals.' He could tell the people they should not work on the Sabbath day; they should not lie, swear, steal, commit adultery, etc., but when he came to teaching the things of God he was as dark as midnight. And so I lived until, finally, I made a profession of religion. I thought to myself I would try to break off my sins and lead a better life and be as moral as I possibly could; for I was pretty sure I should not stay here always. Where I was going to I did not know, but I would like to be as good as I know how while here, rather than run the risk of being full of evil. I had heard a good deal about religion, and what a good nice place heaven was, and how good the Lord was, and I thought I would try to live a pretty good life. But when I reached the years of, I will say, courage, I think that is the best term, I would ask questions. I would say, 'Elder,' or Minister, 'I read so and so in the Bible, how do you understand it?' Then I would go and hear them preach on the divinity of the Son, and the character of the Father and the Holy Ghost and their divinity, and, I will say, the divinity of the soul of man; what we are here for, and various kindred topics. But after asking questions and going to hear them preach year after year, what did I learn? Nothing. I would as lief go into a swamp at midnight to learn how to paint a picture and then define its colors when there is neither moon nor stars visible and profound darkness prevails, as to go to the religious world to learn about God, heaven, hell or the faith of a Christian. But they can explain our duty as rational, moral beings, and that is good, excellent, as far as it goes." [1]

Only a new religion, made to order, would completely satisfy such a mind. But, meanwhile, in his twenty-second year, Brigham Young joined the Methodists. However, he was not so active in their work as his brothers and his father were. He said that when priests had urged him to pray previously to this enrolment as a Methodist, "I had but one prevailing feeling in my mind: Lord, preserve me until I am old enough to have sound judgment, and a discreet mind ripened upon a good solid foundation of common sense." Before joining the Methodists he had at various times attended meetings in Mendon of the Episcopalians, Presbyterians, New Lights, Baptists, Freewill Baptists, Wesleyans, Reformed Methodists and Quakers, "and was more or less acquainted with almost every other ism." Speaking before a meeting of his large family, Brigham Young once said: "I saw them get religion all around me. Men were rolling and bawling and thumping, but it had no effect on me. I wanted to know the truth that I might not be fooled. Children and young men got religion but I could not get it till I was twenty-three years old; and then, in order to prevent my being any more pestered about it I joined Methodism." But, he said,

[1] *Journal of Discourses*, vol. 14, p. 197.

he was looking for something more than mere conformity: "I felt in those days, after I had made a profession of religion, that if I could see the face of a Prophet, such as had lived on the earth in former times, a man that had revelations, to whom the heavens were opened, who knew God and His character, I would freely circumscribe the earth on my hands and knees; I thought that there was no hardship but what I would undergo, if I could see one person that knew what God is and where He is, what was His character, and what eternity was. . . ." This would appear to be a large order, but the opportunity of fulfilling it in some measure was soon after offered to Brigham Young, when Samuel H. Smith, a brother of the Prophet Joseph Smith, Jr., arrived in Brigham's neighborhood, selling the Book of Mormon, which had just been published.

Samuel Smith was the book agent for his religious brother, and in the course of his difficult task of distributing a new bible, he tried to sell a copy of it to the Rev. John P. Green, of Livonia, New York. The Rev. Mr. Green told him to come back in a few weeks after he and Mrs. Green had had a chance to inspect the new bible, and when Smith returned, Mrs. Green told him that her husband had decided not to buy. "It was impressed upon my mind," Samuel Smith said some years later, "to leave the book with her." But the fact that he was not selling his copies very fast and had many more than he could carry conveniently may have had something to do with this impression. He made Mrs. Green a present of the Book of Mormon, asking only that she and her husband would ask God for a sign that it was the truth. They did so and soon afterwards were baptized. Mrs. Green was a sister of Brigham Young. She showed the new bible to her brother Phineas, who took it home to study, and soon afterwards Phineas began to preach the new religion. He showed the book to his brother Brigham, who said later that he first saw it two or three weeks after it was published in 1830.

Brigham was not so hasty as his brother Phineas. In a sermon he once told of his first reaction to this new religion:

"The man that brought it to me, told me the same things: says he, 'This is the Gospel of salvation; a revelation the Lord has brought forth for the redemption of Israel; it is the Gospel; and according to Jesus Christ and his Apostles, you must be baptized for the remission of sins, or you will be damned.' 'Hold on,' says I. The mantle of my traditions was over me, to that degree, and my prepossessed feelings so interwoven with my nature, it was almost impossible for me to see at all; though I had beheld all my life that the traditions of the people was all the religion they had, I had got a mantle for myself. Says I, 'Wait a little while; what is the doctrine of the book, and of the revelations the Lord has given? Let me apply my heart to them;' and after I had done this, I considered it to be my right to know for myself, as much as any man on earth." [2]

Brigham Young pondered over the Book of Mormon for two years. He claimed that he adopted towards this new dispensation the same skeptical attitude he had used towards all the other sects. "When 'Mormonism' was first presented to me," he once said, "I had not seen one sect of religionists whose doctrines, from beginning to end, did not appear to me like the man's masonry which he had in a box, and which he exhibited for a certain sum. He opened the main box from which he took another box; he unlocked that and slipped out another, then another, and another, and thus continued to take box out of box until he came to an exceedingly small piece of wood; he then said to the spectators, 'That, gentlemen and ladies, is free masonry.'" But Mormonism was different. The more he wrestled with it, the truer it seemed, and, so he says, he found it impossible to discern its errors: "I found it was from eternity, passed through time, and into eternity again. When I discovered this, I said, 'It is worthy of the notice of man.' Then I applied my heart to wisdom, and sought diligently for understanding." And eventually he came to this emphatic conclusion: "I knew it was true, as well as I knew that I could see with my eyes, or feel by the touch of my fingers, or be sensible of the demonstration of any sense. Had not this been the case, I never would have embraced it to this day."

But there were other considerations that brought Brigham Young to his final conclusions. His financial condition was not good at the time, and he was undoubtedly shrewd enough, skeptical enough, and well enough acquainted with the progress of religious speculation in his neighborhood to realize that as a business proposition this new religion might be worth looking into. Another influence was that of his family and his friends. His brother Phineas and his father were convinced of the truth presented by the Book of Mormon, and his father was actually

[2] *Journal of Discourses,* vol. 3, p. 91.

baptized into the new church a few days before Brigham was. Together with his brother Phineas and his best friend, Heber Kimball, Brigham went in a sleigh to visit a branch of the new church at Columbia, Bradford County, Pennsylvania. They spent a week investigating the religion in action. When he returned home to Mendon, Brigham Young had become convinced of the truth of Mormonism, and he started for Canada, where his brother Joseph, whose opinion on religious matters Brigham respected more than anybody's except his own, was preaching Methodism. Joseph was four years older than Brigham, and he was considered the theological expert of the Young family; it is therefore natural that Brigham should consult him before doing anything about this new opportunity to embrace salvation.

In March, 1832, the two brothers returned from Canada, and on April 15th, when he was thirty years old, Brigham Young was baptized into the Church of Jesus Christ of Latter-day Saints. His father and his brother Joseph had both been baptized a few days before. Brigham Young said later of his baptism: "I recollect the Sunday morning on which I was baptized in my own little mill stream; I was ordained to the office of an Elder before my clothes were dry upon me." In those days of the new church, which was then two years old, elders were scarce, and any male convert who was not hopelessly incompetent in practical matters, was ordained an elder almost immediately after baptism.

Exactly what were Brigham Young's motives for joining the Mormons, it is impossible to determine. His financial condition had something to do with the decision, and his family had a great deal to do with it, but whatever his original motives, it was not long before he had thoroughly persuaded himself that it was the true religion of God. A few months after their baptism Brigham Young and his friend, Heber Kimball, went to Kirtland, Ohio, to meet the new Prophet of God, Joseph Smith, Jr. Brigham Young put in writing many years later the details of this memorable meeting:

"We went to his father's house and learned that he was in the woods chopping. We immediately repaired to the woods, where we found the Prophet, and two or three of his brothers, chopping and hauling wood. Here my joy was full at the privilege of shaking the hand of the Prophet of God, and receiving the sure testimony, by the spirit of prophecy, that he was all that any man could believe him to be as a true prophet. He was happy to see us and bid us welcome. We soon returned to his house, he accompanying us. In the evening a few of the brethren came in, and we conversed upon the things of the kingdom. He called upon me to pray; in my prayer I spoke in tongues. As soon as we arose from our knees, the brethren flocked around him, and asked his opinion concerning the gift of tongues that was upon me. He told them that it was the pure Adamic language. Some said to him they expected he would condemn the gift Brother Brigham had, but he said, 'No, it is of God.' " [3]

Brigham Young had picked up this divine gift of tongues while on his visit to the branch of the new church in Pennsylvania and had used it effectively while preaching in New York. It consisted of a babble of incomprehensible sounds which were supposed to be the spirit of God resting upon the speaker, and these sounds were interpreted by another person in the congregation as soon as the speaker had uttered them.

What Brigham Young thought of Joseph Smith, Jr., after this first meeting is impossible to discover, but Heber Kimball testified that he heard the Prophet Joseph say to those who stood around him, "That man," pointing to Brigham Young, "will yet preside over this church." But the Mormons have always been prone to *ex post facto* prophecy, and there were others, less friendly, who said that they heard Joseph say: "If Brigham Young ever becomes President of the Church, he will lead it to hell." There are some Mormons who believe the latter prediction to have come as true as the former.

Brigham Young returned home to Mendon, where he spent the following few months. His first wife died there of tuberculosis on September 8, 1832. "In her last moments," says a Mormon sketch of her, "the dying wife and mother clapped her hands and gave praise to the Lord, and called on Brother Kimball and all around her to also praise the Lord." She, too, had been baptized into the Mormon Church soon after her husband. Brigham Young and his two young daughters lived with Heber Kimball and his wife, Vilate, for a short time, and then both families migrated to Kirtland, Ohio, to join the new Prophet of God, Joseph Smith, Jr.

It is now necessary to investigate how Joseph Smith became a Prophet of God and why.

[3] *History of the Church,* vol. 1, footnotes, pp. 295, 296, 297.

Chapter II

A YANKEE MOHAMMED

I

ONE of the main issues in social and religious circles of the United States during the first half of the nineteenth century was whether Joseph Smith, Jr., was inspired by God or instigated by the Devil, whether he was divine or insane, and whether he was an honest-to-God Prophet, like some of his illustrious Biblical predecessors, or a swindling impostor, like some of his immediate contemporaries in the business of religion. To-day we are somewhat inclined to believe with James Huneker, who asked in *Steeplejack:* "Query: What is the difference between a false or true prophet? Aren't they both fakirs?" But, during his lifetime, and for many years thereafter, the divine authenticity of Joseph Smith, Jr., was considered of great import, and the controversy which his pretensions began still continues quietly, but steadily, in books and pamphlets. Now sufficient years have passed since his violent death in 1844 to allow us to consider what he was, and why, rather than whether or not he should have been that.

In his study of Mohammed Carlyle wrote what can be applied with equal significance to our own American Prophet: "A false man found a religion? Why, a false man cannot build a brick house! If he do not know and follow *truly* the properties of mortar, burnt clay and what else he works in, it is no house that he makes, but a rubbish-heap. It will not stand for twelve centuries, to lodge a hundred and eighty millions; it will fall straightway. . . . This Mohammed, then, we will in no wise consider as an Inanity and Theatricality, a poor, conscious, ambitious schemer; we cannot conceive him so." The personality and the religion of Joseph Smith, Jr., of Vermont and points west, have not yet survived twelve centuries, but it is now only a few years short of a century since he published the Book of Mormon, and

15

there are in this country and in Europe some 450,000 men, women, and children who think of him solemnly as one of the few elect of God, and who profess to believe that he died that they may live in the future. He has even been considered important enough to create schisms among his own followers, and for a religious leader that is almost insurance of immortality.

Many legends, with more or less basis of fact, have grown around the personality of Joseph Smith, but it is significant that no miraculous events surrounded the birth and infancy of this latter-day prophet. Even his mother, who had a taste for the marvelous and the visionary, and who wrote a book about her illustrious offspring and his forebears, offered no instances of unusual manifestations at the time of his arrival. In this, as in more important respects, he differed from some of the prophets and messiahs of old.

Joseph Smith, Jr., was born at Sharon, Vermont, two days before Christmas in 1805. He came into an ultra-poor family, where there were already three children older than he, and where there were destined to be six more before he was a man. When he came to write the Book of Mormon—with the help of God— Joseph Smith accounted himself a direct descendant of the original Joseph, of Israel. The Second Book of Nephi of the Book of Mormon contains the prediction that a descendant of the Jewish Joseph will one day arise, who will also be named Joseph, and who in the latter days will save the world by his revelations of the will of the Lord. It is also predicted therein that a Moses will arise, and undoubtedly God had Brigham Young in mind, but, unfortunately, his parents named him Brigham before they knew that the Lord had chosen him.

Whether or not Joseph Smith, Jr., was a direct descendant of the ancient Hebrew family of Egypt, is an open question, but his immediate ancestors were equally interesting. His father, Joseph Smith, Sen., was born in Topsfield, Massachusetts, on July 12, 1771, where the family had resided since 1638, when Robert Smith, an English Puritan, settled there. Numerous attempts have been made to prove that Joseph Smith was descended from depraved, degenerate, and disreputable persons, but it has been established that several of his early American ancestors were considered gentlemen by their contemporaries and took active part in the government of their communities, as well as in the War of the Revolution. On his mother's side, from which we can trace more direct influence than from that of his father, Joseph Smith's ancestors were sturdy Scotch Covenanters, Puritans and Crusaders, of uncompromising principles, who helped to found colonies in this country, and who fought in the colonial wars and the Revolutionary War.

There are interesting details of the religious idiosyncrasies of many of Joseph Smith's ancestors. His paternal grandfather, Asahel Smith, was subject to fits, and he was familiarly known as "Crook-Necked Smith," because of the inability to keep one shoulder as high as the other: A contemporary said that his religious opinions were so free, "that some regarded his sentiments as more distorted than his neck." Solomon Mack, Joseph Smith's maternal grandfather, wrote a short but pregnant narrative of his experiences, according to which he was at various times a farmer, sailor, soldier, sutler, privateer, proprietor of ocean vessels, manufacturer of saltpeter, landowner, and beggar. It is said that *A Narrative of the Life of Solomon Mack* was written and published by the author for the furtherance of the last-named occupation, for he hawked it as a Yankee beggar's chap-book, so that he might have something to gain sympathy for his mendicancy. If we can believe this narrative, Solomon Mack met with a series of most unfortunate accidents: he broke his wrists, was knocked down by a passing trooper's horse, fell on the water-wheel of a sawmill, was shipwrecked several times, and was once knocked down by a powerful tree. But his most interesting ailment from our point of view was his fits and trances: "I afterwards was taken with a fit," he wrote, "when traveling, with an ax under my arm, on Winchester hills, the face of the land was covered with ice. I was senseless from one until five p.m. when I came to myself I had my ax still under my arm, I was all covered with blood and much cut & bruised. When I came to my senses I could not tell where I had been, nor where I was going; but by good luck I went right and arrived at the first house, was under the Doctor's care all winter." At the age of seventy-six Solomon Mack began to think of God and his own salvation, because that winter he was "taken with Rheumatism and confined me all winter in the most extreme pain." From his bed of pain the old man saw bright lights on dark nights and was certain that he heard voices calling him. These visitations made him so fearful for his salvation that, "I literally watered my pillow with tears." These verses from Matthew passed through his mind again and again: "Come unto me all ye that labor and are heavy laden and I will give you rest. Take my yoke upon you, and learn of me; for I am meek and lowly in heart: and ye shall find rest unto your souls. For my yoke is easy and my burden is light." Solomon Mack gave this pathetic description of his visitations:

"About midnight I saw a light about a foot from my face as bright as fire, the doors were all shut and no one stirring in the house. I thought by this that I had but a few moments to live, and O! what distress I was in; I prayed that the Lord would have mercy on my soul and deliver me from this horrible pit of sin. . . .
"Another night soon after I saw another light as bright as the first, at a small distance from my face, and I thought I had but a few moments to live, and not sleeping nights, and reading, all day I was in misery; well you may think I was in distress, soul and body. At another time, in the dead of the night I was called by my christian name, I arise up and answer to my name. The doors all being shut and the house still, I thought the Lord called and I had but a moment to live. Oh, what a vile wretch I had been. . . . I called upon the Lord the greatest part of the winter and towards spring it was reviving and light shined into my soul."

He also records that towards spring the Lord miraculously appeared to be with him, for his rheumatism was cured; perhaps, however, the absence of damp weather was a contributory cause.

Lucy Mack Smith, Joseph's mother, had a brother, Uncle Jason, who believed many of the things Joseph later expressed. Jason Smith was a member of the sect known as Seekers, and as such he believed that by prayer and faith a man could receive the same gifts which God gave to the ancient Apostles. He also believed, what Joseph Smith claimed a few years later, that the Scriptures are not complete. Lucy Smith's sister, Joseph's Aunt Lovisa, was miraculously healed of a two years' illness by a vision from God, and she preached to the neighbors about it.

Both Joseph Smith, Sen., and his wife dreamed in religious parables, the purport of which almost invariably proved to be that there was no true church representative of Jesus Christ and the ancient Apostles. This seems to have been a fixed idea with them, which they handed on to their son Joseph, who, with a practical ability which his parents lacked, started the machinery in motion for the establishment of the one true church, the lack

Lucy Smith

of which his parents had bemoaned so much, both sleeping and waking. About three years before the birth of the Prophet, Lucy Smith became very ill; it was decided that she was suffering from tuberculosis and could not possibly live. Her husband, she wrote in her book of reminiscences, came into her room one day, and, taking her thin, pale hand, said:

" 'Oh, Lucy! my wife! my wife! you must die! The doctors have given you up; and all say you cannot live.' . . . During this night I made a solemn covenant with God, that, if he would let me live, I would endeavor to serve him according to the best of my abilities. Shortly after this, I heard a voice say to me, 'Seek, and ye shall find; knock, and it shall be opened unto you.' In a few moments my mother came in, and, looking upon me, she said, 'Lucy, you are better.' "

When Lucy Smith recovered, she went to preachers and deacons for spiritual aid, but she found them practically useless:

"I therefore determined to examine my Bible, and, taking Jesus and his disciples for my guide, to endeavor to obtain from God that which man could neither give nor take away. . . . At length I considered it my duty to be baptized, and, finding a minister who was willing to baptize me, and leave me free in regard to joining any religious denomination, I stepped forward and yielded obedience to this ordinance; after which I continued to read the Bible as formerly, until my eldest son had attained his twenty-second year."

Joseph Smith, Jr., as we shall see, went through a similar religious experience in his youth. Meanwhile, the financial struggles of the Smith family were acute. Joseph Smith, Sen., labored continually without success; some of his neighbors have testified that he did not labor continuously enough. But the struggle to maintain a family of ten children was too great for a man who was too much of a mystic to be a successful farmer, and too much of a farmer to be a successful mystic. Lucy Smith was a vibrant, vigorous personality, and she seems to have exhibited considerable practical ability in the face of difficulties. In the various removals from farm to farm, she had the responsibility of devising ways and means for transporting her large family and their meager effects. She also at one time increased the family earnings by her talent for painting oil-cloth covers for tables and lamp-stands. Joseph's father, when he did get a little money, invested it in a speculation to send ginseng to China, where great spiritual and physical healing properties are attributed to it. But he was defrauded of his money by his partner.

When Joseph Smith was ten years old, his father moved the family to Palmyra, Wayne County, New York, where he bought and cleared a farm, which he lost because of his inability to pay the last instalment on it. He then moved to a smaller farm in the neighboring village of Manchester. At one time the Smith family is said to have kept a beer and cake shop in Palmyra, where the future prophet peddled both those commodities to the neighbors. Speaking of Joseph's father and mother, a Utah resident once said: "She and her husband looked like a pair of splendid gypsies."

II

There is an attempt upon the part of some of his followers with literary ambitions to make out that the Prophet Joseph Smith, Jr., as a boy, was a good, true, brave, and upright storybook hero, but it is impossible, after reading the large body of inaccurate fact and anecdote brought forth by both his friends and enemies, to get rid of the impression that he was more of a Huckleberry Finn. The Mormons would do better to accept this picture of him, which wins him our sympathy by virtue of his roguery. However, it outrages the moral sensibilities of stern religious enthusiasts to admit that Huckleberry Finn could have grown up into a Prophet of God.

A choice example of the attitude of his followers towards their Prophet as a boy is found in Elder Edward Stevenson's *Reminiscences of Joseph, the Prophet:*

"At about the age of eight years, he passed through an ordeal which gave remarkable evidence of heroic fortitude and indomitable power of will, under intense bodily suffering. After recovering from a severe typhus fever, a fever sore affected his leg and threatened him with the loss of the limb. Under these circumstances, a consultation of physicians was held, and after making an incision eight inches in length, and examining the bone, they decided that, if his life was to be saved, amputation of the member was absolutely necessary. This operation, however, was so strongly opposed by both parents and son that the doctors finally concluded to remove the affected parts of the bone. Accordingly, they called for a strong cord to bind the lad, and were intending to give him a stimulant; but to all this our young hero most decidedly objected, saying, 'I will not touch one particle of liquor, neither will I be tied down; but I will have my father sit on the bed and hold me in his arms, and then I will do whatever is necessary to have the bone taken out.' By drilling into the bone on each side of the part affected, three pieces of bone were extracted, the removal being made with a pair of forceps. The manhood and will power of this noble youth of eight years, under so trying an ordeal, foreshadowed the story of his life—a life fraught with matchless heroism, under all manner of persecution, trials, imprisonments, hardships and finally martyrdom."

It is a pity for his reputation among the strait-laced members of the community with whom he was compelled to associate, that as a young man the Prophet did not continue to practise the abstinence from liquor with which he is so heroically credited as a boy of eight, for, if we can believe the testimony of his neighbors, the Prophet was frequently seen about Palmyra drunk.

Joseph Smith received few educational opportunities. He knew how to read and to write imperfectly, and he understood elementary arithmetic. Among the sayings of the Prophet which have been carefully preserved is this: "I am a rough stone. The sound of the hammer and chisel was never heard on me until the Lord took me in hand. I desire the learning and wisdom of heaven alone." Two books are alleged to have been favorites of the boy Joseph Smith. One of these was the *Memoirs of Stephen Burroughs,* a traveling preacher who was a cause of much trouble in New England because he preached for a living without having been regularly ordained a clergyman. If Smith read Burroughs's confessions, as is not at all unlikely, for there was much talk of Burroughs in the neighborhood, he may possibly have got from them the germ of his idea, or the incentive of his inspiration, to enter the field of practical religion; however, if this was his inspiration, Joseph Smith improved upon his master, for Burroughs only set himself up as an independent itinerant preacher without the proper seminary credentials, while Smith became a Prophet with full credentials from God. The other book in which Joseph Smith is said to have been interested when he was a boy was the autobiography of Captain Kidd, and his favorite lines from this work, which he repeated often to himself and sometimes recited aloud were:

"My name was Robert Kidd,
   As I sailed, as I sailed
And most wickedly I did,
God's laws I did forbid,
   As I sailed, as I sailed."

Joseph's enemies say that this was his favorite part of Captain
Kidd's book, but it is likely that he found more to interest him
in the accounts of buried treasure, for Joseph's father was convinced that money could be found in the ground by aid of a
divining rod or a sprig of witch hazel. Much of the time of the
Smith boys, according to their neighbors' testimony, given after
they became notorious, was spent in searching for money.
Joseph, Jr., was said to be particularly adept at money-digging
with the aid of a peep-stone, which he placed in his hat, but
there is no record of any money actually having been found by
the Smiths. William Stafford, one of their neighbors, gave
this testimony at the request of an anti-Mormon writer, concerning the Smith family's money-digging activities:

"I have heard them tell marvelous tales, respecting the discoveries
they had made in their peculiar occupation of money-digging. They
would say, for instance, that in such a place, in such a hill, on a
certain man's farm, there were deposited keys, barrels and hogs-
heads of coined silver and gold—bars of gold, golden images, brass
kettles filled with gold and silver—gold candlesticks, swords, etc.,
etc. They would say, also, that nearly all the hills in this part of
New York, were thrown up by human hands, and in them were
large caves, which Joseph, Jr., could see, by placing a stone of singular appearance in his hat in such a manner as to exclude all
light; at which time they pretended he could see all things within
and under the earth,—that he could see within the above-mentioned
caves, large gold bars and silver plates—that he could also discover
the spirits in whose charge these treasures were, clothed in ancient
dress. At certain times these treasures could be obtained very
easily; at others, the obtaining of them was difficult. The facility of
approaching them depended in a great measure on the state of the
moon. New moon and good Friday, I believe, were regarded as
the most favorable times for obtaining these treasures."

Another neighbor has testified that Joseph never did any of the
actual digging, confining himself to the spiritual and temporal
direction of the work. When no treasure was found, the young

man had to think of reasons, and he usually maintained that an evil spirit had removed it to deeper ground. On one occasion Joseph is said to have insisted that in order to get the buried treasure he must sacrifice the blood of a black sheep. There was a fine black wether in the flock of one of the neighbors, which he had been fattening for market. "Fresh meat," wrote one anti-Mormon writer, "was a rarity at his father's home." Late at night the blood of the black wether was shed in a circle, and the digging began. But, according to Smith, the Devil interfered, and the treasure was not found. It is said, however, that the Smith family had mutton for dinner several days thereafter.

The most important events of Joseph Smith's youth were his religious experiences. When he was fifteen years old, there was stirring religious excitement in his neighborhood. Revivals were flourishing in that section of the country; priest fought with priest for converts, and feverish, if not permanent, religious interest was exhibited by the ignorant population. People changed their religions every week, with the arrival of new preachers. Joseph's father and his mother, his brothers, Hyrum and Samuel, and his sister, Sophronia, who were older than he, all became Presbyterians together. Joseph was very much disturbed by this religious excitement, and the result of it on his adolescent mind was perplexity and melancholy worry for his salvation. A few years before he had been a rough boy, with battered hat, ragged clothes, and mussed yellow hair, joining in Yankee practical jokes with other farm boys, as he ran barefooted about Palmyra and Manchester. But now vague forebodings of the future were beginning to disturb his placid mind. He has left an interesting record in writing of his first religious experience at the age of fifteen:

"While I was laboring under the extreme difficulties, caused by the contests of these parties of religionists, I was one day reading the Epistle of James, first chapter, and fifth verse, which reads, 'If any of you lack wisdom, let him ask of God, that giveth unto all men liberally and upbraideth not, and it shall be given him.' . . . At length I came to the conclusion that I must either remain in darkness and confusion, or else I must do as James directs, that is, ask of God. I at length came to the determination to ask of God, concluding that if he gave wisdom to them that lacked wisdom, and would give liberally and not upbraid, I might venture. So, in accordance with this my determination to ask of God, I retired to the woods to make the attempt. It was on the morning of a beautiful clear day, early in the spring of eighteen hundred and twenty. It was the first time in my life that I had made such an attempt, for amidst all my anxieties I had never as yet made the attempt to pray vocally."

According to their autobiographies, the woods have always played a prominent part in the development of religious enthusiasts. The impressive quality of solitude in the midst of mysterious life have frequently turned mystic minds to thoughts of God, and, especially in the period of adolescence, from thoughts to visions is an easy transition. The beautiful clear spring day may also have had something to do with Joseph Smith's state of mind, for psychologists have established that in spring when young men's fancies do not turn to thoughts of love, they usually find relief in religion. But, whatever the complex mental circumstances, for Joseph Smith the fact remained that after he had looked about to make sure that he was alone and had kneeled in prayer, he "was seized upon by some power which entirely overcame me, and had such astonishing influence over me as to bind my tongue so that I could not speak. Thick darkness gathered around me, and it seemed to me for a time as if I were doomed to sudden destruction." He prayed fervently to God, and then: "Just at this moment of great alarm, I saw a pillar of light exactly over my head, above the brightness of the sun, which descended gradually until it fell upon me. When the light rested upon me, I saw two personages, whose brightness and glory defy all description, standing above me in the air. One of them spake unto me, calling me by name, and said, pointing to the other, THIS IS MY BELOVED SON, HEAR HIM."

As soon as he could talk, Joseph asked the two glorious personages which of all the religious sects in the United States he should join, and he was told that they were all wrong and all corrupt. The Son of God, for it was none other, also told Joseph Smith many things which he could not repeat when he wrote his account of this vision, for God had not yet released them for publication. "When I came to myself again," Joseph wrote, "I found myself laying on my back looking up into heaven." [1] He finally recovered strength enough to stagger home, for his vision had left him

[1] The account of this vision is taken from the *History of the Church of Jesus Christ of Latter-day Saints: Period I: History of Joseph Smith, the Prophet, by Himself*, vol. I.

limp, and when he entered the house, he leaned against the fire-place, dazed. His mother anxiously asked what was the trouble, and he answered: "Never mind, all is well—I am well enough off." And then he added, "I have learned for myself that Pres-byterianism is not true."

After his vision Joseph began to argue with visiting clergy-men, but he was always reviled, and whenever he dared to tell of the vision, he was informed that visions were things of the past, that there were enough of them in the Bible, and that those would do very well for the present day. To refute this argument, Orson Pratt, one of Joseph Smith's main adherents in later years, argued that angels were often in the habit of visiting the earth. Two angels, he pointed out, had taken dinner with Abraham; Jacob had wrestled with one all of a night; several stayed with Lot and his wife at their house; Moses, Joshua, Manoah, Gideon, David, Daniel, Zechariah, Joseph, the husband of Mary, the Shepherds, the Apostles, Philip, Paul, and Cornelius had all been visited by angels, and Orson Pratt saw no reason therefore why two angels should not visit Joseph Smith, Jr., in the year 1820 at the town of Manchester, Ontario County, New York. It does not matter so much whether or not angels actually visited the boy Joseph Smith as it does that by the time he had grown to man's estate he had thoroughly convinced himself that his visions were reali-ties.

After this first stirring vision, with a charming sense of irre-sponsibility, Joseph Smith continued his everyday life of odd jobs, money-digging, loafing, and dreaming, until September 21, 1823. Meanwhile, according to his own later admission, he had yielded to various temptations, "to the gratification of many appetites offensive in the sight of God," was the way he put it. Although he does not specify in detail what these sins were, he tells us that they were grievous enough to weigh heavily on his conscience, and on the night of September 21, 1823, when he went to bed, he prayed fervently for forgiveness. A light suddenly filled the small bedroom, until "it was lighter than at noonday." A personage appeared beside Joseph's bed, and the curious thing about him, the thing which first attracted the young man's attention, was that he was "standing in the air, for his feet did not touch the floor." "He had on a loose robe of most exquisite white-ness . . .; his hands were naked, and his arms also, a little above the wrist; so, also, were his feet naked, as were his legs, a little above the ankles. His head and neck were all bare. I could discover that he had no other clothing on but this robe, as it was open, so that I could see into his bosom. Not only was his robe exceedingly white, but his whole person was glorious beyond description, and his countenance truly like lightning."

The visitor called Joseph by name and introduced himself. He was, he said, a messenger from God, and his name was Moroni. "He said there was a book deposited, written upon gold plates, giving an account of the former inhabitants of this continent, and the source from whence they sprang. . . . Also, that there were two stones in silver bows—and these stones, fastened to a breastplate, constituted what is called the Urim and Thummim—deposited with the plates; and the possession of these stones were what constituted Seers in ancient or former times, and that God had prepared them for the purpose of translating the book." Then Moroni quoted Scripture, with slight variations from the common Bible text, perhaps to show that he was an authority. He explained in detail to the eighteen-year-old boy lying in bed before him how the prophecies of Isaiah and others would be fulfilled. "Again, he told me that when I got those plates of which he had spoken, for the time that they should be obtained was not yet fulfilled, I should not show them to any person, neither the breastplate with the Urim and Thummim, only to those to whom I should be commanded to show them; if I did, I should be destroyed." While the angel was talking, Joseph was visited with a visionary picture of the place where the plates were buried, so that he should know it when he finally saw it.

After the angel had finished speaking, the light in the room began to concentrate around his figure, until everything in the room was very dark, except his blinding whiteness. "When instantly I saw," wrote Joseph Smith, "as it were, a conduit open right up into heaven, and he ascended up till he entirely disappeared, and the room was left as it had been before this heavenly light had made its appearance." Joseph lay in bed, "musing . . . and marveling greatly at what had been told me by this extraordinary messenger." Suddenly the room began to grow light again, and Moroni returned. "He commenced, and again related the very same things which he had done at this first visit, without the least variation." But this time he added a few predictions of famines and plagues which would eventually descend upon the earth if its inhabitants did not watch out, and again he left for heaven. A third time he returned and repeated what he had said twice before, adding that Satan would tempt Joseph in every way in order to persuade him to get possession of the valuable plates before the time was ripe, and Moroni warned Joseph not to yield. The cock crew, and day began to break.

Many years later Joseph Smith gave his followers this infallible talisman for discovering whether an angel is a real angel of God or an emissary of the Devil:

"When a messenger comes saying he has a message from God, offer him your hand, and request him to shake hands with you. If he be an angel, he will do so, and you will feel his hand. If he be the spirit of a just man made perfect, he will come in his glory; for that is the only way he can appear. Ask him to shake hands with you, but he will not move, because it is contrary to the order of heaven for a just man to deceive; but he will still deliver his message. If it be the devil as an angel of light, when you ask him to shake hands, he will offer you his hand, and you will not feel anything: you may therefore detect him."

A short time afterwards when Joseph was working with his father in the fields he suddenly fainted. While unconscious he saw the same angel, who delivered his heavenly message a fourth time, and added that Joseph might tell it to his father if he wished. Joseph told his father everything, and the son wrote that Joseph Smith, Sen., was sure that the messages were from God, and he urged that young Joseph proceed at once to where the plates were buried. This was conveniently located near the Smith farmhouse, between the towns of Palmyra and Manchester, and was known as the Hill of Cumorah. After removing some earth and the large stone which covered the hiding-place, Joseph found the plates in a golden box, with the Urim and Thummim lying next to them. As he was about to take them away, God's messenger suddenly appeared and told him that the time was not yet come, and that it would not come until four years after date. He made an appointment with Joseph to meet him every year at Cumorah Hill until the end of four years. These appointments with the angel Joseph Smith kept sedulously, and at each of the annual conferences he was told what God had in mind for the peoples of the earth in general and for Joseph Smith, Jr., in particular.

This is the version of the incident which Joseph Smith gave in the history of it which he wrote for his church, but the neighbors said that he told them a different story, according to which he was knocked down twice when he first went to get the plates. When he inquired why he could not have them, he saw a man standing over the spot where they lay, who seemed to Joseph to be a Spaniard with a long beard extending to his breast; his

JOSEPH SMITH, JR. AND AN ANGEL OF GOD INSPECTING THE
GOLDEN PLATES OF THE BOOK OF MORMON AT
CUMORAH HILL
From a contemporary woodcut

throat was cut from ear to ear, and the blood was streaming down. This weird character told Joseph that he could not get the plates alone but must get them in the company of his wife, whom he had not yet met. Joseph's father also told this story and added concerning the gold bible, "I weighed it, and it weighed thirty pounds."

Meanwhile, the Smith family was finding it ever more difficult to earn a living, and the young Prophet was compelled to continue at menial labor until such time as God should see fit to relieve him. One of his jobs was digging in search of a silver mine at Harmony, Pennsylvania, for one Josiah Stoal. Joseph maintained that Stoal had hired him for this job and informed him of the existence of the silver mine, but the neighbors said that Josiah Stoal first heard of the silver mine from Joseph Smith, who had promised to show the old gentleman its exact location.

While he was in Harmony, Pennsylvania, when he was twenty years old, Joseph met Emma Hale, the daughter of a prosperous farmer, Isaac Hale. Isaac Hale later described the Prophet as "a careless young man—not very well educated, and very saucy and insolent to his father." Joseph Smith, Sen., was also employed digging for the mythical silver mine. Joseph Smith visited the Hale house often and finally asked Isaac Hale for permission to marry his daughter. Isaac Hale refused, giving as his reasons that Joseph was a stranger, and that he followed a business which Isaac Hale could by no means approve. Soon afterwards Joseph and Emma went secretly into the State of New York and were married.

The time finally arrived for unearthing the golden plates, and on September 22, 1827, Joseph Smith met the angel of God at Cumorah Hill, and they were delivered into his hands, to be kept until the angel called for them. On the night when the golden plates of the Book of Mormon were delivered to Joseph Smith, Brigham Young, who lived about fifteen miles away, saw strange lights in the heavens, although it was a dark night with no moon. He described the phenomenon many years later: "I gazed at it in company with my wife. The light was perfectly clear and remained several hours. It formed into men as if there were great armies in the West; and I then saw in the northwest armies of men come up. They would march to the South West and then go out of sight. It was a very remarkable occurrence. It passed on, and continued perhaps about two hours."

Persecution and efforts, prompted by the Devil, to get the golden plates are said to have begun immediately after Joseph received them, and he was forced to take his possession in a bean bag to Harmony, Pennsylvania. But his father-in-law testified that the trip was made for Emma's clothes and for financial aid.

There is another story of the origin of the golden plates. Peter Ingersoll, one of Joseph Smith's friends at Palmyra, testi-

THE ANGEL MORONI DELIVERING THE GOLDEN PLATES AND THE
URIM AND THUMMIM TO JOSEPH SMITH, JR.

From a contemporary woodcut

them. Martin Harris never saw the plates, for he was separated from the Prophet by a curtain when he took down Joseph Smith's words. They were working at the house of Isaac Hale, Joseph Smith's father-in-law, in Harmony, Pennsylvania. When pressed by his father-in-law, who was supporting him, for a sight of the golden plates, Joseph Smith replied that his commands from heaven were that the first to see the plates must be a male child who would be born to his wife Emma. Emma conceived and bore a child, but he died before the plates could be shown to him.

Meanwhile, Martin Harris had begged to be allowed to take as much of the manuscript as had been finished to show his doubting wife and thereby convince her once for all that there were plates, and that there would be a book. Joseph Smith inquired twice of the Lord whether he should entrust the manuscript to Martin Harris to take to Palmyra, and the Lord answered in the negative. But Martin Harris was insistent and probably threatened to withdraw his financial support. Joseph asked God a third time, at the request of Martin Harris, and apparently this time the necessity for conciliating the majority stockholder dawned upon the Lord, for He changed His mind and answered in the affirmative. God said that Martin Harris could take the manuscript, if he promised to show it to no one except his wife, his brother, Preserved Harris, his father, and his mother, and his wife's sister, Mrs. Cobb. But what man could resist the temptation to show a new Bible? Joseph Smith always maintained that it was because Martin Harris violated this solemn covenant that the calamity which ensued was visited upon them. Martin Harris took the 116 pages of manuscript which had been completed and left for Palmyra. Joseph Smith awaited his return to Harmony impatiently, and when, after three weeks, he did not return, Joseph hurried to Palmyra. Martin met Joseph at the house of Joseph's father, and Martin reluctantly admitted to the Prophet that he had lost the manuscript. Joseph's mother, in her book, gave this description of the scene:

"'Oh, my God!' said Joseph, clinching his hands. 'All is lost! all is lost! What shall I do? I have sinned—it is I who tempted the wrath of God. I should have been satisfied with the first answer which I received from the Lord; for he told me that it was not safe to let the writings go out of my possession.' He wept and groaned and walked the floor continually. At length he told Martin to go back and search again.

" 'No,' said Martin, 'it is all in vain; for I have ripped open beds and pillows; and I know it is not there. . . .' "

"I besought him not to mourn so," wrote Mrs. Smith, "for perhaps the Lord would forgive him, after a short season of humiliation and repentance. But what could I say to comfort him, when he saw all the family in the same situation of mind as himself; for sobs and groans, and the most bitter lamentations filled the house. However, Joseph was more distressed than the rest, as he better understood the consequences of disobedience. And he continued, pacing back and forth, meantime weeping and grieving, until about sunset, when, by persuasion, he took a little nourishment.

"The next morning he set out for home. We parted with heavy hearts, for it now appeared that all which we had so fondly anticipated, and which had been the source of so much secret gratification, had in a moment fled, and fled for ever."

But Mother Smith was right, and her consoling words came true. Before long the Lord gave Joseph Smith, Jr., a revelation in Harmony, Susquehanna County, Pennsylvania, in which He told him to take up from page 117 and not to worry about the 116 lost pages, which had been stolen by his enemies to confound him. Smith and Harris both believed that Mrs. Martin Harris had stolen the 116 pages, and that she had burned them, but, tantalizingly, she refused to admit or to deny the accusation. Her only answer to all her husband's threats and entreaties was, "Joe Smith may peek for it." It might be thought that since he still had the golden plates, and since he still had the Urim and Thummim, Joseph Smith could begin at the beginning and retranslate the lost pages, but he was afraid that after he had published the Book of Mormon the 116 pages would be made public, and it would be discovered that they were not exactly the same as those contained in the Book of Mormon. However, the Lord conveniently solved the difficulty by commanding Joseph Smith to begin his bible at page 117.

Sobs and groans and bitter lamentations filled the Smith household when its members heard of the loss of the manuscript, for they were depending upon Joseph's theological enterprise to improve the family fortunes. Mother Smith concludes her account of the sad episode with this miracle:

"It seemed as though Martin Harris, for his transgression, suffered temporally as well as spiritually. The same day on which the foregoing circumstance took place, a dense fog spread itself over his fields, and blighted his wheat while in the blow, so that he lost about two-thirds of his crop, whilst those fields which lay only on the opposite side of the road, received no injury whatever.

"I well remember that day of darkness, both within and without. To us, at least, the heavens seemed clothed with blackness, and the earth shrouded with gloom."[3]

When Joseph Smith returned to his family in Pennsylvania after his disheartening loss, he did not begin translating immediately. He was discouraged; he felt as Thomas Carlyle must have felt when the maid burned the French Revolution. It required another insistent revelation to Joseph Smith direct from God to persuade him to take up once more the important prophetic work he had begun. Meanwhile, he labored with his hands on a small farm to support his family. When he finally obeyed the Lord and began to translate the golden plates again, he was assisted by Oliver Cowdery. Cowdery had been a schoolmaster and a blacksmith, and in the course of his travels in New York State he met Joseph Smith's father, who told him of the gold bible. Cowdery visited Smith at Harmony, Pennsylvania, and two days after his arrival Joseph and his new amanuensis began to translate. Soon afterwards Joseph received by revelation from the Lord an appointment for Oliver Cowdery, by which Cowdery was instructed to act always as Joseph Smith's assistant. However, differences of opinion arose. Cowdery's job, according to the Lord, via Joseph Smith, was to translate the Prophet's translations into literate and grammatical English, but he seems to have had higher theological aspirations. There was one little difference, for example, about John the Apostle: whether he had died, or whether he had tarried on earth until the second coming of Jesus. Joseph Smith used his spiritual spectacles, the Urim and Thummim, to settle the matter, and the answer was that he had tarried, which was what Joseph Smith had contended from the first. Another difference of opinion arose concerning baptism for the remission of sins. Smith and Cowdery went into the woods to inquire of the Lord, and a messenger appeared from

[3] *Biographical Sketches of Joseph Smith, the Prophet, and His Progenitors for Many Generations by Lucy Smith, Mother of the Prophet.* This book is said to have been written by another from the material supplied by Mrs. Smith. It was called in by Brigham Young some years after its publication because of the information it contained about the Prophet's early life. It was later revised and reissued. First edition, Liverpool, 1853.

heaven and told Joseph to baptize Oliver and Oliver to baptize Joseph. He also commanded them to "lay hands on" each other and ordain each other into the Aaronic Priesthood. The messenger soon proved to be no other than John the Baptist, who, since he knew more about baptism than any one else, had been sent from heaven to enlighten them on the subject. He said that "he acted under the direction of Peter, James, and John, who held the keys of the Priesthood of Melchisedek," which priesthood, the highest of all, would be conferred on Smith and Cowdery in due time. When they came up out of the water after baptism, they felt spiritual improvement: "We were filled," wrote Joseph Smith, "with the Holy Ghost, and rejoiced in the God of our salvation." They immediately began to prophesy many things to each other, but what these were they did not say.

Soon afterwards Smith and Cowdery began to make converts, but only among members of the Smith family. Joseph's older brother, Hyrum, and his younger brother, Samuel Harrison Smith, visited him, and after special revelation from the Lord for their benefit, were convinced of their brother's divine inspiration, and thereafter became his enthusiastic followers. At this period revelation upon revelation came to Joseph Smith, and sometimes jointly to Joseph Smith and Oliver Cowdery, from God. Each revelation began with the sentence, "A great and marvelous work is about to come forth among the children of men." It was as if God, through his agent, Joseph Smith, Jr., were planning an advertising campaign and had hit upon that phrase as an advance slogan.

In June of 1829 Smith and Cowdery went to Fayette, Seneca County, New York, where they were invited by Peter Whitmer and his sons to board with them free of charge. One of the Whitmer boys also offered to help them in their writing. Gradually the divine translation was finished. The actual writing appears to have taken about seven months, from December, 1827, to February, 1828, from April 12, 1828, to June 14, 1828, and from April 7, 1829, to June 11, 1829. Taking the first edition of 588 pages as a guide, this allows about two or three pages each day. In order to insure privacy during the proceedings, a blanket, which served as a portière, was stretched across the Whitmer family living-room, to shelter the translator and the golden plates from the eyes of any who might call while the work was in progress. Sometimes Emma Smith, sometimes Oliver Cowdery, and sometimes Christian Whitmer acted as scribe to Joseph's dictation. David Whitmer in an interview published in the Chicago *Tribune* of December 15, 1885, gave this description of the method of work:

"After prayer Smith would sit on one side of a table and the amanuenses, in turn as they became tired, on the other. Those present and not actively engaged in the work seated themselves around the room and then the work began. After affixing the magical spectacles to his eyes, Smith would take the plates and translate the characters one at a time. The graven characters would appear in succession to the seer, and directly under the character, when viewed through the glasses, would be the translation in English. Sometimes the character would be a single word, and frequently an entire sentence. In translating the characters Smith, who was illiterate and but little versed in Biblical lore, was ofttimes compelled to spell the words out, not knowing the correct pronunciation, and Mr. Whitmer recalls the fact that at that time Smith did not even know that Jerusalem was a walled city. Cowdery, however, being a school-teacher, rendered invaluable aid in pronouncing hard words and giving their proper definition."

Joseph Smith once said that he could see the printed characters which he translated into the Book of Mormon just as well with his eyes shut as with his eyes open. Whenever he was asked in what language the characters were engraved, Joseph always replied. "Reformed Egyptian."

FACSIMILE SPECIMEN SUBMITTED BY JOSEPH SMITH AS "CARACTORS"
ENGRAVED ON THE GOLDEN PLATES

At last Joseph Smith and his earthly collaborators finished their translation; they secured the copyright of the book in the name of "Joseph Smith, Jun., author and proprietor," and made arrangements for printing five thousand copies for three thousand dollars. Just at this time Joseph Smith received an interesting revelation which was called, "A Commandment of God and not of man, to Martin Harris, given, Manchester, New York, March, 1830, by Him who is Eternal." The first part of the revelation takes many awful paragraphs to establish the eternity of God and the potency of his punishments. Then it proceeds:

"Wherefore I command you [Martin Harris] to repent, and keep the commandments which you have received by the hand of my servant, Joseph Smith, Jun., in my name;

"And it is by my almighty power that you have received them;

"Therefore I command you to repent—repent, lest I smite you by the rod of my mouth, and by my wrath, and by my anger, and your sufferings be sore—how sore you know not, how exquisite you know not, yea, how hard to bear you know not! . . .

"And again, I command thee that thou shalt not covet thy neighbor's wife; nor seek thy neighbor's life.

"And again, I command thee that thou shalt not covet thine own property, but impart it freely to the printing of the Book of Mormon, which contains the truth and the word of God. . . .

"Behold, this is a great and the last commandment which I shall give unto you concerning this matter; for this shall suffice for thy daily walk, even unto the end of thy life."

God said, in effect, that He did not want to have to speak of it again, and then He concluded with this command: "Pay the debt thou hast contracted with the printer. Release thyself from bondage." [4] And Martin Harris repented of his sins, ceased to covet his own property, and pledged $3,000 to Joseph Smith for the expense of printing the Book of Mormon.

The manuscript was guarded carefully. So that there might be no danger of loss by fire, Oliver Cowdery took only a few pages each day to the printer's shop, and on these trips to the printer, he was accompanied by a bodyguard. It seems that no dependence at all could be placed on God to protect His sacred work. Meanwhile, the people of Palmyra organized a mass meeting and pledged themselves before it was printed not to buy the Book of Mormon after it was published. This caused the printer

[4] *The Doctrine and Covenants of the Church of Jesus Christ of Latter-day Saints.* Section 19. That book contains all the published revelations from God to Joseph Smith, Jr.

to cease work until he was assured that he would receive the rest of his money. Martin Harris, in spite of the strict warning from God, had delayed raising all the money, but he was trying to sell his farm in order to pay the printer. Hyrum Smith, Joseph's older brother, became impatient, and he suggested that the money be raised in another way. David Whitmer, who was then closely associated with the enterprise, wrote later:

"Brother Hyrum said it had been suggested to him that some of the brethren might go to Toronto, Canada, and sell the copy-right of the Book of Mormon for considerable money: and he persuaded Joseph to inquire of the Lord about it. Joseph concluded to do so. He had not yet given up the stone. Joseph looked into the hat in which he placed the stone, and received a revelation that some of the brethren should go to Toronto, Canada, and that they would sell the copy-right of the Book of Mormon. Hiram Page and Oliver Cowdery went to Toronto on this mission, but they failed entirely to sell the copy-right, returning without any money. . . . Well, we were all in great trouble; and we asked Joseph how it was that he had received a revelation from the Lord for some brethren to go to Toronto and sell the copy-right, and the brethren had utterly failed in their undertaking. Joseph did not know how it was, so he inquired of the Lord about it, and behold the following revelation came through the stone: *Some revelations are of God: some revelations are of man: and some revelations are of the devil.* So we see that the revelation to go to Toronto and sell the copy-right was not of God, but was of the devil or the heart of man." [5]

It was the will of the Lord that the money must be raised by Martin Harris, and He would have it no other way.

Daniel Hendrix, who read proof on the Book of Mormon, testified that the penmanship of the manuscript was good, but that the grammar and spelling were hopelessly inaccurate, and that punctuation and paragraphs were entirely missing.

Many impartial non-Mormons have wondered what became of Joseph Smith's golden plates of the Book of Mormon after he had translated them into English. Joseph Smith always maintained that the same angel of God who had given them to him conveniently took them back again, and in a sermon delivered many years later in Utah Brigham Young gave this vivid description of the scene of the return of the golden tablets, which seems to rival the magic phenomena of the Arabian Nights:

[5] *Address to Believers in Christ,* by David Whitmer, pp. 30-31.

"When Joseph got the plates, the angel instructed him to carry them back to the hill Cumorah, which he did. Oliver says that when Joseph and Oliver went there, the hill opened, and they walked into a cave, in which there was a large and spacious room. He says he did not think, at the time, whether they had the light of the sun or artificial light; but that it was just as light as day. They laid the plates on a table; it was a large table that stood in the room. Under this table there was a pile of plates as much as two feet high, and there were altogether in this room more plates than probably many waggon loads; they were piled up in the corners and along the walls. The first time they went there the sword of Laban hung upon the wall; but when they went again it had been taken down and laid upon the table across the gold plates; it was unsheathed, and on it was written these words: 'This sword will never be sheathed again until the kingdoms of this world become the kingdom of our God and his Christ.' " [6]

Brigham Young concluded his sermon with this assurance of his faith in the incident: "I tell you this as coming not only from Oliver Cowdery, but others who were familiar with it, and who understood it just as well as we understand coming to this meeting, enjoying the day, and by and by we separate and go away, forgetting most of what is said, but remembering some things."

Towards the end of their work Joseph Smith and his assistant translators discovered a notation on the golden plates that they were to be shown to three witnesses, who would thereafter testify before the world that they had seen real, gold plates. It seemed to Oliver Cowdery, Martin Harris, and David Whitmer that they had earned this privilege, and they requested Smith to ask God if He was willing that they should be The Three Witnesses. Accordingly, Joseph Smith received a revelation in June, 1829, that if Oliver Cowdery, Martin Harris, and David Whitmer would remain faithful they would see the golden plates, the Urim and Thummim, and the Sword of Laban. The second paragraph of this revelation is significant. "And it is," said God, "by your faith that you shall obtain a view of them, even by that faith which was had by the prophets of old." It is a question whether the three men were to accept the plates by faith or to see the plates as a reward for their faith.

A few days later the four retired to the woods to seek fulfilment of this revelation. They prayed but received no answer.

[6] *Journal of Discourses*, vol. 19, p. 38.

They prayed again, separately and in rotation, but received no answer. Then Martin Harris suggested that he withdraw, for he felt that his profane presence was the obstacle. He withdrew, and the remaining three prayed again, "and," wrote Smith, "had not been many minutes engaged in prayer, when presently we beheld a light above us in the air, of exceeding brightness; and behold, an angel stood before us. In his hands he held the plates which we had been praying for these to have a view of. He turned over the leaves one by one, so that we could see them, and discern the engravings thereon distinctly." They heard a voice "from out the bright light above us," saying: "These plates have been revealed by the power of God. The translation of them which you have seen is correct, and I command you to bear record of what you now see and hear."

Joseph Smith then went to seek Martin Harris, whom he found at some distance, "fervently engaged in prayer." He asked Joseph to join him, and after they had prayed together they received the same vision and the same message as the others had just received. Mormons have explained that because Martin Harris lost part of the translation he was not forgiven without an extra prayer, and that his pride and self-will in delaying to pay the expenses of printing the Book of Mormon were responsible for the delay in the spiritual manifestation to him. According to his mother, Joseph Smith returned from the woods very happy that he had witnesses besides himself to bear the burden before the world of the authenticity of the golden plates.

Another version of this memorable scene has it that Joseph Smith opened a box which he said contained the golden plates and showed it to his three witnesses. They could see nothing in the box and said, "Brother Joseph, we do not see the plates." The Prophet flew into a rage. "O ye of little faith!" he said, "how long will God bear with this wicked and perverse generation? Down on your knees, brethren, every one of you—and pray God for the forgiveness of your sins, and for a holy and living faith which cometh down from heaven." The disciples dropped to their knees and began to pray fervently. For two hours this continued with fanatic earnestness, and at the end of that time they were fully persuaded that they saw golden plates.

David Whitmer in an interview in the Kingston, Missouri, *Times,* December 27, 1887, thus described the scene of the plates:

"[The plates] were shown to us in this way—Joseph, Oliver and I were sitting on a log, when we were overshadowed by a light more glorious than that of the sun. In the midst of this light, but a few feet from us, appeared a table, upon which were many golden plates. . . . I saw them as plain as I see you now, and distinctly heard the voice of the Lord declaiming that the records of the plates of the 'Book of Mormon' were translated by the gift and the power of God."

Professor Woodbridge Riley has contended that the vision of The Three Witnesses is "that form of hallucination which may occur either in the normal state, or be induced in the state of light hypnosis. . . . The ideas and interests which were uppermost in the mind were projected outwards. Harris had received the first 'transcription of the gold plates;' Whitmer had been saturated with notices of ancient engravings; Cowdery, for weeks at a time, had listened to the sound of a voice translating the record of the Nephites. When that voice was again heard in the grove, when the four sought 'by fervent and humble prayer to have a view of the plates,' there is little wonder that there arose a psychic mirage, complete in every detail. Furthermore, the rotation in praying, the failure of the first two attempts, the repeated workings of the prophet over doubting Harris, but serve to bring out the additional incentives to the hypnotic hallucination. Repetition, steady attention, absence of mistrust, self-surrender to the will of the principal,—all the requisites are present, not as formulæ but as facts." [7]

Martin Harris was questioned by a lawyer in Palmyra concerning his view of the golden plates:

" 'Did you see the plates, and the engravings on them with your bodily eyes?' Harris replied, 'Yes, I saw them with my eyes—they were shown unto me by the power of God and not of man.' 'But did you see them with your natural,—your bodily eyes, just as you see this pencil-case in my hand? Now say *no* or *yes* to this.' Harris replied, 'Why I did not see them as I do that pencil-case, yet I saw them with the eye of faith; I saw them just as distinctly as I see any thing around me, though at the time they were covered over with a cloth.' "

[7] *The Founder of Mormonism, A Psychological Study of Joseph Smith, Jr.,* by I. Woodbridge Riley, pp. 227-228.

And I saw another angel fly in the midst of heaven, having the everlasting gospel to preach unto them that dwell on the earth, and to every nation, and kindred, and tongue, and people.—Rev. 14:6.

And he shall set up an ensign for the nations and shall assemble the outcasts of Israel, and gather together the dispersed of Judah from the four corners of the earth.—Isa. 11:12.

OLIVER COWDERY.

DAVID WHITMER.

MARTIN HARRIS.

"YE ARE MY WITNESSES"

THE THREE WITNESSES

The simplicity of Martin Harris throughout his connection with the Book of Mormon frequently resembled that of Bottom, the Weaver. He was never sure just how he had seen the plates, or whether he had seen plates at all, but he was sure that he had seen something. Concerning this testimony of The Three Witnesses, Mark Twain wrote in *Roughing It:*

"Some people have to have a world of evidence before they can come anywhere in the neighborhood of believing anything; but for me, when a man tells me that he has 'seen the engravings which are upon the plates,' and not only that, but an angel was there at the time, and saw him see them, and probably took his receipt for it, I am very far on the road to conviction, no matter whether I ever heard of that man before or not, and even if I do not know the name of the angel, or his nationality either."

In every edition of the Book of Mormon there is printed this testimonial:

THE TESTIMONY OF THREE WITNESSES

Be it known unto all nations, kindreds, tongues, and people, unto whom this work shall come, that we, through the grace of God the Father, and our Lord Jesus Christ, have seen the plates which contain this record, which is a record of the people of Nephi, and also of the Lamanites, his brethren, and also of the people of Jared, which came from the tower of which hath been spoken; and we also know that they have been translated by the gift and power of God, for his voice hath declared it unto us; wherefore we know of a surety, that the work is true. And we also testify that we have seen the engravings which are upon the plates; and they have been shewn unto us by the power of God, and not of man. And we declare with words of soberness, that an Angel of God came down from heaven, and he brought and laid before our eyes, that we beheld and saw the plates, and the engravings thereon; and we know that it is by the grace of God the Father, and our Lord Jesus Christ, that we beheld and bear record that these things are true; and it is marvellous in our eyes: Nevertheless, the voice of the Lord commanded us that we should bear record of it; wherefore, to be obedient unto the commandments of God, we bear testimony of these things.—And we know that if we are faithful in Christ, we shall rid our garments of the blood of all men, and be found spotless before the judgment seat of Christ, and shall dwell with him eternally in the heavens. And the honor be to the Father, and to the Son, and to the Holy Ghost, which is one God. Amen.

OLIVER COWDERY,
DAVID WHITMER,
MARTIN HARRIS.

The Testimony of Three Witnesses was followed by a testimonial of eight additional witnesses. This was in conformity with the policy of the early Mormons to make everything as it was in the early days of the Christian religion. The total number of witnesses, eleven, is the same number as those who bore witness to the original Christian miracles. The eight additional witnesses saw the plates without any special spiritual manifestations on the part of God, and they had the plates in their hands, according to their testimony:

AND ALSO THE TESTIMONY OF EIGHT WITNESSES

Be it known unto all nations, kindreds, tongues, and people, unto whom this work shall come, that Joseph Smith, Jr., the Author and Proprietor of this work, has shewn unto us the plates of which hath been spoken, which have the appearance of gold; and as many of the leaves as the said Smith has translated, we did handle with our hands; and we also saw the engravings thereon, all of which has the appearance of ancient work, and of curious workmanship. And this we bear record, with words of soberness, that the said Smith has shewn unto us, for we have seen and hefted, and know of a surety, that the said Smith has got the plates of which we have spoken. And we give our names unto the world, to witness unto the world that which we have seen: and we lie not, God bearing witness of it.

CHRISTIAN WHITMER,
JACOB WHITMER,
PETER WHITMER, JR.,
JOHN WHITMER,
HIRAM PAGE,
JOSEPH SMITH, SEN.,
HYRUM SMITH,
SAMUEL H. SMITH.[8]

[8] The Testimony of Three Witnesses and The Testimony of Eight Witnesses are quoted from The Book of Mormon, first edition, 1830.

Concerning this testimonial, which Professor Riley said "has the suspicious uniformity of a patent medicine testimonial," Mark Twain wrote:

"And when I am far on the road to conviction, and eight men, be they grammatical or otherwise, come forward and tell me that they have seen the plates too; and not only seen those plates but 'hefted' them, I *am* convinced. I could not feel more satisfied and at rest if the entire Whitmer family had testified."

Although all three of the main witnesses to the authenticity of the golden plates were either expelled from the Church or left it in anger a few years after their testimony was published, each of them retained his superstitious belief in the Book of Mormon's divine origin, and each of them maintained that belief on his deathbed. Newspapers awaited the deaths of these men eagerly, in the hope that as they were dying they would confess to fraud, and many attempts were made after their apostasy to persuade them to reveal the truth. All such attempts were unsuccessful. Oliver Cowdery's last words, given to David Whitmer, were: "Brother David, be true to your testimony of the Book of Mormon." That, at least, is what Brother David said. Martin Harris was rebaptized into the Mormon Church, and his last words when he died at the age of ninety-two were: "Book! Book! Book!" This is taken by the Mormons to refer to the Book of Mormon, for Martin Harris had never been a great reader. David Whitmer's deathbed scene was described in the Richmond, Missouri, *Democrat*. He called his family and his doctor to his bedside and said: "Dr. Buchanan, I want you to say whether or not I am in my right mind, before giving my dying testimony." The doctor answered, "Yes, you are in your right mind." Then the old man said: "I want to say to you all, the Bible and the record of the Nephites *is true*." On his tombstone there is this inscription: "The Record of the Jews and the Record of the Nephites *are one*. Truth is eternal." The Record of the Nephites is another name for the Book of Mormon.

The Mormons regard these dying testimonials with great self-satisfaction, but they are not difficult to explain. Men superstitious enough once to have accepted Joseph Smith sincerely as a Prophet of God would, with the prospect of death and its uncertain after-effects before them, prefer to maintain their early faith rather than kick away from under them all props and hurl from their perplexed and sick minds all safe comforts. It is also a source of great satisfaction to the Mormons that during the many years between their break with the Church and their deaths these men never exposed the Church. But this too is not difficult to explain. To expose the Church would have meant to expose themselves, and it is not likely that men would ever again trust a man who admitted that he had helped to create a fantastic speculation in the image of God. To denounce the Church was to denounce themselves in certain terms as men without honor, who would stoop to any deception for a living, and therefore, if they had consciously deceived others, it was wisdom in them to say nothing about their past in the hope that men would forget it in the light of their future. However, it is more likely that these men had nothing to expose, for their extreme simplicity had aided in their own sincere deception.

Orson Pratt, who, as we have seen, sprang so valiantly to the defense of the Prophet's angels, also came to the defense in the matter of the witnesses to the Book of Mormon. In his *Divine Authenticity of the Book of Mormon* he admitted that none but the Prophet's eleven hand-picked witnesses had seen the golden plates, but, he pointed out, the tablets which Moses brought down from Sinai were kept in the secret places of the Holy of Holies, "and none but the high priest had the privilege of going in there, and he only once a year." When some complained that no one had seen the manuscripts of the Book of Mormon except Smith's friends, Orson Pratt asked his opponents to bring forth one living witness "that has seen even one of the original manuscripts of the books of the Bible." And Pratt's opponents believed in the divine origin of the Bible. When Christ arose from the dead, Pratt pointed out, he did not show himself publicly but only to a few of his best friends, and they were instructed to testify to the rest of the world concerning his resurrection. In the matter of the golden plates of the Book of Mormon Joseph Smith had only followed his eminent example. Because of his powers of thought and literary ability, Orson Pratt was considered the philosopher of Mormonism.

Of course, even if Orson Pratt proved the Bible to be a snare and a delusion, he would not thereby have established the divine authenticity of the Book of Mormon, but his rhetorical questions gave his contemporaries many uncomfortable moments, for they could never admit to themselves that the Bible was a chronicle rather than a revelation, and Pratt's comparisons seemed to have elements of truth which they dared not admit. Almost everybody between the years 1830 and 1850 took the Bible literally, but not quite so literally as the Mormons, who, as we shall see, wished to revive some of the practices as well as the precepts of the children of Israel and the contemporaries of Christ.

IV

Much time and thought have been spent in disproving the divine origin of the Book of Mormon from external evidence. The merits or demerits of the book itself have been somewhat obscured in the frantic effort to prove it either a sacred work or a wicked fraud. Even assuming that Joseph Smith saw an angel of God who showed him golden tablets with a golden clasp and gave him the spiritual spectacles whereby to translate his possession, the Book of Mormon must still be condemned because in it there is none of what William James called that "true record of the inner experiences of great-souled persons wrestling with the crises of their fate." If the Book of Mormon was inspired by God, it was His second-rate work.

The Book of Mormon is the story of the wanderings of three ancient peoples. One of them, the Jaredites, came directly from the Tower of Babel, and the other two came originally from Jerusalem or thereabouts. These people, after prolonged sufferings, dissensions, and wars, finally arrived on the American continent. The two tribes from Jerusalem were headed by one Lehi, who led his people forth about the year 600 B.C. He died in the wilderness and bequeathed the leadership of the expedition to his youngest son, Nephi. But the other brothers disputed their father's will, and the family split into the Nephites, advocates of the youngest son, and the Lamanites, followers of the eldest son, Laman. There was constant war between these two peoples, and finally the wicked Lamanites wiped out their righteous brothers, after both tribes had arrived in America. In 420 A.D. the whole American continent was in possession of the Lamanites, from whom, according to the Book of Mormon, the American Indians are descended. It was the task of Joseph Smith, Jr., to redeem the continent, which, by the way, is the Promised Land, for the righteous Nephites. Thus the Book of Mormon has an unhappy ending, but it offers the promise that everybody will live happily forever after the time of the proper redemption.

Before they were annihilated the Nephites had kept accounts on metal tablets of their wanderings and their wars. Mormon, who was the last of his race, and who lived about 400 A.D., was commanded by God to take care of all the plates deposited by his ancestors from the time of the first Lehi. He was also appointed by God to be editor of these plates, and it was the abridgment of them which he made that Joseph Smith, Jr., found deposited in the Hill of Cumorah near Palmyra, N. Y. Mormon died before his work was finished, but his son, Moroni, carried it on and eventually completed it.

When he was asked the meaning of the name Mormon, Joseph Smith was not content to let it rest as a proper name. He said that it was derived from the English "more," and the Egyptian "mon," the latter meaning good, and that therefore Mormon means "more good." Smith's complete philological explanation was: "We say from the Saxon good; the Dane god; the Goth goda; the German gut; the Dutch goed; the Latin bonus; the Greek kalos; the Hebrew tob; and the Egyptian mon. Hence, with the addition of more, or the contraction mor, we have the word Mormon, which means, literally, more good." One of Joseph Smith's minor weaknesses was a pretension to philological erudition.

In the first edition the Book of Mormon took 588 closely printed pages to tell its simple story. The book is padded with material from the Old Testament and the New Testament and with predictions of ruin and accounts of famine. It is one of the dullest books in world literature, and, according to one writer who was a faithful Mormon for many years, even many devout Mormons have been unable to read it through consecutively. Mark Twain said of it: "It is chloroform in print. If Joseph Smith composed this book, the act was a miracle—keeping awake while he did it was, at any rate." Sir Richard Burton, who took a great interest in the Mormons, and who spent some time among them in Salt Lake City, was unsuccessful in his attempts to read all of the Book of Mormon:

"Surely," he wrote, "there never was a book so thoroughly dull and heavy: it is monotonous as a sage-prairie. Though not liable to be terrified by dry or hard reading, I was, it is only fair to own,

steel many centuries before it was used and the use by the Jaredites of a compass centuries before that instrument was known.

The attempt to ape the Bible is followed carefully in the style of the Book of Mormon. It is filled with "And it came to pass." Mark Twain said of Joseph Smith as an author: "Whenever he found his speech growing too modern—which was about every sentence or two—he ladled in a few such Scriptural phrases as 'exceeding sore,' 'and it came to pass,' etc., and made things satisfactory again. 'And it came to pass' was his pet. If he had left that out, his Bible would have been only a pamphlet."

The errors in grammar, punctuation, and spelling in the new bible were on almost every page of the first edition, and it was found advisable later to revise these. The modern editions contain more than 2,000 changes, mainly grammatical, but it is said that a few "And it came to passes" have been taken out.

Orson Pratt, the philosopher of Mormonism, wrote: "The nature of the message in the Book of Mormon is such, that if true, no one can possibly be saved and reject it; if false, no one can possibly be saved and receive it. Therefore, every soul in all the world is equally interested in ascertaining its truth or falsity." At the time this challenge was written it was comparatively true. Men and women were then tremendously exercised in public over the future, and some men proved to themselves that the Book of Mormon was true, and others proved to their neighbors that it was false. After approximately a hundred years of this process, nothing material has happened, and the passions of the controversy have been softened by history. At the time when Pratt wrote his statement, and when Brigham Young ruled, the issue was vitally interesting, for then men largely believed that there was a future life, and that it was necessary to adopt the best means of arriving at it in state. There is, of course, another alternative to Orson Pratt's dilemma. We can rest in comfort, if not in security, with the determination not to cross such a bridge until we come to it. But in order to understand the attitude of the period, we must put aside for the occasion this agnosticism, and to realize the state of mind of the people of the United States in 1830, we must allow them to beg the question of the hereafter.

V

The people who surrounded Joseph Smith and Brigham Young in their youth accepted the presence of a heaven and hell much as we to-day accept the presence of a Republican and a Democratic party. Therefore, no matter how indifferent they may have been to the doctrines and dogmas of specific sects, sooner or later they were all faced with a most troublesome difficulty. They suddenly felt themselves unprepared for their inevitable death, and that meant, as a matter of course, an eternity with real flames and ten thousand devils in the cast, in which spectacle each one felt that he or she occupied the unenviable position of the subject of torment.

A good example of the temper of the times is found in the autobiography of Charles G. Finney, who was the most inspiring evangelist of the period of Joseph Smith's and Brigham Young's adolescence. Finney was addressing a congregation in a village of western New York—much the same kind of village in which both Brigham Young and Joseph Smith grew up. Finney offered his audience the choice of accepting Christ by making peace with God in exactly the manner in which Finney directed, or of rejecting Christ. Those who were willing to accept the Finney God were asked to stand up. The entire congregation sat still in hesitant bewilderment. Finney looked down at them with his deep-set, fierce, hypnotic eyes and said: "Then you are committed. You have taken your stand. You have rejected Christ and his Gospel; and ye are witnesses one against the other, and God is witness against you all. This is explicit, and you may remember as long as you live, that you have thus publicly committed yourselves against the Saviour, and said, 'We will not have this man, Christ Jesus, to reign over us.'" The congregation was awestruck as Finney left the pulpit and hurried from the building. When they went home that night, people all over the town were in fearful distress. One young woman was dumb with terror for sixteen hours. The entire village was converted immediately, and a prayer meeting was held every night thereafter in the village barroom by the barkeeper, who had previously been the most notorious blasphemer in the community. The people did not seem to realize that there were any alternatives except the Charles G. Finney God or damnation for eternity. By urging upon them the fear of the Devil, Finney had succeeded in persuading them of the love of God.

Western New York in 1830 was bare of intellectual and social resources. The church was also the club for men and women, the theater, the library, and, when revival meetings were held, the motion picture performance. Men, women, and children took an earnest interest in the personalities of Moses, Abraham, Jacob, Joseph, David, Saul, and Jesus. The Bible narratives were the only fictions available for their entertainment and study, and the Bible was accordingly accepted as both human and divine. The people were as much interested in the special traits of their favorite Bible characters as their descendants are in those of their favorite motion picture actresses. It is easy to understand, therefore, how Joseph Smith, however ignorant he may have been of other literature, obtained the intimate knowledge of the lives of the men and women of the Bible, which served him so well when he came to write, or, as he preferred to call it, to translate the Book of Mormon.

One reason why the religious condition of the United States in 1830 was so unsettled is found in the absence of any established church, in the lap of which the common people could comfortably rest their convictions concerning the other world while they went about making the most of this one. In March, 1829, while Joseph Smith was still at work on his Book of Mormon, Robert Southey wrote what has since proved a remarkable prophecy concerning the religious condition of the United States. In his work on Sir Thomas More, Southey wrote:

"America is in more danger from religious fanaticism. The Government there not thinking it necessary to provide religious instruction for the people in any of the New States, the prevalence of superstition, and that, perhaps, in some wild and terrible shape, may be looked for as one likely consequence of this great and portentous omission. An Old Man of the Mountain might find dupes and followers as readily as the All-friend Jemima; and the next Aaron Burr who seeks to carve a kingdom for himself out of the overgrown territories of the Union, may discern that fanaticism is the most effective weapon with which ambition can arm itself; that the way for both is prepared by that immorality which the want of religion naturally and necessarily induces, and that Camp Meetings may be very well directed to forward the designs of Military Prophets. Were there another Mohammed to arise, there is no part of the

world where he would find more scope or fairer opportunity than
in that part of the Anglo-American Union into which the older
States continually discharge the restless part of their population,
leaving Laws and Gospel to overtake it if they can, for in the march
of modern colonization both are left behind."

Within one year after Southey's prediction Mormonism was
launched, the Yankee Mohammed had arisen and was finding
customers in the migratory population of the small towns. The
future history of Mormonism, as we shall see, paralleled to a
remarkable degree Robert Southey's prediction.

The absence of any established church with official religious
instruction resulted in confusion. The various sects of Christianity were dividing and subdividing, so that, by a sort of process
of fission, each sect became many little sects with slight family
differences and many family quarrels. This wild dissension and
uproarious misunderstanding were likely to breed a state of bewilderment in an adolescent mind, and both Brigham Young and
Joseph Smith confessed to such a state of mind in their youth.
They asked themselves often, Which is the right religion? And
it is not difficult to understand how Smith soon arrived at the
simple conclusion that there was none, and that it was time some
one started one. That is the way in which most great business
enterprises have originated. Brigham Young's mind being of a
more practical turn, he could not conceive of himself as a prophet
so easily as the more mystic Smith.

During Joseph Smith's youth there were great revival meetings
at Palmyra and in the surrounding towns and villages. That
whole section of the country was in such a continual state of
orgiastic religious ferment that it was known as the "burnt-over
district." It was not only fashionable in that crude society to
suffer a "saving change of heart," but it was considered radical
not to do so. The religious revivals were the most powerful
imaginative influence of their time. The first large-scale revival
was that of the Presbyterians in Kentucky, which began in Logan
County in 1800. Twenty thousand people were present on one
night. Camp fires gleamed at various spots in the huge enclosure
cleared for the purpose by zealous Kentucky woodsmen. Around
them was blackness and an ominous forest. As it grew darker
the voices of the preachers, with their prophecies of a lurid and

a terrifying doom, grew louder. Hysterical song burst from them and their congregations; shouts of religious ecstasy penetrated the undertone of moans, sobs, and groans. Men and women remained all night, rushing from group to group at the rumor that livelier things were happening here or there. Then those who caught the spell began to fall. They writhed and finally became rigid, in what was regarded as a religious trance. The preaching went on unconcerned as the bodies fell under the eyes of the preachers. Spontaneous preaching began from the congregation. At the Kentucky revival a little girl of seven was propped on a man's shoulders, so that the huge mass of men and women might hear her lisping testimony of new-found grace, until finally she sank exhausted on the man's head.

At the height of their frenzy converts were seized with strange manifestations of divinity. Their muscles contracted and contorted; they enjoyed what was known as "the jerks," consisting of spasmodic wriggling of the head or feet, so that the victim either hopped about like a demented frog or wagged his head back and forth like a neurotic horse. One minister estimated proudly that in his rather small congregation more than five hundred persons were "jerking" at once. Some were seized with "the barks," which, as the name implies, consisted of hopping about on hands and feet and barking furiously like an irritated mastiff, completing the imitation by snapping the teeth or by growls. There was also the holy laugh. As the minister was preaching, members of the congregation broke out into solemn laughter, not of criticism, but of devotion. Speaking of the effects of revivals, an English clergyman who witnessed them remarked: "Sometimes, even, in endeavoring to make a convert the unwise and frantic preacher would make a madman." And at the meetings in the night, with the surroundings of concealing woods and the excitement of religious ecstasy, ministers complained that the men and women of their congregation formed into couples and wandered off into the woods for inexplicable diversion and relief, so that it became necessary to station night watches at various places in the enclosures in an effort to stem the tide of sexual promiscuity.

The rumors of these huge religious conversions spread from the mountains which at first confined them to all the communities of the sparsely settled country, and religion became an excitement.

The region in western New York where Joseph Smith and Brigham Young lived was a particularly fertile field for religious enthusiasm. During a period of twenty years it was the scene of the origin of three religious movements which stirred American life at the time. Besides the Mormons, the Millerites also originated in this "burnt-over district." Under the influence of a Vermont farmer, William Miller, thousands of people climbed to the tops of high hills one day in the eighteen-forties and waited confidently for the trumpet call that was to proclaim the end of the world. And then they came down again and waited some more, just as confidently. The Rochester spiritualist rappers arose in the same neighborhood. The Followers of Christ ·were passing through on their way west. Their prophet, who came from Canada, was described as a man of austere habits, who rejected surnames, forbade marriage, allowed his followers to cohabit promiscuously, and had not changed his clothes in seven years.

This religious enthusiasm was a reaction from a period of religious indifference, and even antagonism, which in turn had been a reaction from the hell-fire period of Jonathan Edwards and his colonial associates. Just before the Revolutionary War, during that war, and after the war, there was widespread infidelity, and what the clergy chose to regard as immorality in the form of sexual aberration and drinking. Tom Paine had supplied a definite demand in his crystallization of the common unbelief in the *Age of Reason,* which, in spite of its attempted suppression, was circulated widely. Students at Yale College boasted of their infidelity and went about calling themselves Diderot, D'Alembert, Voltaire, Rousseau, Robespierre, and Danton, instead of their own names. At Bowdoin College during this period only one student had the courage to admit that he was a Christian in the technical sense of the term. It was the common belief in the intellectual circles of the time that Christianity, so called, could not survive two generations. In 1811 when the Rev. Dr. E. D. Griffin took up his position as a minister of an evangelical church, "The current of prevailing thought was so averse to evangelical religion, that to raise a voice in its defense was to hazard one's reputation among respectable people." Men of intelligence and culture were attracted by reports of Dr. Griffin's eloquence and the powers of his mind, but such was the prejudice against religion that they wandered into his church for his Sunday evening lectures in partial disguise, and sat in obscure, dark corners with their caps over their faces and their coats turned inside out.[10] The result of the prevalent unbelief was the opposite of what the agnostics expected. It produced, not the disappearance of Christianity, but its multiplication and division under new, and sometimes weird, forms. One of these, destined to survive most of the others, was Mormonism. The time was ripe for a man who offered practical and at the same time fulsome interference of God in the affairs of men to their economic and political benefit as well as for their spiritual salvation. People were expecting a Daniel, or at least the four horsemen of the Apocalypse, to come along almost any day. Joseph Smith listened to the tumult of religious controversy, and, as one writer has pointed out, he was controlled by its influence much as a boy of 1849 was influenced by tales of gold in California. He read the Bible and retained much of it. He listened to country store discussions of religion and politics, and in his mind these influences ripened into the Book of Mormon and the establishment of his own church.

VI

There is a theory that the Book of Mormon was a plagiarization, and since its invention a few years after the Book of Mormon was published, that theory has been widely held to explain the authorship. According to this story the latter-day bible was based on a manuscript written by a literary clergyman whose name was Solomon Spalding.

Solomon Spalding was born in Ashford, Connecticut, in 1761. His brother said that early in life Solomon was interested in writing. At first, however, he studied law, but soon gave that up because religion suddenly interested him, and he entered Dartmouth College with the intention of qualifying for the ministry. He was regularly ordained and preached for three or four years, but he abandoned the ministry to become a merchant. He was not successful and moved to Conneaut, Ohio, where his brother found him building a forge. He was considerably involved in debt, and when his brother visited him to offer aid, Solomon Spalding told him that he had been writing a book, and that he was depending upon the returns from this book to pay his debts and establish him in comfort for the rest of his life. The book was entitled *The Manuscript Found*. It was an historical romance of the first settlers of America, and Solomon Spalding adopted the then prevalent theory that the American Indians were direct descendants of the lost tribes of Israel. The book was said to contain an account of their wanderings similar to that in the Book of Mormon. Spalding is said to have believed that his romance would explain the presence of mounds and fortifications on the American continent before the arrival of white men, and he also told his neighbors that in one hundred years his book would be believed as readily as any history of England. Relatives and neighbors said that Solomon Spalding finished his book and took it to the print shop of Patterson and Lambdin in Pittsburgh. Patterson and Lambdin retained the manuscript for a long time, but finally decided not to publish it, and it is said that while the manuscript was lying in their offices, it came to the attention of Sidney Rigdon, who was soon to become the right-hand man of the Prophet Joseph Smith. Meanwhile, Solomon Spalding died.

Sidney Rigdon was born February 19, 1793, on a farm about twelve miles south of Pittsburgh. Early in life he showed a great interest in religion, but first he practised the trade of printer and is said to have worked for Patterson and Lambdin, but he himself denied the connection. He was ordained a pastor in the Baptist church and held a pulpit in Pittsburgh during 1822. Here he met Alexander Campbell, the founder of Campbellism, a form of the Baptist religion. Rigdon joined Campbell and preached in favor of the restoration of the ancient order of things, and especially the old doctrine of consecration of all temporal possessions to the church. But his parishioners did not take readily to this doctrine, and Rigdon left Pittsburgh to preach Campbellism in Kirtland, Ohio. He is said to have taken Solomon Spalding's manuscript, or at least a copy of it, with him from Pittsburgh, and it is claimed that he later gave it to Joseph Smith, who, with the aid of Rigdon, used it in the composition of the Book of Mormon.

There are many flaws in this theory of the origin of the Book of Mormon. There is absolutely no evidence worthy of consideration that Sidney Rigdon and Joseph Smith ever met before more than a year after the publication of the Book of Mormon; it has also been impossible to establish definitely, in spite of desperate efforts, that Sidney Rigdon ever worked for the printing firm of Patterson and Lambdin. Solomon Spalding's manuscript was returned to him some time before his death in 1816, according to the admission of his widow, from whom the originators of the Spalding story were careful to get affidavits. Rigdon's residence in Pittsburgh was during 1821, five years after Spalding's death.

The Spalding theory was originated by Philaster Hurlburt, who was associated with the Mormons during their early history, but who was cut off from the Church for adultery and the attempted murder of the Prophet Joseph Smith. Hurlburt lectured against the Mormons soon after his excommunication, and he visited Spalding's widow, who gave him her husband's manuscript, which he told her he intended to publish in order to confound the Mormons. Later she received a letter from Hurlburt that the manuscript did not read as he had expected, and that therefore it would not be printed, but it was not returned to Mrs. Spalding. The manuscript was found many years later in a trunk in Honolulu. The trunk had once belonged to E. D. Howe, a newspaper publisher, and the author of the first book of importance against the Mormons, *Mormonism Unveiled,* in which book the Spalding theory was originated and maintained. Spalding's manuscript is now in the library of Oberlin College, and a facsimile of it was published. It bears no relation to the Book of Mormon in subject matter or in style.

The Spalding story was an attempt on the part of the first ardent anti-Mormons to discredit the divine origin of the Book of Mormon. It was based on the testimony of neighbors and relatives of Solomon Spalding given more than twenty years after the events of which they were said to be witnesses. These men and women said that the Book of Mormon sounded to them like the Spalding manuscript, which Solomon Spalding used to read to them twenty years before, while he was still at work on it, and in this long stretch of memory they were aided by those who took their testimony. The very questions which Hurlburt and Howe asked suggested the answers for which they hoped. Spalding's brother, John Spalding, expressed himself as "amazed" and moved to tears that his brother's innocent manuscript had been used for the purpose of founding a fraudulent religion, but he only experienced that amazement and shed those tears after it had been suggested to him by his interlocutors that such was the purpose for which the manuscript had been used. The whole Spalding story is an instance of the feverish efforts of anti-Mormons to prove that Joseph Smith was incapable of writing the Book of Mormon without the aid of God, and they refused to admit for a moment that he did so with the aid of God. It is my conviction that Joseph Smith wrote the Book of Mormon without the aid of God, and that the book itself shows evidence of being a product of Smith's environment.

When a man says that God was his collaborator in a literary work, and that he had visions in which angels appeared before him and promised delightful special privileges, we who do not receive angels are inclined to dismiss him with an epithet instead of an argument. But there is nothing extraordinary in the visionary phenomena of Joseph Smith's life, however remarkable they may be in detail. He is a good example of what has happened to thousands of adolescent boys and girls between the ages of fourteen and seventeen in all nations and climates. Psychologists who have specialized in religious experience have found hundreds of potential Joseph Smiths, who did not find it necessary to found religions around their conversions, but who passed through almost identical experiences. The frequency of this sudden, adolescent phenomenon of religious enthusiasm led Professor Starbuck to define religious conversion as "in its essence a normal adolescent phenomenon, incidental to the passage from the child's small universe to the wider intellectual and spiritual life of maturity."

The symptoms which most religious converts indicate are those which assailed Joseph Smith as a boy and as a young man. He experienced a sense of incompleteness and imperfection, brooding, depression, morbid introspection, conviction of sin and anxiety about the hereafter. Only a spontaneous spark was needed to light the tinder of spirituality which had been accumulating in Joseph Smith's mind for some years. Where that spark came from, and how it did its final work, are matters of detail, which, unfortunately, it is impossible to discover. Joseph Smith was sure that it came from God, and he gave details of the appearance of visiting angels; others have maintained that it came from the Devil, or from the Rev. Solomon Spalding. The important thing, however, is the background of environment, heredity, and experience which made it plausible, and almost inevitable, that Joseph Smith should act as he did. We have seen how conducive his heredity and environment were to religious enterprise, and we shall now see how he used definite bits of his experience in the composition of the Book of Mormon.

One of the principal matters of speculation in Joseph Smith's youth was the origin of the American Indian, and the most prevalent theory was that he was a direct descendant of the lost tribes of Israel. Josiah Priest published in 1824 *The Wonders of Nature and Providence* in which he presented an elaborate argument to prove that the Indians came originally from Israel. This book was copyrighted in the office of R. R. Lansing, Clerk of the Northern District of New York, the same office in which the Book of Mormon copyright was registered five years later. Meanwhile, Josiah Priest's book had circulated widely throughout western New York, and Joseph Smith may very easily have seen it during the time when he was composing the Book of Mormon. Joseph's imagination had always been stirred by the frequent discoveries of bones and pottery, old spear heads and ancient relics on the neighboring farms. There were also ancient mounds and earthworks in the neighborhood which aroused his curiosity and bewilderment. His mother wrote:

"During our evening conversations, Joseph would occasionally give us some of the most amusing recitals that could be imagined. He would describe the ancient inhabitants of this continent, their dress, mode of travelling, and the animals upon which they rode; their cities, their buildings, with every particular; their mode of warfare; and also their religious worship. This he would do with as much ease, seemingly, as if he had spent his whole life with them."

When he came to write the Book of Mormon, Joseph Smith found this facility of imagination very useful. He also used more tangible experience, however. The vision of Lehi in the first book of Nephi of the Book of Mormon parallels to a remarkable degree a vision which, according to his mother's book, Joseph's father received in a dream. This is the only detailed instance of exact duplication, but the Book of Mormon also contains discussions of most of the problems which were agitating minds in western New York during the first twenty-five years of the nineteenth century. It discusses infant baptism, ordination, the trinity, regeneration, repentance, the fall of man, the atonement, republican government, the rights of man and free masonry. During Joseph Smith's youth New York State was aroused by violent anti-Masonic riots. This influence shows markedly in the Book of Mormon, which contains several terms used in the ritual of free masonry. Masonry was always popular with the Mormons until Joseph Smith claimed that an angel of the Lord had brought him the lost key-words of several degrees, enabling him to progress further than the highest Masons. The charter of the Mormon lodge was then taken away by the Grand Lodge.

Joseph Smith differed from the ordinary revival convert in the important respect that he possessed ambition and an imagination. The tendency of the convert is to follow the leader, but, as we have seen, Joseph Smith was unable to do this. There were any number of revival ministers practising in his neighborhood, and he could have joined one or more of them and eased his mind, but it was impossible for him to be a sheep because he wanted so much to be a shepherd, and this desire was undoubtedly influenced by a realization that it was more profitable to own your own sheep. Joseph Smith's visions and revelations were probably produced by a combination of self-hypnotism and the desire to deceive for the purpose of gaining a living. That he tried often to deceive others is easy to see from some of his revelations, but that he ended by deceiving himself is just as easy to see from his actions. He needed money, and that consideration contributed to the founding of his religion, for his anxiety for his own security is ever-present. But on that account he cannot be set down as a complete fraud, as he was by many of his contemporaries. That he used his religion, sometimes crudely, to contribute to his support is no reason why he did not also believe sincerely in that religion. There was undoubtedly an element of fakery in his faith, but there was also an element of superstitious sincerity in his fakery.

William James wrote: "We may now lay it down as certain that in the distinctively religious sphere of experience, many persons (how many we cannot tell) possess the objects of their belief, not in the form of mere conceptions which their intellect accepts as true, but rather in the form of quasi-sensible realities directly apprehended." Joseph Smith was undoubtedly one of those persons whom we may call gifted or deluded as our interest in religious faith is either hot or cold. Joseph Smith was vividly aware of what William James designated "the consciousness of a presence," and in this respect he was not unusual, as the archives of the Society for Psychical Research and the private collections

JOSEPH SMITH
From a contemporary engraving

A YANKEE MOHAMMED 63

of psychologists indicate. The difference between Joseph Smith and the thousands of people who annually feel a consciousness of a presence is that he thought it either convenient or necessary to act upon his experience and found a religious sect. Had he been a man of extensive education, elegant manners, and some money, he would have been respected for his faith. by the multitude of the thoughtless and followed for his theosophy by those cultivated men and women in the United States who have always joined with the abstruse and the novel. But he was, like his eminent predecessor, Jesus, of lowly origin; he was pitifully poor; he had been known to drink to the point of intoxication; he did not go to school, and he had not read extensively in the evenings after his work on the farm. His pecuniary interest in the foundation of a strong religious community was nearer the surface of his mind and more clearly apparent in his actions than that of other mystic men with religious propensities. However, the fact that he had considerable to gain in material circumstances by the organization of a church does not prove that he was any less a true mystic. He was a Yankee mystic, who, though he had an interest in the main chance, was none the less absorbed in his visions and convinced of their reality.

In his youth Joseph Smith was torn between the fear of not being saved eternally and the desire to have a good time from day to day. Fortunately for his peace of mind he was able to reconcile the two by having himself appointed by God to have a good time. Early in his life he set up a comforting and comfortable system by which he combined faith in himself with faith in God, because he had convinced himself thoroughly that God had faith in him. The rest of his life, as we shall see, was a process of convincing other people of that intangible appointment, and that process led him to do things which were often droll but usually sincere.

The fact that Joseph Smith was uneducated is the greatest argument used in his favor by his followers and against him by his detractors. Once devout Mormons accepted by faith the idea that he was divinely inspired, they were able to point with pride to his lack of education as proof that he was a miracle. But there is nothing in the Book of Mormon that could not have been written by an uneducated man, and the claim that Smith was incapable of writing the Book of Mormon is weakened by his later literary performances. His revelations are as finished as and far more interesting than the Book of Mormon, and during the ensuing years he was the author, or, as he preferred to call it, the translator, of the *Visions of Moses,* a revised translation of the Old and New Testaments, and the *Book of Abraham.* It is true that he then had assistants, but they were useful mainly to correct grammar, for the mark of his personality is indelible in his revelations.

The alternatives in the case of the authenticity of Joseph Smith are: Either God wrote and dictated the Book of Mormon and the revelations of Joseph Smith with the aid of Joseph Smith, or Joseph Smith wrote them alone. One's decision on this point depends on how much one believes in Joseph Smith and how much one believes in God. I prefer to believe that the Book of Mormon is by "Joseph Smith, Jun., Author and Proprietor," as, with a naïve slip of the pen, the title page of the first edition puts it.

The important question is not whether Joseph Smith was divinely inspired, but whether he thought he was divinely inspired, or whether he merely preferred other people to think so to his great financial advantage. It is impossible to determine that exactly without a confession from the accused. It is my impression that he began by discovering that he could fool other people and ended by completely fooling himself. Whatever else he was, however, Joseph Smith was not commonplace. As a boy he was conspicuous for his lack of conformity to the ordinary ways of making a living on a farm by the sweat of his brow, and we shall see that as a man he was conspicuous as a prophet, a general, a lover and a self-constituted candidate for President of the United States.

Chapter III

THE HOUSE OF BONDAGE

I

THE Church of Jesus Christ of Latter-day Saints was organized formally by Joseph Smith, Jr., his two brothers, three Whitmers, and Oliver Cowdery on April 6, 1830. Orson Pratt, who was the mathematician of Mormonism as well as its philosopher, calculated that April 6, 1830, was exactly 1800 years to the day after the resurrection of Jesus Christ. The organizers met at Peter Whitmer, Sen.'s, house in Fayette, Seneca County, New York; Joseph and Oliver ordained each other, and then they gave the gift of the Holy Ghost to the other four. They named the new organization the Church of Jesus Christ, and it was only some years later that they added unto themselves the qualification of latter-day saints. For the occasion of the formal opening God gave Joseph Smith a revelation, which was in the nature of credentials, in which He commanded that Joseph Smith must be obeyed implicitly, for he was God's apostle. Soon after the organization of the Church Martin Harris, Joseph Smith's father and mother, and Orrin Porter Rockwell were baptized in Seneca Lake.

The Book of Mormon had created only a ripple of derisive interest in Palmyra when it was published there, and the Prophet was literally without honor in his own neighborhood. His neighbors refused to believe that the boy whom they had known for so many years as the most ragged and the laziest boy in the place, who had stood up against fences for hours, with his "torn and patched trousers held to his form by a pair of suspenders made out of sheeting, with his calico shirt as dirty and black as the earth, and his uncombed hair sticking through the holes in his old battered hat," could possibly be the elect of God. Young Joseph was convivial, and he had amused them with imaginative stories, but that too was against him as Prophet, for real prophets

in the Bible made fierce predictions and were almost never pleasantly entertaining. Joseph Smith had also smoked cigars and
drunk liquor, and none of the real prophets had ever been known
to do those things. Brigham Young once pointed out with ad-
mirable logic the irrelevancy of these prejudices against the divinity of Joseph Smith:

"I recollect a conversation I had with a priest who was an old
friend of ours, before I was personally acquainted with the Prophet
Joseph. I clipped every argument he advanced, until at last he came
out and began to rail against 'Joe Smith,' saying, 'that he was a
mean man, a liar, money-digger, gambler, and a whoremaster'; and
he charged him with everything bad, that he could find language to
utter. I said, hold on, Brother Gillmore, here is the doctrine, here
is the Bible, the Book of Mormon, and the revelations that have
come through Joseph Smith the Prophet. I have never seen him,
and do not know his private character. The doctrine he teaches
is all I know about the matter, bring anything against that if you
can. As to anything else I do not care. If he acts like a devil,
he has brought forth a doctrine that will save us, if we will abide
it. He may get drunk every day of his life, sleep with his neighbor's
wife every night, run horses and gamble, I do not care anything
about that, for I never embrace any man in my faith. But the
doctrine he has produced will save you and me, and the whole
world; and if you can find fault with that, find it. He said, 'I
have done.' " [1]

This was a good argument, but the personal character of Joseph
Smith cannot be divorced entirely from the spiritual character of
his religion, for his revelations, as we shall see, sometimes coin-
cided strangely with his personal desires.

The progress of the new church was retarded in the villages of
western New York by the fact that Joseph Smith had been heard
using profane language and was known to remark that he was
as good as Jesus Christ. The testimony that Joseph Smith got
drunk frequently cannot be accepted fully. Almost every well-
known man has friends of his youth who used to get drunk with
him, as soon as they have heard that he has become famous, but
it is also true that the famous man sometimes used to get drunk
with them. The whole controversy, which has been the subject
of affidavits for and against, is not important. One of Smith's
followers wrote the most sensible thing about the matter: "And

[1] *Journal of Discourses*, vol. 4, pp. 77-78.

now I ask, who there is that has lived thirty years in this world and at a time when it was fashionable for all people to make use of ardent spirits as a beverage, and have not as much as twice drank too much? But it is said that 'he was quarrelsome when intoxicated.' Well, this is not very strange; most people are; but if he only got intoxicated twice, and only quarreled twice, I think by humble repentance he might be forgiven."

The new Church of six charter members began slowly to make converts of these members' friends. They baptized whole families of Whitmers and Smiths and Rockwells and Jollys. In the beginning families joined in bulk, and we have seen how all of Brigham Young's family were converted together. Joseph Smith ordained all his brothers ministers, even Don Carlos Smith, who was only fourteen years old. Joseph also wrote to all his uncles and invited them to join the Church. One of them, John Smith, when he received the invitation, remarked that "Joseph wrote like a Prophet." Asahel Smith when he heard of the birth of the Book of Mormon said that it was true, "for he always knew that something would turn up in his family that would revolutionize the world. . . . He lived till the Book of Mormon was brought to him, and died when he had read it about half through, being 87 years of age." Joseph Smith's father was in the habit of referring to his talented son as "the genus of the family."

At first it was very difficult to make any converts outside of the families of the founders. In Colesville, New York, the Mormons built a dam for use in baptizing converts. It was destroyed by the townspeople, and, after a mass meeting of indignation, Joseph Smith was arrested on a warrant charging him with disorderly conduct. At the ensuing trial attempts were made to prove that he had obtained a horse and oxen by telling their owners that an angel had authorized him to possess those animals. Some women were also brought to the witness stand to prove his immoral character, but they testified in his favor. He was acquitted, but was immediately rearrested on a warrant from Broome County and hurried away to the court there. He wrote later that as he was brought into a tavern by the constable, the crowd spit upon him, pointed their fingers at him and shouted, "Prophesy, prophesy!" "And thus," wrote Joseph, "did they imitate those who crucified the Saviour of mankind, not knowing what they did." Throughout his lifetime it was a source of great comfort in their tribulations to the Prophet and his followers that he was, as nearly as possible in the nineteenth century, following in the footsteps of his illustrious predecessor. He was acquitted again.

Soon after the Church was organized, efforts were made to sell the Book of Mormon. The price had been fixed by the angel of God at $1.75. Martin Harris, Samuel Smith, and others took to the road in the neighborhood and tried to sell the book at that price, but they found it impossible. Whereupon Joseph received instructions from God that possibly $1.75 was too high, and he was officially authorized to sell the book for $1.25. Eventually, it was sold for anything offered, and the salesmen frequently took merchandise instead of money. Samuel Smith was a good salesman of the Book of Mormon. He soon discovered that it hurt people's prejudices to be offered a new Bible, and he therefore asked them if they did not wish to buy a history of the origin of the Indians. Martin Harris on one occasion was trying to sell a copy to an irascible neighbor. As he grew more insistent the farmer became very angry, and finally he struck Harris a vigorous blow on the right cheek. Martin Harris, happy at the opportunity to reënact a portion of Scripture, with zealous haste shoved out his left cheek and hurriedly read from page 481 of the Book of Mormon: "Whosoever shall smite thee on the right cheek, turn to him the other also." It is not recorded whether the neighbor smote Harris's left cheek or bought a copy of the Book of Mormon. Martin Harris gave up all his time to advertising Mormonism and to trying to sell the book in which he had invested so much of his money. He called public meetings and addressed them himself. He made such extravagant statements to the neighbors that he was generally regarded with the good-humored tolerance accorded the village idiot. He predicted the impending downfall of the United States government and the immediate triumph of Mormonism, and offered that if his prophecies were not fulfilled any one might cut off his head and roll it round the streets of Palmyra as a football. In the first few months of the new Church's existence one of Joseph Smith's unmarried sisters proved to be *enceinte,* and it was immediately declared an immaculate conception, in the course of which a Messiah would be given to the world. Martin Harris was delighted at the prospect of "an immaculate conception in our day and generation." The miracle took place some months later, and, instead of the son who was to be born, resulted in a stillborn girl. The accident was set down to disobedience. It is said that one of Smith's disciples, and not God, was the father of Miss Smith's child, but there is no definite proof on either side.

A few months after the Church was organized Joseph Smith performed his first miracle on the person of one of his devout followers, Newell Knight, who sent for Smith to cure him of possession by the Devil. Joseph Smith wrote that Knight, his body twisted into queer shapes, begged his Prophet to heal him, "saying that he knew that he (the Devil) was in him, and that he also knew I could cast him out. I replied, 'If you know that I can, it shall be done.'" This was a wise answer, and soon afterwards, when Joseph had commanded the Devil in the name of Jesus Christ to be gone, Newell Knight imagined that "he saw the devil leave him and vanish from his sight." The Devil being an over-mastering idea, and Newell Knight having complete faith in Joseph Smith's ability to master him, the first miracle was not difficult to perform. The Mormons have always believed in healing by faith and by the laying on of hands, but, early in the history of the Church, after all the remedies of his new religion had failed, Joseph Smith called in an obstetrician for his wife Emma.

Some of his neighbors have testified that early in his career as a practising theologian Joseph Smith, Jr., attempted to walk upon the water. But in the neighborhood there existed several small boys of mischievous alertness. They discovered the planks which Smith is said to have placed slightly beneath the surface of the body of water he chose to walk upon, and by loosening these just before the miracle was to take place, the boys brought it about that the Prophet went precipitately and ignominiously to the bottom of the lake. The neighbors and the small boys enjoyed the joke hugely, but the Prophet lost none of his few faithful followers as a result of his ducking.

The early converts were not many, and none of them was important until Parley Parker Pratt arrived in Joseph Smith's neighborhood. Pratt had been living in Kirtland, Ohio, where he met Sidney Rigdon and was associated with him in preaching Campbellism. Pratt was enjoying comparative comfort and peace of mind, but one day he held this strange conversation with his brother William. Pratt reproduced it as follows in his autobiography:

"I then unlocked my treasury and drew from thence a large pocket book full of promissory notes like the following: 'Whoever shall forsake father or mother, brethren or sisters, houses or lands, wife or children, for my sake and the gospel's, shall receive an hundred fold in this life, and in the world to come life everlasting.' 'If ye abide in me, and my words abide in you, you shall ask what you will in my name and I will give it you.' 'All things are possible to him that believeth.'

" 'Now, William,' said I, 'are these the words of Jesus Christ, or are they not?'

" 'They certainly are,' said he, 'I always believed the New Testament.'

" 'Then you admit they are genuine bills?'

" 'I do.'

" 'Is the signer able to meet his engagements?'

" 'He certainly is.'

" 'Is he willing?'

" 'He is.'

" 'Well, then, I am going to fulfill the conditions to the letter on my part. I feel called upon by the Holy Ghost to forsake my house and home for the gospel's sake; and I will do it, placing both feet firm on these promises with nothing else to rely upon. If I sink, they are false. If I am sustained, they are true. I will put them to the test. Experiment shall now establish the truth of Christ's promises, or the truth of infidelity.'

" 'Well,' said he, 'try it, if you will; but, for my part, although I always believed the Bible, I would not dare believe it *literally,* and really stand upon its promises with no other prop.' "

Soon afterwards Parley Pratt left his farm and journeyed east with his wife. At Newark, on his way to New York, he heard of the Book of Mormon. He went to refute Joseph Smith's arguments, and, after he heard the new Prophet deliver a sermon, he remained to be baptized. He was an ardent proselyte, and soon after his own baptism in August, 1830, he baptized his brother, Orson Pratt, who was then only nineteen years old. The Pratt brothers were intensely religious and superstitious. They frequently saw signs of the coming of the Son of Man in the skies, and though Parley did not take enough interest in astronomy to make it possible for him to believe that they were anything but spiritual manifestations, his brother Orson, who later became an expert mathematician and a capable astronomer, should have known better. But even mathematicians in those days attributed considerably more to God than they do to-day.

While he was on a mission to convert the Indians of Missouri to Mormonism, Parley Pratt met Sidney Rigdon again and gave him a copy of the Book of Mormon. Rigdon, after some hesitation and doubt, was converted, and he went to Palmyra to visit the Prophet. The result was the decision of Joseph Smith to remove the Church and his followers from Palmyra, where he said he suffered from persecution, and where he certainly was subject to disrespect, to Kirtland, Ohio, an intensely religious community, which offered excellent opportunities for a new religion with enough elements of the old creeds. Here the Church could begin a new life under promising auspices, for at Kirtland Joseph Smith was unknown and Sidney Rigdon was well known.

II

In the first revelation which the Lord gave to Joseph Smith, Jr., at Kirtland, Ohio, on February 4, 1831, there was this significant sentence: "And again, it is meet that my servant Joseph Smith, jun., should have a house built, in which to live and translate." A few days later the Lord said: "And if ye desire the glories of the kingdom, appoint ye my servant Joseph Smith, jun., and uphold him before me by the prayer of faith. And again, I say unto you, that if ye desire the mysteries of the kingdom, provide for him food and raiment, and whatsoever thing he needeth to accomplish the work, wherewith I have commanded him. And if ye do it not, he shall remain unto them that have received him, that I may reserve unto myself a pure people before me."

Early in his career as a prophet Joseph Smith adopted the wise policy of never asking his followers to do anything for him in his own name. He realized that the will of the Lord was much more powerful than his own. The Lord signed everything for Joseph Smith, and, such was the faith at the time, few of the faithful dared to risk salvation by crying forgery. And Joseph Smith never seemed to realize that to the unbiased mind it looked often as if Joseph Smith had prompted God rather than that God had prompted Joseph Smith; therefore his revelations sometimes sound incredibly naïve. He also never gave an order on his own authority, but invariably went into conference with the Lord whenever a problem arose, and usually he came out of conference with a fully developed decision. Smith preferred to put everything up to God and to let Him take the consequences. The result was that whenever there were complaints, he could always tell the grumblers to talk to God, which they did, by means of prayer.

As the only basis for their prayers were the statements of Joseph Smith, God usually supported the Prophet in His answers. When some members of other sects argued that this continual conversation with God was unscriptural, Sidney Rigdon answered: "If you have not familiarity enough with your Creator to ask of him a sign, you are no Christians, and if God will not condescend to his creatures, in this way, he is no better than Juggernaut!"

Soon after the Church was organized, Emma Smith began to fear for the financial security of herself and her distinguished husband; she urged that, since he could not possibly prophesy all day long, a part time job at some more lucrative work would help the family finances, for Joseph promptly received a revelation from God, who said to Mrs. Smith: "Emma, thou art an elect lady and thou needst not fear, for thy husband shalt support thee from the Church." This was revised when the second edition of the revelations was published to read, "thy husband shalt support thee *in* the Church." Emma was also commanded by this revelation to act as scribe for her husband, and to compile an anthology of sacred hymns for the use of the new church.

The Church began to make numerous converts. Nancy Towle, a pious traveler who preached concerning Jesus Christ wherever people would listen to her in America and in Europe, visited Kirtland, Ohio, a few months after Joseph Smith established himself there. She thus described the contents of the community: "Of their numbers, I found, ministers, of different persuasions: and some, it appeared, who had once been eminent for piety. I found, also, many men, of both influence and wealth. Husbands, who had left their wives: and wives, that had left their husbands. —Children, that had left their parents: and parents, their children;—that they might be *'accounted worthy,'* as they said, *'to escape all the things that should come to pass and to stand before the Son of Man.'*" As soon as a man was converted he was sent forth to convert others, and by this means the Church rapidly grew in numbers, until converts from New York and other eastern states began to arrive in Kirtland daily. Curiosity concerning the new religion was aroused in the neighborhood, and on Sundays all the roads leading to Kirtland were crowded with farm waggons on their way to the new Church to hear the new Prophet. There was little entertainment in the villages around Kirtland, and a new Prophet was of major importance. The only other preachers who visited the neighborhood were saddle-bag missionaries, who, in the course of their circuit, arrived perhaps once a month at each village.

The people among whom the early Mormon missionaries worked were ready for what they had to offer. Every village had its boy who had had a vision or its girl who had seen God. The neighbors crowded into a farm house where a child of ten or twelve was forced to repeat and to repeat what he had seen in the night, until finally what had been a dream of unusual mystic force became by elaboration and repetition a visitation from heaven. Then came the Mormons with their Prophet who had had just such visions on a grander scale, with tales of golden plates and promised lands, with daily revelations from God and repeated visits from angels. These things corresponded sufficiently with the experience of their converts to warrant belief and differed enough to allow room for faith in a divinity they knew not of. There is no better example of the combination of faith with mistrust, of the will to believe hampered by a crude but practical knowledge of human nature, than the pathetic statement of Andrews Tyler, an early Mormon convert, to his daughter, who had been converted by Mormon missionaries: Tyler's son wrote: "His remarks to my sister were to the effect that if this new religion was true, it was the best religion in the world, but, if false, it was the worst. 'These men,' said he, 'know whether it is true or false, but I do not.' " Andrews Tyler had threatened to shoot any Mormon elder who baptized his daughter. When he expressed this violent threat to Hyrum Smith, the brother of the Prophet, who was preaching in the neighborhood, Hyrum answered: "Mr. Tyler, we shall not baptize your daughter against your wishes. If our doctrine be true, which we testify it is, if you prevent your daughter from embracing it, the sin will be on your head, not on ours or your daughter's." This terrified Tyler. The responsibility was too much for him. His daughter was baptized, and soon afterwards he and the rest of his family joined the Mormons.

There were many reasons for the rapid spread of Mormonism. One of these was the great zeal of its missionaries, who traveled everywhere without purse or scrip to preach the new revelation. A great appeal was found in the embellishment of the future life so that it became almost eastern in its magnificence and at the same time as exclusive and snobbish as that of the Jews. The Mormons also offered the miracles of primitive Christianity and added to them extemporaneously from their own experience and circumstances. Another great source of the popularity of Mormonism was the refuge which it offered as a new revelation from the confusion of the various Christian sects, which, by their multitude of petty distinctions, befuddled the simple minds of the country people.

When men of education and clergymen of other denominations laughed at the ideas of Mormonism, with its revelations and its latter-day miracles, the Mormons accepted their laughter with complacent resignation; for, they said, had not the savants of Rome, Athens, and Alexandria laughed derisively at Saint Paul? It was only another comforting parallel with the struggles and triumphs of the primitive Christians, whom the Mormons admitted they were trying to emulate and to imitate. And there were millions of Christians, all sprung originally from the perseverance of those early fathers of the Church. Surely, said the Mormons, it was a good omen when philosophers laughed.

Clergymen of other denominations never ceased to write and to talk against the Mormons, for their claim to be the only true faith naturally appeared arrogant to other preachers. Also, the statements of the Mormon leaders in the pulpit were not calculated to make them friends among their competitors. One of the Mormon preachers said: "After a while, you have the beauty, the sublimity of Catholicism. Look at the old mother, seated upon a scarlet-colored beast, boxing the ears of her daughters; and the Church of England in turn boxing the ears of the old mother, assisted by her other numerous offspring, and then mark the bitter contentions and bloody feuds among the children! O, have they not had a sublime time—a beautiful dish of suckertash. What a uniform course they have taken." Joseph Smith was particularly fond of referring to the old established church as the whore of Babylon, an abomination in the sight of righteousness.

The leaders of the Mormon Church took an interest in their followers' temporal possessions as well as in their spiritual welfare, and Joseph Smith received a revelation from God that it was the duty of every rightful heir to the kingdom of heaven to give to the Church all the property that he did not need for his support. The perplexing problem arose of just how much a man needed, and it was met by an edict that a Mormon should consecrate all his property to his bishop and then receive back from the bishop what he needed in order to live, which was determined by him and his bishop in conference. If they disagreed on this important point, the case was to be appealed to a council of high priests, of which Joseph Smith was a member. Smith was rather anxious to make these deeds of consecration follow the letter of the law. He wrote to one of his bishops: "We again say . . . be sure to get a form according to law for securing a gift. We have found by examining the law that a gift cannot be retained without this. . . . You will remember that the power of agency must be signed by the wives as well as the husbands, and the wives must be examined in the matter separate and apart from the husbands, the same as signing a deed, and a specification to that effect inserted at the bottom, by the justice before whom such acknowledgment is made, otherwise the power of attorney will be of no effect." Many of his followers began to think that the Prophet was concerning himself too much with their finances, and some were bold enough to suggest that a Prophet's function was purely spiritual. Brigham Young many years later defended the temporal interference of the Prophet with these arguments:

"What were the feelings of the people, almost universally, in the infancy of this Church? Men of science and talent in this Church believed—or they said they believed—honestly, truly, and with all their hearts, that Joseph Smith did not understand anything about *temporal* matters. They believed he understood *spiritual* things— that he understood the Spirit of the Lord, and how to build up the spiritual kingdom among men; but when temporal matters were talked of, men were ready to decide at once, that *they* knew more than the Prophet about such matters; and they did so decide. . . . For men of principle, and seemingly of good sense, to believe the Prophet Joseph, who was inspired to build up the kingdom of God temporally as well as spiritually, did not know as much about a picayune as about God's spiritual kingdom, about a farm as about the New Jerusalem, is folly in the extreme, it is nonsense in the superlative degree. Those who entertain such ideas ought to have their heads well combed, and subjected to a lively course of friction, that peradventure a little common sense might dawn upon their confused ideas.

"Consult your own judgments in such matters. Do you think that God would set a man to lead his people who does not know as much about a picayune or a farm, as about God's spiritual kingdom, or the New Jerusalem? Shame on those who would entertain such ideas, for they debase and corrupt the hearts of the community who imbibe them. According to the sentiments of some of the

Latter-day Saints, the Lord must have become wonderfully high-minded in the last days; I should think he had become too proud, according to their belief, to notice farms and merchandise, and other little affairs and transactions that pass around us. He used to notice the very hairs of our heads that fell, and the sparrows; He took care of the ravens, and watched over the children of Israel, and supplied all their temporal wants; but we say now, *He* does not condescend to such small matters, having given *us* an understanding, and *we* know what to do. Are not these the feelings of the people? I could refer to some little things by way of example, but it would hit somebody rather too publicly." [2]

But many of the early followers did not take this attitude, and it was found necessary to abandon consecration of property for a system of tithing, by which ten per cent. of a man's possessions went to the Church when he joined it, and ten per cent. of his annual income was to be devoted to the Church. By this time Brigham Young had joined Joseph Smith, and it is said that his more practical mind worked out this system, which was more successful, since it allowed a man control of his own possessions and still insured the Church its revenue. However, since the tithe was purely voluntary, it was not always paid, and Brigham Young spent much of his time in the pulpit in later years urging his people to pay their tithing; usually, by exhortation, he was able to get it. One reason why the Church is wealthy to-day is that Brigham Young never tired of pointing out to his people that since all property came from the Lord originally, no one should hesitate to devote it to His glorification through the instrument of the Church of Jesus Christ of Latter-day Saints.

Joseph Smith also received a revelation from God granting real estate in Kirtland to him, to Sidney Rigdon, and to Oliver Cowdery. God also provided for Joseph Smith, Sen. The son ordained his father Patriarch of the Church, and for the occasion God issued a revelation saying that since the laborer is worthy of his hire, Joseph Smith, Sen., for his services as Patriarch should receive "ten dollars per week and expenses." Later he received three dollars per blessing, for it was his main duty to issue blessings.

Meanwhile, those who had visited Missouri to convert the Indians sent back to their Prophet glowing reports of the fertility of the soil, and Joseph received a revelation from God that the

[2] *Journal of Discourses,* vol. i, pp. 74-76.

future Zion would be in Jackson County, Missouri. One night in March, 1832, Joseph Smith and Sidney Rigdon were dragged from their beds and tarred and feathered by a mob of infuriated Baptists, Campbellites, and Methodists. A week later they left for a tour of inspection of the Saints in Missouri. Although he

A MOB OF RELIGIOUS COMPETITORS TARRING AND FEATHERING
JOSEPH SMITH
From a contemporary woodcut

was favorably impressed with the location of the future Zion, Joseph Smith returned to Kirtland, Ohio, where he had plenty to occupy him, and left others to build up Zion in Missouri.

One of the Prophet's main occupations at this time was a new translation of the Bible, which he was making with the aid of some ancient papyrus. This had come into his possession in a singularly unbiblical manner. Mr. Michael H. Chandler, who was apparently a traveling showman, received some ancient Egyptian mummies, wrapped in papyrus, from his nephew in Paris. The nephew, a French traveler and explorer, had found them in the catacombs of Thebes, so he said. Chandler, the Mormons said, tried to get his papyrus translated by scholars in Philadelphia, but they were unable to translate the characters to his satisfaction. He had heard of the ascension of a new prophet in the west who could decipher strange languages and reveal hidden things, so he sold seven of his mummies and several sheets of papyrus to pay his traveling expenses, and arrived in Kirtland, Ohio, with four remaining mummies and several rolls of papyrus. Joseph Smith, under the inspiration of the Almighty, interpreted some of the ancient writings to the satisfaction of Mr. Chandler, and some friends of the Prophet purchased mummies and papyrus for him. Michael Chandler gave the Prophet the following testimonial, which is reproduced in the *History of the Church* as Mr. Chandler wrote it:

"Kirtland, July 6, 1835.
"This is to make known to all who may be desirous, concerning the knowledge of Mr. Joseph Smith, Jun., in deciphering the ancient Egyptian hieroglyphic characters in my possession, which I have, in many eminent cities, showed to the most learned; and, from the information that I could ever learn, or meet with, I find that of Mr. Joseph Smith, Jun., to correspond in the most minute matters.
"MICHAEL H. CHANDLER,
"Traveling with, and proprietor of, Egyptian mummies."

As soon as the mummies came into his possession, Joseph Smith, with the aid of several of his disciples, examined them more closely, and to their joy they discovered that the papyrus contained the writings of Abraham, of Israel, and Joseph, of Egypt. Joseph Smith set to work immediately to translate them. The mummies were always retained in the Smith household and were exhibited for twenty-five cents by the Prophet's mother. Josiah Quincy, who visited Joseph Smith some years later at Nauvoo, Illinois, described the exhibition of the mummies in his book, *Figures of the Past:*

"'And now come with me,' said the prophet, 'and I will show you the curiosities.' So saying, he led the way to a lower room, where

and superstitious ignorance, but they forget to mention that he had a highly developed sense of humor, which he always delighted to use on those of his followers who made ridiculous demands upon his powers.

Occasionally Joseph Smith asked God for a revelation of advice concerning the private affairs of particular parishioners. Newell Knight, who had already been healed once by a miracle, took a fancy to a quiet girl in Kirtland, named Lydia. She was married to a man who had deserted her, and Newell Knight's wife had died. He asked her one day why they should not comfort each other. Since Lydia knew that Newell knew that she already had a husband, she left the room insulted and ashamed of him. He explained a few days later that his intentions were honorable, that her husband had deserted her for three years, and that therefore she was legally free. But she considered herself spiritually bound. At that point the matter entered the province of the Prophet Joseph Smith. Newell Knight, who knew the Prophet well, took it up with Smith, who spoke to God about it, and the answer sent down from heaven was that Lydia was free from her first husband, and that, in fact, it would be pleasing to God if Newell Knight and Lydia were married. In gratitude, Lydia, who had loved Newell all the time, fell on her knees, and "poured out her soul in thanksgiving to God for His precious blessings." Soon afterwards she heard that her first husband had died, and she took this as "a convincing testimony of the truth of Joseph's word." [5]

One of the favorite subjects of revelation in the days when Joseph Smith's spiritual manifestations were most active was that of the millennium, accompanied by the Second Coming of Christ. The Shakers, the Millerites, and Jemima Wilkinson were making minatory millennial predictions, and Joseph Smith yielded to the temptation to predict the Second Coming, but he was wise enough to set no fixed date. He once discussed the matter with God, and a voice spoke into his ear: "Joseph, my son, if thou livest until thou art eighty-five years old, thou shalt see the face of the Son of Man: therefore let this suffice, and trouble me no more on this matter." This was indefinite enough in time, but to make it absolutely proof against reaction upon himself, the Prophet added this note: "I was left thus, without being able to decide whether this coming referred to the beginning of

[5] *Lydia Knight's History,* pp. 27-29.

the millennium or to some previous appearing, or whether I should die and thus see His face."

On February 16, 1832, Joseph Smith and Sidney Rigdon did see Christ sitting on the right hand of God at Kirtland, Ohio. In this joint vision they were instructed that there were three orders of eternal bliss. The celestial order was conferred only on devout believers such as Smith, Rigdon, and their most faithful followers: "These shall dwell in the presence of God and His Christ for ever and ever." Then there was the terrestrial order, consisting of those who received the testimony of Jesus after they had died, and their boon differed from that of the celestial inhabitants "in glory as the moon differs from the sun." The telestial order came one grade below the terrestrial and consisted of people who had never accepted the testimony of Jesus, such as the Jews, who would only be saved from eternal damnation in the last resurrection. Since there was to be a final resurrection, it was necessary to have some people left to resurrect. All who did not fit into one of these classes were doomed to a Mormon hell with real fire burning for eternity. One of the faithful brethren who saw Joseph Smith and Sidney Rigdon when they came out of this joint revelation said that, "Joseph appeared as strong as a lion, but Sidney seemed as weak as water, and Joseph, noticing his partner's condition smiled and said, 'Brother Sidney is not as used to it as I am.' "

The new converts seemed to accept these revelations and doctrines with faith, no matter how eccentric the conditions under which they were received or promulgated. Occasionally some one revolted. One family apostatized because they were at the Prophet's house when he came down from the translating room and began immediately to play with his children on the floor. They thought a decent interval should have been observed between God and toys. Joseph was finding it a great burden to be a prophet for twenty-four hours each day, and he refused to do so, as this entry in his diary indicates: "This morning I read German, and visited with a brother and sister from Michigan, who thought that 'a prophet is always a prophet'; but I told them that a prophet was a prophet only when he was acting as such. . . . At four in the afternoon, I went out with my little Frederick to exercise myself by sliding on the ice."

There was the case of the doubting Simonds Ryder, who was called upon by the Lord through Joseph Smith to go forth and preach the Gospel. But the Lord spelled his name Rider instead of Ryder, and this led him to doubt the divine origin of the call, for, he argued, if the spirit through which he had been called could err in the matter of spelling his name, it might also have erred in calling him to abandon his home and go forth without purse or scrip as a missionary. Another convert announced one day that he knew Joseph Smith was a false prophet and that the Book of Mormon was a fraud. When he was asked his reason, he answered: "Why, he says, if a man commit adultery, he shall apostatize; and I have done it, and have not apostatized."

There were also several minor schisms at Kirtland. A man named Hoten set up an independent church of ten members. They pretended to share all possessions in common; one day the bishop, who had charge of temporal affairs, charged the president of the new church with visiting his pork barrel without permission, and the president retaliated by charging the bishop with visiting his wife. The church broke up in disorder.

When people began to realize the ease and comfort of prophecy, rival prophets arose, and Joseph Smith found it necessary to insist that to be binding all revelations must come through him. One of Joseph's rivals was a sixteen-year-old boy named James Collins Brewster, who was receiving revelations and converting members of his family and neighbors. Joseph referred to him contemptuously in his diary as "that Brewster boy," and added: "If God ever called me, or spake by my mouth, or gave me a revelation, he never gave revelations to that Brewster boy or any of the Brewster race." That Brewster boy also wrote a book, which he called *The Book of Esdras,* and Smith wrote of it: "Brewster showed me the manuscript he had been writing. I inquired of the Lord, and the Lord told me the book was not true—it was not of Him." There was also Elder Sydney Roberts, who was charged before the High Council with "having a revelation that a certain brother must give him a suit of clothes and a gold watch, the best that could be had; also saluting the sisters with what he calls a holy kiss." He was told that he could retain his membership in the Church, if he would confess his error, but he stubbornly declared that "he knew the revelations he had spoken were from God," and he was therefore excommunicated.

Martin Harris was unconsciously a rival of Joseph's. By his simplicity he embarrassed the true Prophet very much with frequent predictions to the townspeople that Christ would be seen by the faithful in fifteen years, or that within four years not a wicked person would be left in the United States. He had also openly accused the Prophet of getting drunk while translating the Book of Mormon, and it became necessary to expel him from the Church. Many years later Martin Harris repented of his sins, and Brigham Young raised a subscription to bring him to Utah. Elder Stevenson was sent to Kirtland, where Harris was still living, to bring the old man to Salt Lake City. On the way west Harris was used as an advertisement for Mormonism. At Chicago he appeared before several gatherings of people who were anxious to see a man who had seen an angel and the golden plates of the Book of Mormon. He was then eighty years old, and when he arrived in Salt Lake City, he testified before a huge congregation that the Book of Mormon was of divine origin. At a meeting in Salt Lake City Sister M. H. Kimball offered on behalf of the 15th Ward Relief Society to buy Brother Harris a new set of artificial teeth, and to have them made to order. "No, sisters," Martin Harris replied, "I thank you for your kindness, but I shall not live long. Take the money and give it to the poor." When he was driven about Salt Lake City and its suburbs, he was impressed with the gorgeous view, and, according to his companion, Elder Stevenson, he said, "Who would have thought that the Book of Mormon would have done all this!" Apparently he was at last satisfied that his investment had been profitable, at least to others; he lived in Cache Valley, Utah, until he was ninety. A copy of the Book of Mormon was buried with him.

Even Sidney Rigdon could not resist the temptation to rival the Prophet. While Joseph Smith was away from Kirtland, Rigdon prophesied that the keys of the kingdom had been taken from the people and would not be returned until they built Elder Sidney Rigdon a new house. Hyrum Smith doubted the truth of this divine revelation, and he went for his brother, the Prophet. Sidney Rigdon was "delivered over to the buffetings of Satan." The Devil dragged him out of bed three times in one night, he said later. Finally he was granted his former position of trust.

Brigham Young, from the moment he joined the Church, remained steadfast in his professed faith and defended the Prophet against all apostates. Very often he must have felt that what

Joseph Smith did was inexpedient or eccentric, but he told his congregation later that only once did he experience disagreement with the dictates of the Prophet, and he told how he overcame that temptation:

"I can tell the people that once in my life I felt a want of confidence in Brother Joseph Smith, soon after I became acquainted with him. It was not concerning religious matters—it was not about his revelations—but it was in relation to his financiering—to his managing the temporal affairs which he undertook. A feeling came over me that Joseph was not right in his financial management, though I presume the feeling did not last sixty seconds, and perhaps not thirty. But that feeling came on me once and once only, from the time I first knew him to the day of his death. It gave me sorrow of heart, and I clearly saw and understood, by the spirit of revelation manifested to me, that if I was to harbor a thought in my heart that Joseph could be wrong in anything, I would begin to lose confidence in him, and that feeling would grow from step to step, and from one degree to another, until at last I would have the same lack of confidence in his being the mouthpiece for the Almighty, and I would be left, as Brother Hooper observed, upon the brink of the precipice, ready to plunge into what we may call the gulf of infidelity, ready to believe neither in God nor His servants, and to say that there is no God, or, if there is, we do not know anything about Him; that we are here, and by and bye shall go from here, and that is all we shall know. . . . Though I admitted in my feelings and knew all the time that Joseph was a human being and subject to err, still it was none of my business to look after his faults. . . .

"It was not for me to question whether Joseph was dictated by the Lord at all times and under all circumstances or not. . . . He was called of God. God dictated him, and if He had a mind to leave him to himself and let him commit an error, that was no business of mine. . . . He was God's servant and not mine. He did not belong to the people but to the Lord, and was doing the work of the Lord, and if He should suffer him to lead the people astray, it would be because they ought to be led astray. If he should suffer them to be chastised, and some of them destroyed, it would be because they deserved it, or to accomplish some righteous purpose. That was my faith, and it is my faith still. . . . I know that Joseph Smith is a Prophet of God, that this is the Gospel of salvation, and if you do not believe it you will be damned, every one of you. That is one of the most important sermons that ever was preached." [6]

[6] *Journal of Discourses*, vol. 4, pp. 297-298.

This sermon was one of the most important Brigham Young ever preached, because it helps so much to explain how a man of such a practical mind as Brigham Young's could have accepted with any sincerity the pretensions of Joseph Smith. Whenever Brigham Young had doubts of Joseph Smith, as he must have had more often than he cared to admit, he dismissed them with the argument that, granting Joseph Smith inspired of God, which Brigham Young had committed himself to grant, when Joseph Smith did something that appeared wrong, it was in reality something dark and mysterious in the back of the Lord's head. Of course, it was taking a great step to grant that Joseph Smith was inspired by God, but Brigham Young had taken that step, and he could not turn back without destroying his faith completely. The whole fabric of his faith would unravel if he began to pull at that stitch, so he tucked it in carefully and decided to call the cloth perfect. He may have done that sincerely without difficulty, for Brigham Young's idea of God had always been of a being with "body, parts, and passions," and it required less strain on his type of imagination to believe in Joseph Smith than to believe in only an uncommunicative abstraction. Joseph was always doing things that appeared ungodly, or at least ungodlike, it was true, but those were up to the Lord to worry about, who was his master, rather than Brigham Young, who was his servant. Brigham Young once told his people: "I never argued the least against anything Joseph proposed, but if I could not see or understand it, I handed it over to the Lord. There is my counsel to you, my brethren and sisters. . . . What did I do? I handed this over to the Lord in my feelings, and said I, 'I will wait until the Spirit of God manifests to me, for or against.' I did not judge the matter, I did not argue against it, not in the least." And the Spirit of God invariably seemed to take the affirmative in favor of Joseph Smith. It is easy to see that Brigham Young was a model convert. Of course, when reading these statements which Brigham Young made from the pulpit many years after the death of Joseph Smith, we must consider that he realized fully the practical value to himself of an attitude of unquestioning obedience upon the part of his followers.

Soon after he joined Joseph Smith Brigham Young proved very useful as defendant of the Prophet against apostates and dissenters. A secret meeting was held at Kirtland for the purpose of deposing Joseph Smith and making David Whitmer head of the Church. Brigham Young defended the Prophet so vigorously in this meeting that he almost suffered physical violence. "Jacob Bump," Brigham Young wrote, "an old pugilist, was so exasperated that he could not be still. Some of the brethren near him put their hands on him, and requested him to be quiet; but he writhed and twisted his arms and body saying, 'How can I keep my hands off that man?' I told him if he thought it would give him any relief he might lay them on." The meeting adjourned without any action against Smith. Upon another occasion Brigham Young himself used threats of violence in defense of his Prophet. He told the incident in the short history of himself which he wrote for the Church publications:

"A man named Hawley, while plowing his field in the State of New York, had an impression rest down on his mind, with great weight, that he must go to Kirtland and tell Joseph Smith that the Lord had rejected him as a Prophet. He accordingly started right off, with his bare feet, and, on arriving in Kirtland, told Joseph that the Lord had rejected him for allowing John Noah, a Prophet of God, to be cut off from the Church, and for allowing the women to wear caps and the men to wear cushions on their coat sleeves. He was called up before the Bishops' court and disfellowshipped.

"He went through the streets of Kirtland one morning after midnight and cried, 'Woe! woe! unto the inhabitants of this place.' I put my pants and shoes on, took my cow-hide, went out, and laying hold of him, jerked him round, and assured him that if he did not stop his noise and let the people enjoy their sleep without interruption, I would cow-hide him on the spot, for we had the Lord's Prophet right here, and we did not want the Devil's prophet yelling around the streets. The nuisance was forthwith abated." [7]

At Kirtland Brigham Young practised his old trades of painter, glazier, and carpenter, and he built and adorned many houses for the faithful. In February of 1834 he was married by Sidney Rigdon to Mary Ann Angel, a Kirtland girl. During the fall and winter he built houses and painted them, attended Hebrew school and made himself generally useful to the Prophet. During the spring and summer he traveled as a missionary throughout the eastern United States, and as a missionary Brigham Young was more successful than any of his brethren. He had a practical

[7] *Millennial Star*, vol. 25, p. 487.

common sense combined with intense spiritual fervor and a conviction of his own knowledge of absolute truth that was almost irresistible for converts. In later years Brigham Young was proud of his early missionary success. He once said in a sermon:

"I know that when I have travelled with some of the Twelve, and one of them has asked for breakfast, dinner, supper, or lodging, we have been refused dozens of times. Now, you may think that I am going to boast a little; I will brag a little of my own tact and talent. When others would ask, we would often be refused a morsel of something to eat, and so we would go from house to house; but when I had the privilege of asking, I never was turned away—no, not a single time.

"Would I go into the house and say to them, 'I am a "Mormon" Elder; will you feed me?' It was none of their business who I was. But when I asked, 'Will you give me something to eat?' the reply was, invariably, 'Yes.' And we would sit, and talk, and sing, and make ourselves familiar and agreeable; and before our departure, after they had learned who we were, they would frequently ask, 'Will you not stay and preach for us?' and proffer to gather in the members of their family and their neighbors; and the feeling would be, 'Well, if this is "Mormonism," I will feed all the "Mormon" Elders that come.' Whereas, if I had said, 'I am a "Mormon" Elder; will you feed me?' the answer would often have been, 'No: out of my house.' " [8]

Sometimes it was difficult for Brigham Young to keep order in the meetings. At Richmond, Massachusetts, a particularly unruly congregation shouted him down, and when he reproved them, began to burn odoriferous lucifer matches. Brigham Young told them that he would like to send Indians from the West to civilize them, whereupon, at the next meeting some one threw brimstone into the fire and almost succeeded in suffocating Brigham Young and his companion, George A. Smith. He suffered other hardships on his missionary tours, and one of them was the lack of sufficient clothes. During one winter trip through New England he wore a cradle quilt for a coat. Sometimes the accommodations offered by friendly farmers were not good. Brigham Young once told of an unfortunate night spent in an eastern farmhouse: "Brother George A. Smith and I stayed over night with Brother Atkinson, who lived in a very large frame house, said to have stood 150 years, which was so infested with bed-bugs that we could not sleep. Brother George A. Smith gave it as his legal opinion that there were bed-bugs there which had danced to the music at the battle of Trenton, as their heads were perfectly gray. We took our blankets and retreated to the further end of the room, and as the bugs followed us, I lit a candle, and as they approached, caught them and burnt them in the candle, and thus spent the night." [9] Brigham Young visited most of his cousins and other relatives and succeeded in converting the majority of his family.

In February, 1835, Joseph Smith organized the council of the Twelve Apostles, and Brigham Young was appointed one of them. Although he now occupied an important position in the hierarchy of the Church, Brigham Young was not one of the close advisers of the Prophet. When Joseph Smith drew up a plan for the new city of Kirtland, there was a Rigdon Street, a Pratt Street, a Smith Street, a Joseph Street, a Hyrum Street, and a street named for every one of Joseph's brothers, but there was no Brigham Street or Young Avenue.

III

One of the most important projects of the Church at Kirtland was the construction of a Temple for the proper worship of God. God had given Joseph Smith a revelation in which he told him what the dimensions of His house should be: "Verily I say unto you," said God, "that it shall be built fifty-five by sixty-five feet in width thereof and in length thereof, in the inner court." Though God dictated the dimensions, Brigham Young did much of the actual labor, performing carpenter work while it was in the course of construction and painting it after it was built.

In the revelation concerning the Temple God said that the building was not to commence until He gave the word. The Lord was apparently waiting for what was soon started in motion, a subscription for funds. Manna from heaven arrived in the form of John Tanner, a convert from New York. He had been healed of a lame leg by a Mormon elder, and he therefore felt called upon to sell his extensive property in New York State and live in Kirtland. He arrived there just as the mortgage on the Temple ground was about to be foreclosed. It is said that a few days before his arrival the Prophet Joseph and his brethren had assem-

9 *Millennial Star*, vol. 26, p. 280.

bled in prayer-meeting and asked God to send them a brother with means to lift the mortgage. Perhaps this was so, but perhaps some one had whispered to Joseph Smith that John Tanner had just sold two large farms and 2,200 acres of valuable timber land. Nevertheless, the day after his arrival in Kirtland, Tanner was invited by the Prophet to meet with the High Council. The result of the meeting was that he lent Joseph Smith $2,000, and took his note, lent the Temple Committee $13,000 and took their note, and besides these loans made liberal donations to the Temple Fund. A short time later he signed a note for $30,000 worth of merchandise. And they made him an elder; they should have made him a saint. He has achieved, however, a species of canonization, for he is held up as an example of manly righteousness and noble obedience in *Scraps of Biography,* a book published by the Mormon Church for its young.

With the help of God and John Tanner the Temple was finally completed, and elaborate dedication ceremonies were held, in the course of which Joseph Smith washed Brigham Young's feet, and Brigham Young "had the gift of tongues powerfully upon him." The women were not admitted into the Temple while the washing and anointing was going on, and one of the eyewitnesses reported that this made them "right huffy." They considered that they had cause to be "right huffy," besides their exclusion, for many of the elders are reported to have got inordinately drunk that night on sacramental liquor, and the Prophet is said to have needed considerable bracing up before he could face his wife Emma. David Whitmer testified that he saw angels present at the dedication, but others have testified that everybody was drunk enough to see anything. Joseph Smith said later that Jesus had been present at the ceremonies.

While he was busy in the construction of the Temple, the Prophet was also busy organizing a bank. When he first arrived in Kirtland, the Prophet had opened a general store, but he found it impossible to make the business profitable. Brigham Young once explained the cause of failure:

"Joseph goes to New York and buys $20,000 worth of goods, comes into Kirtland and commences to trade. In comes one of the brethren, 'Brother Joseph, let me have a frock pattern for my wife.' What if Joseph says, 'No, I cannot without the money.' The consequences would be, 'He is no Prophet,' says James. Pretty soon Thomas walks in. 'Brother Joseph, will you trust me for a pair of boots?' 'No, I cannot let them go without the money.' 'Well,' says Thomas, 'Brother Joseph is no Prophet; I have found *that* out, and I am glad of it.' After a while in comes Bill and Sister Susan. Says Bill, 'Brother Joseph, I want a shawl, I have not got the money, but I wish you to trust me a week or a fortnight.' Well, Brother Joseph thinks the others have gone and apostatized, and he don't know but these goods will make the whole Church do the same, so he lets Bill have a shawl. Bill walks off with it and meets a brother. 'Well,' says he, 'what do you think of Brother Joseph?' 'O he is a first-rate man, and I fully believe he is a Prophet. See here, he has trusted me this shawl.' Richard says, 'I think I will go down and see if he won't trust me some.' In walks Richard. 'Brother Joseph, I want to trade about 20 dollars.' 'Well,' says Joseph, 'these goods will make the people apostatize; so over they go, they are of less value than the people.' Richard gets his goods. Another makes a trade of 25 dollars, and so it goes. Joseph was a first-rate fellow with them all the time, provided he never would ask them to pay him. In this way it is easy for us to trade away a first-rate store of goods, and be in debt for them." [10]

This may have been a reason for Joseph Smith's failure, but there were others, for he was no more of a success when he tried operating a tannery and a steam sawmill. In his spare moments from revealing the will of the Lord, he also turned to real estate and speculated in land at Kirtland. Throughout the section of the country where he lived, real estate speculation was then a disease, and Joseph Smith was smitten with it to his disadvantage. But the most important of all the Prophet's financial enterprises was the Kirtland Safety Society Anti-Banking Company. The capital stock of this coöperative bank was fixed at four million dollars.

Early in 1837 the Saints began to speculate, apparently with Church money. Because of speculative land ventures and excessive issues of paper money, financial conditions throughout the country were bad. The Kirtland Safety Society Anti-Banking Company issued paper money, which was finally refused by other banks, after Brigham Young had succeeded in disposing of $10,000 worth of it on a missionary trip to the eastern states in the interests of the company. The Church suddenly found itself on the verge of bankruptcy. In June, 1837, Joseph Smith resigned his office of treasurer, and he blamed the subsequent failure of the bank to general business conditions. When the bank

10 *Journal of Discourses*, vol. 1, p. 215.

was established, the Prophet had implied that it was founded by the will of God, and therefore could not fail, but after its failure, he said he had only implied that it could not fail if it were conducted "on righteous principles." He blamed his associates in the enterprise for the lack of these principles.

The people were thoroughly aroused by these financial disasters, and many began for the first time to deny the divine infallibility of Joseph Smith, Jr. Brigham Young had already been compelled to flee from Kirtland. He always maintained that his ardent defense of the Prophet on all occasions had caused threats against his life, but the real reason for his hurried departure was the rage of those who had lost their money in the bank speculation, in which Brigham Young was one of the leaders. A meeting was held in the Temple to investigate the Prophet and his chief associate, Sidney Rigdon. Sidney Rigdon was led into the meeting, for he claimed to be too ill to walk. He made a sick man's plea to the congregation, and the sentimental qualities of his oratory seemed to sway part of the congregation. After he had finished, there was a silence, during which he was slowly led out again. Joseph Smith then arose and declared that the reports of his conduct were false, and he threatened to excommunicate all those who circulated them. The opposition presented its plausible case against him, but before its representative had finished, the Prophet suggested to the congregation that all those opposed to him should be excommunicated first and heard afterwards. During the great disorder which followed this naïve suggestion, it was decided to postpone the hearing for a few days. Meanwhile, towards dusk on the evening of January 12, 1838, Joseph Smith and Sidney Rigdon, now somewhat cured of his ills, left Kirtland on horseback.

In his journal Joseph Smith wrote: "January, 1838—A new year dawned upon the Church in Kirtland in all the bitterness of the spirit of apostate mobocracy; which continued to rage and grow hotter and hotter, until Elder Rigdon and myself were obliged to flee from its deadly influence, as did the Apostles and Prophets of old, and as Jesus said, 'when they persecute you in one city, flee to another.'" Although they may have followed the advice of Jesus, the immediate occasion for their hurried departure was the rumor that warrants were being issued for their arrest on charges of financial fraud. They traveled at night and fast, and they only waited for their families to join them after they had put sixty miles between them and the outraged citizens of Kirtland. Before they had traveled far, they met Brigham Young, and the Prophet told him that he depended upon him to get money for them to continue their journey to Zion in Missouri. All three were so pressed for money, that the Prophet sought a job cutting and sawing wood at Dublin, Indiana. But they soon found easy relief. Brigham Young met a brother in the Church, Brother Tomlinson, who told him that he was trying to sell his farm, but that he could not get an offer. Brigham Young advised Brother Tomlinson to trust in the Lord and the authorities of the Church, and that he would soon be able to sell his farm. Within three days there was an offer for the farm, whether through the efforts of Brigham Young or the Lord, it is impossible to determine. "Brother Brigham," Joseph Smith recorded in his journal, "told him that this was the manifestation of the hand of the Lord to deliver Brother Joseph Smith from his present necessities." Brother Tomlinson thought so too, for he gave the Prophet $300. The three leaders continued their journey in covered waggons until they arrived with their families at Far West, Missouri, where the Mormons had a settlement.

It was also said that some difficulty about a girl hastened the hegira from Kirtland. Oliver Cowdery, who was in a position to know, told some of the brethren that the Prophet had seduced an orphan who was living in his family, and Cowdery claimed that Joseph had confessed his sin to him. Finally, Cowdery withdrew this statement, but he did not do so very emphatically, as this testimonial indicates:

"This may certify, that I heard Oliver Cowdery say, in my house, that Joseph Smith, Jr., never confessed to him, that he was guilty of the crime alleged against him, and Joseph asked if he ever said to him, (Oliver), that he confessed to any one that he, (Joseph) was guilty of the above crime, and Oliver, after some hesitation, answered no.

"GEORGE W. HARRIS." [11]

There is also evidence that polygamy was practised secretly at Kirtland. That this was charged against the Mormons during the Kirtland period is certain, for in the first edition of the *Book of Doctrine and Covenants,* there appears this significant state-

[11] The account of this episode is based on letters in the *Elders' Journal,* of July, 1838, one of the earliest Mormon publications.

ment: "Inasmuch as this Church of Christ has been reproached
with the crime of fornication and polygamy, we declare that we
believe that one man should have one wife, and one woman one
husband, except in case of death, when either is at liberty to marry
again." In a list of questions about his religion which Joseph
Smith answered in the *Elders' Journal* for July, 1838, Question 7
reads:

"Do the Mormons believe in having more wives than one?
"No, not at the same time. But they believe, that if their companion dies, they have a right to marry again. But we do dis-
approve of the custom which has gained in the world, and has been
practised among us, to our great mortification, of marrying in five
or six weeks, or even in two or three months after the death of
their companion.
"We believe that due respect ought to be had, to the memory of
the dead, and the feelings of both friends and children."

It is said that polygamy was first conceived by Joseph Smith
while he was translating the Book of Abraham from his Egyptian
papyrus. The lives of the Old Testament characters, especially
those of Abraham, Jacob, David, and Solomon, made him wonder
why he could not make his life sublime. He suddenly came to
the conclusion that Abraham, Jacob, David, and Solomon were
right, and that the world was wrong: the possession of more than
one wife was not only permissible, but actually necessary to complete salvation. But the time was not yet ripe for public proclamation of this conclusion, even among his own followers. Joseph
Smith stored it away in his mind for use when his people should
become more enlightened and more righteous in the sight of
heaven; meanwhile, however, he practised polygamy surrepti-
tiously, for he himself had attained his full spiritual development.

IV

While Joseph Smith was carrying on extensive religious and
financial operations in Kirtland, Ohio, a number of faithful Mormons were with great difficulty building up the revealed seat of
Zion in Missouri. More than a thousand Saints were gathered
at Independence in Jackson County, Missouri, and were living in
the prosperity which they had created by clearing unsettled territory. But they were not the sole inhabitants of the county, and

before long their neighbors, who were not members of their Church, began to fear the encroachments of this new compact community, who progressed as a whole, and who could not be competed with by individuals. The growing conflict between the Mormons and their neighbors manifested itself at first in petty rows between individuals, and the most serious damage was that done by stones and brickbats, but by the summer of 1833 the non-Mormon citizens of Jackson County decided to organize and to get rid of their Mormon neighbors. Meetings were held and resolutions were passed, in which the main causes of complaint seemed to be that the Mormons boasted that Jackson County, Missouri, was the land God had promised them, and that all non-Mormons would eventually be forced to leave; and that eventually by the increase of their numbers and the power of their community, the Mormons would control the county politics and courts. There were also accusations that the Mormons by fraternizing with the negro slaves and the Indians were causing these two subject races to resent the domination of their self-constituted superiors. The Mormons were asked to abandon the land they had developed and to leave the county. When they appealed to the governor, they were told to resort to the courts, and when they hired lawyers for that purpose, the citizens of Jackson County formed a mob and drove out families, burned houses, and destroyed the printing presses of the Mormon newspaper, the *Star*. After unsuccessful attempts at resistance, the Mormons were driven from their Zion into adjoining counties of Missouri.

During this persecution Joseph Smith was at Kirtland, and when he was asked for advice and aid, he sent his brethren in Missouri consoling messages and revelatory commands. He urged them to hold on to the Promised Land as long as possible, and to refuse always to sell their rights to it, for God intended that they should eventually repossess it. He admitted that God had not yet revealed to him the exact reason for these afflictions, or the definite means by which the lost land would be recovered, but he said that it was evident that God had permitted the persecutions because of transgressions. He added that his heart ached to be with them, but that the Lord willed it otherwise. The Prophet had had some difficulty in persuading the Saints in Missouri to obey his commands from Kirtland, and he was able to point the moral that their afflictions were the result of their disobedience.

Early in May, 1834, Joseph Smith, Brigham Young, and a party of 130 men left Kirtland to aid their Missouri brethren. They had been planning this expedition for some time, but it was impossible to raise the necessary money until May. Once started, however, angels accompanied them all the way, according to Joseph Smith. When the expedition reached Liberty, Missouri, cholera broke out, and the Prophet attempted to heal some of his suffering followers by the laying on of hands, but he soon discovered that cholera was contagious and not religious, for he was stricken with it himself. He offered this ingenious reason for the sudden cessation of his healing activities: "At the commencement, I attempted to lay on hands for their recovery, but I quickly learned by painful experience, that when the great Jehovah decrees destruction upon any people, and makes known His determination, man must not attempt to stay His hand." The great Jehovah was apparently very angry with the Saints, because sixty-eight of the 130 contracted cholera and fourteen of them died of it. When the weakened expedition finally reached their brethren in Missouri, it was discovered that nothing could be done by such a small body of men, and the party was abandoned by Joseph Smith, every man receiving the Prophet's permission to return home, but not the means to do so.

On the way to Missouri Zion's Army, as Joseph Smith called his expedition, passed a large tumulus. The Prophet ordered that it be opened, and it is said that the bones of a human skeleton were discovered. Joseph gathered his brethren around him and, pointing to the bones, said: "He was a Lamanite, a large thick-set man, and a man of God. He was a warrior and chieftain under the great prophet Omandagus, who was known from the hill Cumorah to the Rocky Mountains. His name was Selph. He was killed in battle by the arrow found among his ribs, during the last great struggle of the Lamanites and Nephites." And, after this satisfactory explanation, the expedition continued on its way, comforted by a sight of one of the illustrious ancestors mentioned in the Book of Mormon.

Brigham Young had an interesting encounter with a rattlesnake during the trip. As he was spreading his blankets for the night in the tall prairie grass, he found a rattlesnake close to his hand. He called one of his brethren and said to him: "Take this snake and carry it off and tell it not to come back again; and to say to its neighbors do not come into our camp to-night, lest some one might kill you." Brigham's friend took the snake, carried it some distance from the camp, told it to stay away, and asked it to spread the news to its friends, lest they get killed. The camp was not troubled any more that night with rattlesnakes, and another legend was added to Mormon history.

Joseph Smith and Brigham Young returned to Kirtland after this short and unsuccessful trip to Missouri and continued the activities which have already been described, until, as we have seen, they were driven out by fear of arrest and compelled to join their Missouri brethren permanently.

Meanwhile, the Saints in Missouri who had been driven from their Zion, established themselves in Caldwell County, at the town of Far West, and it was here that their Prophet joined them with Brigham Young and Sidney Rigdon. As a result of the persecutions in Missouri the Church there had become divided; some of the leaders of the Missouri branch were tried by Joseph Smith for selling their land in Jackson County, contrary to the command of the Lord, and several were excommunicated.

For several years the Mormons continued to move from county to county in Missouri and continued to be welcomed at first by the other inhabitants and finally driven out by them. The reasons for these persecutions were numerous. The Mormons have always set them down to the innate and degenerate wickedness of their opponents, but the explanations of that wickedness are far more interesting than the mere assumption of it. The citizens of Clay County, Missouri, assembled in mass meeting, gave some of their reasons for opposition to the Mormons:

"They are eastern men, whose manners, habits, customs, and even dialect, are essentially different from our own. They are non-slave-holders, and opposed to slavery, which in this peculiar period, when Abolitionism has reared its deformed and haggard visage in our land, is well calculated to excite deep and abiding prejudices in any community where slavery is tolerated and protected. . . .

"The religious tenets of this people are so different from the present churches of the age, that they always have, and always will, excite deep prejudices against them, in any populous country where they may locate. . . .

"We do not contend that we have the least right, under the Constitution and laws of the country, to expel them by force. But we would be blind if we did not foresee that the first blow that is struck, at this moment of deep excitement, must and will speedily involve every individual in a war, bearing ruin, woe and desolation in its course. It matters but little how, where, or by whom, the war may begin, when the work of destruction commences, we must all be borne onward by the storm, or crushed beneath its fury."

Another, unexpressed, reason for opposition to the Mormons was the fact that they worked harder than their western neighbors, who preferred a fixed amount of loafing with their work. Accordingly, the Mormons usually prospered more rapidly and more regularly than their neighbors as a community and as individuals. The result was the envy and jealousy of non-Mormons.

That the Mormons were not slaveholders is true, but they had never expressed themselves as opposed to slavery. On the contrary, Joseph Smith issued a statement in which he said, "I do not believe that the people of the North have any more right to say that the South *shall not* hold slaves, than the South have to say the North shall." He then proceeded to defend negro slavery because the Bible acknowledges the practice of slavery, and he traced the descent of the southern negroes directly to the sons of Canaan, of whom the Bible says: "Cursed be Canaan; a servant of servants shall he be unto his brethren." Joseph Smith added: "What could have been the design of the Almighty in this singular occurrence is not for me to say; but I can say, the curse is not yet taken off from the sons of Canaan, neither will be until it is affected by as great a power as caused it to come. . . ." He also advised the missionary elders "not to preach at all to slaves, until after their masters are converted, and then teach the masters to use them with kindness; remembering that they are accountable to God, and the servants are bound to serve their masters with singleness of heart, without murmuring." More than this no slaveholder could ask.

The Mormons were also accused by the people of Missouri of plotting with the Indians for the destruction of non-Mormons. This suspicion arose from the tenet of the Mormon creed which makes the Indian a descendant of the lost tribes of Israel. The Mormons made efforts to convert the Indians and believed that eventually the Indians would return to their heritage. The people of Missouri were very busy at the time driving the Indians from their heritage into unsettled land west of the Mississippi, and they were finding it difficult enough to do without the irritating and counteracting influence of a people who promised that before long the Indians would return. Indian wars were the main excitement of the country at the time, and the settlers of Missouri feared the Indians more than they admired their ancestry and preferred to suppress them rather than to trust them. Any one who regarded an Indian as anything but an enemy could never be popular.

Another reason for the unpopularity of the Mormons was that they looked with eagerness to the day when their enemies would fall, and they would be triumphant over all other sects and creeds. Every earthquake, every great storm, every plague, and every fire were recorded with care in the publications of the Church as signs of the approaching end of wickedness which was not repentant. Individual Mormons irritated their neighbors by urgent invitations to join the only people who would be saved.

One of the immediate causes of mob action against the Mormons in Missouri was a speech delivered by Sidney Rigdon on the Fourth of July, 1838, at Far West. This vehement oration was known thereafter as the "Salt Sermon," because Sidney Rigdon took for his text the verses in the fifth chapter of Matthew: "If the salt have lost its savor, wherewith shall it be salted? It is thenceforth good for nothing, but to be cast out, and to be trodden under foot of men." Rigdon applied this text somewhat freely to the enemies of the Church of Jesus Christ of Latter-day Saints, and expressed it as his firm opinion that such persons would eventually be trodden under foot until their bowels gushed out. Rigdon pointed out the warning that "the apostles threw Judas Iscariot down and trampled out his bowels, and that Peter stabbed Ananias and Sapphira." Then he issued this ultimatum:

"We have proved the world with kindness; we have suffered their abuse, without cause, with patience, and have endured without resentment, until this day, and still their persecution and violence does not cease. But from this day and this hour, we will suffer it no more.

"We take God and all the holy angels to witness this day, that we warn all men, in the name of Jesus Christ, to come on us no more for ever, for, from this hour, we will bear it no more. Our rights shall no more be trampled on with impunity. The man, or set of men, who attempt it, does it at the expense of their lives. And that mob that comes on us to disturb us, it shall be between us and them a war of extermination, for we will follow them till the last drop of their blood is spilled, or else they will have to exterminate us; for we will carry the seat of war to their own houses, and their own families, and one part or the other shall be utterly destroyed. Remember it then, all men. . . . We this day then proclaim ourselves free, with a purpose and a determination that never can be broken, no never, *no never,* NO NEVER."

This was a dare which it was hard for their rough, pioneer neighbors to resist. At the election one month later, it was decided to prevent the Mormons from voting. A fight was the result, and men were killed on both sides. Mobs began to collect rapidly for the avowed purpose of driving the Mormons from Missouri and killing as many as possible in the process.

From that time on all was confusion and violence. Mormons were tarred and feathered in the effort to make them deny their faith in the Book of Mormon. Their farms were burned and their houses destroyed. They also claim that their women were raped and their old men mercilessly murdered. Some of the Mormons took shelter in the woods and others in Haun's Mill. Parties of the mob surrounded this mill and murdered eighteen men, women, and children. When the mill was finally emptied of Mormons by their slaughter or by their escape, the Missourians are said to have found one small boy. One of them urged his companion not to shoot, but the reported reply was: "Nits will make lice; it is best to save them when we can."

The Mormons did not yield without resisting. At this time the notorious Danites were organized by the Mormons. This was a secret order, the existence of which has frequently been denied by the Mormons, but it is established by the testimony of too many men that there was such an organization. It was established in 1837 or 1838 under David W. Patten, a leader of the Church, who was known as Captain Fearnot, because of his reputed courage. The order was first called the Daughters of Gideon, but it soon occurred to some one that it was ridiculous for bearded and violent men to operate under a feminine name, and the name was changed to Destroying Angels. This, too, did not seem exactly appropriate; and finally the name, Sons of Dan, or Danites, was adopted, from the passage in Genesis which reads: "Dan shall be a serpent by the way, an adder in the path, that biteth the horse heels, so that his rider shall fall backward." There were secret oaths and alleged awful penalties, but exactly what these were it is impossible to discover. In the course of a battle with the Missouri mobs Captain Fearnot, David W. Patten, was killed, but the Danites are said to have continued in Mormon history until long after the migration to Utah.

By the treachery of a Colonel Hinkle, whom Joseph Smith thought to be working for his interests, Smith, Rigdon, Parley Pratt, and several other leaders, except Brigham Young, were surrendered to the Missouri militia, who had been called out for the purpose of aiding the Missouri mobs rather than subduing them. General Lucas, commanding the militia, issued the following curt order:

"BRIGADIER-GENERAL DONIPHAN:
"Sir:—You will take Joseph Smith and the other prisoners into the public square of Far West, and shoot them at 9 o'clock tomorrow morning.
"SAMUEL D. LUCAS, Major-General Commanding."

But fortunately for the Prophet he had some weeks before retained General Doniphan as his lawyer, and Doniphan had been teaching Smith and Rigdon law. The General, according to Joseph Smith, thought them good students, and that they could be admitted to the bar within twelve months. General Doniphan, who later became famous in the war between the United States and Mexico, sent the following reply to his commanding officer:

"It is cold-blooded murder. I will not obey your order. My brigade shall march for Liberty to-morrow morning at 8 o'clock; and if you execute these men, I will hold you responsible before an earthly tribunal, so help me God.
"A. W. DONIPHAN, Brigadier-General."

General Lucas decided not to shoot his prisoners, and they were marched into Liberty, Clay County, for trial, and confined meanwhile in the Liberty jail. Eliza Snow, the Mormon poetess, celebrated this arrest of the Prophet in these lines:

> " 'What means your savage conduct?
>   Have you a lawful Writ?
> To any LEGAL process
>   I cheerfully submit.'

> " 'Here,' said these lawless ruffians,
>   'Is our authority';
> And drew their pistols nearer,
>   With rude ferocity."

During the Mormon persecutions Joseph Smith rode along the lines of his followers and said: "God and liberty is the watchword. Fear them not, for their hearts are cold as cucumbers." The Prophet had frequently said that a Gentile could not kill a Mormon, but after it had happened many times, he was compelled to explain why God allowed the outrage. He did so by asking why God had not helped the Saviour down from the cross, and why Paul had not been saved by a miracle from stones and whipping. This did not answer the question, except by asking it again, but it was sufficient answer for Smith's followers, who always believed that there were more things in heaven and earth than they could possibly dream of in their philosophy. The Prophet once said concerning prayers for the destruction of his enemies: "The Lord once told me that what I asked for I should have. I have been afraid to ask God to kill my enemies, lest some of them should, peradventure, repent." However, he did not hesitate to wish for their destruction in a more eccentric manner. Once when he was asked for a toast, he raised his glass and said: "Here is wishing that all the mobocrats of the nineteenth century were in the middle of the sea, in a stone canoe, with an iron paddle; that a shark might swallow the canoe, and the shark be thrust into the nethermost part of hell, and the door locked, the key lost, and a blind man hunting for it."

Brigham Young was the only important leader of the Church to escape arrest. He seemed all his life to have a canny ability to avoid capture. During the persecutions in Missouri he had attained a position of prominence. When the council of the Twelve Apostles was organized at Kirtland, he had been appointed the third apostle, and the succession to the presidency of that body was in numerical rotation. The two men ahead of him were David W. Patten, who had been killed during the battles, and Thomas B. Marsh, who was President of the Twelve Apostles and leader of the Saints in Missouri. Marsh's wife had a quarrel over a pint of milk with another sister. Marsh defended his wife, and when the Church councils decided against her at the numerous trials which followed, Marsh declared "that he would sustain the character of his wife, even if he had to go to hell for it." He apostatized and testified against his former brethren. Many years later, broken in health and finances, Marsh rejoined the Church in Utah.

Brigham Young automatically stepped into the important position left vacant by Marsh's apostasy. Smith and the other leaders were in jail, so it was Brigham Young's job to superintend the removal of the Saints from the State of Missouri. The Governor of Missouri, Lillburn W. Boggs, decided that the Mormons must leave Missouri in a body or be exterminated, unless they were willing to renounce their religion and live as other Missourians. The Mormons, who had been beaten into submission by the combination of mob and militia, were lined up, and the Governor's order was read to them. Brigham Young was present at this ceremony, and he told his congregation many years later in a sermon what his thoughts were at the time:

"Do you want I should tell you what I thought? I do not think I will. I thought a kind of a bad thought, that is, it would be considered so by a very religious person, and especially if he was well stocked with self-righteousness; but I would as soon as not tell what I thought to those who have not much of this and are not very pious, and it was, 'I will see you in hell first.' Renounce my religion? 'No, sir,' said I, 'it is my all, all I have on this earth. . . .' "

The Mormons chose to leave Missouri, and Brigham Young led his people out of the house of bondage into what he could not tell at the time would prove to be the land of Egypt. The exodus was attended with much misery. Valuable farms were traded for old waggons, horses, or yokes of oxen, and it is said that many Mormons were compelled to convey their land at the point of a rifle muzzle. About three thousand of them under the leadership of Brigham Young made their way to Illinois, where there was a small settlement of the Saints. The people of Quincy, Illinois, moved by the stories of their persecutions in Missouri, offered the Mormons sympathy and aid.

The persecutions of the Mormons in Missouri were summed up by Parley P. Pratt in a hymn which has always been popular among the Saints:

"Missouri,
Like a whirlwind in its fury,
And without a judge or jury,
Drove the saints and spilled their blood."

From his cell in Liberty jail the Prophet wrote epistles to his people, in which he said that their misfortunes and his were but signs of the times, and proof positive that the fulfilment of the revelations and predictions concerning the destruction of the wicked would be carried out presently. The prisoners were tried on a composite charge of murder, theft, treason, arson, and several minor crimes. The scene in the court room was one of confusion and interruption. Peter H. Burnett, who, with General Doniphan, defended Smith and his associates, gave this description of the trial in his book, *Recollections and Opinions of an Old Pioneer:*

"I made the opening speech, and was replied to by the District Attorney; and Doniphan made the closing argument. Before he rose to speak, or just as he rose, I whispered to him: 'Doniphan! let yourself out, my good fellow; and I will kill the first man that attacks you.' And he did let himself out, in one of the most eloquent and withering speeches I ever heard. The maddened crowd foamed and gnashed their teeth, but only to make him more and more intrepid. He faced the terrible storm with the most noble courage. All the time I sat within six feet of him, with my hand upon my pistol, calmly determined to do as I had promised him."

Unfortunately, there is no account of what General Doniphan said. Joseph Smith's mother gave a less pleasant, but just as interesting, incident of the trial:

"The opposing attorney tried his utmost to convict Joseph of the crimes mentioned in the writ, but before he had spoken many minutes, he turned sick, and vomited at the feet of the Judge; which, joined to the circumstance of his advocating the case of the Missourians, who are called *pukes* by their countrymen, obtained for him the same appelation, and was a source of much amusement to the court."

The prisoners were granted a change of venue on April 15, 1839, and they were taken under guard to Boone County. Smith bought whiskey and honey for the guards and succeeded in getting them helplessly drunk. The prisoners escaped on horses, making their way to Illinois and their followers. The Prophet had been in jail for six months.

It was estimated that it had cost the State of Missouri $150,000 to wage war against the Mormons, and Joseph Smith soon after he was settled in Illinois drew up claims for $1,381,044.55½, which he presented to Congress. He made a special trip to Washington in 1839 in the interests of this claim and to seek restitution of the rights of his people to their Missouri property. He called on President Martin Van Buren, who listened with impatience to the long recital of the Mormon complaints. When Joseph Smith and his associates had finished, Van Buren said: "Gentlemen, your cause is just, but I can do nothing for you. Were I to take your part, I should lose the support of Missouri." This was frank, but it filled Joseph Smith with a rage against Martin Van Buren that manifested itself whenever the occasion arose during the next few years. The claim for damages was presented to the Senate, where it was attacked with vehemence by the senators from Missouri, Benton and Lynn, and buried without action.

The Missouri persecutions, though they were productive of much suffering and hardship, gained the Mormons considerable sympathy in other parts of the country. Mass meetings were held in large cities in the East, expressing sympathy for them, and money was raised for their relief. Newspapers in many parts of the country blamed Missouri and defended the Mormons.

If we can believe Parley Pratt, terrible things happened eventually to those Missourians who had been most active in persecuting the Saints. Pratt wrote in his autobiography:

"A colonel of the Missouri mob, who helped to drive, plunder and murder the Mormons, died in the hospital at Sacramento, 1849. Beckwith had the care of him; he was eaten with worms—a large black headed kind of maggot—which passed through him by myriads, seemingly a half pint at a time! Before he died these maggots were crawling out of his mouth and nose! He literally rotted alive! Even the flesh on his legs burst open and fell from the bones! They gathered up the rotten mass in a blanket and buried him, without awaiting a coffin!

"A. Mr. ——, one of the Missouri mob, died in the same hospital about the same time, and under the care of Mr. Beckwith. His face and jaw on one side literally rotted, and half of his face actually fell off! One eye rotted out, and half of his nose, mouth and jaw fell from the bones! The doctor scraped the bones, and unlocked and took out his jaw from the joint round to the center of the chin. The rot and maggots continued to eat till they ate through the large or jugular vein of his neck, and he bled to death! He, as well as Townsend, stank so previous to their death that they had to be placed in rooms by themselves, and it was almost impossible to endure their presence, and the flies could not be kept from blowing them while alive! . . .

"These particulars, and many others, were related to me by brother Beckwith previous to his death, and afterwards by his widow and father-in-law, and others who were conversant with them, and are believed to be correct." [12]

There was one important matter to attend to before the Mormons abandoned Missouri to the buffetings of Satan for eternity. God had instructed Joseph Smith to build a Temple there, and He had declared that Jackson County was Zion. The Mormons firmly believed that God always meant what He said. Therefore, Brigham Young and the other eleven Apostles made a secret trip to Missouri, arriving there at midnight on April 26, 1839. The revelation concerning the Temple had said that one year from the date of its issue, April 8, 1838, the Saints must commence to lay the foundation. Young and his associates went at midnight to the chosen site of the Temple, sang a hymn softly, rolled one large stone upon another, and Joseph Smith's prophetic power was vindicated and his pact with God fulfilled.

[12] *The Autobiography of Parley Parker Pratt,* pp. 476-477.

Chapter IV

THE LAND OF EGYPT

I

THE Mormons were received in Illinois with that pity and sympathy accorded to all suffering peoples on their arrival in a country which has heard many sorrowful tales of their hardships. The people of Quincy, through a special committee, recommended that the pitiful strangers be treated with "a becoming decorum and delicacy," and that the regular inhabitants of Quincy should "be particularly careful not to indulge in any conversation or expressions calculated to wound their feelings, or in any way to reflect upon those who, by every law of humanity, are entitled to our sympathy and commiseration." Meanwhile, Brigham Young and the other leaders of the Saints were busy arranging for the people to help themselves. The refugees were not rich in possessions, but their reputation for thrift was productive of credit, and land was sold to them in Iowa and Illinois, on both banks of the Mississippi.

On the east bank of the Mississippi was a town called Commerce. It consisted of five huts, a storehouse, two frame houses, and two blockhouses, with plenty of surrounding farming land and a beautiful outlook over the River. In spite of its rich land and lovely view the place was considered unhealthy, and the Mormons were able to purchase the whole town and its adjoining land for little money. As soon as they took possession the name of the town was changed from the prosaic Commerce, which had been given it by a New York land company, to Nauvoo, which, according to Joseph Smith, meant beautiful. "The name of our city," he said, "is of Hebrew origin, and signifies a beautiful site, conveying besides an idea of repose." Other Hebrew scholars were never able to identify the word, and, as we shall see, the Mormons did not enjoy repose there for very long. One Hebrew scholar remarked concerning Smith's attempt at erudition that it was similar to that of the theological students of Middletown,

109

Connecticut, who used to say that the name of their town was derived from Moses by dropping "iddletown," and adding "oses."

During the strenuous efforts necessary to turn an undeveloped, swampy territory into a neat city, many of the Mormons suffered from malaria contracted while breaking up the new land. Even the Prophet and Brigham Young caught the disease. But Joseph Smith went about healing his people, and it was to his power as a spiritual physician that many of them claimed to owe their salvation. This healing kept him very busy, for one of the early journals records that he was once sent for to heal a pair of twins and could not go himself because of previous appointments. But he sent his red silk handkerchief, and this, we are told, was just as effective. Wilford Woodruff, who was the bearer of the handkerchief, recorded the incident in his journal: "He took a red silk handkerchief out of his pocket and gave it to me, and told me to wipe their faces with the handkerchief when I administered to them, and they should be healed. He also said unto me: 'As long as you will keep that handkerchief, it shall remain a league between you and me.' I went with the man, and did as the Prophet commanded me, and the children were healed. I have possession of the handkerchief unto this day."

The new city began to prosper rapidly, and in what seemed a miraculously short time the new farms were producing crops and the new city had buildings. The neighbors were amazed at the display of energy, but the Mormons attributed everything to the inspiration of God.

Under the leadership of Brigham Young and the Twelve Apostles missionaries went throughout this country and England to preach the glory of God and the beauty of Nauvoo. It is a mystery how these men lived en route, for they themselves have been content to record that God supported them. Brigham Young insisted in later years that when he was traveling in the interests of Mormonism he would put his hand in his pocket or in his trunk and find money which had not been there before, and which he could only account for as a gift from God. George D. Prentice, a humorist of the day, suggested sacrilegiously that perhaps Brigham Young had not always put his hand into his own pocket.

Soon after his family was settled in the new city Brigham Young, accompanied by Heber Kimball, left for a missionary trip to England. Joseph Smith had received a revelation from God that it was the duty of the Church to preach the Gospel in England. Brigham Young was very ill at the time, for the Prophet's healing powers had not been entirely successful in his case; he had to be helped to the ferry from his home, and as the waggon carried him and Heber Kimball out of sight of their weeping families, Kimball suggested that they should give a cheer. Propping himself up, Brigham Young shouted, "Hurrah, hurrah, hurrah for Israel!"

On March 7, 1840, Brigham Young and several of the Apostles sailed as steerage passengers in the *Patrick Henry,* paying eighteen dollars each for their fare. In addition to this they supplied their own food, but Brigham Young did not spend much money on food, for it is recorded that he was seasick practically every day of the twenty-seven-day trip from New York to Liverpool.

A faithful English convert gave Brigham Young 350 pounds, with which he secured the English copyright of the Book of Mormon and printed several thousand copies of it. The *Millennial Star* was started under the editorship of Parley P. Pratt so that the English Saints might know the news of their American brethren. Meetings were held daily in various parts of England. During the year which they spent there Brigham Young and his associates established branches of Mormonism in most of the large towns and cities, converted 8,000 people, sending 1,000 of them to Nauvoo, and published 5,000 copies of the Book of Mormon, 3,000 hymn books and 50,000 tracts. They also established a shipping agency for the convenience of converts who wished to emigrate to the new Zion. While carrying on all this work for the cause, they also managed somehow to get food and lodging for themselves. In a letter to Joseph Smith Brigham Young explained their success:

"The people are very different in this country to what the Americans are. They say it cannot be possible that men should leave their homes and come so far, unless they were truly the servants of the Lord; they do not seem to understand argument; simple testimony is enough for them; they beg and plead for the Book of Mormon, and were it not for the priests, the people would follow after the servants of the Lord and inquire what they should do to be saved."

The Mormon missionaries were particularly successful among the poverty-stricken manufacturing population of English cities, where their offer of a real promised land, with farming possibilities, proved irresistibly attractive. In an Epistle to the Saints in Great Britain Brigham Young urged emigration, giving Biblical precedents for it:

"The spirit of emigration has actuated the children of men, from the time our first parents were expelled from the garden until now. It was this spirit that first peopled the plains of Shinar, and all other places; yes, it was emigration that first broke upon the death-like silence and loneliness of an empty earth, and caused the desolate land to teem with life, and the desert to smile with joy."

But, he hastened to add, it was necessary that men with capital should emigrate first, so that they might establish factories and mills to be worked by their less fortunate brethren.

Mormon missionaries had preceded Brigham Young and his party to England, but they did not possess the energy or temperament necessary to widespread success. In a sermon Brigham Young once told the improper and the proper way to make converts, as illustrated by the temperaments of Brother Wilford Woodruff and Brother Heber C. Kimball:

"When we found them in London, Brother Woodruff was busily engaged in writing his history from morning until evening; and if a sister called on him, he would say, 'How do you do? take a chair,' and keep on writing and laboring to bring up the history of the Church and his own.

"That was all right and well, in its place; but, if a sister asked a question, the answer would be, 'Yes'; and if she asked another, 'No'; and that was the sum of the conversation. If a brother came in, it would be the same. But Brother Kimball would say, 'Come, my friend, sit down; do not be in a hurry'; and he would begin and preach the Gospel in a plain, familiar manner, and make his hearers believe everything he said, and make them testify to its truth, whether they believed or not, asking them, 'Now, ain't that so?' and they would say, 'Yes.' And he would make Scripture as he needed it, out of his own bible, and ask, 'Now, ain't that so?' and the reply would be 'Yes.' He would say, 'Now, you believe this? You see how plain the Gospel is? Come along now'; and he would lead them into the waters of baptism. The people would want to come to see him early in the morning, and stay with him until noon, and from that until night; and he would put his arm around their necks, and say, 'Come, let us go down to the water.'" [1]

[1] *Journal of Discourses,* vol. 4, p. 305.

Brigham Young had great influence in persuading converts not only to devote themselves, but also to devote their money to the new cause, for all the operations of his successful missionary trips were financed by the converts he made in the course of them. He accomplished this, not by asking them for their money, but by bringing them to the point of realization that it was their duty to give it to him. The missionary foundation which was laid in England by Brigham Young has always been the most extensive source of converts to Mormonism. Such was the magnitude of the early success in that country that a few years later Joseph Smith had hopes of converting Queen Victoria and Prince Albert. He ordered Elder Lorenzo Snow to send copies of the Book of Mormon to both of them, and the Mormons seemed to entertain hopes that their majesties would eventually see the light, join the only true church, lend their great influence to the cause, and finally make a pilgrimage to Nauvoo, Illinois. Eliza Snow, the Mormon poetess, celebrated the thought in these lines:

> "Oh! would she now her influence lend—
> The influence of royalty—
> Messiah's kingdom to extend,
> And Zion's nursing mother be,
> Then with the glory of her name
> Inscribed on Zion's lofty spire,
> She'd win a wreath of endless fame,
> To last when other wreaths expire."

But Queen Victoria did not grasp the opportunity, for the Mormons never heard from her concerning their bible.

II

By the time Brigham Young had returned to Nauvoo from his successful missionary trip, Joseph Smith had started several projects of great importance to the community and to the Church. On the 19th of January, 1841, Joseph Smith received a long revelation from God, in which his people were commanded to begin work on two imposing structures, one a Temple for the habitation of the Lord for eternity, and the other a boarding house for the lodging of Joseph Smith and his descendants from generation to generation. The Lord pointed out that He had much to reveal of great importance, but that He could not do so with freedom until the people had a house of worship in which to receive such glorious revelations, where they could carry out appropriately the rites attendant upon their execution. He recommended that the brethren come from afar and bring with them their gold and their silver and their precious stones, and that they gather woods of many varieties for the House of the Lord.

As soon as He had finished speaking of His Temple, the Lord took up the matter of Joseph Smith's boarding house and went into the following details:

"And now I say unto you, as pertaining to my boarding house which I have commanded you to build for the boarding of strangers, let it be built unto my name, and let my name be named upon it, and let my servant Joseph, and his house have place therein, from generation to generation:

"For this anointing have I put upon his head, that his blessing shall also be put upon the head of his posterity after him; . . .

"Therefore, let my servant Joseph and his seed after him have place in that house, from generation to generation, for ever and ever, saith the Lord,

"And let the name of that house be called Nauvoo house, and let it be a delightful habitation for man, and a resting place for the weary traveler, that he may contemplate the glory of Zion, and the glory of this the corner-stone thereof; . . .

"Behold, verily I say unto you, let my servant George Miller, and my servant Lyman Wight, and my servant John Snider, and my servant Peter Haws, organize themselves, and appoint one of them to be a president over their quorum for the purpose of building that house.

"And they shall form a constitution whereby they may receive stock for the building of that house.

"And they shall not receive less than fifty dollars for a share of stock in that house, and they shall be permitted to receive fifteen thousand dollars from any one man for stock in that house;

"But they shall not be permitted to receive over fifteen thousand dollars stock from any one man;

"And they shall not be permitted to receive under fifty dollars for a share of stock from any one man in that house;

"And they shall not be permitted to receive any man as a stockholder in this house, except the same shall pay his stock into their hands at the time he receives stock;

"And in proportion to the amount of stock he pays into their hands, he shall receive stock in that house; but if he pays nothing into their hands, he shall not receive any stock in that house.

"And if any pay stock in to their hands, it shall be for stock in that house, for himself and for his generation after him, from generation to generation, so long as he and his heirs shall hold that stock, and do not sell or convey the stock away out of their hands by their own free will and act, if you will do my will, saith the Lord your God.

"And again, verily I say unto you, if my servant George Miller, and my servant Lyman Wight, and my servant Peter Haws, receive any stock into their hands, in moneys or in properties wherein they receive the real value of moneys, they shall not appropriate any portion of that stock to any other purpose, only in that house;

"And if they do appropriate any portion of that stock any where else, only in that house, without the consent of the stockholder, and do not repay fourfold for the stock which they appropriate any where else, only in that house, they shall be accursed, and shall be moved out of their place, saith the Lord God, for I, the Lord, am God and cannot be mocked in any of these things."

Then the Lord proceeded to give several specific commands concerning the Nauvoo House. He ordered Vinson Knight, Hyrum Smith, whom He called familiarly by his first name, Isaac Galland, William Marks, Henry G. Sherwood, William Law, Almon Babbitt, and Amos Davies to take stock in the Nauvoo House. "And again," God continued, "verily I say unto you, Let no man pay stock to the quorum of the Nauvoo House unless he shall be a believer in the Book of Mormon, and the revelations I have given unto you, saith the Lord your God." There was no prospect that anybody else would pay stock into the hands of the quorum, but God seemed anxious that the control should remain within the Church. In its combination of the language of the Bible and the expressions used in the prospectus of a speculative corporation, this revelation is unsurpassed by any of the Prophet Joseph Smith's other attempts at inspired enterprise. This revelation would lead us to believe that God was not only an inspiration but also a capable corporation promoter. He carefully selected even the name for His boarding house, and in calling it The Nauvoo House, He hit upon the name which every Main Street would recognize at once as most appropriate.[2]

Work progressed slowly on the Temple, apparently because the Lord had not formulated a stock-selling plan for it, but the Nauvoo House was built in a comparatively short time after it

[2] This revelation is printed in full in Section 124 of the *Book of Doctrine and Covenants*.

was commanded. The Prophet made speeches to his people urging them to contribute their money to the fund for building both the Temple and the Nauvoo House. He was getting tired of receiving old clothes and trinkets, and one day on the streets of Nauvoo he made this appeal for cash:

"We want gold and silver to build the Temple and Nauvoo House: we want your old nose-rings, and finger rings, and brass kettles no longer. If you have old rags, watches, guns, &c., go and peddle them off, and bring the hard metal; and if we will do this by popular opinion, we shall have a sound currency. Send home all banknotes, and take no more paper money. Let every man write back to his neighbors before he starts for home to exchange his property for gold and silver, that he may fulfil the scripture, and come up to Zion, bringing his gold and silver with him. . . . If any are hungry or naked, don't take away the brick, timber and materials, that belong to that house [the Temple], but come and tell me, and I will divide with them to the last morsel; and then if the man is not satisfied, I will kick his backside." [3]

Joseph Smith was about six feet two in height, weighed 212 pounds and was always proud of his physical strength; he exhibited it frequently by wrestling with his brethren and his enemies.

In August, 1843, the Prophet moved into the Lord's boarding house, and on October 3 of that year it was formally opened with appropriate resolutions proclaiming the virtues of Joseph Smith and the beauties of Nauvoo. At first the Prophet managed the boarding house himself, but either he found the stress of practical management too great, or he was not successful as a hotel manager, for it was soon leased to Ebenezer Robinson, and Joseph Smith retained a few rooms for himself and his family. In an interview published in the *Universalist Union* for May 4, 1844, the Prophet gave his reason for establishing a boarding house, besides the command of God to do so: " 'I can't stand it to entertain all who come to see me—I wish I could—but I am not able, and so to get clear of it, I am going to keep tavern; then they can come and see me and stay as long as they choose, and when they are satisfied, they can *pay* me and go away. Isn't that right?' said he exultingly." Nauvoo was becoming one of the curiosities of America, and visitors came there every week

[3] *History of the Church*, vol. 5, p. 286.

from the eastern states and from England to examine the latter-day Prophet and to investigate the principles of his new religion. While his hotel was in the course of construction, the Prophet started a grocery store, with a private office adjoining, "where," he wrote, "I keep my sacred writings." He was quite willing to interrupt his translations to sell some canned goods, and his followers, who had practical Yankee training, did not admire their Prophet less because he was sometimes a salesman. But Joseph Smith was no more successful as a storekeeper at Nauvoo than he had been at Kirtland, and a few months after the opening of his store, he took advantage of the bankruptcy law to clear himself of his debts. His brother Hyrum also went into bankruptcy. This action helped to damage the reputation of the Mormons among their non-Mormon neighbors in Illinois.

In spite of all his enterprises Joseph Smith was not personally wealthy. There is other evidence of this besides the unique account of his possessions which he rendered the trustee of church property: "Old Charley, a horse given to him several years before in Kirtland; two pet deer, two old turkeys and four young ones, an old cow given to him by a brother in Missouri, old Major, a dog; his wife, children, and a little household furniture." Brigham Young managed to support a family of eight children in Nauvoo, but all he ever said of the origin of his income was that the Lord gave it to him. But the source of the Prophet's support is suggested by an appeal Brigham Young issued in an epistle to the Saints:

"His family [Joseph Smith's] is large and his company great, and it requires much to furnish his table. And now, brethren, we call on you for immediate relief in this matter; and we invite you to bring our President as many loads of wheat, corn, beef, pork, lard, tallow, eggs, poultry, venison and everything eatable at your command (not excepting unfrozen potatoes and vegetables, as soon as the weather will admit,) flour, etc., and thus give him the privilege of attending your spiritual interest.

"The measure you mete shall be measured to you again. If you give liberally to your President in temporal things, God will return to you liberally in spiritual and temporal things too. One or two good new milch cows are much needed also.

"Brethren, will you do your work, and let the President do his for you before God? We wish an immediate answer by loaded teams or letter. Your brethren in Christ, in behalf of the quorum,
                                                "Brigham Young.

"P.S. Brethren, we are not unmindful of the favors our President has received from you in former days. But a man will not cease to be hungry this year because he ate last year.

"B. Y." [4]

That this epistle to the Saints living at Ramus, Illinois, was successful, can be gathered from two entries in the Prophet's diary a few days later: "Bishop Newel K. Whitney returned from Ramus this evening, with five teams loaded with provisions and grain, as a present to me, which afforded me very seasonable relief. I pray the Lord to bless those who gave it abundantly; and may it be returned upon their heads an hundred fold!" And, a few days later: "Brother David Manhard, of Lee County, Iowa, brought me two loads of corn and one hog; for which may the Lord bless him!" The exclamation marks are Joseph Smith's.

The system of tithing for the support of the Church and its leaders was not so successful under Joseph Smith as it proved later under the superior administrative guidance of Brigham Young. In a sermon many years later Brigham Young described the kind of offerings made by the Saints in Illinois to satisfy their tithing debts:

"In the days of Joseph, when a horse was brought in for tithing, he was pretty sure to be hipped, or ringboned, or have the pole-evil, or perhaps had passed the routine of horse-disease until he had become used up. The question would be, 'What do you want for him?' 'Thirty dollars in tithing and thirty in cash.' What was he really worth? Five dollars, perhaps. They would perhaps bring in a cow after the wolves had eaten off three of her teats, and she had not had a calf for six years past; and if she had a calf, and you ventured to milk her, she would kick a quid of tobacco out of your mouth. These are specimens of the kind of tithing we used to get." [5]

The Prophet's followers had become as dependent upon him as he was upon them, and they seldom concluded any transaction until he had clothed it with sanctity. The negotiations for several farms in Nauvoo for church sites were only begun after fasting and prayer, and when the specific sites had been decided upon,

[4] History of the Church, vol. 5, p. 249.
[5] Journal of Discourses, vol. 8, p. 346.

the men chosen to complete the purchase were ordained by God through Sidney Rigdon for that special purpose. The direct influence of Joseph Smith's revelations on some of his followers is admirably illustrated by a passage in Josiah Quincy's book:

"Near the entrance to the Temple we passed a workman who was laboring under a huge sun, which he had chiselled from the solid rock. The countenance was of the negro type, and it was surrounded by the conventional rays.

" 'General Smith,' said the man, looking up from his task, 'is this like the face you saw in vision?'

" 'Very near it,' answered the prophet, 'except' (this was added with an air of careful connoisseurship that was quite overpowering)—'except that the nose is just a thought too broad.' " [6]

III

When the Mormons arrived in Illinois, the two political parties, the Whigs and the Democrats, were fighting a close contest for control of the State, and it was a distinct advantage for either party to capture the entire vote of the Mormons. Every effort was therefore made by politicians to conciliate the people and their leaders. As the election of 1840 drew near politicians crowded about Joseph Smith, offering him promises, if he would deliver the Mormon vote to their parties. The Prophet proved himself a shrewd politician, for he promised nothing definitely until he was offered definite privileges. What Smith demanded for the Mormon vote, which his influence enabled him to deliver in a body, was a charter for the city of Nauvoo, a charter for the Nauvoo Legion, his militia organization, and a charter for a university to be established at Nauvoo. The Whig Party promised these concessions, and the Mormons all voted for the Whig candidates, cutting the Democratic majority in the State down to the lowest it had ever reached. At the next meeting of the State legislature the charters were promptly granted.

The city charter of Nauvoo gave unlimited powers to Joseph Smith and his associates. The charter provided that the mayor and aldermen of Nauvoo could pass any laws not directly conflicting with the provisions of the Constitution of the United States and the Constitution of Illinois. The charter also granted the mayor and his aldermen power to act as a municipal court. In

[6] *Figures of the Past*, by Josiah Quincy, p. 389.

return for these unlimited privileges Joseph Smith gave only a limited expression of gratitude. He had promised to vote for the Whigs once, but he had not promised to vote for the Whigs always, and it was therefore necessary for the legislators of both parties to conciliate the Mormons constantly by granting whatever they desired in the hope that the vote would go to the highest bidder. Abraham Lincoln, when he was competing for office in Illinois in 1840, sent the Mormons campaign literature and wrote with satisfaction at the time that Joseph Smith was one of his admirers. Lincoln also voted in favor of the Nauvoo charter when he was a member of the Illinois legislature. Stephen Douglas helped to push the charter through the legislature.

Joseph Smith's adviser and aide in his political machinations was John C. Bennett. Bennett had been a professor of midwifery, as he chose to call it, in Willoughby University at Willoughby, Ohio, and a traveling medical practitioner. Governor Ford, of Illinois, characterized him accurately in a few words: "This Bennett was probably the greatest scamp in the western country. I have made particular enquiries concerning him, and have traced him in several places in which he had lived before he had joined the Mormons, in Ohio, Indiana and Illinois, and he was everywhere accounted the same debauched, unprincipled, and profligate character. He was a man of some little talent, and then had the confidence of the Mormons, and particularly that of their leaders." Bennett had written the Prophet a letter suggesting that he might be useful to him in the business of religion if he were to come to Illinois and join the Mormons. His letter was filled with flattery, and Joseph Smith found it interesting. Then, with crude but effective advertising tactics, Bennett followed his letter with one every day for a week, enclosing testimonials of his character and his achievements. All of these letters employed the tone of an unduly exuberant and obviously insincere enthusiast, who was more concerned with his ambitions than with his honesty. But Joseph Smith, who had something of the same quality, felt that such a man could be extremely useful to him, and as soon as Bennett himself followed his advance letters to Nauvoo, he was welcomed and taken into the complete confidence of the Mormon leaders. It was he who carried on the negotiations with politicians, and it was he who talked to legislators in the lobby of the Illinois legislature until the Nauvoo charter was passed. After the charter was passed, Bennett became Mayor of Nauvoo, Master in Chancery for Hancock County, Illinois, Quartermaster-General of the Illinois State Militia, and Major-General of the Nauvoo Legion, which was nominally a branch of the Illinois militia, but actually an independent military force under the absolute control of the Prophet and his associates.

The Nauvoo Legion soon after the legislature granted the charter for its organization consisted of about 5,000 men, and all male Mormons between the ages of eighteen and forty-five were compelled to join it. Drills were compulsory, and a sliding scale of fines was established for those who failed to attend. Generals were fined twenty-five dollars; colonels, twenty dollars; captains, fifteen dollars; lieutenants, ten dollars; musicians and privates, five dollars. The costumes of the Legion were picturesque rather than uniform, for most of the officers and soldiers consulted their individual taste; scarfs, badges, and stripes of varied brilliant colors were attached indiscriminately to the uniforms. The Prophet held the position of Lieutenant-General, and a Mormon writer boasted that after George Washington he was the first man in the United States to hold that exalted rank; but George Washington did not give it to himself. The purpose of the Legion was described in verse by the Mormon poetess, Eliza Snow:

> "The firm heart of the Sage and the Patriot is warm'd
> By the grand 'Nauvoo Legion': The 'Legion' is form'd
> To oppose vile oppression, and nobly to stand
> In defence of the honor, and laws of the land.
> Base, illegal proscribers may tremble—'tis right
> That the lawless aggressor should shrink with afright,
> From a band that's united fell mobbers to chase,
> And protect our lov'd country from utter disgrace. . . ."

Their neighbors, however, did not regard this formidable military force as a source of protection, but ungratefully they began to express the opinion and the fear that Joseph Smith was emulating the career of Mohammed by attempting to propagate his faith, if not by the sword, at least by militia. That Smith would have used his army to spread his creed one cannot establish or deny, for he never enjoyed that opportunity, but its existence was a source of apprehension to the non-Mormon population of Illinois, and it is undoubtedly true that Joseph Smith intended the Nauvoo Legion more for his personal protection from arrest and persecution than for the protection of the inhabitants of Illinois, who needed none at the time.

Whatever his purpose in organizing a private army, Joseph Smith cherished the pomp of his military position. He enjoyed very much riding up and down the lines of brightly colored uniforms, dressed as he was in tight breeches and a swallow-tail coat, ornamented with great areas of gold braid. His large, strong body, clothed in its garish uniform, made as great an impression on himself as it did on his followers. The high title of Lieutenant-General pleased him immensely. Josiah Quincy overheard him make rather incongruous use of it in an argument with a Methodist minister: "Why I told my congregation the other Sunday that they might as well believe Joe Smith as such theology as that," said the Methodist. "Did you say Joe Smith in a sermon?" asked the Prophet. "Of course, I did. Why not?" Smith replied in a tone of quiet superiority, "Considering only the day and the place, it would have been more respectful to have said Lieutenant-General Joseph Smith."

Before long Joseph Smith succeeded John C. Bennett as Mayor of Nauvoo, and in his various positions of Mayor, Lieutenant-General, and Prophet of God he combined in himself all the powers to which man might aspire. "It seems to me, General," Josiah Quincy said to him, "that you have too much power to be safely trusted to one man." "In your hands or that of any other person," Smith answered, "so much power would, no doubt, be dangerous. I am the only man in the world whom it would be safe to trust with it. Remember, I am a prophet!" "The last five words," wrote Quincy, "were spoken in a rich, comical aside, as if in hearty recognition of the ridiculous sound they might have in the ears of a Gentile."

It was not long before Joseph Smith began to abuse his vast power and to arouse the watchful and jealous animosity of his neighbors. The Mormons had increased gradually by foreign immigration and domestic proselytizing until they numbered almost 12,000 and formed the largest city in the sparsely settled State of Illinois. Chicago at the time had a population of about 4,000. The voting strength of the Mormons was greater than the combined voting power of the non-Mormons of Hancock County, and the manner in which Joseph Smith used it is illustrated by a letter he published in the *Times and Seasons,* the weekly Mormon periodical published at Nauvoo:

"To my friends in Illinois—The Gubernatorial Convention of the State of Illinois have nominated Colonel Adam W. Snyder for Governor, and Colonel John Moore for Lieutenant-Governor of the State of Illinois, election to take place in August next. . . . General Bennett informs us that no men were more efficient in assisting him to procure our great chartered privileges, than were Colonel Snyder, and Colonel Moore. They are sterling men, and friends of equal rights, *opposed to the oppressor's grasp, and the tyrant's rod.* With such men at the head of our State, Government will have nothing to fear.

"In the next canvass, we shall be influenced by *no party* consideration . . . *we care not a* FIG for WHIG *or* DEMOCRAT; they are both alike to us, but we shall go for our friends, our tried friends, and the cause of human liberty, which is the cause of God. . . .

"Douglass (Stephen A. Douglas) *is a master spirit, and his friends are our friends.* . . . Snyder and Moore are his friends—they are ours. . . . *We will never be justly charged with* THE SIN OF INGRATITUDE—they have served us, and we will serve them.

"JOSEPH SMITH,
"Lieutenant-General of the Nauvoo Legion."

Both the italics and the capitals are Joseph Smith's. One can readily understand how angry such a document would make the candidates whose election it opposed, and it was impossible for Joseph Smith to switch his support from one party to the other without thoroughly antagonizing both of them. He had lost the friendship of the Whigs, who had granted him his powerful charter, by supporting the Democrats in the campaign for governor in 1842. He lost the friendship of the Democrats by advising his people on other occasions to vote for Whig candidates.

The abuse Joseph Smith exercised of the political influence his position as a Prophet gave him is illustrated by the contest for Congress between Cyrus Walker and Joseph P. Hoge. The Prophet had supported Cyrus Walker, had introduced him to the Mormons whenever he made campaign speeches and had expressed his intention of voting for Mr. Walker, because he had been converted to the wishes of the Mormons. "If he continues converted," Joseph Smith remarked to his entire congregation, "I will vote for him." But some one at the state capital assured the Mormon representative that if the Mormons voted for Hoge, the militia would never be used against them. The Saturday before election the Mormons were called together in a mass meeting. Joseph's brother Hyrum, who was then Patriarch of the Church, told the meeting that God had revealed the command that the Mormons must vote for Joseph P. Hoge for Congress. One of the Mormons, William Law, arose in the meeting and expressed it as his emphatic opinion that God had revealed no such thing. Law pointed out that Joseph Smith, God's Prophet, had supported Cyrus Walker, and that Joseph being the main receptacle of revelation would be more likely to know the mind of the Lord than Hyrum. The people divided upon that question and were uncertain which candidate to vote for. The next day, Sunday, the Prophet appeared in the pulpit and said that he had heard that his brother Hyrum had made public a revelation; personally, he did not believe in revelations concerning elections, but he had known Hyrum since they were boys together, and he had never known Hyrum to tell a lie. If Hyrum said that he had received such a revelation, he had received it, and if the Lord told Hyrum to vote for Hoge, the Lord meant it. "When the Lord speaks," said Joseph, "let all the earth be silent."

The result was that Joseph P. Hoge was elected to Congress the following day, and the Whigs, who had been promised the Mormon vote, were infuriated. The newspapers, and especially those whose politics were Whig, began to devote much attention to alleged Mormon enormities. It was contended that the Mormons were not only dangerous as a body because of the powers granted to them in their charters, but that individually they were thieves and marauders. The Mormons had increased their wealth more rapidly than their neighbors thought possible by honest means, and the conclusion the neighbors drew was that the increase was at the expense of those who lived near them. It was said, too, that the Church encouraged thievery by its doctrine that sooner or later the property of the Gentiles would come into the hands of the Saints, and individuals were charged with anticipating the beneficence of the Lord by taking immediate possession of some of the cattle and farm products which were promised them eventually. The Gentiles maintained that once the thieves got their stolen property within the confines of Nauvoo, they were protected in their possession of it by Joseph Smith's all-powerful municipal court.

The first open expression of opposition to the Mormons in Illinois came at a mass meeting in June, 1841. It was pointed out by the speakers that the Mormons were rapidly increasing in numbers and voting power, that their Church controlled their votes, and that before long the entire county would be subject to a religio-political despotism. The meeting resolved that one-man power was repugnant to those who were not Mormons, and that they would pledge themselves to vote for any candidates for political office who would promise to oppose the growing influence of the new religious sect. It was also resolved that the Nauvoo charter gave the Mormons too much power, and that it was the duty of non-Mormons to vote against any candidates who sought the influence of the Mormon vote.

The breach was thus clearly defined in its political aspects, but there were still other causes of opposition to the Mormons. The Gentiles saw their neighbors, who had been regular Methodists or respectable Baptists, suddenly turn to this new religion, which the Methodist and Baptist clergymen assured them was an abomination in the sight of the Lord. Friends, whose company and common sense they had always valued, became convinced of the truth of Mormonism and joined the new sect. This aroused their neighbors to the spreading danger of this infectious religion, and unless they were baptized themselves, they became virulent anti-Mormons. Another cause of dissension was the fact that the largest numbers of converts the Mormons brought to Nauvoo from Europe were Englishmen and Englishwomen. The War of the Revolution and the War of 1812 had by no means been forgotten, and large numbers of Americans felt that hostility to England and to Englishmen was something of a patriotic duty.

A bill was finally introduced into the Illinois legislature demanding the repeal of the Nauvoo charter. William Smith, a brother of the Prophet, who then held a seat in the legislature, moved an amendment to the title of the measure so that the bill would read, "A bill for an act to humbug the citizens of Nauvoo." The opposition to the Mormons was not yet widespread enough, and their political influence was still too great, so that the measure was not passed.

Meanwhile, Joseph Smith had been arrested several times on charges made by angry Missouri officials, who were still annoyed that the man whom they chose to regard as an archfiend, and who, in their opinion, would be much better dead than alive, had escaped them and was prospering in a nearby state. Ex-Governor

Lillburn W. Boggs, who had been most active in opposition to the Mormons, was then a candidate for the Missouri Senate, and on the sixth of May, 1842, as he was seated by the window of his house enjoying the spring breezes, a pistol charged with buckshot was fired into his face from an adjoining window. Three of the shots lodged in his head, and when his son rushed into the room, he found his father helpless on the floor, with the pistol under the window frame and the footprints of a stranger leading from the window.

As soon as Boggs recovered, he accused Joseph Smith, Jr., of instigating the attempt to assassinate him, and Orrin Porter Rockwell, one of the Prophet's bodyguard, of executing that attempt. Joseph Smith replied to this charge in a letter to the Quincy *Whig*. He. pointed out that Boggs was a candidate for office, and, "I presume, fell by the hand of a political opponent, with his hands and face dripping with the blood of murder." However, even in the Wild West, it was not customary for state senatorial candidates to assassinate each other. Boggs took legal action to extradite Joseph Smith from Illinois so that he might be tried in Missouri for murder.

At the hearing before Judge Pope on this demand for the person of the Prophet, Joseph Smith was attended by his Twelve Apostles, and the Judge, who was described by a contemporary as "a gallant gentleman of the old school," was encircled by ladies, who were defined as both brilliant and beautiful. Mr. Butterfield, the Prophet's attorney, took advantage of the scene in his opening words: "May it please the Court; I appear before you to-day under circumstances most novel and peculiar. I am to address the 'Pope,'" and he bowed low to the Judge, "surrounded by angels," and he bowed still lower to the ladies, "in the presence of the Holy Apostles, in behalf of the Prophet of the Lord," and he began a passionate plea for his client. The Prophet urged that the writ was illegal because it referred to him as Joseph Smith, Jr., whereas he was now Joseph Smith, Sen., owing to the lamented death of his father a few months before. This was not his principal legal objection to the writ, but he seems to have attached great importance to it. When it was proved that Joseph Smith had not been in Missouri, and that there was no evidence to prove that he had sent any one there, the Prophet was discharged, much to the disgust of the Missourians and some of Smith's neighbors. But they did not rest with the decision of this court, and several attempts were made to arrest Smith and carry him off to Missouri on charges varying from murder to treason. When agents were sent to arrest him, the Prophet, who was also the Mayor, retaliated by arresting his arrestors on a charge of false imprisonment, and the ludicrous spectacle was presented of Smith in the custody of an officer who was himself in the custody of a sheriff.

One of the Prophet's trials was held before Stephen A. Douglas, who found it necessary to clear his court of rowdies by the use of a large Kentucky sheriff before he could proceed without interference from people who were more anxious for Smith's punishment than for justice. After the trial, at which the Prophet was acquitted, Douglas invited him to dinner, and Smith related his persecutions for three hours. He also gave Judge Douglas this prophecy: "Judge, you will aspire to the Presidency of the United States; and if you ever turn your hand against me or the Latter-day Saints, you will feel the weight of the hand of the Almighty upon you; and you will live to see and know that I have testified the truth to you; for the conversation of this day will stick to you through life." Fourteen years later Douglas made a speech at Springfield, Illinois. It was at the period in 1857 when opposition to the Mormons was becoming federal instead of a mere neighborly state reaction. In the course of his speech Douglas became virulently oratorical and said concerning the Mormon problem: "Should such a state of things actually exist as we are led to infer from the reports—and such information comes in an official shape—the knife must be applied to this pestiferous, disgusting cancer which is gnawing into the very vitals of the body politic. It must be cut out by the roots, and seared·over by the red hot iron of stern and unflinching law. . . . To· protect them further in their treasonable, disgusting and bestial practices would be a disgrace to the country—a disgrace to humanity—a disgrace to civilization, and a disgrace to the spirit of the age. . . ." Brigham H. Roberts, a Mormon writer, described Douglas's ensuing punishment in the following words:

"Stephen A. Douglas did aspire to the presidency of the United States. He received the nomination for that high office, from a great political party. But he had raised his hand against the Latter-day Saints, the people of the prophet Joseph Smith; and as a consequence he did feel the weight of the hand of the Almighty upon him; for his hopes were blasted; he never reached the goal of his ambition; he failed miserably, and died wretchedly, when his life had but reached high noon. Could anything be more clear than that Stephen A. Douglas felt the weight of the hand of the Almighty upon him? But mark you, these calamities came upon him for striking at the saints of God in Utah. It was for turning his hand against them that he was disappointed in his hopes, blasted in his expectations, and died heart-broken."

But history differs with this firm conviction of the Latter-day Saints; history believes that the Lincoln-Douglas debates and the Dred Scott decision had something to do with the defeat and the subsequent broken heart of Stephen A. Douglas.

Sometimes when he was arrested by Missouri sheriffs, Joseph Smith discharged himself by issuing through his own municipal court of Nauvoo his own writ of *habeas corpus*. He once pleasantly described this process as pulling Missouri to Nauvoo. The municipal council of Nauvoo also passed an ordinance making it an offense, punishable by imprisonment for life in the city prison, to arrest Joseph Smith until after he was tried by the municipal court of Nauvoo. These arbitrary acts aroused the Gentiles to a fury that was all the more dangerous because for the moment it was impotent. And the Prophet himself was also aroused. He was weary of arrest and discharge, sheriffs and writs, and after one of his arrests he delivered before his assembled people a fiery speech in the course of which he offered this angry advice:

"If any citizens of Illinois say we shall not have our rights, treat them as strangers and not friends, and let them go to hell and be damned! If we have to give up our chartered rights, privileges, and freedom, which our fathers fought, bled, and died for, and which the constitution of the United States and of this state guarantee unto us, we will do it only at the point of the sword and bayonet. . . . But before I will bear this unhallowed persecution any longer—before I will be dragged away again among my enemies for trial, I will spill the last drop of blood in my veins, and will see all my enemies in hell! To bear it any longer would be a sin, and I will not bear it any longer. Shall we bear it any longer? (One universal 'No!' ran through all the vast assembly, like a peal of thunder.)

"I say in the name of Jesus Christ by the authority of the holy priesthood, I this day turn the key that opens the heavens to restrain you no longer from this time forth. I will lead you to the battle; and if you are not afraid to die, and feel disposed to spill your blood in your own defense, you will not offend me. Be not the aggressor: bear until they strike you on the one cheek; then offer the other, and they will be sure to strike that; then defend yourselves, and God will bear you off, and you shall stand forth clear before his tribunal. . . . If mobs come upon you any more here, dung your gardens with them." [7]

It is said that Smith's arrest for the attempted assassination of Ex-Governor Lillburn W. Boggs was instigated by John C. Bennett, who had quarreled with the Prophet, and who was then writing articles for newspapers describing the knavery of Nauvoo. These sensational articles were collected by Bennett into a scurrilous book, in which for the first time details of the practice of polygamy among the Mormons were revealed.

IV

We have already noted the rumors that the Mormons before they left Ohio believed in having more wives than one, and they themselves have since admitted that the Prophet Joseph Smith first heard of polygamy from God some time in the year 1831. Although he was not yet permitted to make the doctrine public, he spoke of it to several of his most faithful followers. The frequent denials during the lifetime of the Prophet that polygamy was any part of the Mormon religion, or that it was ever practised, have caused his followers no embarrassment since his death. They blandly admit that the denials were false, and they do not hesitate to make a liar of their Prophet, with the sincere belief that a lie for the cause will be promptly forgiven in heaven, and that it can only be called a real lie by non-Mormons, who are usually wicked and perverse anyway. This attitude on the part of the Mormons is made necessary by the propaganda of a schismatic branch of the Church, the Reorganized Church of Jesus Christ of Latter-day Saints, which was founded on the principle that Joseph Smith never practised polygamy or even preached it. In order to prove their opponents heterodox, the Utah Mormons have produced a wealth of evidence that convicts their Prophet of deception, but they rest comfortably in the assurance that all is fair when God is on the right side, and they offer eminent precedents from the Bible.

[7] *History of the Church,* vol. 5, pp. 466-469.

The Prophet made several early attempts to tell his people something of this new and secret dispensation from heaven. His cousin, George A. Smith, subsequently described one of these attempts: "Whereupon, the Prophet goes up on the stand, and, after preaching about everything else he could think of in the world, at last hints at the idea of the law of redemption, makes a bare hint at the law of sealing, and it produced such a tremendous excitement that, as soon as he had got his dinner half eaten, he had to go back to the stand and unpreach all that he had preached, and left the people to guess at the matter." [8]

It is said that Joseph Smith practised polygamy before he preached it, and that he found it necessary to clear himself in the eyes of his first wife Emma by making his failings divine. This seems the most logical theory. We know that he was always intensely interested in women, and he is credited with the remark to a friend, "Whenever I see a pretty woman I have to pray for grace." The only parts of the Bible which he did not interpret literally were those commandments which forbid adultery and coveting a neighbor's wife. The habits of Abraham, Jacob, Solomon, and David influenced Joseph Smith's own life, and he finally felt that he must know whether they had lived in sin or in promiscuity by the grace of God. Who would know better than God himself? Joseph Smith took the matter directly to Him, and on January 12, 1843, at Nauvoo, he received this reply:

"Verily, thus saith the Lord unto you, my servant Joseph, that inasmuch as you have inquired of my hand, to know and understand wherein I, the Lord, justified my servants Abraham, Isaac and Jacob; as also Moses, David and Solomon, my servants, as touching the principle and doctrine of their having many wives and concubines:

"Behold! and lo, I am the Lord thy God, and will answer thee as touching this matter:"

God then went on to say that there was an universal and eternal law, which all who would be saved must obey, and that all who rejected it would be most assuredly damned. According to this law, all contracts, oaths, vows, and obligations in order to be binding in eternity must be sealed by the Holy Spirit, and Joseph

[8] *Journal of Discourses,* vol. 2, p. 217.

Smith, Jr., was the only person on earth at that time appointed to administer this sealing. This applied especially to the marriage covenant, and unless a man and woman were sealed in marriage according to the Holy Spirit they would not be considered married when they reached heaven and would become the mere servants of those who were so sealed. God then assured Joseph Smith that Abraham had done everything he had done by the command of the Lord, whose purpose was to raise up a populous people unto His name out of the loins of the Patriarch. "Go ye, therefore," said God to Joseph Smith, "and do the works of Abraham; enter ye into my law, and ye shall be saved." Joseph Smith did not have to be told twice.

The Lord also added that Abraham's concubines, Solomon's and David's too, with the single exception of the latter's irregular affair with Uriah's wife, were all recognized as legal in the sight of the Lord, and that they had all gained salvation by obeying His command to cleave unto their righteous husbands. The Lord then said that He gave unto Joseph Smith, Jr., the power to restore all things as they were in the good old days, and that this portion of the restoration was as important as any. God also gave Joseph Smith specific power to take any woman away from a husband who had committed adultery and give her to a faithful, righteous brother. Joseph's decisions on this matter, and also all the plural marriages that he authorized, would be recognized in the celestial kingdom. Then there followed interesting specific commands for Joseph's wife Emma:

"Verily, I say unto you, a commandment I give unto mine handmaid, Emma Smith, your wife, whom I have given unto you, that she stay herself, and partake not of that which I commanded you to offer unto her; for I did it, saith the Lord, to prove you all, as I did Abraham; and that I might require an offering at your hand, by covenant and sacrifice."

This would seem to indicate that Joseph had offered Emma the privileges of polyandry in return for those of polygamy, but that God rescinded that offer by declaring it to be only one of His little Job-like temptations. God also enjoined Emma:

"And let mine handmaid, Emma Smith, receive all those that have been given unto my servant Joseph, and who are virtuous and pure before me; and those who are not pure, and have said they were pure, shall be destroyed, saith the Lord God. . . ."

"And I command mine handmaid, Emma Smith, to abide and cleave unto my servant Joseph, and to none else. But if she will not abide this commandment, she shall be destroyed, saith the Lord; for I am the Lord thy God, and will destroy her, if she abide not in my law;

"But if she will not abide this commandment, then shall my servant Joseph do all things for her, even as he hath said; and I will bless him and multiply him, and give unto him an hundred-fold in this world, of fathers and mothers, brothers and sisters, houses and lands, wives and children, and crowns of eternal lives in the eternal worlds.

"And again, verily I say, let mine handmaid forgive my servant Joseph his trespasses; and then shall she be forgiven her trespasses, wherein she has trespassed against me; and I, the Lord thy God, will bless her, and multiply her, and make her heart to rejoice."

These instructions to Emma Smith were made necessary by her reaction to the practice of polygamy by her husband during the several years before this revelation was received in writing from God. He had before he received this revelation already taken unto himself twelve wives, according to the Mormon records.[9]

All of these twelve wives Joseph married without the consent of Emma, and they all lived in the same house with Emma. "She for some time supposed," one writer recorded, "that his object in having them there was purely a charitable one." Perhaps; but very soon she came to believe that this kind of charity does not begin at home, for she threatened to leave her Prophet husband with full attendant publicity unless the dozen young girls who were living with them left first. The Prophet attempted defiance, but he feared the publicity, for his neighbors were making enough trouble for him at the moment. His more recent wives were removed to other parts of Nauvoo. Finally, after much persuasion Emma did consent to allow her husband two additional wives, if she might be permitted to choose them. She chose Emily Dow Partridge and Eliza M. Partridge, two sisters, who had lived in the Prophet's house because their own family were too poor to support them. They were about nineteen years old and eighteen years old respectively. This was a lucky choice for the Prophet, for he had taken the privilege of marrying these two girls several months before Emma chose them as his future

[9] *The Historical Record*, May, 1887, pp. 233-234.

EMMA SMITH

wives, according to an autobiographical sketch written by one of them. To save family trouble, this sketch said, the Prophet "thought it best to have another ceremony performed," which was done on May 11, 1843, in the presence of Emma Smith. But even after the ceremony and her own choice, Emma could only endure her rivals for several months, and they were then removed to a house elsewhere in Nauvoo.

Sister Emma Smith was described at this time by an impartial observer as "a gaunt, stern, hard-visaged woman of middle age." This fact, perhaps, was the main influence in the trend of Joseph Smith's mind towards polygamy. Naturally her treatment of the young women with whom her husband filled the house was tempered by jealousy and envy. The jealousy of the Prophet's wife and the suspicions of his followers were probably responsible for that part of the revelation on polygamy which makes it clear that the practice was designed purely for utilitarian purposes rather than for the satisfaction of esthetic sensibilities or biological sensations. After He had made clear the relation of Emma to the polygamous wives, God said to Joseph Smith:

"And again, as pertaining to the law of the Priesthood: If any man espouse a virgin, and desire to espouse another, and the first give her consent; and if he espouse the second, and they are virgins, and have vowed to no other man, then is he justified; he cannot commit adultery, for they are given unto him; for he cannot commit adultery with that that belongeth unto him and to no one else;

"And if he have ten virgins given unto him by this law, he cannot commit adultery, for they belong to him, and they are given unto him, therefore is he justified.

"But if one or other of the ten virgins, after she is espoused, shall be with another man; she has committed adultery, and shall be destroyed; for they are given unto him to multiply and replenish the earth, according to my commandment, and to fulfill the promise which was given by my Father before the foundation of the world; and for their exaltation in the eternal worlds, that they may bear the souls of men; for herein is the work of my Father continued, that he may be glorified. . . .

"And now, as pertaining to this law, verily, verily, I say unto you, I will reveal more unto you, hereafter; therefore, let this suffice for the present. Behold, I am Alpha and Omega. Amen." [10]

[10] The complete revelation concerning plurality of wives is published in Section 132 of the *Book of Doctrine and Covenants.*

But God did not keep this promise; He revealed no more concerning plurality of wives, as the Mormons prefer to call polygamy. Whatever developments came afterwards were the result of human trial and error in the practice of the principle.

The actual composition of this remarkable revelation from heaven was described in detail by William Clayton, who acted as the Prophet's amanuensis for the occasion:

"On the morning of the 12th of July, 1843, Joseph and Hyrum came into the office in the upper story of the 'brick store,' on the bank of the Mississippi River. They were talking on the subject of plural marriage. Hyrum said to Joseph, 'If you will write the revelation on celestial marriage, I will take and read it to Emma, and I believe I can convince her of its truth, and you will hereafter have peace.' Joseph smiled and remarked, 'You do not know Emma as well as I do.' Hyrum repeated his opinion and further remarked, 'The doctrine is so plain, I can convince any reasonable man or woman of its truth, purity or heavenly origin,' or words to that effect. Joseph then said, 'Well, I will write the revelation and we will see.' He then requested me to get paper and prepare to write. Hyrum very urgently requested Joseph to write the revelation by means of the Urim and Thummim, but Joseph, in reply, said he did not need to, for he knew the revelation perfectly from beginning to end.

"Joseph and Hyrum then sat down and Joseph commenced to dictate the revelation on celestial marriage, and I wrote it sentence by sentence, as he dictated. After the whole was written, Joseph asked me to read it through, slowly and carefully, which I did, and he pronounced it correct. He then remarked that there was much more that he could write on the same subject, but what was written was sufficient for the present.

"Hyrum then took the revelation to read to Emma. Joseph remained with me in the office until Hyrum returned. When he came back, Joseph asked him how he had succeeded. Hyrum replied that he had never received a more severe talking to in his life, that Emma was very bitter and full of resentment and anger.

"Joseph quietly remarked, 'I told you you did not know Emma as well as I do.' Joseph then put the revelation in his pocket, and they both left the office." [11]

That same evening Joseph Smith showed the revelation to a few leaders of the Church, and Bishop Newel K. Whitney asked if he might make a copy of it. Joseph consented, and it was

[11] William Clayton's testimony in *The Historical Record*, pp. 224-226.

fortunate that he did so, for two or three days later Emma teased Joseph to allow her to destroy the revelation. Brigham Young once described the scene in a sermon:

"After Joseph had been to Bishop Whitney's he went home, and Emma began teasing for the revelation. Said she—'Joseph, you promised me that revelation, and if you are a man of your word you will give it to me.' Joseph took it from his pocket and said—'Take it.' She went to the fire-place and put it in, and put the candle under it and burnt it, and she thought that was the end of it, and she will be damned as sure as she is a living woman. Joseph used to say that he would have her hereafter, if he had to go to hell for her, and he will have to go to hell for her as sure as he ever gets her." [12]

An anti-Mormon writer added a characteristic, fictitious sentimental detail to this scene of the burning of the revelation. He wrote that the Prophet's wife used a tongs, "unwilling, as any pure woman would be, to have her fingers come in contact with the vile document."

The Prophet's wife was not the only one difficult to convince of the divine origin of polygamy. At first it was too revolutionary to appeal even to his most ardent associates, and Joseph Smith quietly and patiently convinced them by personal conversation in the course of long walks in the woods. Even before he had committed the doctrine to writing, the Prophet carried on secret propaganda for it. He was living in polygamy himself, and in order to justify his own conduct, it was necessary that his followers should adopt the practice. William Clayton told the interesting story of how the Prophet first broke the news of the new principle to him:

"During this period the Prophet Joseph frequently visited my house in my company, and became well acquainted with my wife, Ruth, to whom I had been married five years. One day in the month of February, 1843, date not remembered, the Prophet invited me to walk with him. During our walk, he said he had learned that there was a sister back in England, to whom I was very much attached. I replied there was, but nothing further than an attachment such as a brother and sister in the Church might rightfully entertain for each other. He then said, 'Why don't you send for her?' I replied, 'In the first place, I have no authority to send for her, and if I had, I have not the means to pay expenses.' To this he answered, 'I give you authority to send for her, and I will furnish you with means,' which he did. . . . After giving me lengthy instructions and information concerning the doctrine of celestial or plural marriage, he concluded his remarks by the words, 'It is your privilege to have all the wives you want.' . . . He also informed me that he had other wives *living* besides his first wife Emma, and in particular gave me to understand that Eliza R. Snow, Louisa Beman, Desdemona W. Fullmer and others were his lawful wives in the sight of Heaven.

"On the 27th of April, 1843, the Prophet Joseph Smith married to me Margaret Moon, for time and eternity, at the residence of Elder Heber C. Kimball; and on the 22nd of July, 1843, he married to me, according to the order of the Church, my first wife Ruth." [13]

William Clayton was an easy convert to the new doctrine, but some of the others were more difficult to convince of its benefits and righteousness. Even Brother Hyrum did not regard polygamy as expedient when he first heard of it: "He said to Joseph that if he attempted to introduce the practice of that doctrine as a tenet of The Church it would break up The Church and cost him his life. 'Well,' Joseph replied, 'it is a commandment from God, brother Hyrum, and if you don't believe it, if you will ask the Lord He will make it known to you.' " [14] Hyrum asked the Lord, and he received in reply exactly the same revelation that Joseph had committed to paper.

Many years later Brigham Young described his emotions on first learning that polygamy was necessary to salvation:

"Some of these my brethren know what my feelings were at the time Joseph revealed the doctrine; I was not desirous of shrinking from any duty, nor of failing in the least to do as I was commanded, but it was the first time in my life that I had desired the grave, and I could hardly get over it for a long time. And when I saw a funeral, I felt to envy the corpse its situation, and to regret that I was not in the coffin, knowing the toil and labor that my body would have to undergo; and I have had to examine myself, from that day to this, and watch my faith, and carefully meditate, lest I should be found desiring the grave more than I ought to do." [15]

However, these thoughts of the grave did not prevent Brigham Young from doing his duty: he married eight women while he

[13] *The Historical Record*, pp. 224-226.
[14] *Succession in the Presidency*, by Brigham H. Roberts, pp. 123-124.
[15] *Journal of Discourses*, vol. 3, p. 266.

remained in Nauvoo, and in later years, as we shall see, he did not shirk the responsibilities which God had so urgently enjoined. When Joseph Smith first began to discuss polygamy with his followers, Brigham Young and the other eleven Apostles were in England. As soon as they returned, they were taught the new doctrine. John Taylor, a leader of the Church and successor to Brigham Young in the Presidency, wrote his reaction to it:

"Joseph Smith told the Twelve that if this law was not practiced, if they would not enter into this covenant, then the Kingdom of God could not go one step further. Now, we did not feel like preventing the Kingdom of God from going forward. We professed to be the Apostles of the Lord, and did not feel like putting ourselves in a position to retard the progress of the Kingdom of God. The revelation says that 'All those who have this law revealed unto them must obey the same.' Now, that is not my word. I did not make it. It was the Prophet of God who revealed that to us in Nauvoo, and I bear witness of this solemn fact before God, that he did reveal this sacred principle to me and others of the Twelve. . . .

"I had always entertained strict ideas of virtue, and I felt as a married man that this was to me, outside of this principle, an appalling thing to do. The idea of going and asking a young lady to be married to me when I had already a wife! It was a thing calculated to stir up feelings from the innermost depths of the human soul. I had always entertained the strictest regard of chastity. . . . Hence with the feelings I had entertained, nothing but a knowledge of God, and the revelations of God, and the truth of them, could have induced me to embrace such a principle as this.

"We seemed to put off, as far as we could, what might be termed the evil day.

"Some time after these things were made known to us, I was riding out of Nauvoo on horseback, and met Joseph Smith coming in, he, too, being on horseback. . . . I bowed to Joseph, and having done the same to me, he said: 'Stop;' and he looked at me very intently. 'Look here,' said he, 'those things that have been spoken of must be fulfilled, and if they are not entered into right away the keys will be turned.'

"Well, what did I do? Did I feel to stand in the way of this great eternal principle, and treat lightly the things of God? No. I replied: 'Brother Joseph, I will try and carry these things out.'" [16]

And John Taylor swallowed his medicine like a man, for within two years after this conversation he had married Elizabeth

[16] *Life of John Taylor*, by Elder B. H. Roberts, p. 101.

Haigham, Jane Ballantyne, and Mary A. Oakley. Later in Utah he continued to carry forward the Kingdom of God by adding regularly to his household.

In order to reinforce his argument with his associates, the Prophet told them, and they earnestly believed him, that he had delayed practising polygamy as long as possible, until finally an angel of God, carrying a drawn sword, appeared to him and threatened angrily that unless he "moved forward and established plural marriage, his priesthood would be taken from him and he should be destroyed."

Lorenzo Snow, the brother of the Mormon poetess, Eliza Snow, was a bachelor before he heard of divine polygamy, and in her biography of him his sister wrote that he had always regarded marriage as a luxury and an encumbrance for a man whose duty necessitated wandering about the country preaching. But Joseph Smith quickly convinced him that marriage was a multiple necessity. "It is one of his peculiarities," wrote his sister, with sincere admiration and incredible naïveté, "to do nothing by halves; and when convinced of the duty of marriage, and that it was a privilege accorded him in connection with his ministerial calling, he entered into it on an enlarged scale, by having two wives sealed to him in the holy bonds of matrimony, for time and eternity, at the same time; and not long after, another was added to the number, and then another. Thus, all at once, as it were, from the lone bachelor he was transformed into a husband invested with many domestic responsibilities. Probably a realizing sense of the fact that he had arrived at the mature age of thirty-one years in celibacy, suggested to him the propriety of making up for lost time by more than ordinary effort, and out of the old beaten track." [17]

It was rather important that Joseph Smith should convert Lorenzo Snow to plural marriage, for the Prophet had taken the privilege of marrying his sister and biographer while the brother was in England.

If we can believe their testimony, polygamy shocked all of the elders at first, but as soon as they began the actual practice of its privileges, they seemed satisfied of its divine origin. Their Puritan worship of chastity caused them to be revolted at the idea of polygamy, but that barrier was easily overcome by quotations from the lives of Abraham, Isaac, Jacob, David, and Solomon,

[17] *Biography of Lorenzo Snow*, by Eliza R. Snow Smith, pp. 69-70.

and before long the Mormon elders were willing to experiment
with the system themselves; as soon as they had experimented
with it themselves, it took all the legal power of the United States
government, as we shall see, to persuade these elders who had
reluctantly entered upon its practice as part of their duty in this
vale of tears, that polygamy was illegal, even if it were divine.

Heber C. Kimball had a particularly trying experience. Joseph
Smith taught him polygamy as soon as Kimball returned from
England with Brigham Young and the other Apostles. But
Joseph warned him, as he had the others, to tell the secret to
no one, for if he did, the Prophet's enemies would be sure to use
it as an excuse to return him to Missouri for slaughter. Heber
Kimball was forbidden to confide even in the wife he had married many years before. But Kimball was afraid that if he began
to practise polygamy without telling his wife, she might hear of
it from other sources—a very natural fear—and he told Joseph
Smith how terrible such a blow would be to the wife he loved
deeply. The Prophet, sympathizing with him, inquired of the
Lord, whose answer was, "Tell him to go and do as he has been
commanded, and if I see that there is any danger of his aposta-
tizing, I will take him to myself." Kimball's daughter, Helen
Mar Kimball, wrote a description of her father's pitiable situation:

"When first hearing the principle taught, believing that he would
be called upon to enter it, he had thought of two elderly ladies named
Pitkin, great friends of my mother's, who, he believed, would cause
her little if any unhappiness. But the woman he was commanded
to take was an English lady named Sarah Noon, nearer my mother's
age, who came over with the company of Saints in the same ship
in which father and Brother Brigham returned from Europe. She
had been married and was the mother of two little girls, but left
her husband on account of his drunken and dissolute habits.
Father was told to take her as his wife and provide for her and
her children, and he did so.

"My mother had noticed a change in his manner and appearance,
and when she inquired the cause, he tried to evade her questions.
At last he promised he would tell her after a while, if she would
only wait. This trouble so worked upon his mind that his anxious
and haggard looks betrayed him daily and hourly, and finally his
misery became so unbearable that it was impossible to control his
feelings. He became sick in body, but his mental wretchedness was
too great to allow of his retiring, and he would walk the floor till

nearly morning, and sometimes the agony of his mind was so terrible that he would wring his hands and weep like a child, and beseech the Lord to be merciful and reveal to her this principle, for he himself could not break his vow of secrecy.

"The anguish of their hearts was indescribable, and when she found it was useless to beseech him longer, she retired to her room and bowed down before the Lord and poured out her soul in prayer to Him who hath said: 'If any lack wisdom let him ask of God, who giveth to all men liberally and upbraideth not.' My father's heart was raised at the same time in supplication. While pleading as one would plead for life, the vision of her mind was opened, and as darkness flees before the morning sun, so did her sorrow and the groveling things of earth vanish away.

"Before her was illustrated the order of celestial marriage, in all its beauty and glory, together with the great exaltation and honor it would confer upon her in that immortal and celestial sphere, if she would accept it and stand in her place by her husband's side. She also saw the woman he had taken to wife, and contemplated with joy the vast and boundless love and union which this order would bring about, as well as the increase of her husband's king-doms, and the power and glory extending throughout the eternities, worlds without end.

"With a countenance beaming with joy, for she was filled with the Spirit of God, she returned to my father, saying: 'Heber, what you kept from me the Lord has shown me.' She told me she never saw so happy a man as father was when she described the vision and told him she was satisfied and knew it was from God.

"She covenanted to stand by him and honor the principle, which covenant she faithfully kept, and though her trials were often heavy and grievous to bear, she knew that father was also being tried, and her integrity was unflinching to the end. She gave my father many wives, and they always found in my mother a faithful friend." [18]

Mrs. Heber C. Kimball was not of a suspicious nature, for it never seemed to occur to her as of any significance that her husband should be instructed by God to marry the woman with whom he had traveled from Europe upon his return from his mission.

Some women, however, were more incredulous and suspicious than Mrs. Kimball, and they were accordingly difficult to convert. There was, for instance, the case of sixteen-year-old Lucy Walker, whose conversion to polygamy is a unique example of

[18] Statement of Helen Mar Kimball Whitney, published in *The Mormon Prophet's Tragedy*, by Orson F. Whitney, pp. 37-41.

the Prophet's methods with women. In a letter which was published in the *Reminiscences of Latter-day Saints* by Lyman Omer Littlefield Lucy Walker wrote:

"In the year 1842 President Joseph Smith sought an interview with me and said: 'I have a message for you. I have been commanded of God to take another wife, and you are the woman.' My astonishment knew no bounds. This announcement was indeed a thunderbolt to me. He asked me if I believed him to be a prophet of God. 'Most assuredly I do,' I replied. He fully explained to me the principle of plural or celestial marriage. Said this principle was again to be restored for the benefit of the human family. That it would prove an everlasting blessing to my father's house, and form a chain that could never be broken, worlds without end. 'What have you to say?' he asked. 'Nothing. How could I speak, or what could I say?' He said, 'If you will pray sincerely for light and understanding in relation thereto, you shall receive a testimony of the correctness of this principle.'"

Lucy Walker prayed, but her soul was in anguish, and there was nothing but darkness. "No mother to counsel; no father near to tell me what to do in this trying hour." The Prophet visited her again and assured her that polygamy was the will of God. "I will give you until to-morrow," he added, "to decide this matter. If you reject this message the gate will be closed forever against you." "This," wrote Lucy Walker, "aroused every drop of Scotch in my veins. . . . I had been speechless, but at last found utterance and said: 'Although you are a prophet of God you could not induce me to take a step of so great importance, unless I knew that God approved my course. I would rather die. I have tried to pray but received no comfort, no light,' and emphatically forbid him speaking again to me on this subject. Every feeling of my soul revolted against it. Said I, 'The same God who has sent this message is the Being I have worshiped from my early childhood and He must manifest His will to me.' He walked across the room, returned and stood before me with the most beautiful expression of countenance, and said: 'God Almighty bless you. You shall have a manifestation of the will of God concerning you; a testimony that you can never deny. I will tell you what it shall be. It shall be that joy and peace that you never knew.'" Then Lucy Walker prayed for the fulfilment of this prophecy and spent the ensuing nights in sleepless anguish.

"It was near dawn after another sleepless night," she wrote, "when my room was lighted up by a heavenly influence. To me it was, in comparison, like the brilliant sun bursting through the darkest cloud. The words of the Prophet were indeed fulfilled. My soul was filled with a calm, sweet peace that 'I never knew.' Supreme happiness took possession of me, and I received a powerful and irresistible testimony of the truth of plural marriage, which has been like an anchor to the soul through all the trials of life. I felt that I must go out into the morning air and give vent to the joy and gratitude that filled my soul. As I descended the stairs, President Smith opened the door below, took me by the hand and said: 'Thank God, you have the testimony. I, too, have prayed.' He led me to a chair, placed his hands upon my head, and blessed me with every blessing my heart could possibly desire.

"The first day of May, 1843, I consented to become the Prophet's wife, and was sealed to him for time and all eternity, at his own house by Elder Wm. Clayton."

Lucy Walker was married the day after her seventeenth birthday. In that month of May, 1843, the Prophet added four wives to the nine he already had, and all of the four were less than twenty years of age. Lucy Walker's conversion to plural marriage by means of heavenly brilliance and the conviction that it was the will of God was not unusual. Joseph Smith's career furnishes other examples of the same process, and psychologists are familiar with it. Lucy Walker knew what to expect from God, for Joseph Smith had told her how her dark cloud of doubt would be dispelled by the light of inner joy and peace. It required to convert her only a few sleepless nights and the desire, perhaps subconscious, to be one of the wives of the Prophet, whose "beautiful expression of countenance," she had noted even in the anguish of her despair. If it was all right with God, it was all right with her, and she did not have to wait long for God's permission. In fact, Lucy Walker became so convinced of the divinity of plural marriage that after the Prophet's death she became one of the wives of Heber C. Kimball and bore him nine children; but this latter connection was for time only, for she already had an engagement for eternity with the Prophet. In her letter concerning her conversion Lucy Walker added: "In this I acted in accordance with the will of God. Not for any worldly aggrandizement; not for the gratification of the flesh. How can it be said we accepted this principle for any lustful desires? Preposterous! This would be utterly impossible. But, as I said before, we accepted it to obey a command of God, to establish a principle that would benefit the human family and emancipate them from the degradation into which they, through their wicked customs, had fallen." Perhaps so; but Joseph Smith, Jr., was more than six feet tall in his bare feet, and he was universally declared to be handsome, even by his numerous enemies.

Brigham Young once gave this picture of the sealing in marriage to the Prophet of Brigham Young's own reluctant sister:

"I recollect a sister conversing with Joseph Smith on this subject: 'Now, don't talk to me; when I get into the celestial kingdom, if I ever do get there, I shall request the privilege of being a ministering angel; that is the labor that I wish to perform. I don't want any companion in that world; and if the Lord will make me a ministering angel, it is all I want.' Joseph said, 'Sister, you talk very foolishly, you do not know what you will want.' He then said to me: 'Here, Brother Brigham, you seal this lady to me.' I sealed her to him. This was my own sister according to the flesh. Now, sisters, do not say, 'I do not want a husband when I get up in the resurrection.' You do not know what you will want. I tell this so that you can get the idea. If in the resurrection you really want to be single and alone, and live so forever and ever, and be made servants, while others receive the highest order of intelligence and are bringing worlds into existence, you can have the privilege. They who will be exalted cannot perform all the labor, they must have servants and you can be servants to them." [19]

Either Joseph Smith and Brigham Young were quite arbitrary in their sealing activities, or the lady did not protest enough. It was, however, rather easy, on the whole, for the Prophet to persuade pious young women to become his concubines, for he had conveniently made human love a divine institution. In himself he combined both the appeals of sex and religion, for he was a six foot, handsome Prophet of God. It was only those women who happened to maintain control of their emotions by their reason who resisted at all.

The Prophet was not always so successful when he made advances to women who were already married. There was, for example, Sarah Pratt, the wife of Orson Pratt. Orson Pratt was sent to England to convert the heathen, and in the meantime, the Prophet attempted to convert his beautiful wife. John C.

[19] *Journal of Discourses*, vol. 16, pp. 166-167.

Bennett in his scurrilous *Mormonism Exposed* wrote that, "Joe's real object was to CONVERT HER in another way—from virtue, unsophisticated virtue, to vice, soul-damning vice,—from the path of innocence and peace, to the polluted way of the libertine,— from the pure teachings of heaven's high King, to the loathsome caresses of *the beast and the false prophet.*" But John C. Bennett felt strongly on the subject, for he himself was a rival of the Prophet's for the affections of the beautiful lady. This, and another clash over the affection of Sidney Rigdon's daughter Nancy, were the causes of hostility between Smith and Bennett. Each accused the other of lecherous conduct. We know, however, for certain that a scandal resulted when the lady remained indignantly virtuous, for Brigham Young noted in his journal on August 8, 1842: "Assisted by Elders H. C. Kimball and Geo. A. Smith I spent several days laboring with Elder Orson Pratt, whose mind became so darkened by the influence and statements of his wife, that he came out in rebellion against Joseph, refusing to believe his testimony or obey his counsel. He said he would believe his wife in preference to the Prophet. Joseph told him if he did believe his wife and followed her suggestions, he would go to hell." On August 20 Brigham Young noted the failure of his persuasive powers by this brief statement in his journal: "Brother Orson Pratt was cut off from the Church." However, Pratt repented and was reordained one of the Twelve Apostles a few months later.

Joseph Smith's attempt to win Nancy Rigdon, Sidney Rigdon's eldest daughter, resulted in enmity between him and Sidney Rigdon and between him and John C. Bennett, who wanted Nancy Rigdon for his own wife. Bennett said later that Smith offered him $500 in town lots on Main Street, Nauvoo, if he would aid him in persuading Nancy Rigdon to join his spiritual harem. The Prophet had previously attempted to kiss Nancy Rigdon in his private office, and she threatened to rouse the neighborhood by her screams if he did not unlock the door at once. He unlocked the door, and then, realizing the mistake he had made, he wrote her this letter, which was an ingenious attempt to justify his conduct by means of his religion:

"That which is wrong under one circumstance, may be, and often is, right under another. God said, Thou shalt not kill; at another time he said, Thou shalt utterly destroy. This is the principle on which the government of Heaven is conducted, by Revelation adapted to the circumstances in which the children of the kingdom are placed. Whatever God requires is right, no matter what it is, although we may not see the reason thereof till long after the events transpire. If we seek first the kingdom of God, all good things will be added. So with Solomon; first he asked wisdom, and God gave it him, and with it every desire of his heart; even things which might be considered abominable to all who understand the order of Heaven only in part, but which, in reality, were right, because God gave and sanctioned by special revelation. A parent may whip a child, and justly too, because he stole an apple; whereas, if the child had asked for the apple, and the parent had given it, the child would have eaten it with a better appetite; there would have been no stripes; all the pleasures of the apple would have been secured, all the misery of stealing lost. This principle will justly apply to all of God's dealings with his children. Every thing that God gives us is lawful and right, and it is proper that we should enjoy his gifts and blessings, whenever and wherever he is disposed to bestow; but if we should seize upon those same blessings and enjoyments without law, without revelation, without commandment, those blessings and enjoyments would prove cursings and vexations in the end, and we should have to lie down in sorrow and wailings of everlasting regret. . . ." [20]

Joseph Smith asked Nancy Rigdon to burn this letter, but instead she showed it to her father. When the Prophet was accused by Nancy Rigdon before her assembled family of attempting to seduce her, he blandly admitted the charge was true, but he said that he had done so merely to test her virtue. Sidney Rigdon remained an associate of the Prophet for some time, but he was never fully convinced of the efficacy of this kind of test for maidenly virtue, and their relations were thereafter somewhat strained. After the Prophet's death, Brigham Young once said "that Joseph's time on earth was short, and that the Lord allowed him privileges that we could not have."

There were other instances of attempts of the Prophet to appropriate the wives of his leading associates, if they were comely. It seemed impossible to satisfy the indomitable spirit of his youth and vigor, although he was now thirty-seven years old. The more wives he had the more he seemed to want. During his life-

[20] This letter is taken from Bennett's *Mormonism Exposed*, pp. 243-244. It is also printed in part in the Mormon periodical, *Millennial Star*, vol. 19, p. 774, where it is included without any explanation, except the editor's statement that the occasion for its composition is unknown.

time, according to a Mormon estimate, the Prophet married at least twenty-eight women. *The Historical Record,* a carefully compiled official publication of the Church, gathered together the names of the known wives of Joseph Smith and published them in the issue of May, 1887, with this notation: "Summing up the information received from the parties already mentioned and from other sources, we find that the following named ladies, besides a few others, about whom we have been unable to get all the necessary information, were sealed to Prophet Joseph Smith during the last three years of his life." Even the Mormons have been unable to compile a list of all their Prophet's wives, but these are the names of twenty-eight of them, as nearly as possible in chronological order:

Emma Hale Smith	Helen Mar Kimball	Hannah Ells
Louisa Beman	Emily D. Partridge	Flora Ann Woodworth
Fanny Alger	Eliza M. Partridge	Ruth D. Vose
Lucinda Harris	Lucy Walker	Mary Elizabeth Rollins
Zina D. Huntington	Almera W. Johnson	Olive Frost
Prescindia L. Huntington	Malissa Lott	Rhoda Richards
Eliza Roxey Snow	Fanny Young	Sylvia Sessions
Sarah Ann Whitney	Maria Lawrence	Maria Winchester
Desdemona W. Fullmer	Sarah Lawrence	Elvira A. Cowles
	Sarah M. Cleveland	

Occasionally a Saint found it difficult to persuade a sister that he must not marry her. There is one story, true or untrue, which is at least ingeniously pathetic, of "a rather interesting old maid, sister of one of the dignitaries of the church," who traveled sixty miles to tell Brother Rushton that "she had a revelation that he was to be her husband 'right now.'" Brother Rushton, however, remained firm, and "she left him in tears, prostrate with disappointment."

There is another story involving the same Brother Rushton and the Prophet Joseph Smith. Emma Smith used to keep the keys to the Nauvoo House larder above her bed, and Brother Rushton, who opened the house daily, called for them every morning. Emma Smith made a trip to St. Louis to buy supplies— the trip is mentioned in the Prophet's official diary—and the first morning after her departure, Brother Rushton tapped at the door for his keys. When he opened the door to the command of a soft feminine voice, he was startled to find the young wife of Elder Edward Blossom in Emma's bed. She handed him the keys, saying, "I suppose, Brother Rushton, I shall have to be

Sister Emma to you this morning." Joseph Smith, who was also lying in the bed, dressed in a gaudy red flannel nightgown, when he noticed the astonishment on Brother Rushton's face, sat up and in a commanding, prophetic tone told Rushton that everything was as it should be, but that he must not mention what he had seen to any one." [21]

It is interesting that there is no record of children by any of Joseph Smith's wives, except his first wife Emma. The possible explanation of this is contained in the statement of Sarah M. Pratt, the wife of Orson Pratt, to Dr. Wyl that John C. Bennett, who, it will be remembered was a "professor of midwifery" before he became a Mormon, frequently performed abortions at the earnest request of the Prophet. [22]

A significant factor in the career of the Prophet Joseph Smith is that the period of his greatest visionary fecundity was the period of his adolescence, and prior to his marriage to Emma Smith. After his first marriage he ceased to have visions, but he received a great many revelations from God which he wrote down. After his marriages began to multiply, he ceased to receive these, and the revelation on polygamy is the last he ever recorded publicly, although Brigham Young claimed later that the Prophet had many revelations which had never been published. Perhaps, occupied as he was with the intimate friendship of approximately twenty-eight women, he no longer had time for communion with God. Apparently, however, he still had time for dreams, for in his journal he set down several interpretations of dream symbols: "To dream of flying signifies prosperity and deliverance from enemies. To dream of swimming in deep water signifies success among many people, and that the word will be accompanied with power." Dr. Sigmund Freud has attached a quite different significance to these same symbols. The few dreams which Joseph Smith recorded in his journal would interest psychoanalysts. On Wednesday, March 15, 1843, the Prophet wrote: "I dreamed last night that I was swimming in a river of pure water, clear as crystal, over a shoal of fish of the largest size I ever saw. They were directly under my belly. I was astonished, and felt afraid that they might drown me or do

---

[21] *Mormon Portraits*, by Dr. W. Wyl, pp. 65-66. This book is a collection of all the stories of immorality Dr. Wyl, a meticulous German, could gather from the oldest inhabitants of Salt Lake City, in a residence there of several years undertaken exclusively for that purpose.

[22] *Mormon Portraits*, by Dr. W. Wyl, pp. 61-62.

me injury." On February 1, 1844, he had another dream in which he was swimming over huge waves in rough water and eventually conquering.[23]

Although polygamy was practised in 1843 by most of the leaders of the Church and by many of the followers, it was necessary to keep the practice of it a secret and to deny its existence upon every occasion. This is perhaps one reason why there is no record of children by the Prophet's many wives. The Prophet himself claimed that his wives were either adopted daughters or nieces. An English visitor, Edwin De Leon, wrote: "I even ventured, when I became familiar with 'the Prophet,' to comment on the curious variety among his nieces, and the want of any family resemblance among them. There was a sly twinkle in the prophetic eye, as he poked me in the ribs with his forefinger, and rebuked me, exclaiming, 'Oh, the carnal mind, the carnal mind!' and I thought it discreet not to press the subject."[24]

The Prophet even carried the deception into his journal, where he recorded on October 5, 1843, at which time he had about twenty-eight wives, that he gave instructions to bring to trial those persons "who were preaching, teaching, or practising the doctrine of plurality of wives." But he was conscious that some day this journal would be published, and he did not know that some day the revelation on polygamy would also be published. In a sermon which he delivered to his assembled people, as they sat under the trees in the grove near the Temple site, within hearing and view of the rolling Mississippi River, Joseph urged, "Set our women to work, and stop their spinning yarns and talking about spiritual wives." In spite of, or perhaps because of, their faith in polygamy, the Mormons have never believed that woman's place was in the home during the day.

This secrecy concerning polygamy resulted in peculiar social conditions at Nauvoo. One Mormon recorded that a man never knew when he was speaking to a single woman. Brigham Young did not house his wives at the place where he and his legal wife lived. Whether this was for the purpose of avoiding publicity or conciliating his legal wife has not been revealed, but John D. Lee, who was a policeman in Nauvoo and as such bodyguard to the Prophet and to Brigham Young, wrote later: "Many a night

[23] *History of the Church,* vol. 5, p. 255.
[24] *Thirty Years of My Life on Three Continents,* by Edwin De Leon, vol. 1. p. 60.

have I gone with him, arm in arm, and guarded him while he spent an hour or two with his young brides, then guarded him home and guarded his house until one o'clock, when I was relieved. He used to meet his beloved Emmeline at my house." Beloved Emmeline was Emmeline Free, who was the favorite of Brigham Young's early polygamous life. The necessity of visiting seven new wives secretly must have been both annoying and arduous for Brigham Young.

In spite of all their efforts at secrecy, however, polygamy was too sensational to remain unsuspected, and the quarrels of those who practised it resulted in confirmation of the rumor that it existed. Men apostatized and told their tales of Nauvoo, so that the neighboring communities, and the neighboring newspapers especially, began to think of the city as a den of iniquity and a nest of sin. It was, of course, metaphorically referred to as a combination of Sodom and Gomorrah. Some, perhaps, thought that the city should go back to its old name, for when it was a village of a few huts, even before it was prosaically named Commerce, Nauvoo had been named the City of Venus.

People outside the State of Illinois began to hear of what was going on in Nauvoo. Brigham Young wrote in his journal on June 9, 1843, of an argument he had with a southern professor whom he met on a Mississippi River steamboat:

"He then asked me if Joseph Smith had more wives than one. I told him I would admit he had. In order to explain the principle, I asked the gentleman if he believed the Bible, and was a believer in the resurrection. He said he was a believer in the Old and New Testament and in the resurrection.

"I then asked him if he believed parents and children, husbands and wives would recognize each other in the resurrection. He said he did. . . . I then said, 'We see in this life, that amongst Christians, ministers, and all classes of men, a man will marry a wife, and have children by her; she dies, and he marries another, and then another, until men have had as many as six wives, and each of them bear children. This is considered all right by the Christian world, inasmuch as a man has but one at a time.

"'Now in the resurrection this man and all his wives and children are raised from the dead; what will be done with those women and children, and who will they belong to? And if the man is to have but one, which one in the lot shall he have?'

"The Professor replied, he never thought of the question in this light before, and said he did not believe those women and children would belong to any but those they belonged to in this life.

" 'Very well,' said I, 'you consider that to be a pure, holy place in the presence of God, angels, and celestial beings; would the Lord permit a thing to exist in his presence in heaven which is evil? And if it is right for a man to have several wives and children in heaven at the same time, is it an inconsistent doctrine that a man should have several wives, and children by those wives at the same time, here in this life, as was the case with Abraham and many of the old Prophets? Or is it any more sinful to have several wives at a time than at different times?'

"He answered, 'I cannot see that it would be any more inconsistent to have more wives in this life than in the next, or to have five wives at one time than at five different times. I feel to acknowledge it is a correct principle and a Bible doctrine, and I cannot see anything inconsistent in it.' " [25]

The Mormons have defended their secret practice of polygamy in Nauvoo by pointing to the advice of Jesus Christ, which he is said to have given to his disciples on several occasions: "Cast not your pearls before swine, lest they trample them under their feet and turn again and rend you." It was good advice, and had the Mormons been able to follow it indefinitely, they would have avoided considerable difficulty, for as soon as they did cast their pearl, polygamy, before the rest of the country, the attempt was made, as we shall see, to trample them under foot and turn upon them and rend them. It was natural, therefore, from their point of view, that the Mormons should have regarded the rest of the country as swine.

Meanwhile, it was proving impossible to keep such a pearl as polygamy a secret, and, together with the economic and political reasons that have already been stated, it was a source of ominous opposition to the Mormons as a community in Illinois.

V

While the boy Joseph Smith was trying his best to avoid work on a farm for the rest of his days, he may have indulged in ambitious dreams, but by the year 1844 he had accomplished things more extraordinary and more fantastic than any boy could have imagined. By the time of his thirty-eighth birthday he was dic-

[25] *Millennial Star*, vol. 26, pp. 215-216.

tator of more than ten thousand people, who listened to his advice on spiritual matters and took to him the problems of their everyday life; he was mayor of his city, with power to make into a law his wildest fancy; he was general in command of several thousand men, and his uniform was gaudy enough to satisfy the imagination of any boy who wished to be a soldier; and he was beloved by at least twenty-eight women, a consummation no boy in the United States had even dared to wish for. It was therefore only fitting that he should aspire to the alleged ambition of every American boy: to become President of the United States.

The exalted position to which he had attained did not cause Joseph Smith to become arrogant in his relations with his own people; he continued in Nauvoo to be the genial democrat, who won the affection of his followers by his lack of anything but spiritual pretension. He still wrestled good-naturedly with his friends and fought defensive and offensive fist fights with his enemies, when he was not too busy making known the will of the Lord. In his journal for Monday, March 13, 1843, we find: "I wrestled with William Wall, the most expert wrestler in Ramus, and threw him. In the afternoon, held a Church meeting." And a few days later: "Josiah Butterfield came to my house and insulted me so outrageously that I kicked him out of the house, across the yard, and into the street." There are two stories illustrating how readily the Prophet could turn athlete before strangers and thus satisfy his pride in his physical prowess. He wanted very much to wrestle with a United States Army major who visited Nauvoo, and who was taller than the Prophet. Joseph threw off his coat and said, "I bet you five dollars that I will throw you, come on!" The major declined, Joseph laughed and said: "Now you see the benefit of one's being a prophet; I knew you wouldn't wrestle." One of Joseph's faithful followers who witnessed the scene was so shocked at the worldliness of his Prophet that he left the Church forthwith. Upon another occasion two clergymen visited the Prophet at Nauvoo and had an interview with him for the purpose of learning his theological views and principles. Joseph took them to his study, told them his ideas on repentance, baptism for the remission of sins, and the other tenets of his church, all except polygamy. The two clergymen frequently interrupted with argumentative objections, and the Prophet soon became impatient. He suddenly rose to his full height of six feet two inches and said, "Gentlemen, I am not much of a theologian, but I bet you five dollars that I will throw you one after the other." The clergymen fled, and the man who told the story said, "Joseph laughed himself nearly to death." Whenever the Prophet was cornered in an argument, he resorted to the universally human trick of illogically settling it with his fists.

There was one man, however, of whom the Prophet was afraid, and that was his brother William. Joseph and William disagreed frequently, and upon one occasion William knocked down his Prophet brother when the Prophet interfered with William's attempt to set up a debating society. This occurred in Kirtland; after William threw the Prophet on the floor and beat him, Joseph went home and wrote his brother a letter in which he tried to explain the situation:

"I undertook to reason with you, but you manifested an inconsiderate and stubborn spirit. I then despaired of benefiting you, on account of the spirit you manifested, which drew from me the expression that you were as ugly as the devil. Father then commanded silence, and I formed a determination to obey his mandate, and was about to leave the house, with the impression that you was under the influence of a wicked spirit: you replied you would say what you pleased in your own house. Father said: 'Say what you please, but let the rest hold their tongues.' . . . I said, 'I will speak for I built the house, and it is as much mine as yours'; or something to that effect. I should have said, that I helped to finish the house." [26]

There were other fights between the brothers, and William was cut off from the Church several times, but he was always readmitted at the suggestion of the Prophet. William traveled in the eastern states and gathered money for the Temple, which he spent for the satisfaction of his own desires. "In all his missions," wrote the historian of *The Historical Record*, "the course of conduct he pursued towards the females subjected him to much criticism." His Prophet brother could do nothing with him.

Among his followers Joseph Smith took great pains to be considered what so many Americans have desired to be considered above all things, "a regular fellow." In spring he played ball with his brethren, and he engaged in a contest at pulling sticks with Justus A. Morse, reputed to be the strongest man in the

[26] *History of the Church,* vol. 2, pp. 338-343.

country around Nauvoo. One of Joseph Smith's Church biographers reported proudly: "The Prophet used but one hand and easily defeated Morse." Joseph Smith was no sackcloth and ashes Prophet, with long, gloomy beard and melancholy air. On the contrary, Governor Ford, of Illinois, who was close to him at the time we now see him, wrote of him that he "dressed like a dandy, and at times drank like a sailor and swore like a pirate." [27] In a sermon delivered at Nauvoo Joseph Smith once defined his attitude towards his position:

"Many persons think a prophet must be a great deal better than anybody else. Suppose I would condescend—yes, I will call it condescend—to be a great deal better than any of you, I would be raised up to the highest heavens, and who should I have to accompany me? I love that man better who swears a stream as long as my arm, yet deals justice to his neighbors and mercifully deals his substance to the poor, than the long, smooth-faced hypocrite. I do not want you to think I am very righteous, for I am not. God judges men according to the use they make of the light which He gives them." [28]

In order to insure, perhaps, that he would never be in that position of awful, exclusive, aristocratic loneliness in Heaven, the Prophet frequently indulged in sprees on earth. A visiting English clergyman once asked him how he, a Prophet of the Lord, could get drunk. Joseph replied that it was necessary for him to do so occasionally, so that his followers might not worship him as a god. Dr. Wyl was told many years later that the Prophet usually got drunk on parade days of the Nauvoo Legion, and that he once preached after he had recovered: "Brethren and sisters, I got drunk last week and fell in the ditch. I suppose you have heard of it. I am awfully sorry, but I felt very good." Upon another occasion he said in the pulpit that he got drunk to show the elders who were in the habit of doing so, "how bad it looked." There is something engaging about this Prophet, which his more godlike predecessors lack entirely. Sometimes the Prophet experienced all the anguish of the most miserable penitent, humbled himself in begging forgiveness for his sins, and endured the darkest forebodings of eternal woe.

But melancholy moods did not last long. The cause was triumphing and confounding its enemies. Converts poured into

[27] *History of Illinois,* by Thomas Ford, p. 355.
[28] *The Rise and Fall of Nauvoo,* by Brigham H. Roberts, p. 212.

Nauvoo from England on every ship, and missionaries wrote letters detailing their divine victories in their skirmishes in behalf of God's kingdom. "The Marquis of Downshire," wrote a missionary in England, "who had persecuted the Saints at Hillsborough, in Ireland, had the felicity of seeing his son, Lord William, killed by a fall from his horse while hunting; and Mr. Reilly, his agent, who had aided him in persecuting the Saints, had suffered a third attack of paralysis, while his son, who had headed an outbreak against our Church, has fallen ill without hope of recovery. *So much for them.*" The Prophet entertained the idea of a triumphal missionary tour of the world to be undertaken by him and his Twelve Apostles. "If I live," he wrote in his journal on January 20, 1843, "I will yet take these brethren through the United States and through the world, and will make just as big a wake as God Almighty will let me. We must send kings and governors to Nauvoo, and we will do it."

The personal fame of the Prophet Joseph Smith had spread both by the antagonism he had excited and the curiosity he had awakened. In Nauvoo he was visited by mesmerisers, phrenologists, clergymen, physiologists, prophets of minor sects, a Socialist orator, traveling showmen, and politicians of all parties. They found a large, heavy man, nearing forty, but of youthful appearance, with light hair, fair complexion, and agile blue eyes set deep behind his high cheek bones. His head was large, and a phrenologist of the period who examined it reported that it indicated in a high degree "amativeness" and ambition. When he spoke, his voice was loud and coarse, and his language was more impromptu than elegant. Parley P. Pratt wrote in his autobiography that "there was something connected with the serene and steady penetrating glance of his eye, as if he would penetrate the deepest abyss of the human heart, gaze into eternity, penetrate the heavens, and comprehend all worlds." But then, Parley P. Pratt was somewhat biased.

One man who visited Joseph Smith at Nauvoo recorded that, "In his conversation he is uncommonly shrewd, and exhibits more knowledge of books, sacred and profane, than his personal appearance at first seems to promise." The Prophet was not above ludicrous attempts at erudition. James Arlington Bennet, a writer of arithmetic texts and miscellaneous books of all descriptions, wrote to Smith expressing his admiration, comparing him with Mohammed and with Moses, and placing him in a position greater than either because of the fact that he was present, and they were past. Mr. Bennet expressed his intention of settling in Nauvoo, and he hoped that the Prophet would support him for governor of Illinois if he finally decided to come out that way. Bennet had been baptized, not very seriously, in the waters near Coney Island by Brigham Young. Joseph Smith's reply showed that he was discerning enough to sense false flattery, but not sufficiently so to avoid making himself ridiculous in the use of pretentious phrases. After disclaiming all personal credit for the virtues which Mr. Bennet mentioned and giving that credit to God, the Prophet wrote:

"Were I an Egyptian, I would exclaim, Jah-oh-eh, Enish-go-on-dosh, Flo-ees, Flos-is-is; (O the earth! the power of attraction, and the moon passing between her and the sun). A Hebrew, Hauelo-heem yerau; a Greek, O theos phos esi; A Roman, Dominus regit me; a German, Gott gebe uns das licht; a Portuguese, Senhor Jesu Christo e liberdade; a Frenchman, Dieu defend le droit; but as I am, I give God the glory and say in the beautiful figure of the poet:

" 'Could we with ink the ocean fill;
    Was the whole earth of parchment made;
And ev'ry single stick a quill;
    And every man a scribe by trade;
To write the love of God above,
    Would drain the ocean dry;
Nor could the whole upon a scroll,
    Be spread from sky to sky.' "

If we did not have other examples of Joseph Smith's use of foreign phrases in his letters, it might be possible to believe that the Prophet was pulling James Arlington Bennet's leg. When Bennet wrote that he hoped to become the Prophet's right-hand man, Joseph Smith answered shrewdly: "Why, Sir, Cæsar had his right hand Brutus, who was his 'left hand' assassin, not however applying the allusion to you." Then he added this peroration: "I combat the errors of ages; I meet the violence of mobs; I cope with the illegal proceedings from executive authority; I cut the Gordian knot of powers and I solve mathematical problems of Universities, WITH TRUTH,—*diamond truth, and God is my 'right hand man.' "* [29]

[29] *Correspondence Between Joseph Smith, the Prophet, and Col. John Went-worth, Editor of "The Chicago Democrat," and Member of Congress from*

The loss of so much property and money in Missouri still troubled Joseph Smith, and now that he felt his own political and personal strength, he conceived the notion of writing to all the political candidates for the Presidency of the United States in the campaign of 1844 to ask their attitude towards the Mormons as a people; he informed them that he would be able to guarantee the votes of all his ten thousand followers to the candidate who promised to protect their rights. A few weeks later he addressed another memorial to Congress asking damages for the loss of property in Missouri. He also wrote, "An Appeal to the Freemen of the State of Vermont, The 'Brave Green Mountain Boys,' and Honest Men," in which he asked the support of his native state in the effort to get justice from Missouri, and indulged his love of quotation to the inordinate extent of using phrases from seventeen foreign languages. After denouncing politicians as worse than publicans and sinners, he wrote:

"Were I a Chaldean I would exclaim: Keed'nauh ta-meroon lehoam elauhayauh dey-ahemayaua veh aur'kau lau gnaubadoo, yabadoo ma-ar'gnau comeen tehoat sheamyauh allah. (Thus shall ye say unto them: The gods that have not made the heavens and the earth, they shall perish from the earth, and from these heavens.) "An Egyptian, Su-e-eh-ni. (What other persons are those?) A Grecian, Diabolos bssileuei. (The Devil reigns.) A Frenchman, Messieurs sans Dieu. (Gentlemen without God.) A Turk, Ain shems. (The fountain of light.) A German, sie sind unferstandig! (What consummate ignorance!) A Syrian, Zaubok! (Sacrifice!) A Spaniard, Il sabio muda conscio, il nescio no. (A wise man reflects, a fool does not.) A Samaritan: Saunau! (O stranger!) An Italian: Oh tempa! oh diffidanza! (O the times! O the diffidence!) A Hebrew: Ahtauh ail rauey. (Thou God seest me.) A Dane: Hvad tidende! (What tidings!) A Saxon, Hwaet riht! (What right!) A Swede: Hvad skilia! (What skill!) A Polander: Nay-yen-shoo bah pon na Jesu Christus. (Blessed be the name of Jesus Christ.) A western Indian: She-mo-kah she-mo-keh teh ough-ne-gah. (The white man, O the white man, he very uncertain.) A Roman: Procul, O procul este profani! (Be off, be off ye profane!) But as I am I will only add; when the wicked rule the people mourn." [30]

Illinois; Gen. James Arlington Bennet, of Arlington House, Long Island, and The Honorable John C. Calhoun, Senator from South Carolina. A pamphlet, New York, 1844.
[30] The Voice of Truth. A pamphlet containing some of the writings of Joseph Smith, Jr., pp. 16-17. The translations are Joseph Smith's.

To his letter asking for the views of candidates on the Mormon problem, Joseph Smith received what to him were very unsatisfactory replies from Henry Clay and John C. Calhoun; Lewis Cass, Richard M. Johnson and Martin Van Buren did not think it worth while to reply. Calhoun wrote that he could not offer the Mormons any more protection than he would endeavor to give everybody in the country, irrespective of creed, as required by the Constitution of the United States. "But as you refer to the case of Missouri," wrote Calhoun, "candor compels me to repeat what I said to you at Washington; that, according to my views the case does not come within the jurisdiction of the federal government, which is one of limited and specific powers." Joseph Smith's scathing reply read in part:

"Nauvoo, Illinois, Jan. 2, 1844.

"Sir,—Your reply to my letter of last November, concerning your rule of action towards the Latter Day Saints if elected President, is at hand . . . permit me, as a law abiding man, as a well wisher to the perpetuity of constitutional rights and liberty, and as a friend to the free worship of Almighty God, by all, according to the dictates of every person's conscience, to say *I am surprised* that a man, or men, in the highest stations of public life, should have made up such a fragile 'view' of a case than which there is not one on the face of the globe fraught with so much consequence to the happiness of men in this world, or the world to come. To be sure, the first paragraph of your letter appears very complacent and fair on a white sheet of paper; and who, that is ambitious for greatness and power, would not have said the same thing? Your oath would bind you to support the constitution and laws, and as all creeds and religions are alike tolerated, they must, of course, all be justified or condemned, according to merit or demerit—but why, tell me why, are all the principal men, held up for public stations, so *cautiously careful,* not to publish to the world, *that they* will judge a *righteous judgment*—law or no law: for laws and opinions, like the vanes of steeples, change with the wind. One congress passes a law, and another repeals it, and one statesman says that the constitution means this, and another that; and who does not know that all may be wrong. The opinion and pledge therefore, in the first paragraph of your reply to my question, like the forced steam from the engine of a steam-boat, makes the show of a bright cloud at first, but when it comes in contact with a purer atmosphere, dissolves to common air again.

"Your second paragraph leaves you naked before yourself, like a likeness in a mirror when you say that 'according to your *view,* the federal government is one of limited and specific powers,' and has no jurisdiction in the case of the Mormons. So then, a State can at any time, expel any portion of her citizens with impunity, and in the language of Mr. Van Buren, frosted over with your gracious 'views of the case,' though the cause is ever so just, government can do nothing for them, because it has no power.

"Go on, then, Missouri, after another set of inhabitants, (as the Latter Day Saints did) have entered some two or three hundred thousand dollars worth of land, and made extensive improvements thereon; go on, then, I say, banish the occupants or owners, or kill them as the mobbers did many of the Latter Day Saints, and take their lands and property as a spoil; and let the legislature as in the case of the Mormons, appropriate a couple of hundred thousand dollars to pay the mob for doing the job; the renowned senator from South Carolina, Mr. J. C. Calhoun says the powers of the federal government are so *specific and limited that it has no jurisdiction of the case?* Oh, ye people who groan under the oppression of tyrants; ye exiled Poles, who have felt thē iron hand of Russian grasp; ye poor and unfortunate among all nations, come to the 'asylum of the oppressed,' buy ye lands of the general government; pay in your money to the treasury, to strengthen the army and the navy; worship God according to the dictates of your own consciences; pay in your taxes to support the great heads of a glorious nation; but remember a *'Sovereign State!'* is so much more powerful than the United States, the parent government, that it can exile you at pleasure, mob you with impunity; confiscate your lands and property; have the legislature sanction it; yea, even murder you, as an edict of an Emperor, *and it does no wrong,* for the noble Senator of South Carolina, says the power of the federal government is *so limited and specific* that it has no jurisdiction of the case! What think ye of *imperium in imperio.* . . .

"If the general government has no power to reinstate expelled citizens to their rights, there is a monstrous hypocrite fed and fostered from the hard earnings of the people! A real 'bull beggar' upheld by sycophants; and although you may wink at the priests to stigmatize—wheedle the drunkards to swear, and raise the hue and cry of *impostor false prophet, God damn old Joe Smith,* yet, remember, if the Latter Day Saints are not restored to all their rights, and paid for all their losses, according to the known rules of justice and judgment, reciprocation and common honesty among men, that God will come out of his hiding place and vex this nation with a sore vexation—yea, the consuming wrath of an offended God shall smoke through the nation, with as much distress and woe, as independence has blazed through with pleasure and delight. . . . No! verily no! While I have powers of body and mind; while water runs and grass grows; while virtue is lovely and vice hateful; and while a stone points out a sacred spot where a garment of American liberty once was; I or my posterity will plead the cause of injured innocence, until Missouri makes atonement for all her sins,—or sinks disgraced, degraded, and damned to hell—'where the worm dieth not, and the fire is not quenched.' . . .

"To close, I would admonish you, before you let your 'candor compel' you again to write upon a subject, great as the salvation of man, consequential as the life of the Saviour, broad as the principles of eternal truth, and valuable as the jewels of eternity, to read in the 8th section and 1st article of the Constitution of the United States, the *first, fourteenth,* and *seventeenth* 'specific' and not very 'limited powers' of the federal government, what can be done to protect the lives, property and rights of a virtuous people, when the administrators of the law, and law-makers, are unbought by bribes, uncorrupted by patronage, untempted by gold, unawed by fear, and uncontaminated by tangling alliances—even like Cæsar's wife, not only *unspotted but unsuspected!* and God, who cooled the heat of a Nebuchadnezzar's furnace, or shut the mouths of lions for the honor of a Daniel, will raise your mind above the narrow notion, that the general government has no power—to the sublime idea that Congress, with the President, as executor, is as almighty in its sphere, as Jehovah is in his. With great respect,

"I have the honor to be, your obedient servant,
"JOSEPH SMITH.

"Hon. J. C. Calhoun, Fort Hill, S. C."

This argument between Joseph Smith and John C. Calhoun was only another example of the great battle of the period, the contest between the principle of state sovereignty and the powers of the federal government. The conflict was only settled by a civil war, after which Joseph Smith's view of the problem was triumphant.

It is claimed by his followers that Joseph Smith predicted the Civil War almost thirty years before it broke out, when, on Christmas Day, 1832, he received this revelation from God:

"Verily, thus saith the Lord, concerning the wars that will shortly come to pass, beginning at the rebellion of South Carolina, which will eventually terminate in the death and misery of many souls.

"And the time will come that war will be poured out upon all nations, beginning at this place;

"For behold the Southern States shall be divided against the Northern States, and the Southern States will call on other nations, even the nation of Great Britain, as it is called, and they shall also call upon other nations, in order to defend themselves against other nations; and then war shall be poured out upon all nations.

"And it shall come to pass, after many days, slaves shall rise up against their masters, who shall be marshalled and disciplined for war:

"And it shall come to pass also, that the remnants who are left of the land will marshal themselves, and shall become exceeding angry, and shall vex the Gentiles with a sore vexation;

"And thus, with the sword, and by bloodshed, the inhabitants of the earth shall mourn; and with famine, and plague, and earthquakes, and the thunder of heaven, and the fierce and vivid lightning also, shall the inhabitants of the earth be made to feel the wrath of the Almighty God, until the consumption decreed, hath made a full end of all nations;

"That the cry of the saints, and of the blood of the saints, shall cease to come up into the ears of the Lord of Sabaoth, from the earth, to be avenged of their enemies.

"Wherefore, stand ye in holy places, and be not moved, until the day of the Lord come; for behold it cometh quickly, saith the Lord. Amen."

The Mormons choose to regard this as a marvelous proof of the divine inspiration of their Prophet. He not only predicted the Civil War, they say, but he also foretold that it would begin in South Carolina. It is not so remarkable, however, when we realize that one month before Joseph Smith received this revelation, South Carolina, in November, 1832, had passed resolutions declaring the state free and independent of the federal government, and it looked for a time as if war would begin with that state before the year 1833. The Mormons also ignore the fact that God's statements, through the Prophet, were not borne out by the facts. The Civil War was not followed by universal destruction, Great Britain and other nations of the earth did not join in the universal carnage and there were no famines, plagues, or earthquakes to vex the inhabitants of the earth with the grievous anger of the Almighty. Perhaps these things are yet to come, along with the dire disasters of John of Patmos, still so anxiously awaited by thousands of the hopeful. Meanwhile, the cries of the Saints continued for many years to go up to the ears of the Lord of Sabaoth, and He has not yet seen fit to avenge them upon their enemies.

The Prophet saw many "portentous omens" during the eighteen-forties. He called attention to every one of them in the church weekly newspaper, *Times and Seasons.* There was, for instance, the strange calamity of the chandeliers in the Senate, "weighing about 1,500 lbs., said to have cost $5,000." They came tumbling down and were smashed to atoms. "Again," recorded the Prophet, "it is said that the scroll held in the talons of the eagle, placed over the chair of the presiding officer of the Senate of the United States, and bearing upon it the motto of the Union, 'E pluribus unum,' is stated to have fallen to the earth; and on the same day, the hand of the figure representing the goddess of liberty, standing in front of the Capitol of the United States, holding in it our glorious Constitution, broke off, and came tumbling down." As if this were not enough, when the President-elect, William Henry Harrison, started from his home to the national capital, an earthquake shook the earth; when he reached Baltimore, several banks failed; the cord holding the flags stretched from the White House to the Capitol snapped, bringing to the ground in ignominious disaster the flags of all the states that had voted for him. Simple disasters these were to some, but to Joseph Smith, something more. They were assuredly signs of the eventual Coming of the Son of Man, now so long delayed. "That the explosion of the banks," he wrote, "should have anything to do or part to act in this tragedy, no doubt would be thought strange; but what is better calculated to produce 'a distress of nations with perplexity,' than the monied power of the world? What is better calculated to make 'men's hearts fail them for fear,' &c., than to leave them penniless? . . . consequently there is no doubt but banks will perform their part in the great theater of the world, to bring about the purpose of God, preparatory to the second advent of Christ."

Because of the unsatisfactory nature of the replies he received to his letters to Presidential candidates, Joseph Smith decided that there was only one thing to do; he owed it to his people and mankind to become a candidate for President of the United States himself. At a political meeting held in Nauvoo on January 29, 1844, Joseph Smith was nominated for President of the United States, and Sidney Rigdon for Vice-President. The nominations were ratified by a convention, also held in Nauvoo. Preparations immediately began for an extensive campaign. Another weekly newspaper, the *Nauvoo Neighbor,* was established with the purpose avowed in its prospectus of electing Joseph Smith

President. Elders were appointed to visit every state in the Union during the spring of 1844 to urge Mormonism as their religion and Joseph Smith as their President of the United States. Brigham Young, at the head of the Twelve Apostles, left immediately for the eastern states to superintend this campaign. Three hundred and fifty men, with Brigham Young at their head, traveled throughout the country to spread propaganda for the independent religious candidate. At a political meeting in New York City in the spring of 1844 Parley P. Pratt delivered this campaign plea for his Prophet:

"Who then shall we vote for as our next President? I answer, Gen. Joseph Smith of Nauvoo, Illinois.
"He is not a Southern man with Northern principles; nor a Northern man with Southern principles. But he is an Independent man with American principles, and he has both knowledge and disposition to govern for the benefit and protection of ALL. And what is more HE DARE DO IT, EVEN IN THIS AGE, and this can scarcely be said of many others.

"Come then, O Americans! rally to the Standard of Liberty.
And in your generous indignation trample down
The Tyrant's rod and the Oppressor's crown,
That yon proud eagle to its height may soar,
And peace triumphant reign for-ever more."

Parley P. Pratt was always considered something of a poet by his fellow Mormons. There was another campaign verse by an anonymous Mormon poet which the *Nauvoo Neighbor* published:

"Kinderhoos, Kass, Kalhoun, nor Klay
Kan never surely win the day.
But if you want to know who Kan,
You'll find in General Smith the man."

In another issue the *Neighbor* wrote this of its candidate: "A Washington could save America from utter destruction, and we have a greater than Washington now. Some will say no; but all we ask of those persons, is to become acquainted with General Smith for themselves, and we will risk the matter confidently." The *Times and Seasons* urged its readers to vote for "Joseph Smith, the smartest man in the United States."
The Prophet wrote his own political platform and issued it in

the form of a pamphlet known as *Views of the Powers and Policy of the Government of the United States by General Joseph Smith, of Nauvoo, Illinois.* His political program offered a miscellaneous collection of unique panaceas for the cure of the woes of the United States. Among these were some things which no other candidate in the history of the Presidency had thought of. He urged for one thing the liberation of convicts from the penitentiaries, "blessing them as they go," he wrote, "and saying to them in the name of the Lord, *go thy way and sin no more.*" He suggested that work on roads and public works would be more useful to society and to the prisoners than confinement in cells. "Amor vincit omnia," he recalled, and added for the benefit of those who had not gone to school, "Love conquers all." He also advocated that the number of congressmen should be reduced and their pay reduced to "two dollars and their board per diem; (except Sundays,) that is more than the farmer gets, and he lives honestly." "Curtail the office of government in pay, number, and power," he warned, "for the Philistine lords have shorn our nation of its goodly locks in the lap of Delilah."

The Prophet's proposed solution of the slave problem was the purchase of the slaves from their masters and the abolition of slavery after the year 1850. He hoped to pay for this by the revenue from public lands and by the money saved in the reduction of congressmen's salaries. He also advocated freedom from punishment for deserters from the army and the navy: "If a soldier or marine runs away, send him his wages, with this instruction, that *his country will never trust him again; he has forfeited his honor.*" "Oh! then, create confidence! restore freedom! break down slavery! banish imprisonment for debt, and be in love, fellowship and peace with all the world! Remember that honesty is not subject to law: the law was made for transgressors: wherefore a Dutchman might exclaim: *Ein ehrlicher name is besser als Reichthum* (a good name is better than riches)." But the Prophet did not disdain riches entirely, for in the next sentence he called for the establishment of a national bank with branches throughout the country to safeguard the people's money.

The experience of the Mormons in Missouri led the Prophet to urge power for the federal government to send an army to suppress mobs, and his own experience in courts led him to add immediately afterwards: "Like the good Samaritan, send every lawyer as soon as he repents and obeys the ordinances of heaven, to preach the gospel to the destitute, without purse or scrip, pouring in the oil and the wine; a learned priesthood is certainly more honorable than 'an hireling clergy.' " Oregon, Joseph Smith believed, belonged to the United States and not to Great Britain, and he was in favor of its annexation after the Indians had given their consent; he also advocated the annexation of California, Texas, Canada, and Mexico, if they should desire to join the United States. In addition he declared himself the patron of "liberty, free trade, and sailors' rights," and signed himself the friend of the people and of "unadulterated freedom."

Some Mormon historians have contended that Joseph Smith never seriously believed that his candidacy would be successful. That he had doubts of his success in 1844 is likely, but that he also had serious hopes that he might at some time become President of the United States is undeniable. He had been too successful thus far to believe anything to be impossible. Had he not been a farm boy with nothing in abundance but visions? Had he not established three separate communities in three different states, over which he ruled as benevolent despot by the grace of God? And had not those communities, which had been undeveloped before his arrival, prospered sufficiently to support him and twenty-eight wives, besides more than ten thousand followers? He was exciting the interest of every community in the United States and many in the British Isles by the promises and threats of his new religion. He was general of his own army, mayor of his own city, courted by politicians, and questioned by statesmen. Why should he think it impossible that he might become President of the United States? He had met Presidents of the United States and found them contemptible politicians with whom he would not deign to compare himself. Between Martin Van Buren, courting the votes of Missouri, and Joseph Smith, inviting the favor of God, there was a gulf which Joseph Smith felt to be impassable—for Martin Van Buren. Incidentally, his candidacy, he felt, could do no harm, for the spread of Mormonism always depended upon the power of advertising, and the electioneering Apostles were also, it must be remembered, missionaries of God.

It was unwise, however, of Joseph Smith to set himself up as a candidate for President, for he thus brought into national focus the existence of a close-knit church-state organization within the United States, and the combination of church and state has always been repugnant even to pious Americans, ever since the long and sad experience of it which the early Puritan colonists endured. The fact that the leader of Mormonism dared to aspire to the Presidency of the nation caused thousands of Americans to fear this strange new power as a menace, whereas they had previously dismissed it as merely an entertaining fraud. And it was not unthinkable to thoughtful people that Joseph Smith, Prophet of God, might be elected President of the United States. Had not the people just passed through an emotional political experience in the course of which a log cabin and a keg of cider had elected William Henry Harrison and John Tyler President and Vice-President, respectively? But, unfortunately, Joseph Smith was unable to finish his political campaign. With an overwhelming rapidity events overtook him which obscured completely all political ambitions.

VI

The opposition to the Mormons in Illinois suddenly crystallized into violent antagonism to the Prophet Joseph Smith, which he helped to stimulate by his actions, and which he could no longer control by his powers. Joseph Smith was feeling fine. In addition to the satisfaction to his vanity of the notoriety accorded his self-constituted candidacy for President of the United States, he had just succeeded in establishing beyond a shadow of doubt in his own mind that he was a direct descendant of the Joseph, son of Jacob, who had proved so useful to Pharaoh, of Egypt. His wife, Emma, the Prophet was sure, came from a family of equal age and distinction. He made no attempt to establish the ancient lineage of the other twenty-seven odd, for they were still secrets.

But when Smith coveted the wife of William Law, one of his faithful followers, the trouble began. William Law was described by Governor Ford, of Illinois, as "a deluded but conscientious and candid man." And Mrs. Law admired chastity. The Laws and their few friends rebelled from the rule of the Prophet, whom they now considered lascivious as well as false, and formed an opposition group, whose intention it was to expose him. For that purpose they established at Nauvoo a weekly newspaper known as the *Nauvoo Expositor*.

The first and only issue of the *Nauvoo Expositor* was published on June 7, 1844, with the slogan at its mast-head: "The Truth, The Whole Truth, And Nothing But the Truth." Fortunately a few copies of this extremely rare document exist in libraries, for Joseph Smith in the capacity of Mayor of Nauvoo suppressed the paper a few days after publication of its first number and burned as many copies as his sheriffs could discover.

The *Nauvoo Expositor* published in its one issue a Preamble in which the complaints of the schismatics were fully expressed. They declared themselves believers in the divine origin of the Mormon religion and the Book of Mormon, but they had this to say of the departures from righteousness of its author and proprietor:

"We most solemnly and sincerely declare, God this day being witness of the truth and sincerity of our designs and statements, that happy will it be with those who examine and scan Joseph Smith's pretensions to righteousness; and take counsel of human affairs, and of the experience of times gone by. Do not yield up tranquilly a superiority to that man which the reasonableness of past events, and the laws of our country declare to be pernicious and diabolical. We hope many items of doctrine, as now taught, some of which, however, are taught secretly, and denied openly, (which we know positively is the case,) and others publicly, considerate men will treat with contempt; for we declare them heretical and damnable in their influence, though they find many devotees. How shall he, who has drank of the poisonous draft, teach virtue? In the stead thereof when the criminal ought to plead *guilty* to the court, the court is obliged to plead guilty to the criminal. We appeal to humanity and ask, what shall we do? Shall we lie supinely and suffer ourselves to be metamorphosed into beasts by the Syren tongue? We answer that our country and our God require that we should rectify the tree. We have called upon him to repent, and as soon as he shewed fruits meet for repentance, we stood ready to seize him by the hand of fellowship, and throw around him the mantle of protection; for it is the salvation of souls we desire, and not our own aggrandizement.

"We are earnestly seeking to explode the vicious principles of Joseph Smith, and those who practice the same abominations and whoredoms; which we verily know are not accordant and consonant with the principles of Jesus Christ and the Apostles; and for that purpose, and with that end in view, with an eye single to the glory of God, we have dared to gird on the armor, and with God at our head, we most solemnly and sincerely declare that the sword of *truth* shall not depart from the thigh, nor the buckler from **the** arm, until we can enjoy those glorious privileges which nature's God and our country's laws have guaranteed to us—freedom of speech, the liberty of the press, and the right to worship God as seemeth us good . . . though our lives be the forfeiture . . . ; but our petitions were treated with contempt; and in many cases the petitioner spurned from their presence, and particularly by Joseph, who would state that if he had sinned, and was guilty of the charges we would charge him with, he would not make acknowledgment, but would rather be damned; for it would detract from his dignity, and would consequently ruin and prove the overthrow of the Church. We would ask him on the other hand, if the overthrow of the Church was not inevitable, to which he often replied, that we would all go to Hell together, and convert it into a heaven, by casting the Devil out; and says he, Hell is by no means the place this world of fools suppose it to be, but on the contrary, it is quite an agreeable place: to which we would now reply, he can enjoy it if he is determined not to desist from his evil ways; but as for us, and ours, we *will* serve the Lord our God!

"It is absurd for men to assert that all is well, while wicked and corrupt men are seeking our destruction, by a perversion of sacred things; for all is *not* well, while whoredoms and all manner of abominations are practiced under the cloak of religion. Lo! the wolf is in the fold, arrayed in sheep's clothing, and is spreading death and devastation among the saints: and we say to the watchman standing upon the walls, cry aloud and spare not, for the day of the Lord is at hand—a day cruel both with wrath and fierce anger, to lay the land desolate.

"It is a notorious fact, that many females in foreign climes, and in countries to us unknown, even in the most distant regions of the Eastern hemisphere, have been induced, by the sound of the gospel, to forsake friends, and embark upon a voyage across waters that lie stretched over the greater portion of the globe, as they supposed, to glorify God, that they might thereby stand acquitted in the great day of God Almighty. But what is taught them on their arrival at this place? They are visited by some of the Strikers, for we know not what else to call them, and are requested to hold on and be faithful, for there are great blessings awaiting the righteous; and that God has great mysteries in store for those who love the Lord, and cling to brother Joseph. They are also notified that brother Joseph will see them soon, and reveal the mysteries of heaven to their full understanding, which seldom fails to inspire them with new confidence in the Prophet, as well as a great anxiety to know what God has laid up in store for them, in return for the great sacrifice of father and mother, of gold and silver, which they gladly left far behind, that they might be gathered into the fold, and numbered among the chosen of God.—They are visited again, and what is the result? They are requested to meet brother Joseph, or some of the Twelve, at some isolated point, or at some particularly described place on the bank of the Mississippi, or at some room, which wears upon its front—*Positively No Admittance*. The harmless, inoffensive, and unsuspecting creatures, are so devoted to the Prophet, and the cause of Jesus Christ, that they do not dream of the deep laid and fatal scheme which prostrates happiness, and renders death itself desirable; but they meet him, expecting to receive through him a blessing, and learn the will of the Lord concerning them, and what awaits the faithful follower of Joseph, the Apostle and Prophet of God, when in the stead thereof, they are told, after having been sworn in one of the most solemn manners, to never divulge what is revealed to them, with a penalty of death attached, that God Almighty has revealed it to him, that she should be his (Joseph's) Spiritual wife; for it was right anciently, and God will tolerate it again: but we must keep those pleasures and blessings from the world, for until there is a change in the government, we will endanger ourselves by practicing it—but we can enjoy the blessings of Jacob, David, and others, as well as to be deprived of them, if we do not expose ourselves to the law of the land. She is thunderstruck, faints, recovers, and refuses. The Prophet damns her if she rejects. She thinks of the great sacrifice, and of the many thousand miles she has traveled over sea and land, that she might save her soul from pending ruin, and replies, God's will be done, and not mine. The Prophet and his devotees in this way are gratified. The next step to avoid public exposition from the common course of things, they are sent away for a time, until all is well; after which they return, as from a long visit. Those whom no power or influence could seduce, except that which is wielded by some individual feigning to be a God, must realize the remarks of an able writer, when he says, 'if woman's feelings are turned to ministers of sorrow, where shall she look for consolation?' Her lot is to be wooed and won; her heart is like some fortress that has been captured, sacked, abandoned and left desolate. With her, the desire of the heart has failed—the great charm of existence is at an end; she neglects all the cheerful exercises of life, which gladden spirits, quicken the pulses, and send the tide of life in healthful currents through the veins. Her rest is broken. The sweet refreshment of sleep is poisoned by melancholy dreams; dry sorrow drinks her blood, until her enfeebled frame sinks under the slightest external injury. Look for her after a little while, and you find friendship weeping over her untimely grave; and wondering that one who so recently glowed with all the radiance of health and beauty, should so speedily be brought down to darkness and despair, you will be told of some wintry chill, of some casual indisposition that laid her low! But no one knows of the mental malady that previously sapped her strength, and made her so easy a prey to the spoiler. She is like some tender tree, the pride and beauty of the grove—graceful in its form, bright in its foliage, but with the worm preying at its heart; we find it withered when it should be most luxuriant. We see it drooping its branches to the earth, and shedding leaf by leaf, until wasted and perished away, it falls in the stillness of the forest; and as we muse over the beautiful ruin, we strive in vain to recollect the blast or thunder-bolt that could have smitten it with decay. But no one knows the cause except the foul fiend who perpetrated the diabolical deed.

"Our hearts have mourned and bled at the wretched and miserable condition of females in this place; many orphans have been the victims of misery and wretchedness through the influence that has been exerted over them, under the cloak of religion, and afterwards, in consequence of that *jealous disposition* which predominates over the minds of *some* have been turned upon a wide world, fatherless and motherless, destitute of friends and fortune; and *robbed of that which nothing but death can* restore. . . . It is difficult—perhaps impossible—to describe the wretchedness of females in this place, without wounding the feelings of the benevolent, or shocking the delicacy of the refined; but the truth shall come to the world. . . ." [31]

After this impassioned plea for the rights of outraged maidenhood, any other argument sounds like an anti-climax, but the *Expositor* went on for columns to protest against Joseph Smith's political ambitions, declaring them to be not at all seemly, since the Saviour had never mixed in politics. The *Expositor* then denounced as unjust various excommunications, and especially those of the editors and owners of the *Expositor*. Fifteen resolutions were passed, denouncing Joseph Smith, the doctrines of plural wives and plural gods, which they also claimed to be part of the neo-Mormon heresy, and the union of church and state. Two of the resolutions protested against Joseph Smith's financial activities and land speculations, and particularly accused him of using for his personal needs the funds collected by the missionaries for building the Temple.

These accusations, though the tone of their presentation was highly inflated, were largely true, and Joseph Smith knew them

[31] *Nauvoo Expositor*, p. 1, column 5; p. 2, columns 1, 2, 3, and 4. A copy of this rare newspaper of one issue is in the Berrian Collection on Mormonism of the New York Public Library.

to be so. A few days after the *Expositor* appeared on the streets of Nauvoo, Joseph Smith called a meeting of the municipal council of Nauvoo. Evidence was offered that the *Nauvoo Expositor* was libelous and a public nuisance. The councilors testi-fied to each other that the proprietors of the paper were "sinners, whoremasters, thieves, swindlers, counterfeiters, and robbers." Thomas Ford, then Governor of Illinois, who was watching the reports of the controversy with intense interest, wrote later in his *History of Illinois:* "It was altogether the most curious and irregular trial that ever was recorded in any civilized country; and one finds difficulty in determining whether the proceedings of the council were more the result of insanity or depravity." Councilor Hyrum Smith declared it his honest opinion that the best course was to smash the presses and pi the type of the offensive paper. The minutes of the hearing read that the following resolution was passed "unanimously, with the exception of Councilor Warrington":

"Resolved by the City Council of the City of Nauvoo, that the printing office from whence issues the 'Nauvoo Expositor' is a public nuisance, and also all of said Nauvoo Expositors, which may be, or exist in said establishment, and the Mayor is instructed to cause said printing establishment and papers to be removed without delay, in such manner as he shall direct. Passed June 10th, 1844.
"GEO. W. HARRIS,
"Prest. pro. tem."

Then Joseph Smith changed his coat and, as Mayor of Nauvoo, immediately issued the following order:

"State of Illinois, ⎰ To the Marshal of said city,
City of Nauvoo, ⎱   GREETING.

"You are hereby commanded to destroy the printing press from whence issues the 'Nauvoo Expositor' and pi the type of said printing establishment in the street, and burn all the Expositors and libelous handbills found in said establishment, and if resistance be offered to your execution of this order, by the owners or others, demolish the house, and if anyone threatens you, or the Mayor, or the officers of the city, arrest those who threaten you, and fail not to execute this order without delay, and make due return thereon.
"By order of the City Council.
"JOSEPH SMITH, Mayor."

The Marshal returned this brief report: "The within named press and type is destroyed and pied according to order on this 10th day of June, 1844, at about 8 o'clock P.M. J. P. Green, C.M." Meanwhile, Joseph Smith had changed his coat again, and, as lieutenant-general commanding the Nauvoo Legion, he issued this order to his major-general:

"HEAD QUARTERS. ⎫
Nauvoo Legion, ⎬
June 10, 1844. ⎭

"To Jonathan Dunham, acting Major General of the Nauvoo Legion.

"You are hereby commanded to hold the Nauvoo Legion in readiness forthwith to execute the city ordinances, and especially to remove the printing establishment of the Nauvoo Expositor, and this you are required to do at sight, under the penalty of the laws; provided the Marshal shall require it, and need your services.

"JOSEPH SMITH,
"Lieut. General Nauvoo Legion." [32]

Besides these assaults on the newspaper, the city councilors took testimony tending to defame the characters of its owners. Hyrum Smith swore that William Law had confessed to him that he had been guilty of adultery, "was not fit to live," and "had sinned against his own soul." Hyrum Smith also inquired rhetorically: "Who was Judge Emmons? When he came here he had scarce two shirts to his back, but he had been dandled by the authorities of the city, &c., and was now editor of the *Nauvoo Expositor,* and his right hand man Francis M. Higbee, who had confessed to him [Hyrum Smith] that he had had the P * *," as the *Nauvoo Neighbor* modestly put it.

That fine spring day, June 10, 1844, was the busiest and, in its ultimate effects, the most disastrous of Joseph Smith's life. The entire country surrounding Nauvoo was aroused to mob fury by his arbitrary acts of suppression and by his violent means of executing them. The press and materials of the *Nauvoo Expositor* had been tumbled into the street, smashed with sledge hammers, and then set on fire. The Prophet himself is said to have led the attack on Higbee's grocery store, where the press was housed, and when a large man, hired by Higbee for his pro-

[32] These documents are reprinted from the June 19, 1844, issue of the *Nauvoo Neighbor,* the Mormon weekly newspaper.

tection, knocked down three of Smith's followers, the Prophet sent the protector sprawling with a hard punch under the ear, "saying that he could not see his men knocked down while in the line of duty, without protecting them."

While all this stirring action was taking place, Brigham Young was busy in New York and nearby states urging the election of his Prophet as President of the United States. He was ignorant of everything that was taking place in Nauvoo, for the electric telegraph was still an experiment. Had he been present in Nauvoo, he might have influenced the Prophet towards moderation, for, as we shall see, Brigham Young understood mobs and governments, and he knew when to compromise. Hyrum Smith had written a letter to Brigham Young on June 17, 1844, in which he told him of the activities of the mob and urged him to return to Nauvoo with as many of the brethren as he could gather as soon as possible. The letter read in part:

"It is thought best by myself and others for you to return without delay, and the rest of the Twelve, and all the Elders that have gone out from this place, and as many more good, faithful men as feel disposed to come up with them. Let wisdom be exercised; and whatever they do, do it without a noise. You know we are not frightened, but think it best to be well prepared and be ready for the onset; and if it is extermination, extermination it is, of course.

"Communicate to the others of the Twelve with as much speed as possible, with perfect stillness and calmness. A word to the wise is sufficient; and a little powder, lead, and a good rifle can be packed in your luggage very easy without creating any suspicion." [33]

Joseph Smith wrote in his journal that he advised Hyrum not to mail that letter immediately. Three days later Joseph wrote a letter to Brigham Young and addressed it to Boston, asking him and the rest of the Twelve Apostles to return to Nauvoo immediately. However, the mails were slow in those days, and Brigham Young was traveling. Meanwhile, events moved rapidly.

After the forcible suppression of their newspaper, William Law and his associates left Nauvoo for the neighboring city of Carthage, which was composed largely of anti-Mormon people. They swore out a warrant for the arrest of Joseph Smith and his Nauvoo Common Council. Joseph Smith's municipal court,

[33] *History of the Church*, vol. 6, pp. 486-487.

with powers under the extraordinary Nauvoo charter, promptly released the Prophet and his associates by a writ of *habeas corpus.* This use of the charter whipped the mob into a fury. The Carthage leaders contended that if the Nauvoo charter allowed suppression of newspapers and an independent military organization to carry it out, those who were against such arbitrary powers were forced to use any means to overcome the advantages obtained when the charter was jammed through the Illinois legislature by politicians with purely personal interests. First the Carthage people asked Governor Ford for the militia. Ford visited Carthage, and when he arrived there on June 21 he found an armed force of citizens ready to arrest Smith and his common councilors. There was also a rumor that the Prophet intended to suppress the *Warsaw Signal,* the county newspaper, which was attacking Smith vigorously. The Prophet had taken offense at a mild editorial in the *Signal,* which had argued that no one wished to deny the Mormons freedom of worship, but that they were not entitled to political supremacy over their neighbors. Under the heading, "HIGHLY IMPORTANT!!! A NEW REVELATION *from* JOE SMITH, *the Mormon Prophet, for the especial benefit of the Editor of the 'Warsaw Signal,' "* the Warsaw newspaper published this letter from Smith in answer to its editorial:

"Nauvoo, Ill., May 26, 1841.
"Mr. Sharp, Editor of the Warsaw Signal:
"Sir—You will discontinue my paper—its contents are calculated to pollute me, and to patronize the filthy sheet—that tissue of lies— that sink of iniquity—is disgraceful to any moral man.
"Yours, with utter contempt,
"Joseph Smith.
"P.S. Please publish the above in your contemptible paper.
"J. S."

The *Signal* commented: "Now, as one good turn deserves another, we annex below, for the benefit of the aforesaid Prophet, a revelation from our books, in this wise:

"Warsaw, Ill., June 2, 1841.
"Joseph Smith, Prophet, &c. &c.,
"To Sharp and Gamble, Dr.
"To one year's subscription to 'Western World,' $3.00.
"Come Josey, fork over, and for mercy's sake don't get a reve-

lation that it is not to be paid. For if thou dost we will send a prophet after thee mightier than thou."

During the three years between this exchange of sentiments and the suppression of the *Nauvoo Expositor* Joseph Smith and the *Warsaw Signal* had reviled each other.

Underlying the popular antagonism against the Mormons, and fomenting it, was the resentment of those leaders in the community who had felt the political menace of Mormon solidarity. Those politicians who could not obtain the powerful Mormon solid vote, or who felt they were above asking for it, were particularly anxious to destroy its controlling influence. Public meetings, with inflammatory speeches, were held in and around Carthage, and exaggerated rumors were spread about degenerate practices of the Mormons. Parodying these rumors, a Mormon writer once wrote: "It is an error, the prevalent opinion that we all cleanse the nasal orifice with the big toe, and make tea with holy water." Almost overnight, committees arose whose members rode day and night throughout the neighboring countryside, spreading the news of latest Mormon outrages, and soliciting the aid of the adjoining counties in the campaign against this strange and offensive people. Any who were courageous enough to defend the Mormons against some of the ridiculous charges were known as "Jack" Mormons, and they occupied the same uncomfortable position as the Tories during the War of the Revolution.

Illinois was still a pioneer state in 1844, and Hancock County was only fourteen years old. Governor Ford, who was intimately acquainted with the inhabitants of Illinois for many years, wrote that, "with some honorable exceptions," they "were, in popular language, hard cases." The people had been accustomed to take the law into their own hands when they did not feel that it was playing into them. Seven years before this difficulty with the Mormons, the Rev. Elijah P. Lovejoy had come to Alton, Illinois, to edit a religious newspaper, with an anti-slavery bias. He was allowed to edit a religious newspaper, but as soon as he expressed his sentiments concerning slavery, his press and types were thrown into the Mississippi River. He ordered another press and more types and defended them with Abolitionists, armed with rifles. The mob attacked the building, and a shot was fired which killed a boy in the mob. The building with the press was promptly burned, and the Rev. Mr. Lovejoy and all his Abolitionists were shot dead. In addition to this lively method of expressing differences of opinion, horse-stealing, murder, counterfeiting, and robbery were common throughout Illinois, according to Governor Ford. Citizens were in the habit of banding together for protection, because they could not get it from intimidated or dishonest juries; there were also insufficient jails, and illegal changes of venue or eternal legal delays were frequently resorted to in the courts. The last resort in any controversy had been the calling of the militia, which usually was a vehement partisan of one side or the other. In the case of the Mormons professional jealousy, in addition to the other reasons, was sufficient to turn the soldiers against a people who had their own private militia.

Governor Ford addressed a meeting of mob and militia at Carthage, and assured them that Joseph Smith would be made to answer charges for the suppression of the *Nauvoo Expositor,* but he also insisted that no personal harm must come to him until the law had authorized it, and he sent Smith notice to appear at Carthage to answer the charges made against him. Meanwhile, the Prophet had called out the Nauvoo Legion, declared Nauvoo to be under martial law, and no one was allowed to enter or to leave the city without strict search.

The Prophet had made all plans for flight to the Rocky Mountains, and he and his brother Hyrum, with several close friends, crossed the Mississippi River to Montrose, Iowa, and went into hiding. One of the Prophet's bodyguard, Orrin Porter Rockwell, was sent back to Nauvoo to inform their families of the plans for flight. At one o'clock in the morning Emma Smith sent Rockwell and Reynolds Cahoon with a letter to her husband. A copy of this letter does not exist, but there is reason to believe that Emma urged in vigorous terms that the Prophet return immediately to Nauvoo to protect his family and his people instead of abandoning them to the fury of a disappointed mob. The messengers found Joseph, Hyrum, and Willard Richards seated in the room of a farmhouse, which was filled with flour and other provisions, ready for packing. They delivered their letters and reported that some of the brethren in Nauvoo were openly accusing the Prophet and his brother of cowardice. "Like the fable, when the wolves came the shepherds ran from the flock, and left the sheep to be devoured," was the way one of the Prophet's followers frankly put the situation. To which Joseph wearily replied, "If my life is of no value to my friends, it is of none to myself." Then he asked the advice of those who were in the room filled with flour and provisions, ready for packing. "Brother Hyrum," said Joseph, "you are the oldest, what shall we do?" "Let us go back and give ourselves up, and see the thing out," suggested Hyrum. Joseph was silent for a few minutes; this advice did not seem to satisfy him. He was disappointed, but he finally said, "If you go back, I will go with you, but we shall be butchered." Hyrum replied: "No, no; let us go back and put our trust in God, and we shall not be harmed. The Lord is in it. If we live or have to die, we will be reconciled to our fate." But, at the moment, the Prophet Joseph Smith was not thinking of the Lord. The flour and provisions were ready. The *Maid of Iowa,* the little river steamer which the Church owned, was waiting with steam up to take him down the Mississippi River to safety. Reluctantly, he consented to recross the river to Nauvoo. On the way back he was sullen and discontented. He lagged behind the others, with Orrin Porter Rockwell, his trusted bodyguard, and when he was urged to hurry, he answered, "It is no use to hurry, for we are going back to be slaughtered." [34]

On Monday, June 24, 1844, Joseph Smith, his brother Hyrum, and all the members of the Municipal Common Council of Nauvoo went to Carthage to surrender themselves on charges of riot. All except Joseph Smith and his brother Hyrum were discharged on bail, but the two leaders were held in jail on a charge of treason, because Smith had declared Nauvoo under martial law, which, the charge said, amounted to a declaration of war against the State of Illinois.

The State of Illinois was out of joint, and it surely was cursed spite that ever Thomas Ford was born to set it right. He was a small, timid man, with a sharp nose, bent slightly to one side. His manner was "plain and unpretending," according to one of his contemporaries, and he was a very poor orator. His small, squeaky, unimpassioned voice came from a frail, unimposing body. He had a clear, logical mind, which knew the law and realized how it should be applied, but the physical application of it in a pioneer state of civilization was beyond his personality. Ford, like another Illinois lawyer, Lincoln, was not particularly interested in the details of religion, and he was of the opinion

[34] *History of the Church,* vol. 6. *Succession in the Presidency,* by B. H. Roberts, pp. 116-117.

that any religious sect ought to be allowed to live, if its members
desired religious life. It was entirely due to the interest in him
and faith in him of his more worldly half-brother, George For-
quer, that Ford had been elected a judge of the Supreme Court
of Illinois. He was finally selected as a compromise candidate for Governor of Illinois in 1842. Ford's contemporaries
said that in order to fortify his feeble courage, he used whiskey
in large doses. After his retirement from the office of Governor,
Ford went to a farm in Hamburgh, Illinois, where, his health
wrecked, and a financial bankrupt, he wrote his *History of Illinois,* which is far superior to most of the histories of our states
because of its liberal attitude of mind and its careful literary
workmanship. For a few years after he finished the history,
Ford and his wife, both afflicted with incurable diseases, lived as
objects of public charity. Many years later a monument to
Thomas Ford was erected at Peoria, Illinois.

Governor Ford had promised Joseph Smith and his brother
that he would give them protection from the mob, and he had
persistently refused to call the state militia to Carthage to aid
that mob. The militia used to guard the prisoners was a local
Carthage body, known as the Carthage Greys. Joseph Smith had
confidence in Governor Ford, but the Governor was not equally
appreciated by the anti-Mormons, who did not find him firm
enough for their purposes. The women of Hancock County
formed a committee and waited upon the Governor. They presented him with a package, which the nervous little man opened
before them with embarrassed suspense. He expected no doubt
a token of their regard. The women intended the gift to be such,
for the package contained a petticoat.

At Governor Ford's suggestion the Smith brothers were
allowed a large room in the Carthage jail, where they could see
some of their friends. On the evening of June 26 the Prophet
felt uneasy, and Hyrum read to his brother a passage from the
Book of Mormon concerning the deliverance of God's servants
from prison; but, somehow, this passage did not seem to satisfy
Joseph Smith, for he remained uneasy. The next day, Thursday,
June 27, was a sultry summer day. Governor Ford had gone to
Nauvoo with a force of voluntary soldiers to address the Mor-
mons and assure them that their Prophet would have fair play.
The prisoners, meanwhile, spent the afternoon listening to John
Taylor, who was visiting them, sing "The Poor Wayfaring Man

of Grief." Joseph was so pleased with the song that he asked that it be repeated. Hyrum Smith then read extracts from Josephus. At about five o'clock in the evening there was a noise in the compound outside the jail, followed by a few rifle shots. Then men rushed up the stairs of the jail to the room in the second story where the prisoners were sitting. The door of the room was pushed open, and shots were fired at the prisoners and their visitors. Hyrum Smith was hit in the face and the head, and fell, crying, "I am a dead man." As he was falling, three more

THE ASSASSINATION OF JOSEPH SMITH
From a contemporary woodcut

bullets struck him and killed him. Joseph Smith had a revolver, which a friend had smuggled into the jail, and with this he wounded three of the mob. When he could no longer keep them from entering the room, he rushed for the window to jump out, when a ball struck him, and he fell out of the window, shouting, "O Lord, my God!" It is said that when the Prophet's body hit the ground he was still alive. One of the assailing mob propped it up against the wall of a well, four men advanced eight paces and fired their rifle balls into it, and Joseph died. A bareheaded, barefoot man, with his pants rolled up above his knees and his shirt sleeves above his elbows, is said to have approached the body with a long bowie knife, with the intention of cutting off the Prophet's head, when, according to the Mormons, just as he had raised his arm with the knife in his hand, a blinding flash of lightning struck him with terror, and his arm fell powerless to his side. The assassins hurried away without the head of the Prophet. According to Mormon accounts, the mob that killed their Prophet and their Patriarch was made up of about one hundred and fifty men, whose faces were disguised by terrifying black paint.

Meanwhile, Governor Ford had finished his speech of reassurance to the Mormons in Nauvoo and started back eighteen miles to Carthage. A few miles from Nauvoo his party met two men hurrying from Carthage, who told them that the Prophet and his brother had been killed, and that John Taylor had been seriously wounded. Ford took the two messengers back to Carthage with him in order that the Mormons might not be aroused to a sanguinary fury at this awful, unexpected news. It was the Governor's opinion that the mob had planned its attack on Smith for the exact time that Ford was in Nauvoo, with the intention of inciting the Mormons to retaliate by killing the Governor, so that it might kill two birds by hurling only one stone itself, for the mob hated Ford almost as much as it hated Smith. Then the national excitement which would have been created by the assassination of the Governor by Mormons would have made a war of extermination against those people a natural result.

Willard Richards, who was also in the jail room entertaining the Prophet when the assassination took place, sent this message to Nauvoo, which Governor Ford intercepted:

> "Carthage jail, 8 o'clock 5 min. p.m.,
> "June 27th, 1844.
> "Joseph and Hyrum are dead. Taylor wounded, not very badly. I am well. Our guard was forced, as we believe, by a band of Missourians from 100 to 200. The job was done in an instant, and the party fled towards Nauvoo instantly. This is as I believe it. The citizens here are afraid of the 'Mormons' attacking them; I promise them no.
> "W. RICHARDS.
> "N.B.—The citizens promise us protection; alarm guns have been fired.
> "JOHN TAYLOR."

Joseph Smith, as we have seen, had premonitions of disaster, but the Mormons have produced since his death several instances of the extent of his advance knowledge. Elder Stevenson brought forth the inevitable comparison:

"At this time, our beloved Prophet was impressed with a sad foreboding somewhat similar to that experienced in Gethsemane by the Saviour just previous to the crucifixion, when he called upon the Father and said: 'Father, if thou be willing, remove this cup from me: nevertheless, not my will, but thine be done.' The Prophet Joseph said, while on his way to Carthage, 'I am going like a lamb to the slaughter; but I am calm as a summer's morning; I have a conscience void of offence towards God and towards all men. I shall die innocent, and it shall be said of me, "he was murdered in cold blood."' Elder Bates Nobles, now living, authorizes me to say that he heard the Prophet utter those very words." [35]

There is also a description of the scene of the Prophet's journey to Carthage. As he was leaving Nauvoo, he passed the Masonic Hall, which he had built, and, waving to some men who were standing outside, he said: "Boys, if I don't come back, take care of yourselves. I am going like a lamb to the slaughter." When he passed his own farm, he stopped and looked at it for a long time. When the party finally moved on, he turned and looked back at the farm several times. Some one commented on this, and Smith said: "If some of you had such a farm, and knew you would not see it any more, you would want to take a good look at it for the last time." All of these scenes are somewhat apocryphal. And against them we must place another statement, credited to the Prophet a short while before his death: "I defy all the world to destroy the work of God, and I prophesy they never will have power to kill me till my work is accomplished, and I am ready to die." The question of whether his work was accomplished, and whether he was ready to die in 1844 has never been settled. Elder Stevenson estimated that at the time of his death the Prophet was thirty-eight years, six months and six days old, and that it was just fourteen years, two months and twenty-one days after the foundation of the Mormon Church when its Prophet was killed. "Strange as it may appear," wrote Elder Stevenson, "our Lord and Saviour was murdered when only a few years younger than Joseph, and both were put to death for the same cause, namely, establishing of the Church of

[35] *Reminiscences of Joseph, the Prophet,* pp. 7-8.

Christ on the earth, the one in the former and the other in the latter days."

The bodies of Joseph and Hyrum were removed from the jail to Hamilton's Hotel in Carthage. As soon as Governor Ford arrived in Carthage, he consulted John Taylor and Willard Richards, and, at his suggestion, they sent this hurried message to their people:

"The governor has just arrived; says all things shall be inquired into, and all right measures taken. I say to all citizens of Nauvoo— My brethren be still, and know that God reigns. Don't rush out of the city—Don't rush to Carthage—stay at home and be prepared for an attack from Missouri mobbers. The governor will render every assistance possible—has sent orders for troops. Joseph and Hyrum are dead, will prepare to move the bodies as soon as possible.

"The people of the county are greatly excited, and fear the 'Mormons' will come out and take vengeance. I have pledged my word the violence will be on their part, and say to my brethren in Nauvoo, in the name of the Lord, be still; be patient, only let such friends as choose come here to see the bodies. Mr. Taylor's wounds are dressed, and not serious. I am sound.

"WILLARD RICHARDS."

A few days later the bodies of the Prophet and Patriarch were taken to Nauvoo and greeted with wailing and lamentation. Mother Smith recorded this scene in her book:

"I had for a long time braced every nerve, roused every energy of my soul, and called upon God to strengthen me; but when I entered the room, and saw my murdered sons extended both at once before my eyes, and heard the sobs and groans of my family, and the cries of 'Father! Husband! Brothers!' from the lips of their wives, children, brother, and sisters, it was too much, I sank back, crying to the Lord, in the agony of my soul, 'My God, my God, why hast thou forsaken this family!' A voice replied, 'I have taken them to myself, that they might have rest.' " [36]

The authoress of Mother Smith's book outdid herself, or else Mother Smith was especially favored, for there is no record that Christ ever received any answer to his similar question.

The bodies were concealed for a few days for fear of an attempt to cut off the heads for exhibition purposes in Carthage.

[36] *Biographical Sketches*, by Lucy Smith, p. 279.

Then they were buried near Joseph Smith's former home. He had expressed a wish to be buried in a tomb near the Temple, but Emma Smith objected and refused to allow the Church to carry out that wish. Eight thousand Mormons gathered around the bodies of their dead leaders and resolved their trust in the Lord to revenge the foul murder.

The memory of the Prophet was perpetuated a few days later. The rough boards which had been used as temporary coffins were sawed in pieces and distributed among Joseph's and Hyrum's friends, who had canes made of them, each with a lock of the Prophet's hair set in the top. These canes are considered sacred relics to-day.

Eliza Snow, one of the Prophet's wives and Mormonism's poet, composed a long poem which appeared in the *Nauvoo Neighbor* a few weeks after the assassination. The last two stanzas read:

"Now Zion mourns—she mourns an earthly head:
The Prophet and the Patriarch are dead!
The blackest deed that men or devils know
Since Calv'ry's scene, has laid the brothers low!
One in their life, and one in death—they prov'd
How strong their friendship—how they truly lov'd:
True to their mission, until death, they stood,
Then sealed their testimony with their blood.
All hearts with sorrow bleed, and ev'ry eye
Is bath'd in tears—each bosom heaves a sigh—
Heart broken widows' agonizing groans
Are mingled with the helpless orphans' moans!

"Ye Saints! be still, and know that God is just—
With steadfast purpose in his promise trust:
Girded with sackcloth, own his mighty hand,
And wait his judgments on this guilty land!
The noble martyrs now have gone to move
The cause of Zion in the courts above."

In a poem called "The Seer," John Taylor expressed the Mormons' appreciation in simpler fashion:

"The Saints, the Saints, his only pride,
For them he lived, for them he died.
Their joys were his, their sorrows too:
He loved the Saints, he loved Nauvoo."

The general sentiment of the Mormon commemorative verse
was the same: that their Prophet had died, like Christ, a martyr
to the most glorious of all causes. By their reckless shots on
that June day the men of Carthage set a new religion on a firm
basis, and instead of aiding to exterminate Mormonism, which
was their avowed object, they created in the minds of many thousands a latter-day Jesus Christ. Mormonism had developed all
the paraphernalia for a parallel with ancient Christianity; it only
lacked a martyr, and the mob supplied the final touch with un-
intentional generosity. John Brown once said, "I am worth in-
conceivably more to hang than for any other purpose." So far
as Mormonism was concerned, Joseph Smith could have said the
same. He was assassinated at exactly the right time for his
religion, however cruel and unfortunate his death was for himself. Had he lived a few years longer, and had he conducted
himself as he did during the few last years of his life, in all
probability his church would have been broken into splinters by
the impact of his own ambitious pretensions, or smashed into
kindling by the rage of hostile mobs. Joseph Smith had become
more ambitious than the angels and more dictatorial than the
Hebrew God. His vision of himself as President of the United
States, and his picture of himself as lord of a harem, were not
only inconsistent with each other, but productive of opposition
from Gentiles and dissension among Mormons. He was between
these two smoldering fires when the rabble of Carthage made of
him a martyr to be worshiped for many years to come by hundreds of thousands of sincere people.

Governor Ford sensed this result of the martyrdom of Joseph
Smith, when he wrote, somewhat sadly, in his *History of Illinois:*

"Sharon, Palmyra, Manchester, Kirtland, Far West, Adam-on-
Diahmon, Ramus, Nauvoo and the Carthage Jail, may become holy
and venerable names, places of classic interest, in another age; like
Jerusalem, the Garden of Gethsemane, the Mount of Olives, and
Mount Calvary to the Christian, and Mecca and Medina to the
Turk. And in that event, the author of this history feels degraded
by the reflection, that the humble governor of an obscure State,
who would otherwise be forgotten in a few years, stands a fair
chance, like Pilate and Herod, by their official connection with the
true religion, of being dragged down to posterity with an immortal
name, hitched on to the memory of a miserable impostor. There
may be those whose ambition would lead them to desire an immortal

name in history, even in those humbling terms. I am not one of that number."

But the days of Gethsemane and the days of Nauvoo are different. With the invention of the printing press times have changed somewhat, and in order that Joseph Smith might attain to the dignity and legendary significance of Christ, it would be necessary for too many books, pamphlets, and newspapers to be destroyed. There is a lack of romantic glamor about Palmyra, New York, Kirtland, Ohio, Carthage and Nauvoo, Illinois, which makes it impossible to drink in the events that took place in those towns as one absorbs unquestioningly the tales of the Bible. There is a crass lack of vagueness about Mormonism which detracts from its charm and throws into glaring reflection its crude and shiny newness. Its traditions are not built for hundreds of years, but look rather as if they are ready to fall at the hands of the wrecking company whenever the land on which they are located becomes more valuable for other purposes. And, although Governor Ford played the part of Pontius Pilate in this dangerous western miracle play, like Pilate, he seems to have tried his best to save his prisoner from a mob that had its own reasons for his slaughter.

Many of Joseph Smith's followers were certain that he was about to rise again from the dead, and they watched daily for signs of this phenomenon. Some reported that they had seen him, attended by a celestial army, riding through the air on a great white horse. These rumors persisted for many years, and in 1857 Brigham Young delivered this denial in the Tabernacle at Salt Lake City:

"Joseph is not resurrected; and if you will visit the graves you will find the bodies of Joseph and Hyrum yet in their resting place. Do not be mistaken about that; they will be resurrected in due time. . . . As quick as Joseph finishes his mission in the spirit world he will be resurrected.

"I do not know that any news would come to my ears so sad and discouraging, so calculated to blight my faith and hope as to hear that Joseph is resurrected and has not made a visit to his brethren. I should know that something serious was the matter, far more than I now apprehend that there is. When his spirit again quickens to his body, he will ascend to heaven, present his resurrected body to the Father and the Son, receive his commission as a resurrected

being, and visit his brethren on this earth, as did Jesus after his
resurrection. . . . As quick as Joseph ascends to his Father and
God, he will get a commission to this earth again, and I shall be
the first woman that he will manifest himself to. I was going to
say the first man, but there are so many women who profess to
have seen him, that I thought I would say woman. . . .

"When Jesus was resurrected they found the linen, but the body
was not there. When Joseph is resurrected, you may find the linen
that enshrouded his body, but you will not find his body in the grave,
no more than the disciples found the body of Jesus when they looked
where it was lain." [37]

But of Joseph Smith's eventual position in heaven, and of the
certainty of his resurrection on earth, Brigham Young never had
any doubt. Several years after the foregoing sermon, he told
his congregation:

"From the day that the Priesthood was taken from the earth to
the winding-up scene of all things, every man and woman must have
the certificate of Joseph Smith, junior, as a passport to their entrance into the mansion where God and Christ are—I with you and
you with me. I cannot go there without his consent. He holds the
keys of that kingdom for the last dispensation—the keys to rule in
the spirit-world; and he rules there triumphantly, for he gained full
power and a glorious victory over the power of Satan while he was
yet in the flesh, and was a martyr to his religion and to the name of
Christ, which gives him a most perfect victory in the spirit-world.
He reigns there as supreme a being in his sphere, capacity, and calling, as God does in heaven. Many will exclaim—'Oh that is very
disagreeable! It is preposterous! We cannot bear the thought!'
But it is true.

"I will now tell you something that ought to comfort every man
and woman on the face of the earth. Joseph Smith, junior, will
again be on this earth dictating plans and calling forth his brethren
to be baptized for the very characters who wish this was not so, in
order to bring them into a kingdom to enjoy, perhaps, the presence
of the Father and the Son; and he will never cease his operations,
under the directions of the Son of God, until the last ones of the
children of men are saved that can be, from Adam till now. . . .

"It was decreed in the counsels of eternity, long before the foundations of the earth were laid, that he should be the man, in the
last dispensation of this world, to bring forth the word of God to
the people, and receive the fulness of the keys and power of the

[37] *Journal of Discourses*, vol. 4, pp. 285-286.

Priesthood of the Son of God. The Lord had his eye upon him, and upon his father, and upon his father's father, and upon their progenitors clear back to Abraham, and from Abraham to the flood, from the flood to Enoch, and from Enoch to Adam. He has watched that family and that blood as it has circulated from its fountain to the birth of that man. He was foreordained in eternity to preside over this last dispensation, as much so as Pharaoh was foreordained to be a wicked man, or as Jesus to be the Saviour of the world because he was the oldest son in the family." [38]

Those who refused to believe this were in grave danger of eternal damnation, and Brigham Young at another time illustrated that danger by telling his own version of the story of Noah and the Ark:

"Did you ever hear the story of an old man that came to Noah when he was building the ark? 'What, Mr. Noah, are you still at the ark? You are a veritable old fool, building an ark far away from any water! How are you going to float it?' 'Wait a little while, and I will show you: by-and-by the Lord will break up the mighty deep and send forth the waters and drown the wicked.' 'Oh, you are a fool, Noah! You had better build a good house, and plant and till the earth. I am going home,' &c. 'Go on,' said Noah; 'by-and-by you will learn that I am right.' They waited year after year, and by-and-by the fountains of the great deep were broken up, and the rain began to descend. The old man came along, and Noah said to him, 'What do you think now, neighbor?' 'Oh, this is only a shower; it looks like clearing up; it will soon be over.' In a short time the old man came again, wading in water to his knees, when Noah said, 'Well, what do you think now?' 'Oh, it will soon clear away.' He came again, and that time he was paddling along in water up to his neck, and said, 'Won't you take me in, Noah?' 'I have got my load; all who have received tickets are aboard, and those who have not tickets cannot come aboard. What do you think of it now, old man, is it only a little shower?' Then it was not, 'Damn old Noah!' but they were crying, 'Oh, Mr. Noah, take us in.' By-and-by it will be, 'Mr. Smith, won't you have a little compassion on us?' 'No,' Joseph will say; 'you would not take a ticket when I offered it to you by my brethren; you refused my tickets, and said it was "nothing but a shower, we guess it will pass off." ' According to the words of the Saviour, 'As it was in the days of Noah, so it will be in the days of the coming of the Son of Man.' " [39]

[38] *Journal of Discourses*, vol. 7, pp. 289-290.
[39] *Journal of Discourses*, vol. 8, pp. 229-230.

Meanwhile, Joseph Smith's body is still resting in his grave at Nauvoo, but his followers have not given up hope that, as it was in the days of Noah, so will it be at some indefinite time in the future.

Governor Ford made an effort to discover the murderers of Joseph and Hyrum Smith, and to bring them to trial. But the mob was determined that they should not be punished, and more than a thousand men, under arms, guarded the court room to keep away Mormons who might sit on the jury or bear testimony. The accused were all acquitted. One of the accused was Judge Thomas C. Sharp, editor of the *Warsaw Signal*. Many years later he spoke to Kate Field, the journalist, when she visited him. "They say I helped to kill Joe Smith," said the judge, laughingly. "Did you?" asked Miss Field. "Well, the jury said not," and then the good old judge laughed louder.

VII

When Joseph Smith's body fell from the window ledge to the ground outside Carthage jail on that sultry afternoon in June, 1844, Brigham Young was in the railway station at Boston, waiting for the train to Salem. His journal, which was written some time after the event, has this entry: "In the evening, while sitting in the depot waiting, I felt a heavy depression of Spirit, and so melancholy I could not converse, with any degree of pleasure. Not knowing anything concerning the tragedy enacting at this time in Carthage jail, I could not assign my reasons for my peculiar feelings." Parley P. Pratt, who at the same moment was on a canal boat near Utica, on his way to Nauvoo, experienced peculiar feelings too, he wrote later. He and his brother William were talking on deck, when, suddenly, "a strange and solemn awe came over me, as if the powers of hell were let loose. I was so overwhelmed with sorrow I could hardly speak; and after pacing the deck for some time in silence, I turned to my brother William and exclaimed—'Brother William, this is a dark hour; the powers of darkness seem to triumph, and the spirit of murder is abroad in the land; and it controls the hearts of the American people, and a vast majority of them sanction the killing of the innocent. My brother, let us keep silence and not open our mouths. If you have any pamphlets or books on the fullness of the gospel lock them up; show them not, neither open your mouth to the people; let us observe an entire and solemn silence, for this is a dark day, and the hour of triumph for the powers of darkness. O, how sensible I am of the spirit of murder which seems to pervade the whole land.' " This was said, Parley Pratt wrote in his autobiography, at the same hour, "as nearly as I can judge," as the assassination of the Smiths. Brother William did not write an autobiography.

Almost two weeks after Joseph Smith was killed, Brigham Young first heard the news, and he hurried to Nauvoo with the others of the Apostles whom he could gather on the way. He met Orson Pratt, Orson Hyde, and Wilford Woodruff at Albany and traveled the rest of the journey with them. It would be of great value to know their conversation as they sat impatiently in the railroad cars that were taking them back to a community without a leader, which, when they left it, had been a city with a king. Brigham Young wrote that the first thing he thought of upon hearing of the death of the Prophet was, who now had the keys of the kingdom: "The first thing that I thought of was whether Joseph had taken the keys of the kingdom with him from the earth. Brother Orson Pratt sat on my left; we were both leaning back on our chairs. Bringing my hand down on my knee, I said, 'The keys of the kingdom are right here with the church.' " Perhaps Brigham Young meant to imply by that gesture that the keys of the kingdom were right there in his pocket; but, be that as it may, he soon decided that if they were not there, he was going to pick the lock.

While Joseph Smith was being assassinated, Sidney Rigdon was in Pittsburgh. During the last two years of his life Joseph Smith and Sidney Rigdon had not been in agreement, and upon one occasion the Prophet accused Rigdon at a Sunday meeting before the people of conspiring to betray him to the Missourians. Several attempts were made by Smith to "disfellowship" Sidney Rigdon, but by the clever use of sentimental oratorical appeals, reminiscent of the good old days when he and Smith suffered together, Rigdon had always been able to move the general conference of the people, and they would not vote to disfellowship him. Once, when the people had failed to approve the Prophet's desire to get rid of Rigdon, Joseph Smith said to them: "I have thrown him off my shoulders, and you have again put him on me. You may carry him, but I will not." Rigdon had proved of great service to the Prophet. He exerted considerable influence on the theology of Mormonism, for he had enjoyed experience with several sects before he joined the Mormons. He had also influenced Joseph Smith's revelations to some extent. It was he, too, who must have supplied the Prophet with his foreign phrases and their translations, for Rigdon knew Hebrew, Latin, and Greek, and he had read considerably more English literature than any of the other Mormon leaders. During the last year at Nauvoo Sidney Rigdon was fifty-one years old, while his Prophet and superior was only thirty-eight; Sidney Rigdon was opposed to polygamy, at least so far as it concerned his own daughter, and there is no record that he had taken unto himself additional wives; the Prophet had adopted polygamy as the most important tenet of his religion, and he coveted Rigdon's daughter. It was natural that Rigdon should lose the Prophet's confidence.

As soon as he heard of Joseph Smith's death, Sidney Rigdon hurried back to Nauvoo. He arrived there on August 3, 1844, almost a week before Brigham Young, and he set about with unseemly haste to capture the control of the headless church. He urged that a conference of the people be called at once, and he was very anxious that his succession to the leadership should be settled before Brigham Young had time to arrive in Nauvoo. He told the people that he had been appointed by heaven to be their guardian, and he received several appropriate visions to corroborate the appointment. He finally succeeded in arranging a conference of the people for August 8. The conference was first set for August 6, but it was postponed, and it was this delay which was fatal to Sidney Rigdon's plans, for Brigham Young and the Apostles reached Nauvoo at 8 o'clock in the evening of August 6. If the conference had taken place that day, Sidney Rigdon would have been by virtue of his oratory president of the Church, and Brigham Young would have been in the strategically disadvantageous position of the leader of a schism.

At 10 o'clock in the morning on August 8 the people met in the large open-air grove overlooking the Mississippi River. It was a windy day, and there was difficulty in hearing the speakers. Sidney Rigdon arose in a waggon placed so that he spoke with the wind. He was nervous and embarrassed, for the unexpected return of the Apostles had disconcerted him. For an hour and a half he spoke, but his oratory was not up to his usual standard, and the people showed evident signs of restlessness. Meanwhile, Brigham Young had quietly taken a seat in the regular speaker's stand, which placed him with the backs of the people towards him. As soon as Rigdon's last words had fallen, Brigham Young arose and addressed the people. They had not expected to hear his voice; many of them did not know that he was in Nauvoo; and several thousand backs were suddenly turned towards Sidney Rigdon, and with pleased wonder the people faced Brigham Young. The effect was magnetic. An observer wrote: "If Joseph had risen from the dead and again spoken in their hearing the effect could hardly have been more startling. It seemed to be the voice of Joseph himself; and not only that: but it seemed in the eyes of the people as though it was the very person of Joseph which stood before them." Many wrote later that the scene reminded them of that transformation in the Bible, when the mantle of Elijah fell upon Elisha. The voice, some said, *was* the voice of Joseph. "If I had not seen him with my own eyes," wrote Wilford Woodruff, "there is no one that could have convinced me that it was not Joseph Smith; and any one can testify to this who was acquainted with these two men." Orson Hyde said in a sermon many years later:

"I know that when President Young returned with the Twelve to Nauvoo, he gathered them around him, and said he, 'I want you to disperse among the congregation and feel the pulse of the people, while I go upon the stand and speak.'

"We went among the congregation, and President Young went on the stand. Well, he spoke, and his words went through me like electricity. 'Am I mistaken?' said I, 'or is it really the voice of Joseph Smith?' This is my testimony; it was not only the voice of Joseph, but there were the features, the gestures and even the *stature* of Joseph before us in the person of Brigham. And though it may be said that President Young is a complete *mimic,* and can mimic anybody, I would like to see the man who can mimic another *in stature,* who was about *four or five inches higher than himself.* Every one in the congregation—every one who was inspired by the Spirit of the Lord—felt it. They knew it. They realized it." [40]

Eliza Snow commemorated the extraordinary scene in this verse:

"Brigham Young, the Lord's anointed,
　　Loved of heav'n and fear'd of hell;
Like Elijah's on Elisha,
　　Joseph's mantle on him fell."

[40] *Journal of Discourses,* vol. 13, p. 181.

Brigham Young first told the people that he was astonished that instead of mourning the death of their great leader, he found them holding meetings to choose his successor. He himself, he said, would rather sit in sackcloth and ashes for a month than appear before the people, but he pitied their loneliness and felt constrained to step forward. He pointed out that there was a regular, ordained body whose duty it was to obtain the will of the Lord on such questions, and he wondered that the people had not delegated this question of the succession to the quorums of Apostles and elders to which it belonged by virtue of their authority. He urged that the general conference of the people adjourn, and that a meeting of the quorums be held that afternoon. The people acquiesced. By deftly reminding them of the death of their Prophet, and by the implication that they were out of order, Brigham Young made the people feel ashamed of themselves. That afternoon the quorums of the Church leaders met, and Brigham Young addressed them. He said:

"I do not care who leads this church, even though it were Ann Lee; but one thing I must know, and that is what God says about it. I have the keys and the means of obtaining the mind of God on the subject. . . . Joseph conferred upon our heads all the keys and powers belonging to the apostleship which he himself held before he was taken away, and no man or set of men can get between Joseph and the Twelve in this world or in the world to come. . . .

"You cannot fill the office of a Prophet, Seer and Revelator: God must do this. You are like children without a father and sheep without a shepherd. You must not appoint any man at our head: if you should, the Twelve must ordain him. You cannot appoint a man at our head, but if you do want any other man or men to lead you, take them and we will go our way to build up the kingdom in all the world. . . . I will tell you who your leaders or guardians will be. The Twelve—I at their head!" [41]

Brigham Young did not once mention himself as the possible head of the Church or as successor to Joseph Smith. He merely contended that the Twelve Apostles, as ordained by God through the dead Prophet, Joseph Smith, were the heads of the Church, and that no man could alter that eternal position. This position of the Twelve Apostles as immediately in line of succession to the Prophet had always been recognized. He then offered them the alternatives: Sidney Rigdon, or the Twelve Apostles. Since

[41] *The Rise and Fall of Nauvoo,* by Brigham H. Roberts, p. 330.

Brigham Young asked nothing for himself, and since Sidney Rigdon had asked in his speech that he be appointed to succeed Joseph Smith, whose first counselor he had been for many years, the contrast was fatal to Rigdon. As Brigham Young was head of the Twelve Apostles, he had nothing to lose by their succession to authority. He then asked the people to vote whether they would sustain the Twelve, and when the negative was called for only a few dared raise their hands. The meeting then adjourned until the Church conference of the following October, and the Church was in the hands of the Twelve, who were in the hands of Brigham Young.

Gradually, during the last years of the Prophet, Brigham Young had become his trusted adviser. After Young's return from his successful missionary tour of England, and after he led the people from Missouri to Illinois, he was taken into the confidence of the Prophet to a much greater extent than formerly, and he is mentioned more often than any of the other leaders in the latter part of the Prophet's journal. When the Nauvoo charter was passed, Brigham Young became one of the city councilors. There is only one instance of a disagreement between the Prophet and Brigham Young. This was over the question of the money collected by the Apostles for the Temple and the Nauvoo House. At a conference of the Church Joseph Smith urged that a rule be passed requiring the Twelve Apostles to receipt for all money they collected on their travels. Brigham Young objected to the implied reflection on his honesty and that of his associates. He asked the conference not to "muzzle the ox that treadeth out the corn." To which Joseph Smith replied, "We will make the ox tread out the corn first, and then feed him." Nothing definite was decided, but about a month later there is record of Brigham Young signing a bond of $2,000, and pledging himself by this security to deliver to Joseph Smith all money collected.

The Prophet had considered the missionary work of great importance, for he realized that in its success lay his strength and his financial welfare. He was wise, therefore, to place at its head a man of Brigham Young's practical abilities, and this decision was of great value to Brigham Young also. It not only gave him an outlet for his great administrative talent, but it also removed him from too close contact with his eccentric leader. If Brigham Young had spent all his days as the right-hand man of

BRIGHAM YOUNG IN MIDDLE AGE
From a daguerreotype, 1850

the Prophet at Nauvoo, sooner or later there would have been a conflict, for their personalities differed too much. Brigham Young was practical, efficient, and loved order; Joseph Smith was more fond of words and parades than work and plans. Although Brigham Young was in many respects naïve, there must have been things about Joseph Smith which he doubted were divine. There are no definite hints in his sermons or his conversation of these doubts, but his personality was such that if he was ever deluded, he deluded himself. In Mormonism Brigham Young discovered an opportunity for himself to rise to the position of a leader of men, which his practical abilities led him to suppose to be his natural right. Once he had joined the religion, he accepted its doctrines and dogmas unqualifiedly. The question of other world salvation was not one on which he had ever had any very definite ideas of his own, and therefore he could with ease and with sincerity accept what another man formulated for him concerning the other world, if that was in accord with his very definite ideas concerning this one. Very often during the first ten years of his association with the Mormon Church Brigham Young must have felt that his opportunity for preëminence would never come, but the only alternative to his position of pleasant and influential subordination to Joseph Smith was a return to the struggles of an itinerant painter, glazier, and carpenter. So far as the religion itself was concerned, Brigham Young had undoubtedly succeeded in convincing himself while he was so busy persuading others, and after the assassination of Smith he was too busy with executive affairs and the task of preserving the lives of his people to worry much about his soul. His religion now became so involved in his everyday life that it became impossible to abandon the one without ruining the other completely. Brigham Young literally lived his religion, as he so often begged his people to do, and it was a religion easy for him to live, because, according to its precepts, God took a hand in every phase of practical life, and, strangely enough, seemed to command what His people wanted most to do.

Brigham Young's first problem as head of the Church was the security of his own position and the necessary dispersal of his rivals. Of these Sidney Rigdon was the first. Rigdon had a few friends, whom he had convinced that Brigham Young, in spite of his high-sounding words about wishing nothing for himself, had stolen the leadership of the Church. Secretly, Rigdon began to organize a schism, and he told his few followers that he had received a vision in which God ordered him to lead the Church to Pittsburgh, the new Promised Land, which also happened to be Sidney Rigdon's home town. He made extravagant speeches, in one of which he predicted that the time would come when he would be so powerful that: "I will cross the Atlantic, encounter the Queen's forces, and overcome them—plant the American standard on English ground, and then march to the palace of Her Majesty, and demand a portion of her riches and dominions, which if she refuse, I will take the little madam by the nose, and lead her out, and she shall have no power to help herself. If I do not do this, the Lord never spake by mortal." Rigdon did not ordain his followers mere prophets or priests, but kings. He began his secret propaganda in Nauvoo on Monday, September 2, 1844, and on Tuesday, September 3, Brigham Young knew all about it. Tuesday night Brigham Young called on Sidney Rigdon and tried to persuade him to repent, but he refused, and a few days later he was excommunicated by the Twelve Apostles, an act which the people later approved in special conference. By the united voice of the whole Church Sidney Rigdon was "delivered over to the buffetings of Satan," until such time as he might repent and humble himself before God and his brethren.

In a speech against Sidney Rigdon, Orson Hyde compared him to a young man who has paid his respects to a young lady, and "has got the mitten," and who then, in order to cover his own shame and disgrace impugns the virtue of the young lady. "We preferred his room to his company," said Orson Hyde. "This plain talk made him angry: 'Now,' said he, 'I will tell all your wickedness, your secret abominable acts—your midnight doings— for you are the worst, the most abominably corrupt people on the earth. You are not fit to live.' Well, well, Sidney; fall down, and like Judas let your bowels burst out; and let the world see how much filth you had in you."

A short time after his excommunication Sidney Rigdon left with his followers for Pittsburgh, where he established a Mormon church of his own and published a newspaper advocating his cause, but before long his church fell into decay and his newspaper was discontinued. Sidney Rigdon himself lived for many years in obscurity, and he did not prosper. Efforts were made

THE LAND OF EGYPT

to persuade Rigdon to admit that the Book of Mormon was founded on the Spalding manuscript, but he always denied that charge.

Other dissenters from the leadership of Brigham Young were members of Joseph Smith's family. The Prophet's mother claimed that she had visions in the course of which she was told that William Smith, Joseph's wayward brother, should be the new prophet. William Smith claimed only that he was president *pro tempore* of the Church, holding that office in trust for young Joseph Smith, the eldest son of the Prophet by his first wife, Emma. This young man, however, was not anxious to go into his father's business. According to his autobiographical sketch, he tried keeping a store, worked as a railroad contractor, studied law, practised farming, and served as a justice of the peace, but he found difficulty making a living at any of these occupations, and finally, in February, 1860, he took his place at the head of the church which had organized many years before to maintain his right of succession. This church, the Reorganized Church of Jesus Christ of Latter-day Saints, is still in existence, with more than fifty thousand members, and its main difference from the Utah Mormons, as we have noted, is the belief that Joseph Smith never preached or practised polygamy.

Emma Smith, the Prophet's widow, refused to acknowledge the ascendancy of Brigham Young, and she openly stated that she had never for a moment believed the "apparitions and visions" of her late lamented husband. Two and a half years after the death of the Prophet she married L. C. Bidamon, with whom she kept a tavern in Nauvoo.

Another branch of the Mormon Church was started after the death of Joseph Smith. This schism was headed by James Jesse Strang, one of the most picturesque characters associated with Mormonism. Strang was born on a farm in Scipio, New York. He was educated at Fredonia Academy, Hanover, New York, and was more learned than most of the Mormon leaders. He once began an autobiography, which it is a pity he did not finish, for, if we can judge from the fragment which is preserved, it would have been an extraordinary human document. Writing of his childhood, Strang said: "I learn from many sources that in childhood I exhibited extraordinary mental imbecility. Indeed, if I may credit what is told me on the subject, all who knew me, except my parents, thought me scarcely more than idiotic." He started his autobiography with that frank statement, and he added: "Long weary days I sat upon the floor, thinking, thinking, thinking! occasionally asking a strange, uninfantile question and never getting an answer. My mind wandered over fields that old men shrink from, seeking rest and finding none till darkness gathered thick around and I burst into tears and cried aloud, and with a voice scarcely able to articulate told my mother that my head ached." [42]

While he was working on his father's farm, Strang studied law and was admitted to the bar. He wandered from town to town, changing his occupation almost as often as his abode. He taught a country school, edited a newspaper, and became a temperance lecturer. Finally he settled in Wisconsin with his wife's brother and practised law at Burlington. A judge before whom he appeared, William P. Lyon, said of Strang that he was interested mainly in unusual points of law and cases of quaint interest. Once he brought suit for a client to recover the value of honey stolen by his neighbor's thievish bees, and Strang made an eloquent charge against the bees, for he was above all an orator. "I think," said Judge Lyon, "he liked the notoriety that resulted from that sort of thing."

Mormon missionaries visited Burlington, Wisconsin, about one year after Strang settled there, and their arguments appealed to his temperament. He immediately threw all his energy and oratorical ability into the Mormon movement. In January of 1844 he was baptized, and Joseph Smith liked him so much that in February he gave him authority to establish a stake of Zion in Wisconsin. Strang, inspired by the success of Joseph Smith, who was then at his zenith, planned great things for himself, and he worked hard to make his small stake of Zion populous. When Joseph and his brother were assassinated, Strang hurried to Nauvoo and exhibited a letter which he claimed the Prophet had written to him, by which he was appointed successor to Joseph Smith's spiritual and temporal powers as head of the Church. The postmark on Strang's letter was black, and Brigham Young's followers pointed out that all letters left the Nauvoo post office with a red post mark. But when Strang attempted to verify the dispatch of his letter by reference to the Nauvoo post office register, the register strangely disappeared. Strang was excommunicated and delivered over to "the buffetings of Satan."

[42] *Michigan Historical Society Collections,* 1903, pp. 203-204.

Angry at his lack of success, Strang returned to Voree, Wisconsin, where he set up an independent Mormon kingdom. He imitated the late Prophet's methods by receiving revelations regularly from God, by means of which he silenced all objections to his powers and policies. He even capped the parallel by discovering some buried plates, from which he translated *The Book of the Law of the Lord*. Strang realized early what Joseph Smith did not realize until it was too late, that if he was not to be molested by persecution, he must take his followers to an isolated spot. Accordingly, he chose Beaver Island, far away in Lake Michigan. There was plenty of timber on the island, and the waters teemed with fish; he was cut off from neighbors, but he could always get to large towns by steamer. With four men Strang started for Beaver Island, and they explored the place. Slowly his followers increased to sixty-two, only seventeen of them men, for polygamy was also practised under Strang's leadership. Twelve Apostles were sent out into the world to make converts, while Strang and his followers spent their time building a schooner, a steam sawmill, and printing *The Book of the Law of the Lord* at the royal press, for Strang had decided to call himself king, and he was respectfully addressed by his followers as King Strang. The harbor of Beaver Island was named St. James, after Strang, and nearby a river was called Jordan, while a hill in the interior was named Mount Pisgah. The Jordan discharged its waters into the Sea of Galilee.

By 1850 Strang's community had increased slightly, and he was ready to be crowned King Strang. The 8th of July, 1850, was Coronation Day. The ceremony, according to Mrs. Cecilia Hill, who was an eyewitness, took place in a log tabernacle. Strang was dressed in a bright red robe, and was followed in regal procession by his councilors and his Twelve Apostles. George A. Adams, who was six feet tall, and who had been an actor of heavy parts in Boston, crowned James Jesse Strang, King Strang. Adams later testified that he was called upon to play the part of the Apostle Paul, and he reluctantly admitted in court that when he played the Apostle Paul, he used the costume he had formerly worn in Boston as Richard III. The King's red robe was also one of Adams's former Shakespearean costumes. As the Apostle Paul, Adams placed a circlet, with a cluster of stars in front, on Strang's red hair. The King was small and heavy; he wore a red beard, and his dark eyes were set close under wide brows and a huge forehead. Every July 8 was thereafter kept as a holiday, and for the occasion each family was commanded to bring the King a fowl, and the burnt offering of a heifer was made at the expense of the community. King Strang soon began to hand down dictatorial mandates. He prohibited the use of intoxicants and tobacco, coffee and tea. He required his subjects to pay tithes. Gambling was prohibited. The women were required to wear bloomers. Neighbors on adjacent islands, mainly fishermen, began to resent Strang's powers and habits, and they planned concerted action against him, but before they could carry out their plans, an important quarrel arose within the community. Thomas Bedford and Alexander Wentworth had been publicly whipped by command of the King because they had upheld their wives' refusal to wear bloomers. This was in June, 1856. The *Michigan,* a United States ship, was anchored in the port of St. James, and King Strang had been invited to go abroad. As he was stepping onto the pier, Bedford and Wentworth shot him in the back and beat him over the head and face with their weapons. Then they ran aboard the *Michigan* and were taken to Mackinac, where they were welcomed as heroes and never brought to trial. For several days King Strang lay dying, and he gave last instructions to his followers for the government of the kingdom. He asked that his body be removed to Voree, Wisconsin, and he died there on July 9, 1856, and was buried in an unmarked grave.

Soon after Strang's death the Gentiles invaded Beaver Island, burned the Mormon houses, and destroyed the printing press which had published a newspaper and *The Book of the Law of the Lord*.[43] An example of the literary quality of the *Gospel Herald,* which Strang published at Voree, Wisconsin, is the following verse from the issue of Thursday, November 25, 1847:

"CHEWING TOBACCO IN THE HOUSE OF GOD

"A word I would drop to the Church-going folk
Of country and town, and not in a joke.
Now chewing tobacco and spitting the juice
In the House of the Lord, can find no excuse;

---

[43] In the destruction of the Royal Press at Beaver Island and the burning of the houses, most of Strang's works were destroyed. His pamphlets and the few remaining copies of *The Book of the Law of the Lord* are excessively rare and form one of the valuable items of Americana.

But want of politeness, or rather of grace,
Or want of respect for the hallowed place:
Yet here it is practiced by A, B, and C,
And there it is followed by E, F, and G,
You never need ask where these gentry sit,
Just look on the wall and you'll see by the spit;
In dark filthy puddles it spreads on the floor,
From the pulpit all round each way to the door.
The scene is disgusting! and how must you feel
If, in such a place, you're expected to kneel?
Yet often it happens these men are so good,
They bend on their knees while others have stood.
This done, they return to their labor again,
Still chewing their quid and spreading the stain.
A scandal to men!—a scandal to grace!
Here decency blushes and covers her face!
Do throw out your *chew* ere you enter the door,
And never so rudely behave any more;
But down with your cash for the sand and the soap,
And the horrible job of cleaning all up."

King Strang was the author, besides his religious publications, of a report on *The Natural History of Beaver Island,* published by the Smithsonian Institution.

After his death the Mormons of Strang's community scattered to neighboring islands and to other parts of the United States. Strang's life, like Joseph Smith's, had ended in assassination, and this was taken by many of his followers as an indication that he was the rightful successor. When Strang wrote to John Taylor and Orson Hyde, challenging the orthodox followers of Brigham Young to discuss publicly Strang's authority, they replied: "Sir—After Lucifer was cut off and thrust down to hell, we have no knowledge that God condescended to investigate the subject or right of authority with him. Your case has been disposed of by the authorities of the Church. Being satisfied with our own power and calling, we have no disposition to ask from whence yours came." The followers of Brigham Young regarded Strang's fatal end as only another instance of the divine truth of their new leader's prophetic utterance, for soon after the death of Joseph Smith, Brigham Young said: "All that want to draw away a party from The Church after them, let them do it if they can, but they will not prosper."

VIII

In spite of these few schisms, Brigham Young was able to keep the main body of the Mormon Church faithful to his leadership. Other and more important difficulties, however, soon beset him, for the mob that had murdered Smith discovered that the death of the Prophet would not affect the growth of his community and its consequent political and economic power. Appeals urging the expulsion of the Mormons from Illinois appeared regularly in the newspapers, and the Madison *Express* reported the prevailing sentiment of Hancock County to be that, "Every Saint, mongrel or whole-blood, and every thing that looked like a Saint, talked or acted like a Saint, should be compelled to leave." It was contended specifically that the Mormon leaders were counterfeiters, and that their followers were chronic thieves. At Lima, Illinois, a mob assembled and warned the Mormons to leave town. They refused, and the mob burned down 175 houses and forced the inhabitants to flee to Nauvoo for shelter. Murders were committed on both sides in the course of riots and individual quarrels, for the Mormons did not believe in non-resistance.

One method of protection which the Mormons adopted was akin to non-resistance, but it embodied visible warning of danger. The boys of Nauvoo all carried large bowie knives, and when a man came to town who was regarded by the authorities as a suspicious character, the boys were sent to visit him. They took out their large knives and began whittling pine shingles, accompanying their action with quiet, but suggestive, whistling. Frequently, they followed the undesirable stranger wherever he went, and sometimes their knives came close to his body. When he objected, they pretended neither to hear nor to see. Eventually, the victim would make his way to the ferry, accompanied by a crowd of boys whittling and whistling, but saying nothing. When one of the men who had voted for the repeal of the Nauvoo charter, which was repealed by the legislature at this time, complained to Brigham Young that a crowd of whittling boys followed him everywhere, and that his life was in danger, Brigham Young replied: "I am very sorry you are imposed upon by the people: we used to have laws here, but you have taken them away from us: we have no law to protect you. 'Your cause is just,

NAUVOO TEMPLE

KIRTLAND TEMPLE

but we can do nothing for you.' Boys, don't frighten him, *don't*." It was Brigham Young's policy, however, to avoid open conflict between his people and their enemies, for he wished to demonstrate to the rest of the country that the Mormons were persecuted without provocation. Finally, however, after the burning of many houses, and after some people were murdered, he and his associates realized that it was both useless and dangerous to remain in Illinois. They agreed to remove all Mormons from Nauvoo by the spring of 1846. An armed force was stationed in Nauvoo during the preparations for the removal.

During the winter of 1846-1847 almost every house in Nauvoo was turned into a workshop, and property of all kinds was exchanged for waggons and animals. Meanwhile, frantic efforts were made to finish the Nauvoo Temple, for God had commanded that it be built. For years money had been collected for this Temple, and the Mormons estimated its cost at $600,000. They also maintained that the construction and divine design of the Temple exhibited "more wealth, more art, more science, more revelation, more splendor, and more God, than all the rest of the world." Many Gentiles marveled that the Mormons continued to expend money and effort on a structure they were about to abandon, but the completion of the Temple was a wise move on Brigham Young's part. God had decreed that a house be built for Him in Nauvoo, and Brigham Young argued that it was up to the Saints to build Him one, no matter what had happened between the time of the revelation and the time for its execution. If this revelation had been left unfulfilled, it would always have been a source of skeptical inquiry upon the part of earnest Saints. Revelation was the foundation of the Mormon religion, and Brigham Young was always careful to carry out prophecies whenever it was humanly possible to do so. He also felt that a completed building would be possible to sell, while a half-finished building was only fit to be abandoned. The following advertisement appeared in the *Nauvoo New Citizen* soon after the departure of the Mormons:

"TEMPLE FOR SALE

"The undersigned Trustees of the Latter Day Saints propose to sell the Temple on very low terms, if an early application is made.

The Temple is admirably designed for Literary or Religious purposes. Address the undersigned Trustees.

"Nauvoo, May 15, 1846.

"ALMON W. BABBITT,
"JOSEPH L. HEYWOOD,
"JOHN S. FULMER."

The Temple was examined and admired by members of several Catholic organizations, but there were no purchasers. Perhaps this was due somewhat to the architectural method employed in its construction. Joseph Smith had insisted that God was its designer, and that He revealed His plans daily in the course of construction. Governor Ford found the building a symbol of the Mormon theology, "a piece of patch-work, variable, strange and incongruous." As soon as the Nauvoo Temple was practically completed in October, 1845, Brigham Young and Parley Pratt worked day and night giving people their promised endowments for eternity, which could only be done in the Temple. In two months more than 1,000 Mormons "received the ordinances."

Early in the spring of 1846 some of the Mormons were ready to leave Nauvoo. Their removal was expedited by several indictments brought against Brigham Young and the Twelve Apostles on charges of counterfeiting. The Twelve Apostles, with about 2,000 followers, crossed the Mississippi River early in February, before the ice had broken. It was thought by the leaders that if the Mormons showed signs of their sincerity by starting west with 2,000 of their people, the anti-Mormons would be satisfied to allow the rest to remain in Nauvoo until such time as they could leave with convenience. But this was an error. Posses of citizens of Hancock County were organized for the purpose of removing the Mormons by force. The leader of the anti-Mormon party was the Rev. Thomas S. Brockman, whom Governor Ford described as "a large, awkward, uncouth, ignorant, semi-barbarian, ambitious of office, and bent upon acquiring notoriety. . . . To the bitterness of his religious prejudices against the Mormons, he added a hatred of their immoral practices, probably because they differed from his own." Brockman had eight hundred men under his leadership, and he led them in an attack on the Mormons for the purpose of removing them from Nauvoo immediately. Those Mormons who were left in Nauvoo raised a company of one hundred and fifty men, threw up breastworks, and firing began on both sides; but its animosity was greater than its accuracy, for little damage was done. The anti-Mormons exhausted their ammunition and retreated. In a few days they returned with more cannon balls,. and the firing was resumed. This time one Gentile and three Mormons were killed, and a few men were wounded on both sides, and to accomplish this result between seven hundred and nine hundred cannon balls were fired and many more rifle bullets. Both sides kept very far apart. Finally, at the suggestion of some of the more moderate of the Gentiles, it was agreed that the Mormons should give up their arms and remove from the state immediately. They were allowed two hours to pack up and evacuate Nauvoo. This battle occurred in September, 1846, when the Church leaders and their 2,000 followers were en route to the West.

The mob parodied with crude cruelty the rite of Mormon baptism. In a letter to Franklin Richards, Elder Thomas Bullock described this scene: "They seized Charles Lambert, led him into the river, and, in the midst of cursing and swearing, one man said—'By the Holy Saints I baptize you, by order of the commanders of the temple,' (plunged him backwards) and then said—'the commandments must be fulfilled, and God damn you, you must have another dip' (then threw him on his face), then sent him on the flatboat across the river, with the promise that, if he returned to Nauvoo, they would shoot him."

When the anti-Mormon mob entered Nauvoo, they found a literally deserted city, lying as if in a doze from the summer heat. There were no sounds except those made by the rolling Mississippi and by the birds in the trees. Workshops and smithies were empty of men, but filled with fresh shavings and coals. No dogs barked, and inside the empty houses were white ashes lying in the fireplaces. Col. Thomas L. Kane, who visited Nauvoo three days after the last Mormons had left, said that he felt it necessary to tread on tiptoe, "as if walking down the aisle of a country church, to avoid rousing irreverent echoes from the naked floors."

About two years after the Mormons left Nauvoo, Étienne Cabet, the French communist, took over the city for his Icarian communistic society. He purchased the abandoned Temple. On November 10, 1848, an incendiary set fire to the Temple, and the tower was destroyed. Two years later a tornado blew down the north wall, and the rest of the building was later removed.

The Icarians did not prosper, and they eventually left Nauvoo. It was a source of satisfaction to the Mormons that no community was able to raise the city to its former level of prosperity, and they profess to see in this an omen of the hand of God.

The Mormons were reluctant to leave the successful city they had established and the rich farms they had cleared. Their attitude and that of their enemies was aptly expressed in a sermon many years later by George A. Smith:

"We were quite willing to go, for the best of all reasons, we could not stay. There was no chance under the heavens for us to stay, and be protected, in any State in the Union; and I suppose some of them felt as the pious old Quaker did when he was on board a vessel which was attacked by pirates—he was too pious to fight, it was against his conscience, but when one of the pirates started to climb a rope and get upon the vessel, the old Quaker picked up a hatchet and said, 'Friend, if thee wants that piece of rope, thee can have it and welcome,' and immediately cut the rope and let him drop into the sea, where he was drowned. So our enemies thought they would let us go into the heart of the Great American Desert and starve, as they compelled us to leave every thing that would make life desirable."

Where the Mormons were going was a problem that Brigham Young had not solved. He and his followers always have said that God knew all the time, but if this was so, God did not see fit to tell the Mormons their ultimate destination. Before his death Joseph Smith had planned to remove the Church to the Rocky Mountains, and for this purpose he selected an advance exploring party. He sent Orson Hyde and Parley P. Pratt to Washington with a petition asking for the right to settle in Oregon, and asking also for an armed escort of 100,000 soldiers. Meanwhile, the mob became active, and there was no time to send out the exploring party. While they were in Washington, Pratt and Hyde received from Stephen A. Douglas a copy of Colonel Frémont's report of his explorations in the West, and this proved useful to Brigham Young. When Henry Clay had suggested a few years before that Joseph Smith transport his people to Oregon, Smith had replied with this invective:

". . . the renowned Secretary of State, the ignoble duellist, the gambling Senator, and Whig candidate for the Presidency, *Henry Clay:* the wise Kentucky lawyer, advises the Latter-day Saints to go

EXPULSION OF THE MORMONS FROM NAUVOO
From a contemporary engraving

JOSEPH SMITH AT THE HEAD OF THE NAUVOO LEGION
From a contemporary engraving

to Oregon to obtain justice and set up a government of their own; O ye crowned heads among all nations, is not Mr. Clay a wise man, and very patriotic! why Great God! to transport 200,000 people through a vast prairie; over the Rocky Mountains, to Oregon, a distance of nearly 2,000 miles, would cost more than *four millions!* or should they go by Cape Horn, in ships to California, the cost would be more than *twenty millions!* and all this to save the United States from inheriting the disgrace of Missouri, for murdering and robbing the saints with impunity!" [44]

In the passion of the controversial moment the Prophet, his church historians admit, made a slight error. There were not 200,000 Saints in all the world, and the population of Nauvoo to be transported over the Rocky Mountains did not reach 15,000, according to the highest Mormon estimates. The fact that this could be done was proved by Brigham Young, as we shall now see.

[44] *The Voice of Truth*, p. 58.

Chapter V

EXODUS

I

When he was asked by Senator Overman whether he thought the laws of God superior to the laws of man, Senator Reed Smoot answered, cautiously, that he considered the laws of God superior upon the conscience of man. When Senator Overman pressed the point, Mr. Smoot, who was fighting for his seat in the Senate, added that if the law of God conflicted with the law of the country in which he lived, "I would go to some other country where it would not conflict." That essentially was the Mormon attitude from the beginning of Mormon history, and when their country thought their God was wrong, the Mormons moved from one unpopulated region to another. Finally, in 1846 they began their trek to the West, which they believed to be inhabited by God, whose laws they considered themselves chosen to administer, and by the Indians, who had no laws with which they could come into conflict. Just where in the West they were going, the Mormons did not know, but Oregon and California were in the mind of Brigham Young. He knew that he wanted to take his people beyond the jurisdiction of the United States, and when he left Nauvoo, California was a part of Mexico, and Oregon was a subject of dispute between the United States and Great Britain. As we have seen, the alternatives were a Mormon exodus or a Mormon massacre, and Brigham Young once expressed tersely the whole purpose of the migration of his people: "To get away from Christians."

At eleven o'clock on the morning of February 15, 1846, Brigham Young crossed the Mississippi River and camped with his 2,000 Saints on Sugar Creek. Snow still covered the ground, and the river was still frozen hard. The temperature was twenty degrees below zero. Nine babies were born in the camp of freezing, shivering people. One of them was born in a hut by the side of the road, where some women held dishes over the mother to prevent the heavy rain from soaking her and her new child while she was giving birth to it.

While Brigham Young was encamped on Sugar Creek with his two thousand followers, a letter arrived from Elder Samuel Brannan, the Mormon representative in New York. He wrote that a syndicate of gentlemen in New York, including Amos Kendall, formerly postmaster-general of the United States, and A. G. Benson, had convinced him that the United States government had the right to disarm the Mormons and prevent them from moving into the West. These men assured Brannan that this would happen, unless political influence was used in Washington, and they offered to exercise the necessary influence if the Mormons would agree in writing to assign every alternate lot of land in the new home they chose to the syndicate of gentlemen in New York. The President of the United States, Mr. Polk, they said, was a member of their syndicate, "though his name was not to be used in the matter." Elder Brannan had signed the agreement with the syndicate, which he forwarded to Brigham Young for his approval. In his letter urging this approval Brannan wrote: "I am aware it is a covenant with death, but we know that God is able to break it, and will do it. The Children of Israel, in their escape from Egypt, had to make covenants for their safety, and leave it for God to break them; and the Prophet has said, 'As it was then, so shall it be in the last days.' And I have been led by a remarkable train of circumstances to say, amen; and I feel and hope you will do the same." But Brigham Young refused to be intimidated, and he did not depend upon God to break the covenant, but simply ignored it himself.

For two weeks the Mormons remained in the camp on Sugar Creek, building and repairing waggons, and gathering together sufficient provisions by working for Iowa farmers. On March 1 the camp was broken up, and the whole party moved forward five miles. Mud was deep in the roads, and during the first days of the journey the Mormons exchanged their horses for oxen whenever possible. Even with oxen, however, the progress was pitifully and distressingly slow, and during the first month of travel they never made more than six miles each day. The camps lived, meanwhile, on wild turkeys, prairie hens, and deer brought in by the hunters of the party.

During April it rained every day, and besides the ordinary

discomforts of rain in an open camp, it also subjected the emigrants to floods, swollen streams, and high rivers, which were
impossible to cross until they had subsided. There were long,
miserable delays in rain-swept camps, with nothing to do but
wait and try to keep dry. During the rain the cold continued
and froze the mud fast around the waggons at night, so that each
morning it required considerable effort to pull them out of frozen
ruts. Orson Pratt wrote in his journal for April 9: "With great
exertion a part of the camp were enabled to get about six miles,
while others were stuck fast in the deep mud. We encamped
at a point of timber about sunset, after being drenched several
hours in rain. The mud and water in and around our tents were
ankle deep, and the rain still continued to pour down without
cessation. We were obliged to cut brush and limbs of trees, and
throw them upon the ground in our tents, to keep our beds from
sinking in the mire." The rain made it almost impossible to
keep camp fires lighted. Twice the roads were so bad that the
people had to remain in camp for two weeks without fires. At
other times they were only able to travel one mile during the
day.

The nights were so cold that grass could not grow, and the
teams of oxen and horses had to live on bark and the limbs
of trees. The animals became so weak from lack of fodder that
progress was even slower. Then rattlesnakes became common,
and many of the animals were poisoned.

The Mormons, however, maintained their faith that God was
looking after them. Those who had been ruthlessly expelled from
Nauvoo by the mob after the departure of Brigham Young and
the first party, were now encamped on Sugar Creek and were suffering from lack of food. Suddenly, flocks of quail came across
the sky and settled near their tents, waiting docilely for the hungry Mormons to capture and eat them. The people praised God
and ate the quail. When Brigham Young heard of this miracle,
he exclaimed in his journal: "Tell this to the nations of the
earth! Tell it to the kings and nobles and great ones." In the
distress of their circumstances the Mormons forgot that quail
were common in the neighborhood and had been seen to settle
peacefully at that season in other years.

In Brigham Young's party, which was progressing slowly
through Iowa, another miracle was performed. A horse became
violently ill, and one of the brethren decided to cure him by the

laying on of hands. Some doubted if this were proper, but the owner of the horse quoted the words of the Prophet Koel, "that in the last days the Lord would pour out His spirit on all flesh." This quotation satisfied the orthodox, and six of the brethren laid hands on the horse and prayed for his instant recovery. "The horse," wrote the author of *The Historical Record*, "immediately rolled over twice, sprang to his feet, and was soon well."

The worries of Brigham Young, as responsible leader of this band of misery, were great, and George Q. Cannon reported that by May, 1846, Brigham Young's coat, which in Nauvoo he found difficulty in buttoning, "lapped over twelve inches." Brigham Young himself remarked in a public meeting that he could scarcely keep from lying down and awaiting the resurrection. Besides the constant difficulty of finding food for his people, he was worried by the impatience of those who wished to travel faster than their brethren, and by the despair of those who could not travel so fast. Some who became discouraged turned their waggons back east.

The journey was not entirely gloomy, however, for Brigham Young had brought along with his expedition not only apostles and priests, but also Captain Pitt's brass band. It is said that members of this band were found by a Mormon missionary in an English town, and that after they had listened to his arguments, and he had listened to their music, they took up their instruments and followed the missionary to the United States. To the music of this band, whenever the weather permitted, the people danced quadrilles, polkas, Scotch reels, and minuets, led by Brigham Young, and preceded by prayer. The waltz was banned as unseemly. A member of the party had a copy of Mme. Cottin's *Elizabeth, or The Exiles of Siberia,* which was a favorite sentimental novel of the first half of the nineteenth century. It was particularly comforting to the Mormons, because it described in florid language the sufferings of a despised people and the heroics of a virtuous maiden. The book was very popular throughout the world, but in the Mormon camp this one copy received wide circulation, for it was one of the few books besides the Bible in possession of the people. Men and women read it with delight by moonlight in their waggons and passed it on to the next waggon after they had finished. Psalms and hymns were also a source of entertainment, and the Mormons had a few songs composed by their own people. One of them went:

"In upper California, O that's the land for me—
It lies between the mountains and the great Pacific sea.
The Saints can be protected there, and enjoy their liberty
In upper California, O that's the land for me."

And another comfort was polygamy. By this time the numbers of wives had increased, in spite of the secrecy with which the divine command had to be executed. On Tuesday, May 5, 1846, William Clayton made this entry in his journal: "Went over to J. D. Lee's and learned that some of the clerks had been to the President and told him that I had ordered that they should include in their reports each wife a man has. I did not do any such thing, only requested each name should be in full according to the order of a previous council. The President said it did not matter about the names being in full but I think it will prove it does. Dr. Richards thinks as I do. The President, I understand, appeared quite angry." William Clayton was Clerk of the Camp of Israel, which was the name the Mormons gave their expedition. In the course of the day he kept a very complete journal of their travels, to which we owe credit for the most intimate details of the daily life of the Mormons during this period. In an introduction to his journal, which was published by his descendants, William Clayton is thus described: "He was methodical, always sitting in his own armchair, having a certain place at the table, and otherwise showing his love for order, which he believed the first law of heaven. His person was clean and tidy; his hands small and dimpled. He wore very little jewelry but what little he had was the best money could buy. He would not carry a watch that was not accurate, and his clothing was made from the best material." It is fortunate that such a man accompanied the expedition in a position where he could observe and record his observations, and it is also easy to understand that the omission of the full names of all the wives would prove distressful to him.

The people of Iowa, through whose towns and villages the Mormons passed, told Colonel Thomas L. Kane that they did not seem despondent, "but at the top of every hill, before they disappeared, were to be seen looking back, like banished Moors, on their abandoned homes and the far-seen temple and its glittering spire."

Brigham Young ruled every action of his people. William

Clayton had a music box and a set of china which he thought of selling to an Iowa family, but before doing so, he went to Brigham Young's waggon to ask permission. The President was busy, but Heber Kimball, his first counselor, gave Clayton permission to sell his possessions. Frequently the band was requested to play by the people of the towns and villages near which the Mormons camped. The members of the band earned money and provisions in this way. Once they played for a pail of honey and again for eight bushels of corn. At one town they earned $25 and their meals, but at another, owing to the opposition of priests, they earned only $7. Before the band played in any town, it was necessary for Clayton, who was its manager, to get the permission of Brigham Young.

In June the rain stopped, but then the mosquitoes became a distracting pest. On June 13, 1846, Clayton wrote that they were very troublesome, "there being so many of them and so bloodthirsty." Plague and fever now attacked the camp, for they were in the marshy section of the country on the east bank of the Missouri River, known as "Misery Bottom." So many of the Mormons died that it was impossible to dig graves fast enough to bury them, "and you might see women sit in the open tents keeping the flies off their dead children, sometimes after decomposition had set in." [1]

There was much grumbling upon the part of some of the people, and the usual amount of friction which results when personalities are thrown together. Clayton wrote on Sunday, June 14: "I camped here and in the evening told the men a part of what I thought of their conduct." Later he recorded: "Pelatiah Brown went swimming all the forenoon and when Corbitt asked him to help with the teams he swore he would not if Jesus Christ would ask him." Most of the grumbling was because of short rations.

In the summer the Mormons arrived near the present site of Council Bluffs, Iowa, and established themselves in winter quarters there and across the Missouri River on the present site of Florence, Nebraska. Here the band played for the Indians, who were practically the only inhabitants of the country, and pleased them so much that they raised $10.10 as a token of their appreciation.

At Winter Quarters the people built log cabins and dugouts,

[1] *The Mormons,* by Thomas L. Kane, p. 50. Col. Kane was a member of the camps for a time, although he was not a Mormon.

and planted crops, for it was the plan of Brigham Young to use this temporary location as a halfway settlement until he had succeeded in transporting all his people to their indefinite home near the Rocky Mountains. Brigham Young had intended to start for the Rocky Mountains with a small advance party in 1846, but he was detained at Winter Quarters by the necessity for superintending a settlement there. Under his direction a mill to grind their corn was built, and he also set the people to work building a council house, for it was his object to keep them as busy as possible in order to prevent dissension. They manufactured wash-boards and willow baskets, which were sold in the nearest Missouri towns. Regular religious meetings were held, and dances and parties kept the people amused. Brigham Young was delighted with the sight of what he described in his journal as "the 'Silver Greys' and spectacled dames, some nearly a hundred years old, dancing like ancient Israel." On the whole, however, life was difficult. The lack of vegetables resulted in "black-leg" scurvy; provisions were scarce, and the prospect of getting fresh supplies before the crops could grow were slight.

At the camp in Winter Quarters Brigham Young received his first, and one of his few revelations, which he issued publicly on January 14, 1846. It told the Saints to do all that Brigham Young had already urged them to do and thereby approved all that he had already done for their welfare. The revelation also promised that the Lord would stretch forth His hand and save the Mormons from hardship. Brigham Young always resisted the temptation to get revelations, which Joseph Smith never could resist; as Artemus Ward put it, "Smith used to have his little Revelation almost every day—sometimes two before dinner. Brigham Young only takes one once in a while." Early in his career as President of the Church, Brigham Young announced that Joseph Smith had left enough revelations to guide the people for twenty years, and that no new ones were required until all the old had been obeyed.

Brigham Young's business at Winter Quarters also consisted of negotiations with the Indians and the United States Indian agents for permission to remain on the Winter Quarters site, which legally belonged to the Pottawattomie Indians. The Indian superintendent of the district denied this request, and insisted that the Mormons must move on, but Colonel Kane, who had been nursed by the Mormons when he was taken ill in their camp, used his influence at Washington and obtained permission for them to remain. Brigham Young sent Big Elk, the chief of the local tribe, some presents and a letter requesting that he restrain his people from stealing Mormon cattle. Big Elk visited Brigham Young and apologized for the conduct of some of his tribe; he expressed gratitude for the presents and promised that there would be no more thefts. The Mormons did not experience any of the melodramatic Indian horrors which made the early development of the West a subject of fiction for so many years. This was due to Brigham Young's policy of catering to the wishes and respecting the rights of the skilled original inhabitants of the country. He developed their good will by his gifts and his consideration; the result was that only two horses were lost to the Indians in the original Utah pioneer party, and no men, women, or children were killed.

There was one instance of a difficulty with a half-breed Indian, recorded by the notorious Bill Hickman, who wrote a book of confessions in which he established himself as the chief gun man of Brigham Young. At Winter Quarters this half-breed had an argument with Brigham Young, and swore that he would have the President's scalp, and that he would hold a war dance over that scalp. "Brigham sent me word," wrote Hickman, "to look out for him. I found him, used him up, scalped him, and took his scalp to Brigham Young saying—'Here is the scalp of the man who was going to have a war-dance over your scalp; you may have one over his, if you wish.' He took it and thanked me very much. He said in all probability I had saved his life, and that some day he would make me a great man in the Kingdom. This was my first act of violence under the rule of Brigham Young. Soon after this, I was called upon to go for a notorious horse thief, who had sworn to take the life of Orson Hyde. I socked him away, and made my report which was very satisfactory." [2]

II

While the Saints were encamped at Winter Quarters, Captain James Allen, of the United States Army, rode into camp one day

[2] *Brigham's Destroying Angel: Being the Life, Confession, and Startling Disclosures of the Notorious Bill Hickman, The Danite Chief of Utah. Written by Himself, with explanatory notes by J. H. Beadle, Esq., of Salt Lake City*, p. 47.

towards the end of June, 1846, and had a conference with Brigham Young. Captain Allen showed Brigham Young the request of President Polk for five hundred Mormons to serve in the war against Mexico, which had just begun. Once more luck was against the Mormons. They had expected to find territory in the West which was not under the jurisdiction of the United States, and to establish there an independent theocracy. While they were en route, the United States captured all the available territory from Mexico, and the Mormons found themselves by the time they reached Utah still under the government they were endeavoring to leave behind them. However, their objections to the government of the United States were not strenuous, for their conflicts had been almost entirely with state governments and local mobs; they accepted their inevitable subordination to the United States without complaint.

In speaking of this requisition for five hundred of his followers Brigham Young said in the Tabernacle at Salt Lake City on Sunday afternoon, September 13, 1857, more than ten years after the event:

"There cannot be a more damnable, dastardly order issued than was issued by the Administration to this people while they were in an Indian country, in 1846. Before we left Nauvoo, not less than two United States senators came to receive a pledge from us that we would leave the United States, and then, while we were doing our best to leave their borders, the poor, low, degraded curses sent a requisition for five hundred of our men to go and fight their battles! That was President Polk; and he is now weltering in hell with old Zachary Taylor, where the present administrators will soon be, if they do not repent." [3]

In the heat of the moment Brigham Young intentionally falsified the circumstances, for at the time he delivered that sermon he was engaged, as we shall see, in defying all the force of the United States government. The request for five hundred Mormons to join the Mexican War was not unwelcome to the Mormons at the time and was the direct result of their own solicitation. In his letter of appointment to J. C. Little as eastern representative of the Mormon Church, Brigham Young had written on January 20, 1846: "If our Government shall offer any facilities for emigrating to the Western coast, embrace those

[3] *Journal of Discourses,* vol. 5, pp. 231-232.

facilities, if possible, as a wise and faithful man." Mr. Little called on President Polk in Washington. President Polk's diary for that day, June 3, 1846, contains this entry:

"Held a conversation with Mr. Amos Kendall & Mr. J. C. Little of Petersborough, N. H. (a mormon) to-day. They desired to see me in relation to a large body of Mormon emigrants who are now on their way from Nauvoo & other parts of the U. S. to California, and to learn the policy of the Government towards them. I told Mr. Little that by our constitution the mormons would be treated as all other American citizens were, without regard to the sect to which they belonged or the religious creed which they professed, and that I had no prejudices towards them which could induce a different course of treatment. Mr. Little said that they were Americans in all their feelings, & friends of the U. S. I told Mr. Little that we were at war with Mexico, and asked him if 500 or more of the mormons now on their way to California would be willing on their arrival in that country to volunteer and enter the U. S. army in that war, under the command of a U. S. officer. He said he had no doubt they would willingly do so. He said if the U. S. would receive them into the service he would immediately proceed and overtake the emigrants now on the way and make the arrangement with them to do so. . . . It was with the view to prevent this singular sect from becoming hostile to the U. S. that I held the conference with Mr. Little, and with the same view I am to see him again to-morrow. . . ." [4]

President Polk was particularly anxious to conciliate the Mormons at the moment because he had enough difficulties to contend with. The United States was at war with Mexico, and Great Britain was disputing the claim of the United States to Oregon. War with Great Britain was feared, and President Polk did not wish the large body of Mormons in the West to become allies of either Mexico or Great Britain. The Mormons, on their part, were anxious to get west, and the opportunity to transport five hundred men, not only at the expense of the government, but with the additional advantage of salaries en route appealed to Mr. J. C. Little, and he knew that it would appeal also to Brigham Young's practical mind. It was Little who urged President Polk to enlist the Mormons while they were en route rather than wait until they had arrived in California. At first President Polk was

[4] *The Diary of James K. Polk During His Presidency, 1845-1849,* vol. 1, pp. 445-446.

opposed to this plan because he did not wish the Mormons to be the first troops to reach California, for, as he said in his diary a few days later, the few settlers of California were already alarmed at the rumor that the Mormons were on their way. However, President Polk changed his mind and consented finally to the enlistment of Mormons. At the time Brigham Young was so grateful for the favor President Polk conferred upon his people by enlisting five hundred of them, with the understanding that they would not fight in Mexico, but would proceed to California, that the Mormons voted the Democratic ticket at the next election. It is said that the Mormons did more than this: that they voted the Democratic ticket three or four times. Brigham Young and the Mormons contended a few years later that this request for five hundred men was not only persecution, but that it was also a trap. They said that it was the plan of the federal government to exterminate the Mormons by force if they should refuse the request for five hundred men. This contention of Brigham Young's is not supported by any evidence.

Immediately after his conference with Captain James Allen Brigham Young made efforts to raise a Mormon Battalion. A mass meeting was held at which Brigham Young addressed the people. Among other things he said: "Now, I would like the brethren to enlist and make up a battalion, and go and serve your country, and if you will do this, and live your religion, I promise you in the name of Israel's God that not a man of you shall fall in battle." This was not such a rash promise as it sounds, for the understanding with the government was that the Mormon Battalion would not fight Mexicans, but would merely guard California. In his speech Brigham Young also said: "After we get through talking, we will call out the companies; and if there are not young men enough we will take the old men, and if they are not enough we will take the women. I want to say to every man, the Constitution of the United States, as formed by our fathers, was dictated, was revealed, was put into their hearts by the Almighty, who sits enthroned in the midst of the heavens; although unknown to them, it was dictated by the revelations of Jesus Christ, and I tell you, in the name of Jesus Christ, it is as good as ever I could ask for. I say unto you, magnify the laws. There is no law in the United States, or in the Constitution, but I am ready to make honorable." Then an old American flag was hurriedly brought out of the storehouse of things rescued from the mob at Nauvoo, hoisted to the top of a tree mast, and in three days the Mormon Battalion was mustered and ready to march. Brigham Young ordered the men "to take their Bibles and Books of Mormon, and if they had any playing cards to burn them." The thing that interested Brigham Young very much about this enlistment was the allowance the United States made in advance of forty-two dollars for each man for clothing. This amounted to $21,000 for the five hundred men, and most of this money went to their families or to the Church treasury. In addition the men sent their salaries as soldiers back to their families and to their church. Brigham Young sent men to Santa Fé to get the soldiers' money.

The Mormon Battalion marched from Winter Quarters at Council Bluffs, Iowa, to Fort Leavenworth. After drawing arms and equipment, they started for California, traveling along the Arkansas River to Santa Fé. Many of them became ill with fever, and some died in the course of the long march. The main body continued along the Rio Grande to Albuquerque and finally arrived in California in January, 1847. Eliza Snow commemorated their hardships in this verse:

"When 'Mormon' trains were journeying thro'
To Winter Quarters, from Nauvoo,
Five hundred men were called to go
To settle claims with Mexico—
To fight for that same Government
From which, as fugitives we went.
What were their families to do—
Their children, wives, and mothers too,
When fathers, husbands, sons were gone?
Mothers drove teams, and camps moved on.

"And on the brave battalion went
With Colonel Allen who was sent
As officer of government.
The noble Colonel Allen knew
His 'Mormon boys' were brave and true,
And he was proud of his command
As he led forth his 'Mormon band.'
He sickened, died, and they were left
Of a loved leader soon bereft!
And his successors proved to be
The embodiment of cruelty.

> Lieutenant Smith, the tyrant, led
> The cohort on, in Allen's stead
> To Santa Fé, where Colonel Cooke
> The charge of the battalion took."

But the truth of the matter seems to be that the Mormon boys, like other soldiers, were ever ready to complain. One source of their complaints was a certain Dr. Sanderson, the company physician. He was from Missouri, which was enough to arouse Mormon suspicion and hatred, and he insisted upon dosing them with calomel for all diseases. He was also opposed to the laying on of hands and anointing with blessed oil as curatives. The determination of the Mormon soldiers to take no calomel, and another medicine which they maintained was arsenic in disguise, was strengthened by a letter from Brigham Young, in which he said: "If you are sick, live by faith, and let surgeons' medicine alone if you want to live." But Dr. Sanderson stood by the troops with his iron spoon and insisted that his calomel be thrown nowhere but down Mormon throats. One of the soldiers immortalized the incident in the following verse:

> "A doctor which the government
> Has furnished proves a punishment.
> At his rude call of 'Jim along Joe'
> The sick and halt to him must go.
> Both night and morn this call is heard,
> Our indignation then is stirred.
> And we sincerely wish in hell
> His arsenic and calomel."

The song which maintained in the soldiers a sense of their grievance and deprivations, and to the tune of which they marched from Santa Fé to California, was also the effort of one of their number, and contained these two lines:

> "How hard, to starve and wear us out
> Upon this sandy desert route."

Some one in commenting on this strenuous march of the Mormon Battalion to California said: "Bonaparte crossed the Alps, but these men have crossed a continent." The Mormons have always been certain which was the greater achievement.

At the end of its period of enlistment, the Mormon Battalion was mustered out in California. Some of the company reën-listed in San Diego and built up that town. Others proceeded to northern California, where they heard that their brethren had established themselves in the valley of the Great Salt Lake, and they proceeded there to join them.

III

Brigham Young held the semi-annual conference of the Church at Winter Quarters on April 6, 1847, and the next morning he left Winter Quarters with a party of 148 of his people, to find a place of settlement in the Far West. The party was made up mainly of sturdy men, but three women accompanied them. One of these was Clarissa Decker Young, one of Brigham Young's wives, another was Harriet Page Wheeler Young, one of the wives of Brigham's brother, Lorenzo, and the other was Ellen Saunders Kimball, one of the wives of Heber C. Kimball. Two children also accompanied the party. The train consisted of seventy-two prairie schooners, ninety-three horses, fifty-two mules, sixty-six oxen, and there were also nineteen cows, seven-teen dogs, a few cats, and some chickens. Some of Brigham Young's personal equipment for the trip was received by him as gifts from devoted subordinates. John D. Lee wrote in his memoirs that he presented Brigham Young with seventeen ox teams: "He accepted them and said, 'God bless you, John.' But I never received a cent for them—I never wanted pay for them, for in giving property to Brigham Young I thought I was loan-ing it to the Lord."

The waggons of this pioneer party were of all descriptions. Heavy carts rattled along, followed by two-wheeled trundles, large enough to carry a baby or a sack of meal. Many of the large prairie schooners had wooden hoops instead of iron, for iron was scarce in Nauvoo, and as they rattled over the rough roads and hilly trails, they broke down and delayed their drivers. One of the women in the party discovered that the jolting of these heavy waggons would churn milk, and all the Mormon parties thereafter made butter en route. By digging hollows in the hill-sides, they made ovens in which to bake the dough which they prepared as the waggons jogged along. Whenever the camp halted, the shoemakers set up stone benches and repaired the men's boots, the gunsmiths fixed rifles, and some of the men did weaving and dyeing. Knitting, spinning, and weaving kept the women busy during the long afternoon journeys.

As soon as the Mormons reached the prairies, their difficulties began. Large prairie fires made it necessary to alter the course by many miles to keep the waggons and animals from the fire. "The prairie," wrote Clayton in his journal, "is all burned bare, and the black ashes fly bad, making the brethren look more like Indians than white folks." The fires also burned the grass and destroyed the cattle feed. But, in spite of all such difficulties, there was a mystic quality to a journey into the wilderness, which was only added to by the difficulties encountered. Among the vast sand heaps, the stubby sage-brush, the salt and the saleratus, there, if anywhere, men would be impressed with the solemnity, or at least the insecurity, and perhaps the terror, of the world. And it was a great comfort for the Mormons to feel that a Being, with rain at His command to extinguish prairie fires, and with bounties in the form of buffalo and other game, was keeping in constant touch with their progress. "During the night," wrote William Clayton, "the Lord sent a light shower of rain which has put the fire out except in one or two places and made it perfectly safe traveling."

There was, however, an inescapable, depressing quality to the prairies, which was felt by even the most sanguine dispositions. There were no roads. The lines of dusty waggons stumbled awkwardly along the faint trail made by previous lumbering waggons, and meanwhile coarse and ugly prairie grass had grown in these paths of sandy, gray dirt. To the left, to the right, behind and in front were the same slight hills, studded with prairie grass and sage brush, and stretching, seemingly, in infinite monotony. In such an atmosphere a coyote was a relief and a buffalo a miracle. Only that type of contemplative seaman so familiar in fiction and so rare in life could find grandeur in the limitless redundancy of those wearying plains. They were, in fact, very like the sea, and most travelers on them, like those who travel the ocean, learned to love them only after they had crossed them. Sir Richard Burton wrote that opium was indispensable to relieve the gloom of his journey on the prairies, which lasted only five days and five nights in a stage coach. "Nothing, I may remark," Burton wrote of these American prairies, "is more monotonous, except perhaps the African and Indian jungle, than those prairie

tracts, where the circle of which you are the center has but about
a mile of radius; it is an ocean in which one loses sight of land.
You see as it were the ends of the earth, and look around in
vain for some object upon which the eye may rest: it wants the
sublimity of repose so suggestive in the sandy deserts, and the
perpetual motion so pleasing in the aspect of the sea." [5] These
plains were enough to make strong men weep; their almost unerr-
ing sameness required a placidity for their appreciation which
most men cannot achieve. The Mormons were placid enough for
lack of subtle sensibility, but their ambition to arrive at last at
the Promised Land and to begin to make it fulfil its promise,
made the agonizingly slow journey a torture.

Some little relief of beauty broke the desolation. Occasionally
a grove of cottonwood trees rose up in pleasant decoration of the
neighboring wilderness, but these, surrounded as they were by
miles of waste land, were only melancholy reminders of what men
had left behind to make this heart-breaking journey. Another,
more lugubrious, item of interest was a grave. Frequently the
rolling prairies were broken by isolated graves, which added a
touch of terror to the deepening sense of despair. The Mormons
stopped to read the inscriptions of those who had not reached
their destinations, and, either in the spirit of superstition or fatal-
ism, wished themselves better luck, and prayed to God for it.

At times the prairies in front of the Mormons grew black with
buffaloes. These herds sometimes reached fifty thousand head,
and sometimes even a hundred thousand. They formed a valuable addition to the Mormon diet, and even supplied the fuel by
which they were cooked, for wood was scarce, and the fires were
made of the chips of buffalo dung. Brigham Young, hating
waste, prohibited his men from killing any more buffaloes than
they needed for food.

As soon as the waggons halted their banging pace for the day,
the work of feeding and corraling the cattle began, and when
that was finished the men had to feed and corral themselves.
Usually the party halted at four o'clock in the afternoon. When
the work was finished, some men, and especially William Clayton,
wrote in their diaries, while others sang and talked until eight-
thirty, when everybody, after prayers, went to bed, for the bugle
was blown at five o'clock in the morning, and the party started
again at seven. The evenings on the prairies were sometimes

[5] *The City of the Saints,* by Sir Richard Burton, p. 22.

varied with games of cards and dice, but Brigham Young objected to these iniquities, as well as to other manifestations of evil conduct on the part of his pioneers. William Clayton preserved in his journal a sermon Brigham Young delivered at half-past ten in the morning on May 29. Instead of starting for the day at the usual hour, Brigham Young had the bugle blown late, gathered the men around his waggon, and in a vehement, angry voice, began:

"I remarked last Sunday that I had not felt much like preaching to the brethren on this mission. This morning I feel like preaching a little, and shall take for my text, 'That as to pursuing our journey with this company with the spirit they possess, I am about to revolt against it.' This is the text I feel like preaching on this morning, consequently I am in no hurry. . . . Nobody has told me what has been going on in the camp, but I have known it all the while. I have been watching the movements, its influence, its effects, and I know the result if it is not put a stop to. . . . I do not mean to bow down to the spirit that is in this camp, and which is rankling in the bosoms of the brethren, and which will lead to knock downs and perhaps to the use of the knife to cut each other's throats if it is not put a stop to. I do not mean to bow down to the spirit which causes the brethren to quarrel.

"When I wake up in the morning, the first thing I hear is some of the brethren jawing each other and quarreling because a horse has got loose in the night. I have let the brethren dance and fiddle and act the nigger night after night to see what they will do, and what extremes they would go to, if suffered to go as far as they would. I do not love to see it. The brethren say they want a little exercise to pass away time in the evenings, but if you can't tire yourselves bad enough with a day's journey without dancing every night, carry your guns on your shoulders and walk, carry your wood to camp instead of lounging and lying asleep in your waggons, increasing the load until your teams are tired to death and ready to drop to the earth. Help your teams over mud holes and bad places instead of lounging in your waggons and that will give you exercise enough without dancing. Well, they will play cards, they will play checkers, they will play dominoes, and if they had the privilege and were where they could get whiskey, they would be drunk half their time, and in one week they would quarrel, get to high words and draw their knives to kill each other. This is what such a course of things would lead to. Don't you know it? Yes. Well, then, why don't you try to put it down? I have played cards once in my life since I became a Mormon to see what kind of spirit would attend it, and I was so well satisfied, that I would rather see in your hands the dirtiest thing you could find on the earth, than a pack of cards. You never read of gambling, playing cards, checkers, dominoes, etc., in the scriptures, but you do read of men praising the Lord in the dance, but who ever read of praising the Lord in a game of cards?

"If any man had sense enough to play a game at cards, or dance a little without wanting to keep it up all the time, but exercise a little and then quit it and think no more of it, it would do well enough, but you want to keep it up till midnight and every night, and all the time. You don't know how to control your senses. Last winter when we had our seasons of recreation in the council house, I went forth in the dance frequently, but did my mind run on it? No! To be sure, when I was dancing, my mind was on the dance, but the moment I stopped in the middle or the end of a tune, my mind was engaged in prayer and praise to my Heavenly Father and whatever I engage in, my mind is on it while engaged in it, but the moment I am done with it, my mind is drawn up to my God. . . .

"Joking, nonsense, profane language, trifling conversation and loud laughter do not belong to us. Suppose the angels were witnessing the hoe down the other evening, and listening to the haw haws the other evening, would not they be ashamed of it? I am ashamed of it. I have not given a joke to any man on this journey nor felt like it; neither have I insulted any man's feelings but I have hollowed pretty loud and spoken sharply to the brethren when I have seen their awkwardness at coming to camp. . . . Now let every man repent of his weakness, of his follies, of his meanness, and every kind of wickedness, and stop your swearing and profane language, for it is in this camp and I know it, and have known it. I have said nothing about it, but I now tell you, if you don't stop it you shall be cursed by the Almighty and shall dwindle away and be damned. . . .

"I understand that there are several in this camp who do not belong to the Church. I am the man who will stand up for them and protect them in all their rights. And they shall not trample on our rights nor on the priesthood. They shall reverence and acknowledge the name of God and His priesthood, and if they set up their head and seek to introduce iniquity into this camp and to trample on the priesthood, I swear to them, they shall never go back to tell the tale. I will leave them where they will be safe. If they want to retreat they can now have the privilege, and any man who chooses to go back rather than abide the law of God can now have the privilege of doing so before we go any farther.

"Here are the Elders of Israel, who have the priesthood, who have got to preach the Gospel, who have to gather the nations of the earth, who have to build up the kingdom so that the nations can come to it, they will stop to dance as niggers. I don't mean this as debasing the negroes by any means. They will hoe down all, turn summersets, dance on their knees, and haw, haw, out loud; they will play cards, they will play checkers and dominoes, they will use profane language, they will swear! . . . If we don't repent and quit our wickedness we will have more hindrances than we have had, and worse storms to encounter. I want the brethren to be ready for meeting to-morrow at the time appointed, instead of rambling off, and hiding in their waggons at play cards, etc. I think it will be good for us to have a fast meeting to-morrow and a prayer meeting to humble ourselves and turn to the Lord and He will forgive us." [6]

This speech must have been impressive, even if it did not stop all future poker games. Uttered in Brigham Young's sonorous voice, which could be hard and biting in tone when he was angry, it undoubtedly made his transgressors feel ashamed of themselves and afraid of him. After he had finished, he lined up his flock, including the high priests, the bishops, the elders, and the seventies, and asked them to raise their right hands if they were willing "to cease from all their evils and serve God according to His Laws." Every man, of course, held up his right hand. Then Heber C. Kimball arose and said the same things in different words that Brigham Young had said. Orson Pratt then urged the brethren to spend their spare time reading some of the books in the camp, the names of which he did not mention. After the sermons were finished, Colonel Markham arose before his brethren and confessed "that he had done wrong in many things," that he had played cards and checkers and dominoes. The enormity of these sins worried him greatly, for Clayton reports, "while he was speaking he was very much affected indeed and wept like a child." All promised to be better men, and in the recklessness of their repentance, some one even suggested burning every pack of cards, checker board, and set of dominoes in the camp; but it is not recorded that this was done. At half-past one in the afternoon the meeting broke up, and the slow journey across the plains was resumed. The next day, Sunday, the whole camp fasted and prayed.

It is not strange that the Mormon pioneers should forget their religion occasionally during their long, uncomfortable, and dan-

[6] *William Clayton's Journal*, pp. 189-201.

gerous journey. There were the sun and the dust, which made
the men dirty and grimy and hot, for there was rarely water
enough for anything but drinking purposes, so that for days at a
time the travelers could not wash the dirt of the road or of the
prairie fires from their faces and hands. When they came to a
river or a stream, the halt was joyously welcomed. William
Clayton took advantage of the opportunity for a physical and a
spiritual bath on Sunday morning, May 9:

"We arrived here," he wrote, "at nine-fifty and shall stay till
morning. Soon as the camp was formed, I went about three quarters of a mile below to the river and washed my socks, towel and
handkerchief as well as I could in cold water without soap. I then
stripped my clothing off and washed from head to foot, which has
made me feel much more comfortable for I was covered with dust.
After washing and putting on clean clothing I sat down on the banks
of the river and gave way to a long train of solemn reflections respecting many things, especially in regard to my family and their
welfare for time and eternity. I shall not write my thoughts here,
inasmuch as I expect this journal will have to pass through other
hands besides my own or that of my family but if I can carry my
plans into operation, they will be written in a manner that my family
will each get their portion, whether before my death or after, it
matters not."

The Indians did not prove troublesome. The Mormons often
saw their tracks but met very few Indians until they got beyond
the Platte River. This caused Clayton to reflect: "But we are
satisfied the Lord hears the prayers of his servants and sends
them out of the way before we come up to them." However, the
Mormons also carried a cannon on wheels, the purpose of which
was to impress the Indians that they were the chosen people.

Innocent amusement, approved by Brigham Young, was provided by mock trials and dances, preceded always by prayer. In
the mock trial of The Camp *vs.* James Davenport, the defendant
was charged with blockading the highway and turning ladies out
of their course. Dances were usually held on Saturday nights,
for the camp did not travel on Sunday unless it was absolutely
necessary to do so in order to reach water or good grazing
ground. As there were only three women in camp, the men
danced with each other.

Along the route the Mormons set up guide posts and placed

letters in them for the Saints who were to follow them later. Whitened buffalo bones and skulls were also used for messages, and on these the Mormons wrote advice about the roads and the streams. The grease for the waggon wheels they obtained from the fat of the wolves they killed for protection. William Clayton thought of the possibility of a speedometer. It was his job to keep a record of the distance covered, and it occurred to him that an attachment on a waggon wheel would be more accurate and less burdensome than his guesses, based on counting the revolutions of the wheel all day. He wrote in his journal: "I walked some this afternoon in company with Orson Pratt and suggested to him the idea of fixing a set of wooden cog wheels to the hub of a waggon wheel, in such order as to tell the exact number of miles we travel each day. He seemed to agree with me that it could be easily done at a trifling expense." Nothing was done about Clayton's idea at first, but finally Brother Appleton Harmon, a mechanic, was set to work making a speedometer after William Clayton's directions. Later William Clayton made this entry in his diary: "I discovered that Brother Appleton Harmon is trying to have it understood that he invented the machinery to tell the distance we travel, which makes me think less of him than I formerly did. He is not the inventor of it by a long way, but he has made the machinery after being told how to do it. What little souls work." In spite of professional jealousies, the instrument was finished and was called the "roadometer."

As soon as the Mormons had crossed the prairies and arrived in the foothills of the mountains, their daily life improved in variety and ease. West of the Platte River the dull prairie grass was replaced by green clumps of sage brush, growing in the sandy hills, and out of these clumps gray sage-hens scurried as the rumbling waggons disturbed their solitude. Clear springs and streams became more numerous, and the air was perfumed in some places with the delicate odor of wild mint. It was June. Gradually the gray sand of the trail before them turned to red earth, the color of the rocks and bluffs which began to rise around them. The red glare of the road and the rocks hurt their eyes. They now made better time, averaging fifteen miles each day instead of ten.

Frequently now they met other emigrants on their way to Oregon and to California. As much as they enjoyed the sight of fellow travelers, the Mormons were careful to avoid those from Missouri, for Missourians were still their traditional enemies, and Brigham Young preferred to travel ahead a few miles, rather than camp on the same ground with them. A party of Missourians came to inspect Clayton's roadometer. "They expressed a wish," he wrote, "to each other to see inside and looked upon it as a curiosity. I paid no attention to them inasmuch as they did not address themselves to me." The Missourians gave the Mormons information about the route and paid them $1.50 per load to ferry their goods across the Platte River in the boat of skins, known as the Revenue Cutter, which the Mormons had made. Ferrying Missourians yielded so much profit in flour that Brigham Young decided to leave a party of nine men at the river to continue the work.

North of the Platte River the Mormons branched off from the regular trail. Previously they had followed the route used by emigrants who had preceded them to Oregon, and this regular trail would have taken them to the valley of the Great Salt Lake, but Brigham Young thought it wiser to blaze a trail to the north, so that his people might not be subject to competition for fodder and to conflict with Missouri emigrants. This trail, which Brigham Young and Heber Kimball established by going ahead each day to search out the easiest route, was known for many years as the "Old Mormon Road" and was followed by all the Mormon emigrants who came after the original pioneers. To-day part of the Union Pacific Railroad runs across it.

Late in June Brigham Young and his party began to reach the high, irregular rock hills. The highest of these, Independence Rock, was even at that early date scrawled in black, red, and yellow paint with the names and initials of hundreds of men and women who had arrived there, climbed the rock and thought it important to leave an indelible impression of their lack of taste. This was near the Sweet Water River, and the scenery now began to take on an imposing, romantic grandeur. The country seemed fortified with huge, overhanging hills of burnt sienna, sandy rock. Snow and ice were found in some of the mountain pools and springs. The mornings became bitingly cold, and during the nights drinking water froze in the pails. At the beginning of July the mountain fever started, and many of the Mormons were stricken with its violent headache, burning temperature, and fantastic delirium. On July 12 Brigham Young was afflicted with mountain fever, and in the evening of that day he was raving in a mad delirium. Mosquitoes in huge armies made the cattle restless and the men frantic.

Near Green River and Bear River members of the Mormon Battalion met their brethren, and Elder Samuel Brannan arrived from California to consult with Brigham Young. On the day in February, 1846, when the Mormons left Nauvoo, the ship *Brooklyn,* carrying 238 Saints left New York to travel around Cape Horn to California, where it was assumed their brethren would join them. This expedition was in charge of Elder Samuel Brannan, who combined great enthusiasm with some ability and very little principle. On the long sea journey four leading men of the party were excommunicated by Brannan for crimes which he later described as "wicked and licentious conduct." Two children were born on the ship, and they were named Atlantic and Pacific, respectively; Atlantic was a boy, born before the *Brooklyn* had rounded the Horn, and Pacific was a girl, born after the ship had passed the Cape. Elder Brannan settled the Mormons under his charge in a location near the present city of San Francisco, and then he proceeded overland to meet Brigham Young. By this time Brigham Young had heard a great deal about the valley of the Great Salt Lake, which he had made up his mind might be the most suitable place for his settlement. Brannan urged strenuously that the Mormons should not stop at the Salt Lake Valley, which, he assured them, was desolate and would never bear grain. He insisted that the Saints must come on to California, where the climate was incomparable and the soil of an amazing fertility. One could grow anything, could accomplish anything in California, he argued. But Brigham Young quietly laughed at his enthusiasm and refused to act upon it, for he felt that to take his people to California, where living was easy, would be to subject them, sooner or later, to association with competitive neighbors, who would adopt eventually the same attitude of opposition that had made it impossible for them to live in Ohio, Missouri, and Illinois; and from California they could only move west into the sea. The valley of the Great Salt Lake was irresistibly attractive to a man of Brigham Young's foresight: it was, to his mind, by reason of its lack of attraction for those who wished to get rich quickly, the very place to build up a powerful, isolated community, which would grow without molestation until it was powerful enough to resist it. If the land was at all fertile, he realized that it was the place for his Mormons.

Sam Brannan became disgusted with Brigham Young's lack of interest in the California climate and the California soil. He made up his mind that Brigham Young was pig-headed, and he returned himself to California, where he appears often in the pages of the history of that state. It is said that when Brannan came into San Francisco Bay with his party of Mormons, the American flag was floating over the Presidio, which had recently been captured from the Mexicans. Eyewitnesses reported that Brannan threw his hat on the deck of the *Brooklyn* in disgust, and shouted, "There's that damned rag again." He had sailed thousands of miles only to run into what he had planned to avoid. But he soon adapted himself to the disappointment, and made the best of his opportunities in a sparsely settled community. In January, 1847, he established a newspaper, known as the *Yerba Buena California Star;* San Francisco was then called Yerba Buena. Many of his party of Mormons remained in California with Brannan, and he collected tithes from them regularly for the Church, but Brigham Young never received any of the money. This led ultimately to Brannan's resignation from the Mormon Church. After the discovery of gold in California, Sam Brannan was one of the first to hear about it. He then had a store at Sutter's Fort, where gold was first found. Brannan's enthusiasm overran his discretion, and he rode on horseback through California communities, carrying with him gold dust and nuggets, and shouting to the startled inhabitants, "Gold! Gold! Gold from the American River!" He, more than any one man, spread the interest in California gold which was so soon to assume the proportions of a mania.

As his party neared the valley of the Great Salt Lake Brigham Young's interest in it grew. He had read about it in Colonel Frémont's reports of his explorations; Father De Smet, the famous French missionary traveler among the Indians, had met Brigham Young at Winter Quarters, and they had held long conversations, during which Father De Smet described to Brigham Young this strange valley, with its stranger lake. It is clear, however, that Brigham Young had only a vague idea of his ultimate destination and an instinctive feeling that Salt Lake valley was the right place. In a sermon he delivered in 1857, when he was fighting the United States government, Brigham Young said:

"When I was written to in Nauvoo by the President of the United States, through another person, enquiring, 'Where are you going, Mr. Young?' I replied that I did not know where we should land. We had men in England trying to negotiate for Vancouver's Island, and we sent a ship-load round Cape Horn to California. Men in authority asked, 'Where are you going to?' 'We may go to California, or to Vancouver's Island.' When the Pioneer company reached Green River, we met Samuel Brannan and a few others from California, and they wanted us to go there. I remarked, 'Let us go to California, and we cannot stay there over five years; but let us stay in the mountains, and we can raise our own potatoes, and eat them; and I calculate to stay here.' We are still on the backbone of the animal, where the bone and the sinew are, and we intend to stay here, and all hell cannot help themselves." [7]

Whenever Brigham Young was asked by one of the pioneer party where they were going, he remarked that he would recognize the site of their new home when he saw it, and that they would continue as the Lord directed them. Near South Pass, the dividing point of the waters which run into the Pacific Ocean, and those which flow east into the Atlantic, Brigham Young met T. L. Smith, a trapper and explorer, better known as "Pegleg" Smith. He had explored Salt Lake in August, 1826, and he advised Brigham Young to settle slightly farther west in Cache Valley, Utah. He also offered to meet them two weeks later and guide the Mormon emigrants there, but for some reason he did not keep his appointment, and Erastus Snow was sure that God had His mind set on Salt Lake Valley, that "Pegleg" Smith's failure to arrive was "a providence of an all-wise God." Near South Pass Brigham Young also talked with Jim Bridger, the famous trapper and trader, who had also explored Salt Lake. He tried to discourage Brigham Young from settling there, and he offered him $1,000 for the first bushel of wheat or ear of corn grown in that great salt basin.

The roads now became mountain passes; the noise of the heavy waggon wheels was given back in a sharp echo, like the sound of hundreds of carpenters hammering their planks against the

[7] *Journal of Discourses,* vol. 5, pp. 230-231.

MORMON EMIGRANT TRAIN

sides of rocky mountains. Rifle shots resounded with cracks, and the lowing of the cattle and the braying of the mules were answered in uncanny mockery by the surrounding hills. The Mormon band played music, every note of which was echoed weirdly. During the nights the mules were disturbed in their sleep by the answers to their own noises. The waggons ascended hilly passes, overhung by huge, irregular, red, dusty rocks which took on dream shapes, or descended into cañons surrounded by different, but no less weird, red rocks.

Brigham Young became very ill with mountain fever. It was necessary for him to halt his waggon and remain behind with a few men to care for him, while Parley Pratt led an advance party into the valley of the Great Salt Lake, which they were now approaching, but which he had not yet seen. It looked very much for a time as if his career might terminate with the last, fatal parallel with that of Moses, as if he were to see the Promised Land, but never enter it. When the advance party came to his waggon to get last instructions, Brigham Young rested his elbow on his pillow and, with difficulty, sat up to talk to them. "My impressions are," he said, "that when you emerge from the mountains into the open country, you bear to the northward and stop at the first convenient place for putting in your seeds." He did not say whether this impression was based on a revelation of God or the map of Colonel Frémont.

On Saturday, the 24th of July, 1847, Brigham Young drove in Wilford Woodruff's carriage into the open valley of the Great Salt Lake. Still weak from mountain fever, he was lying on a bed in the carriage. "When we came out of the cañon into full view of the valley," Wilford Woodruff recorded, "I turned the side of my carriage around, open to the west, and President Young arose from his bed and took a survey of the country. While gazing on the scene before us, he was enwrapped in vision for several minutes. He had seen the valley before in vision, and upon this occasion he saw the future glory of Zion and of Israel, as they would be, planted in the valleys of these mountains." But all he said was, "It is enough. This is the right place. Drive on." [8]

The scene which lay before Brigham Young's heavy, tired eyes was of a quality to inspire visions, for it is one of the most impressive sights on the American continent. As Sir Richard

[8] *The Utah Pioneers*, p. 23.

Burton said of this view, "Switzerland and Italy lay side by side." Beneath was a great plain, stretching almost as far as the eye could see, surrounded on all sides by a spacious semi-circle of sun-burned, snow-capped mountains. In the far distance was a hazy expanse of salt water, glistening an invitation in the sunlight. The air was soft, clear, and had a faint, sweet, virgin odor. The plain was studded with low, brown and red, bare hills; a gray desert, with alkaline sinks extended in one direction, and stretches of burning red sandstone wandered off into another place. To his left were green trees hiding themselves in the cañons, as if fearful to come out into such a waste land. Azure, purple, and silver of sky and mountains overhung the gleaming turquoise of the lake. And there was not a building, not a sign of man, to break the fearful charm of virgin solitude.

It was impossible that, catching a glimpse of this sight from the plateau which overlooked it, the Mormons should regard it as anything but the Promised Land. After their dreary journey of one hundred and two days from the Missouri River, crossing prairies, climbing mountains, fording troublesome, treacherous, depressingly dirty rivers, this was a promise of paradise, and it occurred to them that none but God had fulfilled it. Brigham Young, far from jealous, encouraged that attitude. When General Garfield asked him how he happened to choose Salt Lake valley, Brigham Young answered: "Why, we were traveling along, and I was lying in a wagon, and all of a sudden I called out, 'Halt! the Lord says "stop here"'; and there on that hill (pointing to one) an angel of the Lord stood, and pointed down this valley, and said, 'Stay there.'" Brigham Young had made good the boast of his Church biographer that "he was 'every inch' the Moses of the last days." He did better, for he was granted the privilege not only of leading his people out of the land of Egypt and out of the house of bondage, but, like Joshua, he also ruled them in the Promised Land for many years.

As the Mormons rode into the valley from the flat tableland from which Brigham Young got his first view of it, their romantic sentiments changed to practical considerations, and a bitter tinge of disappointment seized them. Their new home, when they came to examine it closely, proved to be sandy and absolutely nude of timber, except for that in the cañons some miles away. The only plant that seemed able to survive the salt and drought, was the tall, careless sunflower, and even its yellow face was covered with parasitical, black and brown crickets. The potentialities of this stubborn looking soil worried them dreadfully. On the first day, before he took his dinner, Wilford Woodruff hurried to plant the half bushel of potatoes he had brought with him. The air seemed ominously hot, and the dry ground gave indication of chronic lack of rain. But that first night something of a minor miracle occurred. It rained, and as rain in that valley in July was notoriously rare, the Saints took this as a comforting assurance of special dispensation in their favor. But their melancholy did not disappear. From the point of view of the valley the mountains above and around seemed rugged and forbidding, and the lack of anything green brought memories of verdant Illinois. Under foot was still the maddening sage brush, the eternal, haunting companion of their dismal journey. The three women, overcome with a sense of wretchedness, desolation, and loneliness, and that first feeling of despair at unfamiliar, foreign sights, broke down and wept.

But the people did not have much time for melancholy. On the same day of their arrival in the valley the men began to plow the land and to plant their seed. The blacksmith set up his forge and began to repair the plows and other farm machinery. Some of the men set out on exploring parties into the surrounding country, and they were filled with joy at varieties of surprises in the nature of hot springs, mountain streams of sweet, cold water, and cañons covered with green trees. The Indians came into camp and proved friendly, trading buckskins and ponies for powder and muskets.

After he had been in the valley four days, Brigham Young recovered from his illness and was able to ride about the country in a carriage. He was satisfied that this valley was the ideal home for his people, and the very desolation and loneliness which depressed so much his wife and his sister-in-law impressed him with the advantages of isolation. As soon as he had looked about, Brigham Young addressed his followers, and he told them that their present camp was the ideal site for their future city. "He said," wrote Clayton, "they intended to divide the city into blocks of ten acres each with eight lots in a block of one and a quarter acres each. The streets to be wide. No house will be permitted to be built on the corners of the streets, neither petty shops. Each house will have to be built so many feet back from the street and all the houses parallel with each other.

The fronts are to be beautified with fruit trees, etc. No filth will be allowed to stand in the city but the water will be conducted through in such a manner as to carry all the filth off to the River Jordan. No man will be suffered to cut up his lot and sell a part to speculate out of his brethren. Each man must keep his lot whole, for the Lord has given it to us without price. The temple lot will be forty acres and adorned with trees, ponds, etc." These plans were carried out almost exactly in every detail as Brigham Young formulated them that day, although some of his brethren must have been extremely doubtful of the possibility of carrying such a vision into execution in such a barren land. Brigham Young set the men to work immediately building a road to the mountains, to be used for hauling timber, and as soon as they got the timber, he superintended the building of a stockade as a precaution against the Indians, and a boat to be used on the one-hundred-mile lake of salt water that glistened in the distance.

Before the beginning of August the Saints had built a bowery for their Sunday services, and Brigham Young had selected the site for the Temple and several sites for himself and his associates. He chose for himself a square block near the proposed Temple. Realizing the scarcity of timber, the Saints built houses of adobes, sun-burned clay bricks.

Meanwhile, a new party of Saints had left Winter Quarters and was en route to Salt Lake. Brigham Young made preparations to return to Winter Quarters for the purpose of leading the rest of his people to their new home. First, however, he laid the foundations himself of four adobe houses, which he wished for his family and business use. On August 26, after blessing his pioneers, Brigham Young left them in the new city, and accompanied by several of his leading associates and the members of the Mormon Battalion who were anxious to return to Winter Quarters and bring their families back to the valley, he started on the return journey.

The main characteristic of this journey was the scarcity of food, and the grumbling of the men on that account. Their breadstuffs were exhausted, and they were compelled to live almost entirely on the buffaloes they could kill en route. Clayton wrote: "John Pack has got flour enough to last him through. We have all messed together until ours was eaten, and now John Pack proposes for each man to mess by himself. He has concealed his flour and beans together with tea, coffee, sugar, etc., and cooks after the rest have gone to bed. Such things seem worthy of remembrance for a time to come." [9] Some of those who killed buffaloes kept the meat and tallow and refused to share with their less lucky companions. Dissension was rife in the small group with which Clayton was traveling ahead: "Young Babcock shook his fist in Zebedee Coltrin's face and damned him and said he could whip him." Brigham Young had warned these men not to travel ahead, but his advice had been disregarded. Clayton records that the small party met some Indians, who bullied the Mormons, took some horses, oxen, knives, and a sack of salt, "and we concluded," wrote Clayton, "to turn about and go back to the company. . . . After traveling back about six miles, we met the company, told the story, and bore their slang and insults without saying much, but not without thinking a great deal." After a journey of nine weeks and three days, they arrived back at Winter Quarters. At the command of Brigham Young Clayton had supervised a new roadometer, and the registered distance from Florence, Nebraska, Winter Quarters, to the new site of Salt Lake City was 1,031 miles. About halfway, Brigham Young had met the two thousand Mormons who were en route to the valley; he had dinner with them, told them the nature of their new home, and left them. This second party arrived in the valley in good health, only seven people, three of them infants, having died en route.

Brigham Young arrived back at Winter Quarters on October 31, 1847. He spent the winter there, planning for the emigration of his people the following spring. At Winter Quarters there was a small log cabin in the center of the settlement, the walls of which were covered with turf two feet thick. The windows were in the roof, and no one could look in or hear what was being said inside. Into this council chamber Brigham Young called his Apostles about a month after his return and suggested that it was time for him to be elected President of the Church. As yet he was only President of the Twelve Apostles. Several of the Apostles suggested that since, according to Brigham Young, the succession to the supreme leadership rested with the Twelve Apostles, it was not necessary to elect a President of the Church, who would also become "Prophet, Seer, and Revelator," in succession to Joseph Smith. But Brigham

[9] *William Clayton's Journal,* pp. 361-362.

Young insisted that his position as President of the Twelve Apostles was not sufficient authority or sufficient security, and he finally won his followers to submission. There was nothing for them to do but submit, for to take the question before the people in open assembly would produce a disrupting wrangle, from which everybody would suffer and nobody would benefit. Besides, they needed the guiding genius of Brigham Young now more than ever, for their new settlement had been selected, not developed. The appointment was ratified, and then taken before the people for their approval. At the public voting, it has been claimed, the Apostles all raised their hands first, and the faithful brethren followed their leaders.

By the end of May, 1848, Brigham Young had organized his second exodus, which consisted this time of 2,417 men, women, and children. There were also in the party pigs, chickens, cats, dogs, goats, geese, doves, ducks, five beehives, and a squirrel, as well as the many horses, oxen, and mules used to pull the waggons. In a sermon Brigham Young once described the miscellaneous character of the Mormons' possessions and animals:

"We had to bring our seed grain, our farming utensils, bureaus, secretaries, sideboards, sofas, pianos, large looking glasses, fine chairs, carpets, nice shovels and tongs, and other fine furniture, with all the parlor, cook stoves, etc.; and we had to bring these things piled together with the women and children, helter skelter, topsy turvy, with broken down horses, ring-boned, spavined, pole evil, fistula and hipped; oxen with three legs, and cows with one tit. This was our only means of transportation, and if we had not brought our goods in this manner we should not have had them, for there was nothing here." [10]

The second Brigham Young party arrived without unusual hardship in their new home on September 20, 1848. Brigham Young was escorted into the new city by those he had left in charge and those who had followed. A hymn of welcome, composed especially for the occasion by Eliza Snow, was sung in the Bowery. There were now four hundred and fifty houses of adobes and logs, three saw mills, and a flour mill in the new city. Those who returned from Winter Quarters with Brigham Young were all satisfied with the activities of their brethren, all except Bill Hickman, who wrote in his book of confessions:

[10] *Journal of Discourses,* vol. 12, p. 287.

"I had in the Winter just previous to leaving Nauvoo, taken me a second wife, whose father was going with this Company, and she wanted to go with them. I sent her along, and when I reached Salt Lake next year, was not surprised to find she had helped herself to a youngster a few days old. Believing her virtue to be easy going before this let me off. I never had any children by her." [1]

[1] *Brigham's Destroying Angel*, p. 48.

Chapter VI

SINAI

I

THOSE Mormons who remained in the valley of the Great Salt Lake during the winter of 1847, while Brigham Young was preparing his followers for the second exodus, endured a winter of great difficulties. They had arrived late in July, and it was impossible to get much from the soil that year because of lack of water. Their vegetables were almost exhausted, and the food situation became so serious that a pound of gold was offered for a pound of flour, and the owner refused to sell. Lorenzo D. Young, Brigham's brother, traded some oxen for a steer, and after all the meat was eaten by his family, he cut the hide into strips, soaked these in the creek, scraped off all the hair, and turned them over to Mrs. Young, who boiled them into a glue soup, to which she added salt and served. Even the fine set of china which she brought out to use for this soup did not altogether succeed in making it palatable. From the Indians the new settlers learned how to use the roots and herbs of plants which grew along the river that Brigham Young and his associates had decided to call the River Jordan. But the community did not despair. They succeeded in remaining industrious, planting spring crops, building several saw mills and grist mills, fencing in twelve miles of farming land, and giving birth to one hundred and twenty babies. One of these children, born early in August, 1847, to John and Catherine Steel was named Young Elizabeth Steel, after Brigham Young and Queen Elizabeth, of England.

When Brigham Young returned to the new settlement, to remain there for the rest of his life, he was satisfied with the labors of his flock. He recalled to them the prophecy of Isaiah: "The wilderness and the solitary place shall be glad for them; and the desert shall rejoice, and blossom as the rose." Meanwhile, the efforts to make this prophecy come true became necessarily greater, for the arrival of two thousand additional Saints

made food scarcer for every one. Some of the new arrivals
lived for three months on the cattle that had carried them across
the prairies and the mountains. Clothes began to wear out, and
farming implements soon needed repair and replacement. Tea
and coffee disappeared entirely from the diet, not because of the
ban against them, but because they were unobtainable, for the
nearest shop was a thousand miles away. At the height of this
scarcity of all things material Heber Kimball arose in the pulpit
and announced a prophecy he had just received. He predicted
that in a short time the Saints would be able to buy everything
they needed in the valley cheaper than they could buy the equiva-
lent articles in the States. Many of the Saints did not believe
him, and they felt that it would be a miracle indeed if this
prophecy should be fulfilled. It redounded very much to his
credit, and to that of God, when, less than a year later, his miracle
began to be consummated in an unexpected manner.

Brigham Young decided that at first a large common farm
would be of greater advantage to both individuals and the community than separate farms, and he urged this coöperative enterprise to prevent starvation. This was the first step in the execution of his general economic policy; he always preferred co-
operative work to individual speculation, and so far as he was
able, he refused to allow the rise in land values due to community
development to be appropriated as unearned increment by individual owners. One enterprise particularly he safeguarded carefully from monopoly. The land of Utah was valueless without
irrigation, and many urged that a large private company should
irrigate the entire territory and charge for the use of water.
Brigham Young wisely insisted that every farmer should build
his own furrows and canals. The result was that no one owned
the indispensable water supply, and the farmers paid tribute to no
one. Those parts of the irrigation system which required greater
labor than individuals or families could perform were built co-
operatively by groups of farmers and their families. Irrigation
was one of the great triumphs of the Mormons over their environment, and was developed largely by their own ingenuity;
their efforts were the first large-scale irrigation projects in the
United States. So grateful are they to the value of this process
that in recent years a Mormon organist wrote and composed a
song known as the "Irrigation Ode."

Among the other dangers and difficulties of life in the valley were the wild animals. Wolves, foxes, and catamounts prowled about the adobe houses, and, after he had spread strychnine one night about his doorstep, Lorenzo Young said he found fourteen dead white wolves lying there next morning. There were also swarms of mice, who found it easy to cut cavities in the shelters of logs and clay. It was sometimes necessary to catch fifty or sixty of them in an evening before the family could go to sleep. There were only a few cats in the community, and one device for destroying mice was the ingenious arrangement of a bucket of water, with a greased sloping board at each end, down which the mice slid to death by drowning. Another great irritation were the thousands of bedbugs, who lived in the fresh, green mountain timber and remained after their homes were transformed into log cabins.

These annoyances, however, were of minor importance compared with the plague of grasshoppers and crickets. When the Mormons arrived, they found the land covered with destructive crickets, and equally destructive grasshoppers soon swarmed in clouds all over the territory of Utah. "Often they fill the air for many miles of extent," wrote Lieutenant Warren in his government report, "so that an inexperienced eye can scarcely distinguish their appearance from that of a shower of rain or the smoke of a prairie fire. To a person standing in one of these swarms as they pass over and around him, the air becomes sensibly darkened, and the sound produced by their wings resembles that of the passage of a train of cars on a railroad when standing two or three hundred yards from the track. The Mormon settlements have suffered more from the ravages of these insects than probably all other causes combined." [1]

Brigham Young once expressed greater fear of grasshoppers and crickets than the enemies of the Mormons in Missouri and Illinois; "the crickets and the grasshoppers," he said, "are the greatest plague, for we can hit men, but when you hit one cricket or grasshopper, the air is at once alive with them, and if you kill one, two come to bury him." The insects alighted in the fields on the heads of wheat stalks, and the crops were quickly destroyed. Sometimes, however, they made a fortunate error, which Brigham Young described in a letter: "Myriads of grasshoppers, like snowflakes in a storm, occasionally fill the air over

[1] Reports of Secretary of War. Reports of Lieutenant Gouverneur K. Warren, U. S. Topographical Engineers, 1855, 1856, 1857.

the city, as far as the eye can reach, and they are liable to alight wherever they can distinguish good feed. A great portion of them, however, alight in the Great Salt Lake, which appears green at a distance, and the shore is lined with their dead, from one inch to two feet thick, and which smell exactly like fish." Another observer described the crickets as "wingless, dumpy, black, swollen-headed, with bulging eyes in cases like goggles, mounted upon legs of steel wire and clock spring, and with a general personal appearance that justified the Mormons in comparing them to a cross of a spider and the buffalo."

The men, women, and children of the settlement organized into squads, armed with willow bush brooms, with which they attempted to sweep the armies of crickets and grasshoppers into the creeks, where coffee sacks were placed, which were buried in trenches as soon as they were full. But this was slow and laborious battle. Suddenly, as the Mormons were beginning to despair of saving any of their crops, flocks of beautiful white, glossy gulls, with bright red beaks and feet, and looking like doves in form and motion, swept down gracefully upon the valley. At first the Mormons, looking up at the sky in anxious bewilderment, considered this another torment for their unknown transgressions, but soon they noticed that the gulls began to eat the crickets as rapidly as they could swallow them. At early dawn they came each day from the islands of Great Salt Lake and feasted all day long. When they became stuffed to the red beaks with this food, which they seemed never to get enough of, like Roman nobles at their saturnalia, they disgorged themselves and returned to the feast immediately.

The Mormons came to the conclusion that this was the greatest miracle of all they had yet witnessed, and they eased their troubled minds with the consolation that God was still watching over them with curious care. But, if it was a miracle, it was one which God fortunately repeated with seasonal periodicity; during the next ten years the crickets and grasshoppers several times damaged the crops, and several times the gulls saved them from utter destruction; the gulls even arrived sometimes when the grasshoppers and crickets had forgotten to come.

Another miracle took place during the famine of 1856, when food was so scarce that Brigham Young's large family, and every family in the community, were on short rations. One of the brethren who needed bread asked Heber Kimball's advice how to get it. "Go and marry a wife," was Brother Heber's terse reply, which was accompanied with a few charitable measures of flour for immediate wants. "Thunderstruck at receiving such an answer," wrote Heber Kimball's church biographer, "at such a time, when he could hardly provide food for himself, the man went his way, dazed and bewildered, thinking that President Kimball must be out of his mind. But the more he thought of the prophetic character and calling of the one who had given him this strange advice, the less he felt like ignoring it. Finally he resolved to obey counsel, let the consequences be what they might. But where was the woman who would marry him? was the next problem. Bethinking himself of a widow with several children, who he thought might be induced to share her lot with him, he mustered up courage, proposed and was accepted." [2] And fortunately the widow had a lot, and a house, and six months' store of provisions.

It was difficult during the hardships of this first ten years of the pioneer existence of the Mormon community to prevent some of the less scrupulous and the more shiftless from appropriating the fruits of industry of their more fortunate and industrious brethren. Wood disappeared from carefully constructed woodpiles, and even Brigham Young's supply was not safe, according to one of his angry sermons. Timber was so far away that some men believed it was much easier to take it than to cut it, and flour was harder to grow than to steal. Brigham Young was reticent about his own losses and proud of his ability to prevent them. "I have never been troubled with thieves stealing my property," he once said in a sermon. "If I am not smart enough to take care of what the Lord lends me, I am smart enough to hold my tongue about it, until I come across the thief myself, and then I am ready to tie a string around his neck." [3]

The punishment Brigham Young advocated for stealing was drastic:

"If you want to know what to do with a thief that you may find stealing, *I say kill him on the spot,* and never suffer him to commit another iniquity. That is what I expect I shall do, though never, in the days of my life, have I hurt a man with the palm of my

[2] *Life of Heber C. Kimball,* by Orson F. Whitney, pp. 415-416.
[3] *Journal of Discourses,* vol. I, p. 255.

hand. I never have hurt any person any other way except with this unruly member, my tongue. Notwithstanding this, if I caught a man stealing on my premises I should be very apt to send him *straight home,* and that is what I wish every man to do, to put a stop to that abominable practice in the midst of this people.

"I know this appears hard, and throws a cold chill over your revered traditions received by early education. I had a great many such feelings to contend with myself, and was as much of a sectarian in my notions as any other man, and as mild, perhaps, in my natural disposition, but I have trained myself to measure things by the line of justice, to estimate them by the rule of equity and truth, and not by the false tradition of the fathers, or the sympathies of the natural mind. If you will cause all those whom you know to be thieves, to be placed in a line before the mouth of one of our largest cannon, well loaded with chain shot, I will prove by my works whether I can mete out justice to such persons or not. I would consider it just as much my duty to do that, as to baptize a man for the remission of his sins. That is a short discourse on thieves, I acknowledge, but I tell you the truth as it is in my heart." [4]

II

A correspondent wrote Brigham Young asking for frank answers to questions concerning life in Utah so that he might know whether he and one hundred associates would care to emigrate. One of his questions was, "Are you annoyed seriously by the Indians?" Brigham Young answered: "We do not permit anything to seriously annoy us; 'tis true the Indians steal our horses, kill our cattle, sometimes disturb the quiet of some of our settlements for a season, and we are compelled for our safety to keep a good lookout, and sometimes chastise them a little; but our quiet, peace, and security is so much greater here than it was in the States, that we feel grateful to our heavenly father for the exchange of neighbors."

It was true that the Indians proved far better neighbors than any the Mormons had yet encountered, but this was due largely to Brigham Young's policy towards them. It was one of his most earnest convictions that it was cheaper, as well as more humane, to feed the Indians than to fight them, and he urged his followers to teach their brethren, who were after all the

[4] *Journal of Discourses,* vol. I, pp. 108-109.

direct descendants of the Lamanites of the Book of Mormon, the cultivation of the soil, and to make them presents of food and tobacco. He did not, however, consider it wise to pamper them, or to allow them to become too familiar. His whole Indian policy is summed up admirably in a sermon he delivered before the conference of the Church on April 6, 1854:

"I want to say a few words on Indian character. When one tribe of Indians are at war with another, if a few sally out and kill a warrior of the opposite party, that tribe will watch their opportunity, and perhaps go and kill men, women, and children of the other tribe. They do not care whom they kill, if they can kill any of the tribe. This has been taught them from age to age. The inhabitants of the United States have treated the Indians in like manner. If but one person or only a few were guilty of committing a depredation upon a white settlement, they have chastised the whole tribe for the crime, and would perhaps kill those who would fight and die for them. . . .

"As I have done all the time, I tell you again to-day, I will not consent to your killing one Indian for the sin of another. If any of them commit a depredation, tell the tribe to which they belong that they may deliver up the man or men to be tried according to law, and you will make friends of the whole tribe. They have men among them they would be glad to have despatched. For instance, there is a man at Utah called Squash-head: it is said he has made his boast of taking father Lemon's child and killing it. We know the other Indians wish he was dead: they do not like to kill him, for fear of their own lives. They would like to have that man tried and hung up for the murder of that child. . . .

"I have fed fifty Indians almost day by day for months together. I always give them something, but I never forget to treat them like Indians; and they are always mannerly and kind, and look upon me as their superior. Never let them come into your houses, as the whites did in Utah [County]. There they would let them lounge upon their beds, until finally they would quarrel and become angry, if the women would not let them lounge upon their beds. Great, big, athletic fellows would want to go into the wickeups of the 'Mormons,' and lounge upon their beds, and sit on their tables and on their chairs, and make as free as though they belonged to the family. When their familiarities became oppressive to the whites, and they desired them to leave their houses, it made them angry, and I knew it would. This is the true cause of the Indian difficulties in Utah." [5]

Frequently the Indians visited the Mormon settlements and

[5] *Journal of Discourses*, vol. 7, pp. 328-329.

offered Indian boys and girls for sale. At first the Mormons refused to buy, but the Indians insisted that they intended to kill all unpurchased children, and when this threat was several times carried out with cold determination, Brigham Young advised his people to buy any Indian children who could only be saved in that way, so that the Mormons might help the Indians to become the "white and delightsome people" the Book of Mormon said they were destined to become eventually. Another method some Mormons had of making the Indians "white and delightsome" was by breeding with them. Some Mormons considered it their duty to take unto themselves dark-eyed Indian squaws—purely for the sake of the future of the Lamanites.

Although he trusted in God to convert the Indians, as predicted in the Book of Mormon, and had faith in the gratitude of the Indians for good treatment, Brigham Young believed also in taking all precautions against the failure of these assurances. He urged that every Mormon settlement in the outlying districts of Utah build a fort to protect its people, before any other structure was built, and he superintended the building of the fort in Salt Lake City. "I have always acknowledged myself a coward," he said once, "and hope I always may be, to make me cautious enough to preserve myself and my brethren from falling ignobly by a band of Indians. . . . I do not repose confidence in persons, only as they prove themselves confidential; and I shall live a long while before I can believe that an Indian is my friend, when it would be to his advantage to be my enemy." Sometimes the Mormons disliked the labor of building a stockade when all around them seemed so peaceful, and there was so much other work to be done. Brigham Young continually pointed out in his sermons the danger of this criminal negligence, and on one occasion he addressed himself exclusively to their wives: "If they want to drag you off to some place where you will be exposed to the ravages of Indians, tell them you are going to stay where you are, and then ask them what they are going to do about it. It is not my general practice to counsel the sisters to disobey their husbands, but my counsel is—*obey your husbands;* and I am sanguine and most emphatic on that subject. But I never counseled a woman to follow her husband to the devil. If a man is determined to expose the lives of his friends, let that man go to the devil and to destruction alone." [6]

[6] *Journal of Discourses,* vol. i, p. 77.

There was one Indian chief who proved troublesome at times, who was often worth conciliating, but who was above all picturesque. He went by the Anglo-Saxon name of Walker. He spoke English and Spanish, as well as the Ute dialects, was an excellent shot, a good judge of horse flesh, and particularly gifted in the art of pantomime. He executed raids for the purpose of accumulating cattle, and in Mexico, where he did most of his business, he was said to have a collection of the most beautiful black-haired brides in the country. Walker dressed in a brown broadcloth suit, cut in European fashion, a fine cambric shirt and a shining beaver hat. To these he added Indian trimmings and beads; and he was said to cut a fine figure as he rode at the head of his more primitive warriors. Walker and Brigham Young became great friends, and usually the chief treated the Mormons with respect and their property with consideration. When Brigham Young made his annual tours of the Mormon settlements in the north and south of Utah, he always visited Walker and brought him gifts. Upon one occasion Brigham Young laid hands on the Indian chief, at his request, to cure him of a depression of spirit, and sang Mormon hymns to him. "He traveled with us to Iron County," Brigham Young said of this visit, "and had dreams which amounted to revelations. If I could keep him with me all the time, do you suppose he would have an evil spirit? No, he would be filled with the Spirit of the Lord." George A. Smith once said in a sermon:

"I tell you in a country like this, where women are scarce and hard to get, we have great need to take care of them, and not let the Indians have them.

"Walker himself has teased me for a white wife; and if any of the sisters will volunteer to marry him, I believe I can close the war forthwith. I am certain, unless men take better care of their women, Walker may supply himself on a liberal scale, and without closing the war either.

"In conclusion I will say, if any lady wishes to be Mrs. Walker, if she will report herself to me, I will agree to negotiate the match." [7]

On March 13, 1850, assisted by his first counselors, Heber Kimball and Willard Richards, Brigham Young baptized Walker and his brother, Arapeen, into the Mormon Church. This, how-

[7] *Journal of Discourses,* vol. 1, p. 197.

ever, did not prevent the chief from making war on his Mormon brethren three years later. During this war Brigham Young steadfastly refused to attempt the extermination of the band. When the Indians were cornered and helpless, Brigham Young sent Walker tobacco, "to smoke when he is lonely in the mountains." "He is now at war with the only friends he has upon the earth," Brigham Young explained to his people, "and I want him to have some tobacco to smoke." Accompanying the tobacco was this letter:

"Great Salt Lake City, July 25, 1853.

"Capt. Walker:—I send you some tobacco for you to smoke in the mountains when you get lonesome. You are a fool for fighting your best friends, for we are your best friends, and the only friends you have in the world. Everybody else would kill you if they could get a chance. If you get hungry send some friendly Indians down to the settlements and we will give you some beef-cattle and flour. If you are afraid of the tobacco which I send you, you can let some of your prisoners [Mormons] try it first, and then you will know that it is good. When you get good-natured again, I would like to see you. Don't you think you should be ashamed? You know that I have always been your best friend.

"BRIGHAM YOUNG."

In 1855 Brigham Young, as Governor of the Territory of Utah, sent the following message on the Indians to the territorial legislature:

"To retaliate for every outbreak by taking their lives, either through civil or military power, and severely chastising them for every depredation, is actually descending to their grade of conduct, and still more excites them to acts of savage barbarity.

"We witness, in the surrounding territories, the effects of the war policy in an almost constant scene of mutual carnage and bloodshed, while our experience confirms the opinion of many eminent statesmen, that the conciliatory course is far the most humane and successful, as well as the most economical.

"I therefore appeal to you, Gentlemen, to use your influence throughout the Territory to preserve the policy of feeding and clothing the natives, of giving them employment, teaching them to obtain a living by their labor, and exercising patience, perseverance and forbearance towards them, as well as care and watchfulness.

"Let this policy be strictly adhered to in all our settlements, and the chances are that we shall hear of no Indian massacres and depredations, at least not to any great extent." [8]

But in spite of this humane policy, there were occasional Indian difficulties. As the white men began to settle in Utah the Indians lost their pasture lands and hunting grounds, which were turned rapidly into Mormon towns and ranches. They were offered by circumstances the choices of starvation, livelihood by farming with methods unfamiliar to them, and plunder. Farming was not congenial to their migratory habits, practised for centuries, starvation was unthinkable, so that there remained only plunder. The United States government had, it is true, Indian agents, but the appropriations were always insufficient and usually late. They were at best merely palliatives. The Indians lived on roots, reptiles, insects, and grass-seed when they could not steal emigrants' or Mormons' cattle and grain. Whenever they could do so, they did, to the great inconvenience, chagrin and moral indignation of the emigrants and the Mormons. Finally General Connor defeated the Indians at the Battle of Bear River, where more than three hundred Indians were killed. This disaster made the other Indians somewhat timid, and herds and flocks were thereafter safe in Utah. Treaties were finally signed with the Indians in 1863, by which they agreed to keep the peace, and received in return annuities of $21,000 worth of goods for a period of twenty years.

III

Every year Mormons arrived from Winter Quarters, and new converts came from England; a year after the first Mormons arrived in Utah plans were made for new settlements, one ten miles north of Salt Lake City, and the other ten miles south. On July 24, 1849, the anniversary of the arrival of Brigham Young in the valley was celebrated, and every year thereafter July 24 has been observed as Pioneer Day and commemorated with appropriate ceremonies. At the first celebration in 1849 a large American flag, "sixty-five feet in length," we are told, was unfurled "at the top of the liberty pole, which is one hundred and four feet high." "Seventy-four young men dressed in white, with white scarfs on their right shoulders, and coronets on their

[8] *Millennial Star*, vol. 18, p. 260.

heads, each carrying in his right hand a copy of the declaration of independence and the constitution of the United States, and each carrying a sheathed sword in his left hand," were followed by "seventy-four young ladies, dressed in white, and with white scarfs on their right shoulders, and wreaths of white roses on their heads, each carrying a copy of the Bible and the Book of Mormon." At the meeting which followed this procession, the Declaration of Independence was presented to Brigham Young by one of the seventy-four young men in white, and all the people, led by Brigham Young, shouted, "May it live for ever." When the Mormons discovered that the land which they had expected to appropriate from Mexico was already confiscated by the United States, they did not hesitate to declare their loyalty to the government they had hoped to escape.

The new settlement survived crickets, Indians, and drought, but it was early subjected to a more serious test of endurance. The sudden, almost miraculous, discovery that gold lay under the ground in California, a short distance away, was the source of both potential profit and imminent disaster to the struggling Mormon community. The discovery of gold in California is credited to James W. Marshall, who was digging one day early in 1848 with a group of Mormons from the Mormon Battalion at Sutter's Fort, near Sacramento. Marshall, though not a Mormon himself, was in charge of these Mormon laborers, who were digging a mill race for Captain Sutter, when their shovels turned up some small yellow grains with the soft dirt. News of the great discovery was kept quiet at first, but by February, 1849, it had spread sufficiently to bring more than 8,000 emigrants in 137 ships, and by the end of the following month the *New York Herald* said that 18,341 men had left the eastern states by sea for California. By July, 1849, there were said to be 40,000 Americans in California, which just before the war with Mexico had been inhabited by less than 3,000. By January 1, 1850, there were 120,000 Americans and Europeans in California, and 12,000,000 dollars' worth of gold from there had been deposited at the Washington mint. It was estimated that 30,-000,000 dollars' worth had been mined during the year 1849.[9]

The first definite news of the extent of the gold discovery was

[9] These figures of population and mining are taken from *The History of North America*, vol. 13, *Growth of the Nation from 1837-1860*, by E. W. Sikes and W. M. Kenner.

brought to Salt Lake City by members of the Mormon Battalion, who went there from California to join their families. On their way they met emigrants en route to the mines, who were frantic for news of gold. One of the Mormons took out his purse and poured an ounce of gold dust into the palm of his hand, stirring it slowly with his finger, exhibiting its lovely gleam to those who were on their way to make their fortunes. One man of seventy watched this demonstration with intense interest, and when he saw the shining yellow dust, the first concrete indication that his long and arduous journey was not a fool's chase, he threw his old felt hat on the ground, jumped on it with all the vigor his age could command, kicked it high in the air, and shouted, "Glory, hallelujah, thank God, I'll die a rich man yet!"

The members of the Mormon Battalion brought into Salt Lake City gold in metal and in dust; this was used as security for the Kirtland Bank notes, which Joseph Smith had prophesied would be "as good as gold" some day. Brigham Young took this as another instance of the divine authenticity of the late Prophet. Mormon currency consisted at this time, besides these few notes, of blankets, grain, seed, and flour, and for many years after the discovery of gold, currency remained scarce in Salt Lake City, where the system of barter remained in use until 1860. A carpenter was paid for his work with an order on the stores, or, if he worked for the Church, with an order on the central tithing house. With this order he paid his rent and got food. Tithing was paid to the Church in cattle or grain, if the member was a farmer, and in labor, such as shingling church buildings, if the man was not. This system gave Brigham Young a great economic hold on his people, because a man could not easily accumulate riches convertible outside Utah, and it was therefore difficult to leave the territory, even if one became dissatisfied with its government or disgusted with its religion.

The discovery of gold and the immediate rush to mine it were both the greatest blessing and the greatest trial of the community at Salt Lake. The gold rush fulfilled the prediction of Heber C. Kimball that within a short time Mormons would be able to buy goods cheaper in Salt Lake City than in the East, and at the same time it threatened to disrupt the community by the temptation it offered its members to go such a comparatively short distance and get rich quickly. The opportunity to obtain supplies of all kinds from the emigrants who passed through Salt

Lake City was taken advantage of eagerly, and the danger of disruption was prevented by Brigham Young's powers of argument in the pulpit. For one thing, Brigham Young and his associates found great ironic satisfaction in the fact that those people who had reviled their Prophet because he was a money digger, were now engaged on a wholesale scale in the business of digging for money. But they forgot that Joseph Smith, in spite of alleged supernatural assistance, never found any money, while gold in tangible form was being taken daily from the ground in California.

The eager emigrants to California stopped at Salt Lake City to refresh themselves, and usually left as encumbrances much property that was invaluable to the Mormons. In Salt Lake City the forty-niners got their first glimpse of the gleaming little grains of gold dust, and the sight put them in such a frenzy of excitement, and aroused to such an extent the hopes which had been somewhat shattered by the depressing journey over plains, prairies, and mountains, that they wished only to push on as fast as possible, abandoning whatever they did not need to keep them alive. There were auction sales daily in the new streets of Salt Lake City, and a yoke of oxen with three or four heavy waggons would be offered for one light waggon and a horse to carry an emigrant, his shovel and pick, and the food he needed for the trip to the gold fields. · Mormons bought for thirty-seven and a half cents waistcoats which sold in St. Louis for $1.50, and tools which cost $100 in the East were purchased for twenty-five in Salt Lake City. The boon to the Saints was incalculable, for emigrants found plows, which they had brought cautiously in case gold should fail, an encumbrance, and the Mormons were able to replace their worn-out implements for fifty per cent. below their cost at wholesale in the eastern states.

Besides reviving trade and aiding farming, the California emigration had a social effect on the Mormon community, which was once expressed angrily by Elder Orson Hyde in a sermon which he delivered before the men and women at the semi-annual conference of the Church in October, 1854:

"What have I got to say concerning women that will come into the Church and kingdom of God, and bring dishonor upon themselves, and endeavor to bring it upon the whole Church, by cohabiting with those cursed scapegraces who are passing through here to California, who make their boast of what they did in Great Salt Lake City? I know their secret talk in their chambers, for the Spirit of God searcheth all things. . . .

"I am going to say something upon those who dishonor the Church and kingdom of God in this way. I will tell you what shall happen to those men and women who commit lewdness, and go and boast of it, and laugh in the face of heaven. The day shall come when their flesh shall rot upon their bones, and as they are walking it shall drop, and become a nauseous stink upon the highway. Now go and boast that you can get all you want for a dress pattern, or a yard of ribbon; go and boast of it, and the Lord Almighty shall curse you all the day long. (Voice in the stand, 'Amen.') And when you step, chunks of your flesh shall drop off your bones, and stink enough to sicken a dog. . . . For such abominable practices to come in our midst under the robes of sanctity, because there are liberal, holy, and righteous principles practised by the Saints, I say, curse their habitation and their persons; and if this is your mind, let all Israel say amen. (The whole of the congregation at the top of their voices said, 'Amen.') And let these contemptible wretches feel the 'Mormon' spirit, not by 'Mormon' hands, but by the power of God on high.

"I feel charged with the Holy Ghost sent down from heaven, and it burns in my heart like a flame, and this is the testimony I bear. If I do mingle in the streets with the crowd to engage in business as any other man, I am not always asleep, and insensible to what is passing around me. I do not profess to know a great deal, but some things I do know, and some things I do not know." [10]

Brigham Young devoted a sermon to the temptations offered to Mormon women by men on their way to California, and to the fate of those who yielded to them:

"How odious it was last winter [1854], in the sight of certain men who were here, to think that we had more lawful wives than one; yet they would creep into your houses, and try to coax your wives and daughters away from you. What for? Was it to give them a better character in the midst of the inhabitants of the earth, sustain them better, and make them more comfortable, and acknowledge them? No—they wanted to prostitute them, to ruin them, and send them to the grave, or to the devil, when they had done with them.

"I do not know what I shall say next winter, if such men make their appearance here, as were some last winter. I know what I think I shall say, if they play the same game again, let the women be ever so bad, so help me God, we will slay them.

[10] *Journal of Discourses*, vol. 2, p. 86.

but these were not the majority. Brigham Young once told in a sermon of a conversation he had with a gold seeker who was also interested in religion: "A man from Boston on his way to the gold diggings stopped a few days in this city and heard me preach. Soon afterwards I met him in the street, and he asked me if I knew where hell was. I told him I thought he was on the road to that very place; and when he crossed over the Sierra Nevada mountains into the gold diggings of California, if he discovered that he had not found hell, to come back and let me know. As I have not since heard from him, I presume he found it, which I now think a person will who goes East as well as West." [14]

While he was not particularly interested in making gold seekers Mormons, Brigham Young was vitally concerned with the tendency of Mormons to become gold seekers. His sermons at the period of mining activity bristle with denunciation of the lure of gold, and it was one of his greatest triumphs that the Mormons lost comparatively few men to the mines. The magnetic pull towards the mines one would think irresistible for men who were so near to them, compared with eastern rivals, and the opportunity to grow rich quickly was likely to appeal strongly to a people who had worked so hard on meager farms and lost so much in their frequent forced migrations. Brigham Young sensed the danger at once, and with vigorous arguments he appealed constantly to his people to make the wilderness blossom as the rose and enjoy the blessings of their paradise rather than subject themselves to the degrading influences surrounding the underground search for salvation. He was wise enough, however, to realize that if he told his people not to go to California, he would tempt some of the independent spirits towards forbidden pleasures, and therefore, in his rugged language, he told them to go to California and be damned. He thrust into their minds the fear of hell and the desire for salvation, and these two combined enabled the Mormons to resist temptation and at the same time to await patiently the promise of the other world, which Brigham Young constantly dangled before them. It has been said by anti-Mormons, but with no proof offered, that Brigham Young also dangled the threat of the other world before those who wished to leave for the gold mines, and that he, through his henchmen, used violence against them.

[14] *Journal of Discourses,* vol. 5, p. 341.

Brigham Young found it effective on his audience to disparage in his sermons the value of gold. "The true use of gold," he once said, "is for paving streets, covering houses, and making culinary dishes; and when the Saints shall have preached the gospel, raised grain and built up cities enough the Lord will open up a way for a supply of gold to the perfect satisfaction of His people. Until then, let them not be over-anxious, for the treasures of the earth are in the Lord's storehouse, and He will open the doors thereof when and where He pleases." Brigham Young's picturesque Yankee associate, Heber C. Kimball, once told the people in the Tabernacle: "I will tell you a dream which Brother Kesler had lately. He dreamed that there was a sack of gold and a cat placed before him, and that he had the privilege of taking which he pleased, whereupon he took the cat, and walked off with her. Why did he take the cat in preference to the gold? Because he could eat the cat, but could not eat the gold." "Gold," said Brigham Young, "is good for nothing, only as men value it. It is no better than a piece of iron, a piece of limestone, or a piece of sandstone, and it is not half so good as the soil from which we raise our wheat, and other necessaries of life."

After the California mines had been in operation for ten years and his own community had been established for twelve years, Brigham Young pointed with pride to the general prosperity of the Mormons compared with the haphazard fortunes of those who lived in California:

"Men, women and children run to California to get gold," he said. "They were then told what I can now prove. 'Go to California, if you will; we will not curse you—we will not injure nor destroy you, but we will pity you. If you must go for gold, and that is your god, go, and I will promise you one thing: Every man that stays here and pays attention to his business will be able, within ten years, to buy out four of those who leave for the gold-mines.' Since then some of those persons have come back, and thinking, 'O dear, I declare I wish the brethren could not know that I had been away! I want to appear as though I had not gone to California, and to be full of good works and faith.' Poor, ignorant, pusillanimous creatures! They come whining back and want to be considered in full fellowship, after leaving this place to which our God has led us, and after having used their means to feast and build up the Gentiles. . . . You may take all who have unadvisedly gone from this Territory, (and hundreds and thousands have so gone,) and I believe that

I alone am able to buy the whole of them, though when I came here I had but very little property, except what I owed for." [15]

Those Mormons who did leave Salt Lake City for California were warned not to come back there to die in piety, or, as Brigham Young expressed it, "Let such leave their carcasses where they do their work; we want not our burial grounds polluted with such hypocrites." Brigham Young, however, did not have any objections to the return of wealthy prodigals, who lent their money without interest to aid their brethren, but he was particularly vehement against those who refused to use their new riches for the benefit of their friends and the community. He once said in a sermon:

"If at the mines they will listen to the counsel of those men who have been appointed to counsel them, and when they return work righteousness, and do as they would be done unto, and acknowledge God in all their ways, they may yet attain unto great glory; but if they shall cease to hearken to counsel, and make gold their god, and return among the Saints, filled with avarice, and refuse to lend, or give, or suffer their money to be used unless they can make a great speculation thereby, and will see their poor brethren, who have toiled all the day, in want and perplexity, and they will not relieve, but keep the dust corroding in their purses, it had been better for them if a mill stone had been hanged about their necks, and they had been drowned in the depths of the sea, before they departed from the right ways of the Lord; for if they shall continue thus to harden their hearts, and to shut up their bowels of compassion against the needy, they will go down to the pit with all idolators, in a moment they are not aware, with as little pity as they have manifested to their poor brethren, who would have borrowed of them but have been sent empty away." [16]

IV

The economic advantages of the gold rush enabled the Mormons to continue their struggle to make the wilderness blossom as the rose with the odds slightly in their favor. Difficulties continued to present themselves, but the community succeeded in keeping alive and in satisfying the most imperative needs. Occasionally grasshoppers and drought combined to bring famine,

[15] *Journal of Discourses,* vol. 6, pp. 172-173.
[16] *Millennial Star,* vol. 12, pp. 244-245.

as in 1855-1856, when everybody ate only what was apportioned to him, but these periods were not many, and by careful storage of provisions in time of plenty, the community was able to survive in its dangerous isolation from outside aid. The success of the community was attributed by all who watched its early growth to the guiding influence and strict domination of Brigham Young. It was to obtain coöperative endeavor among his people and perseverance in the face of immense difficulties with the natural disadvantages of their environment that Brigham Young had devoted his life. He, and he alone among his people, realized that an autocratic communism was their only salvation, and he fought, sometimes savagely, to maintain this idea, which was to prove so successful economically. The odds were against him at almost every round in the fight.

First, Brigham Young had the powerful force of individuality and personality to batter down, and he did so by subduing all personal and temperamental traits which he could not harness to the community service. Brigham Young believed in education, but only in education which would later prove practically useful to its owner or to his neighbors, and preferably to his neighbors. To know something for the joy involved in finding it out was to his mind a complete waste of valuable time. In his sermons he was frequently contemptuous of pure science and philosophy, and he often ridiculed Professor Orson Pratt, who was the only mathematician and philosopher in the community. "We have few collegians among us," Brigham Young once told the congregation with an air of satisfaction, "but I know that a thoroughly educated man knows no more than you do, when his literature is displayed, though he spreads himself like the green bay tree." It would have been extraordinary indeed if Brigham Young had encouraged the fine arts and the pure sciences, for, as Sir Richard Burton wrote after his visit to the Mormons, "literature will not yet enable a youth to marry and to set up housekeeping in the Rocky Mountains." In order that the community might prosper, it was necessary that the youths should think only of those things which enabled themselves and their neighbors to marry and set up housekeeping in the Rocky Mountains. It was necessary first that the wilderness should blossom as the rose, and then, perhaps, there would be no objection to a little poetry inspired by the roses. But manual labor which was at first a necessity, became imperceptibly in the minds of Brigham Young and his people the greatest of all virtues. In 1901, when the Church was wealthy and at peace with the world, Brigham Young, Jr., made this entry in his diary: "Had a lengthy talk with Pres. Snow. . . . Discussed Bro. —— paintings and his itinery for the next seven months to fulfill his year's contract to paint for the Church. Pres. Snow does not seem to feel the necessity of art among us this is too much of a luxury when we have so many poor wanting the necessities of life, at least this is the way it strikes me." [17]

Sir Richard Burton listened to a mild clash in the Tabernacle between Brigham Young and Professor Orson Pratt. Burton described the situation in these words:

"The Usman of the New Faith, writer, preacher, theologian, missionary, astronomer, philosopher, and mathematician,—especially in the higher branches,—he has thrust thought into a faith of ceremony which is supposed to dispense with the trouble of thinking; and has intruded human learning into a scheme whose essence is the utter abrogation of the individual will. He is consequently suspected of too much learning, of relying, in fact, rather upon books and mortal paper, than that royal road to all knowledge, inspiration from on high, and his tendencies to let loose these pernicious doctrines often bring him into trouble and place him below his position. In his excellent discourse to-day, he had declared the poverty of the Mormons, and was speedily put down by Mr. Brigham Young, who boasted the Saints to be the wealthiest (*i.e.,* in good works and post-obit prospects) people in the world. I had tried my best to have the pleasure of half an hour's conversation with the Gauge, [Orson Pratt was known as 'The Gauge of Philosophy'] who, however, for reasons unknown to me, declined." [18]

Brigham Young took delight in ridiculing the technique of philosophizing, and he once said in a sermon, "When I read some of the writings of such philosophers, they make me think, 'O dear, granny, what a long tail our puss has got!'" It was the language of erudition that irritated Brigham Young more than its ideas. He and Orson Pratt thought alike fundamentally, for Pratt, as Burton pointed out, only used his reading to build up

[17] Manuscript Diary of Brigham Young, Jr., p. 148. In the Manuscript Collection of the New York Public Library.
[18] *The City of the Saints,* p. 429.

a defense of his faith. Brigham Young was annoyed, however, by the variety of human expression, while Orson Pratt had sufficient feeling for words to wish to use them in their shades of meaning. Of the two, however, Brigham Young's sermons are far superior, for they have a simplicity of expression which adds to the charm of his ideas, while Pratt's ideas, much more meager in content, were always hidden in the convolutions of his expression. Once in a sermon Brigham Young gave his idea of human expression:

"The English language, in its *written* and *printed* form, is one of the most prominent now in use for absurdity, yet as a vehicle in which to convey our ideas *verbally*, it is one of the best, for extent and variety it goes before, and far beyond, any other. Its variety is what I dislike. The schools in the Southern, New England, and Eastern States, all teach the English language, yet the same ideas are conveyed with entirely different classes of words, by these separate communities. If there were one set of words to convey one set of ideas, it would put an end to the ambiguity which often mystifies the ideas given in the language now spoken. Then when a great man delivered a learned lecture upon any subject, we could understand his words, for there would be only one word with the same meaning, instead of a multiplicity of words all meaning the same thing, as is the case now. For instance, there are men in this house so technical in their feelings with regard to their choice of words, that when their ideas are formed, and they commence to convey them, they will stop in the middle of a sentence, and introduce another set of words to convey the same idea. If I can speak so that you can get my meaning, I care not so much what words I use to convey that meaning. . . .

"I long for the time that a point of the finger, or motion of the hand, will express every idea without utterance. When a man is full of the light of eternity, then the eye is not the only medium through which he sees, his ear is not the only medium by which he hears, nor the brain the only means by which he understands. When the whole body is full of the Holy Ghost, he can see behind him with as much ease, without turning his head, as he can see before him. If you have not that experience, you ought to have. It is not the optic nerve alone that gives the knowledge of surrounding objects to the mind, but it is that which God has placed in man—a system of intelligence that attracts knowledge, as light cleaves to light, intelligence to intelligence, and truth to truth. It is this which lays in man a proper foundation for all education. I shall yet see the time that I can converse with this people, and not speak to them, but the expression of my countenance will tell the congregation what I wish to convey, without opening my mouth." [19]

In an effort to simplify language, Brigham Young ordered the Board of Regents of the Deseret University, the educational institution established by the Mormons for the education of their own young in the faith, to draw up a system of simplified, phonetic spelling with an entirely new alphabet, known as the Deseret Alphabet. The Book of Mormon was printed in the new characters, but it was found more difficult to read Deseret than to read English, and the plan was finally abandoned.

"Often when I stand up here," Brigham Young once said in the pulpit, "I have the feelings of a person that is unable to convey his ideas, because I have not the advantage of language. However, I do not frequently complain of that, but I rise to do the best I can and to give the people the best I have for them at the time; and if it don't suit them they can go without it, for I am not responsible whether it suits them or not." Crudity and incoherence in speech were preferable, in Brigham Young's opinion, to verbosity. He likened his own and Brother Kimball's discourses to dishes of succotash, in which beans and corn were mixed, and "those who like the beans best can pick them out, and those who prefer the corn can select it out." And it is undeniable that his and Brother Kimball's sermons are, with a few exceptions, the only documents in the more than twenty volumes of the *Journal of Discourses* which have any interest as reflections of personality unvarnished by unsuccessful attempts at conscious erudition.

Brigham Young did not read much; Sir Richard Burton said of him that "his mind was uncorrupted by books." One of his associates, who later left the Church, T. B. H. Stenhouse, wrote in his book, *The Rocky Mountain Saints,* that Brigham Young "probably never read a book, outside of the Mormon faith, in his life. His secretary, or Mr. Cannon, generally reads to him anything considered interesting or amusing. Their enlightenment of his mind is always in the direction of his own prejudices." When Vice-President Schuyler Colfax visited Salt Lake City, Brigham Young delivered a defense of polygamy for the benefit of his distinguished visitor. He argued that Martin Luther had approved of polygamy when he sanctioned the mar-

[19] *Journal of Discourses,* vol. I, p. 170.

riage of Philip, Landgrave of Hesse-Darmstadt, to a second wife while his first wife was still alive and married to him. Brigham Young's history had been prepared for him in advance by his secretaries, and when he looked at his notes, he saw something about Philip Landgrave of Hesse; he spoke to the audience of that eminent polygamist, "Mr. Philip Landgrave, of Hesse," much to the amusement of his Gentile visitors and the mortification of his more educated and more self-conscious brethren. "I will acknowledge," Brigham Young once said in a sermon, "my lack of memory to retain scientific phrases, and the names of places, and of men who have figured in the history of the world. With these exceptions, I am not a whit behind them [the Gentiles] as to a knowledge of things as they are, though I confess that my knowledge is limited." His statement was modest, for, in a knowledge of things as they are, he was far and away ahead of most of his contemporaries.

Sometimes Brigham Young was conscious of his own crudities and those of his people; he once explained them in a sermon:

"It is true that we have not the etiquette here, as a general thing that is in the world; and this is not at all strange when the circumstances in which most of the people have been reared are considered. When I meet ladies and gentlemen of high rank, as I sometimes do, they must not expect from me the same formal ceremony and etiquette that are observed among the great in the courts of kings. In my youthful days, instead of going to school, I had to chop logs, to sow and plant, to plow in the midst of roots barefooted, and if I had on a pair of pants that would cover me I did pretty well. Seeing that this was the way I was brought up they cannot expect from me the same etiquette and ceremony as if I had been brought up at the feet of Gamaliel. . . . Many and many a man here, who is now able to ride in his waggon and perhaps in his carriage, for years and years before he started for Zion never saw daylight. His days were spent in the coal mines, and his daily toil would commence before light in the morning and continue until after dark at night. Now what can be expected from a community so many of whose members have been brought up like this, or if not just like this, still under circumstances of poverty and privation? . . . But I will tell you what we have in our mind's eye with regard to these very people, and what we are trying to make of them. We take the poorest we can find on earth who will receive the truth, and we are trying to make ladies and gentlemen of them. We are trying to educate them, to school their children, and to so train them that they may be able to gather around them the comforts of life, that they may pass their lives as the human family should do— that their days, weeks, and months may be pleasant to them. We prove that this is our design, for the result, to some extent, is already before us." [20]

That Brigham Young's design and its execution were productive of the greatest good to the greatest number cannot be denied, and the very few who chafed under the lack of Epicureanism, as in all pioneer civilizations, had to be sacrificed to the majority, who were Yankee farmers, English miners and mechanics, and Scandinavian peasants, whose ideals were those Brigham Young tried so hard and so successfully to satisfy. Even Orson Pratt, much as he may have preferred higher mathematics to problems in irrigation, was in favor of this sacrifice, for in his periodical, *The Seer,* he went further even than Brigham Young:

"Painting, music, and all the fine arts, should be cherished, and cultivated, as accomplishments which serve to adorn and embellish an enlightened, civilized people, and render life agreeable and happy; but when these are cultivated, to the exclusion of the more necessary duties and qualifications, it is like adorning swine with costly jewels and pearls to make them appear more respectable: these embellishments only render such characters a hundred fold more odious and disgustful than they would otherwise appear." [21]

On one occasion Brigham Young described to his people the mechanism of his practical mind:

"This is my philosophy on thinking; and if I were obliged to think for ten years, and not erect a building, or help build up a city, or in any way put my thoughts into execution, it would materially injure my mental faculty, through want of results for it to rest upon. But let me engage in active operations, even though I do not personally perform one day's manual labor, let me see the result of my thinking budding into existence, and my mind has something to rest upon. . . . Can you go to sleep in one minute, after you have said your prayers and gone to bed? Can you cease reflection, bid good-bye to thought, and say to the body, compose yourself and let us go to sleep? How many now in this house can do that? Whether it is natural or supernatural, mental or mechanical, it matters not, but I have trained myself to go to sleep when I get ready, and when I

[20] *Journal of Discourses,* vol. 14, p. 103.
[21] *The Seer,* p. 187.

am in good health, as a general thing, in about one minute I can be fast asleep." [22]

Brigham Young was Julius Cæsar's ideal; he was neither lean, nor hungry, he did not think too much for his material welfare, and he suffered no one around him to do so. For, as head of the Mormon community, Brigham Young demanded and received implicit obedience. "If this people will do as they are told," he said, "will please those who preside over them, they will do well for themselves. And if they will do this from morning to evening and from evening to morning, all will be right, and their acts will tend to promote the kingdom of God on the earth." He pointed out previously that if the people were really living "in the enjoyment of the Spirit of the Lord Jesus Christ," and had "the testimony of Jesus within them" they would know instinctively when their leaders were taking them astray, and could therefore deliver themselves over to the head of the Church with perfect confidence. When some of them did occasionally protest against some action of Brigham Young or his associates, they were usually told that they lacked the enjoyment of the Spirit of the Lord Jesus Christ, and were in the possession of Satan. On the whole, however, Brigham Young was satisfied with his flock, who usually followed his leadership with unquestioning obedience. After they were in Utah for ten years, he once compared their lot and his position with that of the children of Israel and Moses:

"It will be twenty-seven years on the sixth of next month, since this Church was organized. What do you think about this people? I say that the virtuous acts of their lives beat the whole world. Were the children of Israel ever so obedient to Moses, as this people are to me? No, they never began to be; for obedience they could not favorably compare with this people. Moses led his people forty years in the wilderness in rebellion, fighting, stealing, whoring, and every manner of iniquity; and their evils were so great, that God cut every one of them off in the wilderness, except Caleb and Joshua. He did not suffer one of them to go into the land of Canaan, except the two I have named; they never revolted from Moses, but held up his hands all the time. They never turned away, not even when Aaron, his half-brother and right-hand man, made the golden calf." [23]

22 *Journal of Discourses*, vol. 3, p. 249.
23 *Journal of Discourses*, vol. 4, p. 269.

Heber Kimball, Brigham Young's right-hand man, never tired of comparing the people to clay in the hands of the potter and to iron in the hands of the blacksmith, and it never seemed to occur to any one that the comparison was not flattering. The people were quite content to be as clay and as iron, for they trusted their potter and blacksmith thoroughly.

Brigham Young soon became to his people a combination oracle and nursemaid. An old lady once called at his office to ask whether, according to the word of the Lord, it was better to wear red or yellow flannel next the skin. Brigham Young counseled her by all means to wear yellow. Upon another occasion a woman rushed to him and tearfully complained that her husband had told her to go to Hell. Brigham Young looked at her solemnly and said, "Well, don't go; don't go." He encouraged this tendency to consult him on everything, and he once said in a sermon: "If you do not know what to do in order to do right, come to me at any time, and I will give you the word of the Lord on the subject." They came, and Brigham Young devoted much of his time to their minute troubles, for he realized that such time was not wasted for a man in his position. His patience helped to inform him of the most intimate details of the life of his people, and it increased the confidence which those people reposed in him, their respect for him, and his power over them, for he soon got to know who were his enemies when he became arbiter of the quarrels of the community. There was nothing too small for his attention. In a letter to the elders in England Willard Richards once wrote: "Our president don't stick at any thing that tends to advance the gathering of Israel, or promote the cause of Zion in these last days; he sleeps with one eye open and one foot out of bed, and when any thing is wanted, he is on hand, and his counselors are all of one heart with him in all things." Summing up the manifold duties and privileges of Brigham Young, a less reverent observer once remarked: "In addition to all this, he heals the afflicted by the laying on of hands, and comforts the widow by becoming her husband."

It would seem at first that rugged Yankees, who had heard nothing but talk of independence and liberty in their youth, would not have tolerated the paternal despotism which Brigham Young exercised over them. He himself was conscious of the conflict of his practice with the general superficial philosophy of Americans, and he gave his opinion of the common ideals of independence and individual freedom:

"We are in a land of liberty; and our fathers have taught us—especially those born in America, that every man and woman and every child old enough to speak, argue, read, reflect, etc., must have minds of their own, and not listen to anybody else. They are taught to shape their own opinions, and not depend upon others to direct their thoughts, words, or actions. That system of teaching reminds me of the old saying, 'Every man for himself, and the Devil for them all.' Such views, though entertained by the family at large, must be checked in this people. . . .

"My maxim is, and it is a rule I have established in the Legislature of this Territory, never to oppose anything unless the one making the objection can present something better. Do not oppose when you cannot improve. If you are not capable of dictating your brethren, do not say that you will dictate them until you have found out a better path than the one in which they are walking." [24]

It did not seem to occur to Brigham Young or to any of his followers that it is not necessary to know better in order to distinguish bad. They accepted this binding rule of procedure, and kept silent. The reason why they turned over their independence of thought and action to their leader was contained in his jocular statement in the pulpit once, when he was asked if he regarded himself as a prophet. He replied, "I am of profit to my people," and so long as he remained so, they asked for very little else. They even worshiped him for it. Heber Kimball once said in the Bowery at Salt Lake City: "On account of the breeze that is playing beneath this shade, brother Brigham thought I had better put on my hat, but I never feel as though I wanted to wear my hat when he is present. I consider that the Master should wear his hat, or hang it on the peg that God made for it, which is his head, of course." Brigham Young usually wore a large, black, felt, "stovepipe" hat in public, and he seldom took it off indoors.

Another reason for the success of Brigham Young's domination was his modest insistence that all he was or could ever hope to become was due to the Lord, and that he was nothing in himself without the guidance of God. This appealed strongly to a people who had accepted Joseph Smith as a direct representative

[24] *Journal of Discourses*, vol. 6, pp. 41, 44.

of the Almighty. Brigham Young, however, did not believe in bothering the Lord, directly, too much. His expressed policy was to devote himself to works first with all his ability, and to faith only after the possibilities of his works were exhausted. "It is the Lord," he said once during a drought, "that gives the increase. He could send showers to water our fields, but I do not know that I have prayed for rain since I have been in these valleys until this year, during which I believe that I have prayed two or three times for rain, and then with a faint heart, for there is plenty of water flowing down these cañons in crystal streams as pure as the breezes of Zion, and it is our business to use them. I do not feel disposed to ask the Lord to do for me what I can do for myself. I know when I sow the wheat and water it that I cannot give the increase, for that is in the hands of the Almighty; and when it is time to worship the Lord, I will leave all and worship Him." [25]

Brigham Young insisted that his people follow his example of mixing work with their faith and preparedness with their prayer. Only when artificial circumstances prevented a man from taking care of himself, was he justified in taking his troubles to the Lord. He once expressed this idea in this language:

"When a person is placed in circumstances that he cannot possibly obtain one particle of anything to sustain life, it would then be his privilege to exercise faith in God to feed him, who might cause a raven to pick up a piece of dried meat from some quarter where there was plenty, and drop it over the famishing man. When I cannot feed myself through the means God has placed in my power, it is then time enough for Him to exercise His providence in an unusual manner to administer to my wants. But while we can help ourselves, it is our duty to do so. If a Saint of God be locked up in prison, by his enemies, to starve to death, it is then time enough for God to interpose, and feed him.

"While we have a rich soil in this valley, and seed to put in the ground, we need not ask God to feed us, nor follow us round with a loaf of bread begging of us to eat it. He will not do it, neither would I, were I the Lord. We can feed ourselves here; and if we are ever placed in circumstances where we cannot, it will then be time enough for the Lord to work a miracle to sustain us." [26]

[25] *Journal of Discourses,* vol. 3, p. 331.
[26] *Journal of Discourses,* vol. 1, p. 108.

Brigham Young believed with Oliver Cromwell in trusting to God but keeping the powder dry, and with Mohammed in trusting to Allah but tying up the camels. When he feared the fate of Joseph Smith at the hands of his enemies, Brigham Young used this combination: "I have prayed many times, and had a man at the door to watch for the murderer who thirsted for my blood. Then he would pray, and I would watch. What for? To kill the blood-thirsty villain."

We have seen that Brigham Young believed in hell as well as heaven, and in works as well as faith; he also believed in the virtues of adversity as well as those of prosperity. He retained many of the principles of Puritanism which were inculcated in him by the environment of his youth; but the one which remained all his life, and which he impressed upon his people was the principle that hardship is a blessing, for without it no one could know the value of ease. His sermons were littered with manifestations of this sentiment. "Suppose you were rolling in wealth," he told his congregation one Sunday morning, "and perfectly at your ease, with an abundance around you, you might have remained in that condition until Domesday, and never could have known about the works of God, in the great design of the creation, without first being made acquainted with the opposite." Brigham Young forced his people to believe that adversity was a part of salvation, because it was necessary for the temporal welfare of the Mormons that they should believe in the lessons of hardship, for, unless they could face their discouragements in the form of crickets to eat their crops and Indians to steal their cattle, with the assurance that comfort was in the offing and would be all the more poignant when it came, they were likely to despair, and despair would have wrecked that colony in the valley of the Salt Lake faster than Indians, crickets, or armies. Those who survived the hardships, which were something in the nature of tests, would be saved, said Brigham Young, and those who turned aside from them to search for the vanity of human riches would be damned to eternal damnation. "There is not a hardship, there is not a disappointment, there is not a trial, there is not a hard time, that comes upon this people in this place, but that I am more thankful for than I am for full granaries. We have been hunting during the past twenty-six years, for a place where we could raise Saints, not merely wheat and corn. Comparatively I care but little about the wheat and corn, though a little is very useful." He once described the vanity of attaching too much importance to the things of this world:

"There are hundreds of people in these valleys, who never owned a cow in the world, until they came here, but now they have got a few cows and sheep around them, a yoke of oxen, and a horse to ride upon, they feel to be personages of far greater importance than Jesus Christ was, when he rode into Jerusalem upon an ass's colt. They become puffed up in pride, and selfishness, and their minds become attached to the things of this world. They become covetous, which makes them idolaters. Their substance engrosses so much of their attention, they forget their prayers, and forget to attend the assemblies of the Saints, for they must see to their land, or to their crops that are suffering, until by and bye the grasshoppers come like a cloud, and cut away the bread from their mouth, introducing famine and distress, to stir them up in rememberance of the Lord their God. Or the Indians will come, and drive off their cattle; where then is their wealth in their grain, and in their cattle? *Are these things riches?* No. They are the things of this world, made to decay, to perish, or to be decomposed, and thus pass away." [27]

Fortunately for their peace of mind, neither Brigham Young nor his people ever allowed themselves to believe for one moment that they, perhaps, might be things of this world, made to decay, to perish, or to be decomposed, and thus pass away.

George Bernard Shaw wrote: "The ruler who appeals to the prospect of heaven to console the poor and keep them from insurrection also curbs the vicious by threatening them with hell. In the Koran we find Mahomet driven more and more to this expedient of government; and experience confirms his evident belief that it is impossible to govern without it in certain phases of civilization." Brigham Young used for purposes of government, not only the prospect of hell in the indefinite future, but also the prospect of adversity any day, in order that his people might be humble and docile in their prosperity. The result was that, except for occasional short famines and droughts, they were uncommonly prosperous.

Sooner or later the Mormons expected to extend their successful domain throughout the Far West. When they first petitioned Congress for a government, they asked to be admitted to the United States as the State of Deseret, the land of the honeybee, which was their translation of the name they adopted for their territory, where, as Burton pointed out, "that industrious insect is an utter stranger." They asked that the State of Deseret comprise all the territory from what is now Utah to the west, extending south as far as Mexico, and north as far as the Columbia River, including California and what is to-day the entire Far West. But Congress decided that the Mormons were biting off much more than they should be allowed to chew, and instead of admitting them as the State of Deseret, their domain was contracted to what is now Utah and Nevada, and organized in 1850 as the Territory of Utah. Brigham Young was appointed territorial governor by President Millard Fillmore, and in gratitude he named the capital city of the new territory Fillmore. In 1850 there were 11,354 people in Utah; in 1880, a few years after the death of Brigham Young there were about 120,000. The difference was made up largely by European emigration.

V

Brigham Young gave much attention to the work of the missionaries who were sent forth every year to convert people in England and the Scandinavian countries, as well as in the eastern states. When a missionary wrote to Utah from New York that the prospects for conversion there were bad, and that there was no room for preaching in the East, Brigham Young expressed it as his opinion that the opportunities for conversion were greater in New York than they had formerly been in Galilee: "Had I the choice," he said, "whether to go to the States and gather Saints, or to go where the Gospel was preached by the ancient Apostles of the Lord Jesus Christ, among the children of the people who have formerly had the Gospel preached to them, I would engage to go to the States and gather one hundred Saints to one that could be gathered from among the children of those who heard Peter, Paul, and others of the ancient Apostles preach the Gospel." On the whole, Brigham Young was satisfied with the labors of his missionaries, and he once said that if the mileage they covered was compared with that covered by the ancient Israelite preachers, the Prophets, Jesus Christ, and the Apostles, it would be found that the Mormon missionaries had covered much more ground.

Brigham Young established what was known as the Perpetual

SALT LAKE CITY IN 1853

From a contemporary engraving

Emigration Fund, to which his people contributed money and goods, to be used for the purpose of bringing to Zion foreign converts who could not pay their own traveling expenses. After they arrived in Utah, these converts were given work and were supposed to pay back the cost of their passage. The territory needed laborers and farmers, and women who would marry them and raise large families. This plan of advancing the expenses to converts caused some friction, for usually they were in no hurry to pay back what they owed after they were established on farms in Utah. Brigham Young in his sermons continually exhorted the people to pay their debts to the emigration fund.

Sometimes the elders in Europe took what money converts had and gave them for it drafts on Brigham Young, payable when they arrived in Utah. Brigham Young once described the anxiety for their money which the converts showed:

"There are men who have lately arrived in town who have a draft on me, and who have hunted me up for the cash before they could find time to shave their beards, or wash themselves, saying, 'I have a draft on you at ten days', fifty days', or six months' sight,' as the case may be, with, 'Please pay so and so. Brigham Young, cannot you let me have the money immediately, for I do not know how I can live without it, or get along with my business at all?' This is the kind of confidence some men have in me. I wanted to name this. Why? Because I am hunted; I am like one that is their prey, ready to be devoured. I wish to give you one text to preach upon, 'From this time henceforth do not fret thy gizzard.' I will pay you when I can, and not before. Now I hope you will apostatize, if you would rather do it." [28]

During the first ten years of the residence in Utah about 17,000 emigrants arrived from Europe. Before the gold rush started, the Church transported emigrants from England to Utah for fifty dollars each, including their food, but after the prices went up as a result of the increased traffic across the plains, the price was raised to sixty-five dollars. By 1857 there were seventeen places of worship for Mormons in Great Britain, and four thousand volunteer missionaries combed that country for converts. Denmark was the next best field, for freedom of religious discussion was allowed there. Germany and France, because of the differences of temperament and language, did not contribute many converts to Mormonism. The missionaries were always most suc-

[28] *Journal of Discourses,* vol. 3, p. 3.

cessful in districts where the climate was harsh, wages low, living conditions wretched, and where there were large numbers of illiterate men and women. Wales was a particularly fertile field. The Mormon missionaries made very little effort to convert rich men, for they had nothing to offer the rich man except the difficulty he would experience getting into heaven, and to him their proffer of a lot in Salt Lake City or the right to raise his own food and clothing would not appeal strongly. A table of occupations of Mormon emigrants, selected at random from the lists of several ships, showed that the greatest numbers were blacksmiths, bakers, butchers, bricklayers, shoemakers, boiler makers, carpenters, dyers, engineers, knitters, farmers, gardeners, miscellaneous laborers, miners, millers, masons, mariners, spinners, sawyers, tailors, and wheelwrights. The professions, however, were not altogether unrepresented. There were two butlers in one of the emigrating parties, and six hairdressers in another. Two artists, two confectioners, one doll maker, one dancing master, an interior decorator, two gamekeepers, one haberdasher, two innkeepers, one lawyer, one musician, an omnibus conductor, four stewards, six soldiers, a toll-gate keeper, four umbrella makers, a vellum binder, two valets, two university students, and a perfumer came to Utah to make the wilderness blossom as the rose.[29] A French observer found these nationalities in Salt Lake City, and he set them down in the following order of their numerical importance: "English, Scotch, Canadians, Americans (these are for the most part the original converts of Joseph Smith), Danes, Swedes, Norwegians, Germans, Swiss, Poles, Russians, Italians, French, Negroes, Hindoos, and Australians; we even saw a Chinese there." [30]

In the epistles to the Saints abroad issued by Brigham Young and his Apostles, they were urged to bring with them to Utah seeds of rare plants, "everything that will please the eye, gladden the heart, or cheer the soul of man, that grows upon the face of the whole earth," as well as birds, cotton, wool, flax, and silk machinery, or models for such machinery so that it could be constructed in the valley. An effort was also made to convert weavers and wool carders, so that home industry might be benefited by their association with the Church. The emigrants were also urged to bring with them a copy of every valuable treatise

[29] Statistics of immigration from *Route from Liverpool to Great Salt Lake Valley*, by James Linforth, p. 167.
[30] *A Journey to Great Salt Lake City*, by Jules Remy, vol. 1, p. 199.

on education, book, map, chart, or diagram they could obtain, for use in educating the children, because text books were almost as scarce as teachers in Salt Lake City. "We also want," read one epistle, "all kinds of mathematical and philosophical instruments, together with all rare specimens of natural curiosities and works of art, that can be gathered and brought to the valley—where, and from which, the rising generation can receive instruction; and if the saints will be diligent in these matters, we will soon have the best, the most useful and attractive museum on earth." A library of 2,000 volumes for which Congress had appropriated the money was dragged across the plains in 1852 by ox-teams. In the same year Wilford Woodruff brought to Utah two tons of school books. In 1851 a man brought a grand piano, carefully packed in straw, which he left during the winter on a bank of the Platte River, calling for it the following spring. Women brought as part of their luggage toasting-irons, waffle-irons, and gridirons.

The steady stream of emigration, beginning each spring and ending at Salt Lake City in the autumn, began to make the city a busy place. The population of Utah was doubled in a few years, and in 1856, before the Mormons had been in the Territory ten years, their census gave the population as 76,335, of which there was a surplus of about two thousand women over men. This census was taken by the Mormons, and since they were interested in showing a large enough population to entitle them to a state government, it has been claimed that they counted oxen, cows, the dead, the prospective children of couples who were engaged and would be expected to have children after they were married, and the children that some married people should have had in the estimation of the census takers. However, most estimates agree that the population of Brigham Young's domain after ten years approached 60,000.

A brass band usually went out to greet the emigrants as they arrived near Salt Lake City, and frequently Brigham Young accompanied the party of welcome; anti-polygamists have always intimated that his purpose was to look over the new arrivals among the women, with an eye to future wives, but there is no real evidence of this propensity. Often the emigration parties were late, and then teams were sent out with extra provisions to bring them in rapidly and save them from the hardships of winter in the mountains.

There was one disastrous emigration experience which was not forgotten for generations in Utah. In 1855, the year of its most serious crop failure, the colony found itself short of money and supplies. Large sums had been spent by the Church to build up the new community and to import its population. Brigham Young therefore found it necessary to economize, and he decided that instead of the more expensive ox-teams with prairie schooners, he would bring emigrants to Utah by supplying them with hand-carts, which he designed himself. These were small, light structures, which were loaded with luggage and pulled by the men and women themselves. A hand-cart would hold the clothing of the emigrant, or his baby and clothing, but very little else. The men and women walked beside their carts while one man pulled each cart, instead of riding in covered waggons. This sounded unattractive, but the elders preached the opinion of Brigham Young that the exercise would be beneficial and the speed greater. After the first party of hand-cart emigrants had arrived in Utah, Brigham Young wrote in a letter to England: "It is worthy of notice, that almost all the sisters who have this season crossed the Plains in the hand-carts, have got husbands; they are esteemed for their perseverance. I doubt not but many of their friends in England are already informed of this fact." He also suggested to the elders in charge of emigration that the hand-cart emigrants bring nothing with them except what they needed to wear on the journey and their food. "Thus you will perceive," he wrote, "the money usually spent in England for extra clothing and unnecessary 'fiddle-faddles'—for extra freight on the same, and for hauling this across the Plains, can all be saved; and most assuredly may be more profitably used on the arrival of the Saints here." To reinforce his argument in favor of his hand-carts, and to combat the objection that they did not hold enough, Brigham Young said in a sermon:

"I count the hand-cart operation a successful one, and there is a lesson in it which the people have overlooked. What is it? Let me ask the sisters and brethren here, what better off are you to-day, than as though you had started with a bundle under your arm? You started with an abundance, but have you any oxen, or waggons, or trunks of valuable clothing, or money? 'No.' What have you got? A sister says, 'I have the underclothes I wore on the Plains, and a dress, and a handkerchief which I pinned over my head in the absence of my sun bonnets which were worn out, and I am here.'

Are you here? 'Yes.' Did you come across the Plains? 'Yes.' Do you feel bad? 'O, no; I feel pretty well.' Now reflect, what else do we want of you, and what else do you want of yourselves? 'Why,' says one, 'I want a dress and a pair of shoes.' Well, go to work, and earn them, and put them on and wear them. 'I want a bonnet.' Go to work and earn it, and then wear it as you used to do. "What do you want here but yourselves? Nothing, but yourselves and your religion; that is all you want to bring here. If you come naked and barefooted, (I would not care if you had naught but a deer skin around you when you arrive here) and bring your God and your religion, you are a thousand times better than if you come with waggon loads of silver and gold and left your God behind. If I want to take a wife from among the sisters who came in with the hand-cart trains, I would rather take one that had nothing, and say to her, I will throw a buckskin around you for the present, come into my house, I have plenty, or, if I have not, I can get plenty." [31]

A Hand-Cart Song was composed by one of the Mormons and sung by the emigrants to emphasize the advantages of that mode of travel:

HAND-CART SONG

Tune—A Little More Cider.

Chorus: Hurrah for the Camp of Israel!
Hurrah for the hand-cart scheme!
Hurrah! hurrah! 'tis better far
Than the wagon and ox-team.

Oh, our faith goes with the hand-carts,
And they have our hearts best love;
'Tis a novel mode of travelling,
Devised by the Gods above.

And Brigham's their executive,
He told us the design;
And the Saints are proudly marching on,
Along the hand-cart line.

Who cares to go with the wagons?
Not we who are free and strong;
Our faith and arms, with a right good will,
Shall pull our carts along.

[31] *Journal of Discourses*, vol. 4, p. 203.

The first group of hand-cart emigrants left Liverpool in 1856. There were 1,300 men, women, and children, and at Winter Quarters they divided into five companies. The first of these left early and arrived safely in Utah, with no more than the ordinary hardships of such a long walk, but the last companies left late in August, and by the time they arrived in the mountains the weather was cold and their provisions were practically exhausted. An Oregon traveler who met one of the companies described them:

"We met two trains, one of thirty and the other of fifty carts, averaging about six to the cart. The carts were generally drawn by one man and three women each, though some carts were drawn by women alone. There were about three women to one man, and two-thirds of the women single. It was the most motley crew I ever beheld. Most of them were Danes, with a sprinkling of Welsh, Swedes, and English, and were generally from the lower classes of their countries. Most could not understand what we said to them. The road was lined for a mile behind the train with the lame, halt, sick, and needy. Many were quite aged, and would be going slowly along, supported by a son or daughter. Some were on crutches; now and then a mother with a child in her arms and two or three hanging hold of her, with a forlorn appearance, would pass slowly along; others, whose condition entitled them to a seat in a carriage, were wending their way through the sand. A few seemed in good spirits."

It is easy to imagine the depression of these people, pulling along their food and belongings in thoroughly new and startlingly wild surroundings, unable to enjoy even the comfort of small talk with those whom they met, alert for dangers that required constant presence of mind, and wondering about the nature of the life they were about to lead. When the cold overtook them, many froze to death in the mountains. Dysentery became an epidemic, and food being scarce, they killed their few cattle. Thirteen in one party were found frozen to death one morning and were buried hurriedly in a hole covered with willows and dirt. Parties passing that way the following summer found their bones scattered about by ravaging wolves. Of the four hundred in one division sixty-seven died on the way to Salt Lake City, and a few died afterwards from the hardships of the journey. The cold was so great that the rivers were filled with floating ice, which bruised the shins of the emigrants as they waded across pulling their hand-carts. Many of the people sat near the bodies of the dead to get from them whatever warmth was left.

Brigham Young rallied his people and rushed teams and provisions to the suffering emigrants, but all could not be saved. He insisted that his hand-cart scheme was a success and blamed the disaster entirely on the late start. This was to a certain extent true, but it was also true that with waggons the emigrants could have carried more food and protected themselves from the cold. Brigham Young made this statement concerning the deaths in the mountains:

"Some of those who have died in the hand-cart companies this season, I am told, would be singing, and, before the tune was done, would drop over and breathe their last; and others would die while eating, and with a piece of bread in their hands. I should be pleased when the time comes, if we could all depart from this life as easily as did those our brethren and sisters. I repeat, it will be a happy circumstance, when death overtakes me, if I am privileged to die without a groan or struggle, while yet retaining a good appetite for food. I speak of these things, to forestall indulgence in a misplaced sympathy." [32]

There was no room for sentimentality in Brigham Young's rugged character; the dead were dead, and would win salvation, the greatest of all blessings, and he turned his attention to making the lot of the survivors as comfortable as possible. One of the companies arrived on Sunday; news of the arrival was brought to Brigham Young in the pulpit as he was delivering his sermon, and he dismissed the congregation with these words:

"When those persons arrive I do not want to see them put into houses by themselves. I want to have them distributed in this city among the families that have good, comfortable houses; and I wish the sisters now before me, and all who know how and can, to nurse and wait upon them. . . . The afternoon meeting will be omitted, for I wish the sisters to go home and prepare to give those who have just arrived a mouthful of something to eat, and to wash them, and nurse them up. . . . Prayer is good, but when (as on this occasion) baked potatoes, and pudding, and milk are needed, prayer will not supply their place."

Hand-cart emigration was continued for another season to show that it could be done, for the Prophet, Seer, and Revelator had devised the system, and he must not be allowed to err. How-

[32] *Journal of Discourses,* vol. 4, p. 89.

ever, careful precautions were taken with subsequent parties to prevent disaster, and teams met them with several thousand pounds of flour and a supply of bacon. Finally, the hand-cart system was quietly discontinued.

Although Brigham Young was anxious to increase the population of his territory with laboring men and farmers, he did not offer inducements to individuals, and especially to professional men. Dr. David Adams, a physician of Illinois, wrote asking Brigham Young questions concerning the opportunities and advantages of the new colony, and expressed his desire to join the Mormons with one hundred of his friends and neighbors, if Brigham Young's answers were satisfactory. In his answer Brigham Young refused to promise the doctor comfortable prosperity, and he remarked: "It was the words of Jesus, 'leave all and follow me.' . . . Shall we then offer inducements of earthly prosperity to any man, to unite his destiny with ours? I will answer in the words of our Saviour, 'Seek first the kingdom of heaven and its righteousness, and all these things shall be added unto you.'" He added that at the moment, 1852, the people were prosperous, but that he could not guarantee that it would last, "for the Lord chasteneth whom he loveth." The doctor asked, "Is the Valley healthy? What diseases are most prevalent?" Brigham Young replied: "People die in all countries, in this as well as any other, although there is a difference in different countries, in relation to sickness and the manner of their death. In the first place, and to answer your questions, I do consider this an healthy country, as much so as any in which I ever lived or traveled; yet when disease once gets hold of a person, it is rather apt to terminate one way or the other, sooner than in those low countries, where a man may always be dying and yet be alive, yet never alive but always dying, until some friendly physician shall interpose, and put him quietly away, according to the most approved and scientific mode practised by the learned M.D.'s. . . . The most prevalent diseases here are fevers, sometimes called mountain fever, which are not very common; child-births; and, during the gold excitement, yellow fever; the last two, however, work their own cure; one by proper nursing, the other by a little hard experience." To Dr. Adams's question whether a physician of twenty years' experience could earn a living in Utah, Brigham Young replied that cultivating the soil was the most profitable profession, and that the physicians in Utah were also seen sawing wood, plowing and sowing, which was very good for their health. Then he added: "As an individual, I am free to acknowledge that I should much prefer to die a natural death, to being helped out of the world by the most 'intelligent graduate,' new or old school, that ever scientifically flourished the wand of Esculapius, or any of his followers."

In spite of their natural disadvantages, the Mormons "attached themselves to the soil, and increased with the rapidity of an isolated germ culture," as Professor Riley put it. During their first ten years they not only built up cities and settlements, farms and roads, but also customs and manners, which they practised openly in defiance of the opinion of the rest of mankind. One of these customs was the stern opposition to intoxicating liquor in any form, but Artemus Ward in describing the Salt Lake Hotel said: "It is a temperance hotel. I prefer temperance hotels—altho' they sell worse liquor than any other kind of hotels." Another custom was the far-famed practice of polygamy, which Brigham Young now declared openly and practised extensively.

Chapter VII

PURITAN POLYGAMY

I

DURING the first few years after their arrival in Utah, the fact that the Mormons practised polygamy was an open secret. Visitors who stopped at Salt Lake City on their way to California, and judges who were sent by the federal government to preside in the territorial courts, could not help but notice the multiplicity of wives, and once noticed, the phenomenon was not one which a man was likely to keep to himself. Brigham Young therefore decided in 1852 that the time had come to announce the doctrine publicly and to take the consequences, for he felt that his community was strong enough and sufficiently isolated to prevent any consequences. Besides, he was weary of whispering what he sincerely believed to be divine. Because of the prejudices which the very mention of more wives than one aroused in the minds of Gentiles and prospective converts, Brigham Young had delayed any public pronouncement of Joseph Smith's revelation. Elders abroad were denying every day that the Mormons enjoyed the association of more than one wife, although by this time there was much tangible evidence in the form of children by polygamous marriages; the presence of these children was sometimes difficult to explain to visitors without either admitting polygamy, or admitting what was considered to be worse.

In 1846 at a conference of the Saints in Manchester, England, Parley Pratt had declared polygamy to be "another name for whoredom," and in 1850 at Boulogne, France, John Taylor had denied that the theory or practice of polygamy was part of the Mormon Church doctrine or ritual. To support this denial he had read from the *Book of Doctrine and Covenants* the revelation given to Joseph Smith at Kirtland, in which polygamy was denied and denounced. At the moment in 1850 when he was issuing that vehement denial at Boulogne John Taylor had four wives in

Utah, and was courting a young girl who lived on the Isle of Jersey.

When Brigham Young had finally decided that the time for consistency was ripe, he assembled his people in general conference at ten o'clock on Sunday morning, August 29, 1852. Professor Orson Pratt opened the meeting with a long explanation of the scriptural significance of marriage. He told what God had in mind when He created Adam and Eve, and he gave it as his earnest opinion that the marriage between those two had been for eternity as well as for time. Then he took up the case of Abraham and his wife Sarah, who so generously gave her handmaiden Hagar to her husband, but Pratt forgot to mention that this gift was actually a loan, for breeding purposes only, and that Sarah suddenly said to Abraham one day, "Cast out this bondwoman and her son." Pratt did say that in the case of Hagar God's intentions, whatever Abraham's may have been, were honorable, and that He purposed to raise up multitudinous seed so that eventually there might be enough to inherit the earth. The Mormons, Pratt reminded them, were lineal descendants of Abraham, and it was their divine duty to act as he had done. This sermon, which extended for several hours, consumed the morning session; in the afternoon the meeting reconvened to hear the revelation on plural marriage read for the first time in public. Brigham Young prefaced the rendition with a short explanation of how Sister Emma had, in her jealous wrath, burned one copy of it, but how, fortunately for posterity, Bishop Whitney had preserved the other copy.

Soon after the publication at home and abroad of the revelation on polygamy, marriages for time and eternity took place without secrecy. Some women were married to their husbands for both time and eternity, and in those cases the husbands enjoyed all the marital privileges of this world, and the wives enjoyed the husbands' society in the next. There were also marriages for eternity only. These often took place between a man and a wife who had died, so that he might enjoy her society in heaven when he arrived there. Another form of this marriage for eternity was the sealing, as marriage ceremonies were called, of a woman to Joseph Smith, who was dead, or to Brigham Young, for eternity only. It was considered by the elderly women of Utah a great and sacred privilege to be the spiritual wife of Brigham Young or the Prophet Joseph Smith in the world to come. In this last instance of marriage for eternity, the wife did not enjoy the privileges of one in this profane world. There were no marriages for time only, unless the wives had engagements to other dead husbands for eternity. To marry a woman for time only would imply that the husband did not wish the society of his wife in the next world, and the relation would therefore have been purely temporal, and perhaps purely sensual, which was repugnant to the religious sentiment of the community.

It was also possible for a woman to obtain a divorce for eternity from a husband who had died. George Reynolds, one of the leaders of the Church, testified to this privilege of divorce from the dead before the United States Senate committee which was investigating the right of Reed Smoot to hold his seat in the Senate:

"SENATOR FORAKER: 'Are these divorce proceedings confined to the living? You spoke of marriages after death.'

"MR. REYNOLDS: 'I have known very rarely of a woman seeking to be separated from her husband after he was dead, and the president of the church hearing her statement has directed that the marriage be canceled on the records. . . .'

"SENATOR FORAKER: 'I should like to ask another question before we get away from the matter. It is about these divorces that are granted to women from their husbands who are deceased. Is that divorce, in the few cases you have referred to, granted on account of something that the man did in lifetime or something he is supposed to have done after death?'

"MR. REYNOLDS: 'In lifetime. We do not know anything they do after death.'

"SENATOR FORAKER: 'The proceeding is taken against him without making him a party or giving him a chance to be heard?'

"MR. REYNOLDS: 'That is exactly it, and that is why so few have been granted, because it has been regarded as unjust to the person who could not appear. But when the wife produced evidence sufficient to cause it to be evident that he had done certain things, making him unworthy of being her husband, then the divorce has sometimes been granted.'

"SENATOR FORAKER: 'Is anyone appointed to defend the dead man in such cases?'

"MR. REYNOLDS: 'No, sir.'

"SENATOR FORAKER: 'The proceeding is purely ex parte?'

"MR. REYNOLDS: 'Purely.'

"MR. TAYLER: 'Then the man who dies, the fortunate possessor of a half a dozen wives, has no assurance that he will find them at the end; that is to say, the church on earth has the power to dissolve after a man's death the bonds of matrimony that have tied him to several wives?'

"MR. REYNOLDS: 'Yes, sir.'

"THE CHAIRMAN (SENATOR BURROWS): 'I understand you to say that the power exists and is exercised through the president of the church?'

"MR. REYNOLDS: 'When exercised, it is exercised through the president of the church. He is the only man who has the right to seal and to loose.' " [1]

One would think that Brigham Young would have reserved decision on such cases until the parties met in heaven and the husband enjoyed the opportunity of answering before God.

Secrecy, which had at first been a necessity, was now adhered to as a rite by the Mormons, who, it must be remembered, had also been Masons. The ceremony of sealing was enshrouded in secrecy. Brigham Young once insisted in a sermon that a man who could not keep a secret, even from his wife or wives, was not only an object of ridicule, but one who could never hope to enjoy the eternal blessings of the celestial kingdom:

"Do some men know something that you cannot tell your wives?" he asked. " 'O, I have received something in the endowment that I dare not tell my wife, and I do not know how to do it.' The man who cannot know millions of things that he would not tell his wife, will never be crowned in the celestial kingdom, *never*, NEVER, NEVER. It cannot be; it is impossible. And that man who cannot know things without telling any other living being upon the earth, who cannot keep his secrets and those that God reveals to him, never can receive the voice of his Lord to dictate him and the people on this earth." [2]

Gibbon has described the results of the secrecy practised by the early Christians in words which apply almost exactly to the results of Mormon secret ceremonies:

"It was concluded that they only concealed what they would have blushed to disclose. Their mistaken prudence afforded an opportunity for malice to invent, and for suspicious credulity to believe,

[1] *Proceedings before the Committee on Privileges and Elections of the United States Senate in the Matter of the Protests against the Right of Hon. Reed Smoot, a Senator from the State of Utah, to Hold His Seat*, vol. 2, pp. 28-29.
[2] *Journal of Discourses*, vol. 4, p. 287.

the horrid tales which described the Christians as the most wicked of human kind, who practised in their dark recesses every abomination that a depraved. fancy could suggest, and who solicited the favor of their unknown God by the sacrifice of every moral virtue. There were many who pretended to confess or to relate the ceremonies of this abhorred society. It was asserted, 'that a new-born infant, entirely covered over with flour, was presented, like some mystic symbol of initiation, to the knife of the proselyte, who unknowingly inflicted many a secret and mortal wound on the innocent victim of his error; that as soon as the cruel deed was perpetrated, the sectaries drank up the blood, greedily tore asunder the quivering members, and pledged themselves to eternal secrecy, by a mutual consciousness of guilt. It was as confidently affirmed that this inhuman sacrifice was succeeded by a suitable entertainment, in which intemperance served as a provocative to brutal lust; till, at the appointed moment, the lights were suddenly extinguished, shame was banished, nature was forgotten; and, as accident might direct, the darkness of the night was polluted by the incestuous commerce of sisters and brothers, of sons and of mothers.' "

The details of the confessions and narratives of apostate Mormons and of professional authors, who claimed to have obtained their details from people who had received in the Endowment House the rites of sealing for time and eternity, were almost as lurid, though much less picturesque, as those which Gibbon quotes from Justin Martyr, Athenagoras, and Tertullian.

The polygamous marriage ceremony performed by Brigham Young in the Endowment House consisted of the ordinary marriage ceremony, with the exception that the first wife stood beside her husband and his new wife, and was asked if she consented to give her husband an additional wife. This consent was a formality, almost as superfluous as the question whether a man and woman take each other for husband and wife; usually, if the first wife had any objections, she was left at home during the ceremony. After this formality Brigham Young pronounced the man and woman sealed to each other for time and eternity.

The Endowment ceremony was quite different from that of marriage, and was presented in the form of an allegory; it is this scene which has given rise to many lurid, paper-covered pamphlets concerning the sexual secrets of Mormon knavery. At the ceremony the man and woman appeared in white shifts, with oiled hair and cleansed bodies, the oiling and cleansing, all innuendo to the contrary, being performed by male and female Mormons respectively in separate parts of the Endowment House. The couple then joined each other and entered a room, fitted up to represent the Garden of Eden, with a Devil, and a voice that played the part of God. It was a very amateurish and a very crude ceremonial, designed to instil the fear of the Lord and respect for His wishes, by means of an allegorical representation of the tale of Adam and Eve and the serpent. It was all sexually symbolic, but there was in it nothing in the nature of the primitive orgy which the heated imaginations of anti-Mormons have represented it to be. Even anti-Mormons have only stated that it was a primitive orgy, for their imaginations were not sufficiently powerful to supply the details, which they always hid behind a false decorum.

Combined with this allegory was an oath to avenge the death of Joseph Smith and his brother Hyrum, and it has been said that with this oath was combined the pledge to cherish enmity against the government of the United States until it did something about those deaths. Mormons, on the plea that to reveal the secrets of the Endowment ceremony was to break a most solemn covenant never to tell them, have always refused either to affirm or to deny the existence of such an oath.

When they received their endowments of celestial, eternal happiness, Mormons received a garment which was always to be worn next to the skin. It resembled very much the type of underwear known as a combination, and was fastened with strings at various places. Over the breast was a mystic sign, differing for man and woman. The garment was supposed to protect the wearer from danger to his or her life, and some of Joseph Smith's followers maintain that the only reason why the bullets fired at him were able to penetrate his body was his neglect to wear his Endowment garment that day.

The Endowment oath prescribed that if the covenant not to reveal the details of the ceremony was broken, the apostate was to have his bowels torn out and trampled under foot, his throat cut from ear to ear, and his tongue ripped from his mouth. This, however, was more impressive than practicable, for there is no trustworthy record of bowels that were torn out and trampled under foot, throats that were cut from ear to ear, or tongues that were ripped from tattling mouths; and enough people did tell about the Endowment ceremonies to supply sufficient victims.

The recklessness to carry out their horrible threats seems to have been lacking in the Mormon authorities.

Some one said of the Mormons that their creed was singular and their wives plural. One of the features of the Mormon marriage system which has been somewhat obscured in the emphasis that has always been placed on its plurality is the elaborate excuse which the Mormon theologians invented for the extensive reproductive activities of their people. According to the Mormon theory, God instituted polygamy solely for the purpose of multiplying the number of the righteous, and not to satisfy the carnal desires of man. A large part of the Mormon celestial world is inhabited by spirits, who go about, like Maeterlinck's souls of the unborn in *The Blue Bird,* searching for tabernacles. It is absolutely necessary to their eventual resurrection that these spirits should have tabernacles, or earthly bodies. Brigham Young once described their pitiable situation:

"The spirits which are reserved have to be born in the world, and the Lord will prepare some way for them to have tabernacles. Spirits must be born, even if they have to come to brothels for their fleshly coverings, and many of them will take the lowest and meanest spirit house that there is in the world, rather than do without, and will say, 'Let me have a tabernacle, that I may have a chance to be perfected.'

"The Lord has instituted this plan for a holy purpose, and not with a design to afflict or distress the people; hence an important and imperative duty is placed upon all holy men and women, and the reward will follow, for it is said, that the children will add to our honor and glory. . . ."

In the same sermon he outlined the advantages of many wives, from the point of view of capacity to carry out this holy duty:

"God never introduced the Patriarchal order of marriage with a view to please man in his carnal desires, nor to punish females for anything which they had done; but He introduced it for the express purpose of raising up to His name a royal Priesthood, a peculiar people. Do we not see the benefit of it? Yes, we have lived long enough to realize its advantages.

"Suppose that I had had the privilege of having only one wife, I should have had only three sons, for those are all my first wife bore, whereas, I now [1855] have buried five sons, and have thirteen living.

"It is obvious that I could not have been blessed with such a family, if I had been restricted to one wife, but, by the introduction of this law, I can be the instrument of preparing tabernacles for those spirits which have come in this dispensation. . . ."

Brigham Young made a mistake in this sermon, for his first wife bore two daughters and not three sons, but the extent of his family life, as we shall see, was a bit confusing. He was always certain, however, of one thing, in his sermons at least, and that was the purity of plural marriage, and the necessity for righteous men to do their duty, though all the wicked world raged. In this same sermon he said:

"I foresaw when Joseph first made known this doctrine, that it would be a trial, and a source of great care and anxiety to the brethren, and what of that? We are to gird up our loins and fulfill this, just as we would any other duty.

"It has been strenuously urged by many that this doctrine was introduced through lust, but that is a gross misrepresentation.

"This revelation, which God gave to Joseph, was for the express purpose of providing a channel for the organization of tabernacles, for those spirits to occupy who have been reserved to come forth in the kingdom of God, and that they might not be obliged to take tabernacles out of the kingdom of God. . . .

"I am aware that care and other duties are greatly increased by the law which I am remarking upon; this I know by experience, yet though it adds to our care and labor, we should say, 'Not my will, but thine, O Lord, be done.' . . .

"The Lord intended that our family cares should be greater; He knew they would be, yet He is able to bless us in proportion. I know quite a number of men in this Church who will not take any more women, because they do not wish to take care of them; a contracted spirit causes that feeling. I have also known some in my past life, who have said, that they did not desire to have their wives bear any children, and some even take measures to prevent it; there are a few such persons in this Church.

"When I see a man in this Church with those feelings, and hear him say, 'I do not wish to enlarge my family, because it will bring care upon me,' I conclude that he has more or less of the old sectarian leaven about him, and that he does not understand the glory of the celestial kingdom. . . .

"Now if any of you will deny the plurality of wives, and continue to do so, I promise that you will be damned; and I will go still further and say, take this revelation, or any other revelation that the

Lord has given, and deny it in your feelings, and I promise that you will be damned." [3]

Brigham Young insisted that it was not only man's duty to multiply his wives, but that if he did not do so, the one wife would be taken away from him in heaven and given to some one who had obeyed the commands of the Lord. And, so far as the women were concerned, they could not attain to all the privileges of the celestial kingdom if they remained unmarried or refused to obey their husbands. The Mormon said to his prospective wives, "I will give you the keys of heaven," and the women were so terrified at the prospect of being locked out that they accepted the husband. Heber Kimball once said in the pulpit:

"In the spirit world there is an increase of males and females, there are millions of them, and if I am faithful all the time, and continue right along with Brother Brigham, we will go to Brother Joseph, and say, 'Here we are, Brother Joseph; we are here ourselves are we not, with none of the property we possessed in our probationary state, not even the rings on our fingers?' He will say to us, 'Come along, my boys, we will give you a good suit of clothes. Where are your wives?' 'They are back yonder; they would not follow us.' 'Never mind,' says Joseph, 'here are thousands, have all you want.' Perhaps some do not believe that, but I am just simple enough to believe it." [4]

This system of feminine salvation through attachment to a husband seems to have impressed some of the women with the fact that they could do anything so long as they were sealed to Brigham Young, Joseph Smith, or one of the other leaders of the Church. Jedediah M. Grant, one of Brigham Young's first counselors, refuted this error in a sermon:

"Men and women are saved because they do right. It is nonsense for a woman to suppose, that because she is sealed to some particular man she will be saved, and at the same time kick up hell's delight, play the whore, and indulge in other evil acts and abominations.

"Even some mothers in Israel actually suppose that if their daughters are sealed to a certain man they will be saved, no matter what they do afterwards. That is damned foolery; and I want men

[3] *Journal of Discourses*, vol. 3, pp. 264-266.
[4] *Journal of Discourses*, vol. 4, p. 209.

and women to understand that salvation is based on a better foundation, that it is made up of righteousness, joy, and peace in the
Holy Ghost." [5]

The Mormons used to cling tenaciously to the Bible precedents
for their practice of polygamy. Heber Kimball once said that he
looked forward with joy to meeting and associating with Abraham, Isaac, Jacob, and the other famous polygamists, whom he
was sure he would meet in the next world. Abraham, by his
example, was particularly useful to the Mormons. Orson Hyde
once asked this rhetorical question in the pulpit: "Are we Abraham's seed, or are we bastards and not sons? That is the question." But the example of Abraham was one time a temporary
embarrassment to Brigham Young. G. D. Watt, the reporter of
the Church sermons, came to Salt Lake City from Scotland with
his half-sister. He called upon Brigham Young and asked to be
married to her. Brigham Young objected on the grounds that
the relationship was too close, and Watt pointed out that Sarah
had been the half-sister of Abraham, and he "reckoned he had
just as much right as Abraham." Brigham Young was impressed
with this argument; it is said that he tried to solve the difficulty
by marrying the lady himself for a few weeks. But he finally
came to the conclusion that what Abraham did was legal in the
latter days, and it is said he married Watt to his half-sister. [6]

But, in spite of their distinguished precedents from the Old
Testament, Mormon polygamy outraged the Gentile sense of decency, because the ideals of the Christian world since the publication of the New Testament had been virginity and celibacy. In
the early Christian church marriage was regarded as an unfortunate necessity at best, and the most pious people were those who
avoided it altogether by becoming priests or nuns. For hundreds
of years this attitude was carried on by the veneration and respect showered upon the virginity of Mary and the celibacy of
Jesus. It was somewhat natural that the Mormons should shock
their Christian neighbors, for they insisted that marriage was
not only a sacred act, but a divine duty, and compulsory to salvation. This was revolutionary to the theology of the time, for
even those Christian sects which permitted marriage among the
clergy were forced to admit that no man was a priest to his own

[5] *Journal of Discourses*, vol. 4, p. 128.
[6] *Mormonism: Its Leaders and Designs*, by John Hyde, Jun., pp. 56-57.

wife. The Mormons grasped the bull by the horns and not only recognized but sanctified the relationship of the two sexes. In order to establish precedents, the Mormons searched not only the Old Testament, but also the New Testament, and they usually found what they were looking for. When a congressman said in a speech that monogamy was divine, because Adam and Eve were monogamous, William Hooper, the Mormon territorial delegate in Congress, answered: "As for the illustrious example quoted of our first parents, all that can be said of their marriage is, that it was exhaustive. Adam married all the women in the world."

One would think that the Mormon elders would have had difficulty when they came to the New Testament, but it was not so. Occasionally clergymen of other denominations pointed out passages in the New Testament which seemed to forbid plural marriage to holy men. The most useful of these to the anti-polygamists was that contained in the third chapter of Paul's first epistle to Timothy, in the course of which he wrote: "This is a true saying, If a man desire the office of a bishop, he desireth a good work. A bishop then must be blameless, the husband of one wife, vigilant, sober, of good behavior, given to hospitality, apt to teach. . . ." Brigham Young's exegesis of this passage was ingenious, if not altogether convincing:

"Instead of my believing for a moment that Paul wished to signify to Timothy that he must select a man to fill the office of a Bishop that would have but *one* wife, I believe directly the reverse; but his advice to Timothy amounts simply to this—It would not be wise for you to ordain a man to the office of a Bishop unless he has a *wife;* you must not ordain a *single* or *unmarried* man to that calling. . . .

"I will now give you my reasons why it is necessary that a Bishop should have a wife, not but that he may have more than one wife. In the first place he is, or should be, like a father to his ward, or to the people over whom he presides, and a good portion of his time is occupied among them. . . .

"Paul, knowing by observation and his own experience the temptations that were continually thrown before the Elders, gave instructions paramount to this—Before you ordain a person to be a Bishop, to take the charge of a Branch in any one district or place, see that he has a *wife* to begin with; he did not say, '*but one* wife'; it does not read so; but he must have *one* to begin with, in order that he may not be continually drawn into temptation while he is in the line of his duty, visiting the houses of widows and orphans, the poor, the afflicted, and the sick in his ward. He is to converse with families, sometimes upon family matters, and care for them, but if he has no wife, he is not so capable of taking care of a family as he otherwise would be, and perhaps he is not capable of taking care of himself. Now select a young man who has preserved himself in purity and holiness, one who has carried himself circumspectly before the people, and before God; it would not do to ordain him to the office of Bishop, for he may be drawn into temptation, and he lacks experience in family matters; but take a man who has one wife at least, a man of experience, like thousands of our Elders, men of strength of mind, who have determination in them to preserve themselves pure under all circumstances, at all times, and in all places in their wards. Now, Timothy, select such a man to be a Bishop." [7]

Brigham Young seized upon other statements of Paul for use in defense of polygamy:

"I would now call your attention to some of the sayings of the Apostle Paul. I hope that you will not stumble at them. Paul says: 'Nevertheless, neither is the man without the woman, neither the woman without the man in the Lord, for as the woman is of the man, even so is the man also by the woman, but all things of God.' The same apostle also says, 'The woman is the glory of the man.' Now, brethren, these are Paul's sayings, not Joseph Smith's spiritual wife system sayings.

"And I would say, as no man can be perfect without the woman, so no woman can be perfect without a man to lead her, I tell you the truth as it is in the bosom of eternity; and I say so to every man upon the face of the earth; if he wishes to be saved, he cannot be saved without a woman by his side. This is spiritual wifeism, that is the doctrine of spiritual wives." [8]

Brigham Young would have agreed with Benjamin Franklin, who once referred to man without woman as "the odd half of a pair of scissors."

The Mormons were not content with appropriating Saint Paul for the defense of their doctrine. They went higher and took Jesus himself as an example. In discussing the wives of Jesus, Orson Pratt said: "The Evangelists do not particularly speak of the marriage of Jesus; but this is not to be wondered at, for St. John says: 'There are also many other things which Jesus

[7] *Journal of Discourses*, vol. 2, pp. 88-89.
[8] *New-York Messenger*, vol. 2, no. 10, pp. 75-76.

did, the which, if they should be written every one, I suppose that even the world itself could not contain the books that should be written.' " Orson Pratt was sure, however, that some of these unwritten things concerned the wives of Jesus, and he offered this argument: "One thing is certain, that there were several holy women that greatly loved Jesus—such as Mary, and Martha, her sister, and Mary Magdalene; and Jesus greatly loved them, and associated with them much; and when he arose from the dead, instead of first showing Himself to His chosen witnesses, the Apostles, He appeared first to these women, or at least to one of them, namely, Mary Magdalene. Now it would be very natural for a husband in the resurrection to appear first to his own dear wives, and afterwards show himself to his other friends. If all the acts of Jesus were written, we, no doubt, should learn that these beloved women were his wives." [9] Orson Hyde went even further than Orson Pratt on this subject. He traced a definite marriage, a suspicion, and offered a prediction:

"It will be borne in mind that once on a time, there was a marriage in Cana of Galilee; and on a careful reading of that transaction, it will be discovered that no less a person than Jesus Christ was married on that occasion. If he was never married, his intimacy with Mary and Martha, and the other Mary also whom Jesus loved must have been highly unbecoming and improper to say the best of it.

"I will venture to say that if Jesus Christ were now to pass through the most pious countries in Christendom with a train of women, such as used to follow him, fondling about him, combing his hair, anointing him with precious ointment, washing his feet with tears, and wiping them with the hair of their heads and unmarried, or even married, he would be mobbed, tarred, and feathered, and rode, not on an ass, but on a rail." [10]

Jedediah M. Grant quoted Celsus to prove that Jesus was persecuted because of the number of his wives:

"What does old Celsus say, who was a physician in the first century, whose medical works are esteemed very highly at the present time. His works on theology were burned with fire by the Catholics, they were so shocked at what they called their impiety. Celsus was a heathen philosopher; and what does he say upon the subject of Christ and his Apostles, and their belief? He says, 'The grand

[9] *The Seer*, vol. 1, no. 8, p. 159.
[10] *Journal of Discourses*, vol. 4, pp. 259-260.

reason why the Gentiles and philosophers of his school persecuted Jesus Christ, was, because he had so many wives; there were Elizabeth, and Mary, and a host of others that followed him.' . . . A belief in the doctrine of plurality of wives caused the persecutions of Jesus and his followers. We might almost think they were 'Mormons.' " [11]

Brigham Young and his disciples believed not only that Jesus had wives, but also that he had children. In several sermons on the marriage relation Orson Hyde defended himself from the charge of blasphemy because of his statements concerning Jesus's family:

" 'Mr. Hyde, do you really wish to imply that the immaculate Saviour begat children? It is a blasphemous assertion against the purity of the Saviour's life, to say the least of it. The holy aspirations that ever ascended from him to his Father would never allow him to have any such fleshly and carnal connexions, never, no never.' This is the general idea; but the Saviour never thought it beneath him to obey the mandate of his Father; he never thought this stooping beneath his dignity; he never despised what God had made; for they are bone of his bone, and flesh of his flesh. . . ."

"I discover," he said in another sermon, "that some of the Eastern papers represent me as a great blasphemer, because I said, in my lecture on Marriage, at our last Conference, that Jesus Christ was married at Cana of Galilee, that Mary, Martha, and others were his wives, and that he begat children.

"All that I have to say in reply to that charge is this—they worship a Saviour that is too pure and holy to fulfill the commands of his Father. I worship one that is just pure and holy enough 'to fulfill all righteousness'; not only the righteous law of baptism, but the still more righteous and important law 'to multiply and replenish the earth.' Startle not at this! for even the Father himself honored that law by coming down to Mary, without a natural body, and begetting a son; and if Jesus begat children, he only 'did that which he had seen his Father do.' " [12]

Brigham Young once delivered a sermon in which he told his people once for all the relative positions of the Father, the Son, and the Holy Ghost, which has perplexed mankind for so many centuries since the birth of Christ. Brigham Young insisted that Adam was a God, that he entered the Garden of Eden with Eve,

[11] *Journal of Discourses*, vol. I, p. 345.
[12] *Journal of Discourses*, vol. 2, p. 79; p. 210.

"one of his wives," and that they only became mortal after eating the forbidden fruit. Adam, according to Brigham Young, was also the temporal father of Jesus Christ, while his spiritual father was the Father of all of us. Adam occupied great importance in Brigham Young's theogony, for besides being a God he was also Michael, the Archangel, the Ancient of Days: "He *is our* Father *and our* God, *and the only God with whom* WE *have to do."* This creation of Adam as a God caused a sensation among people who had always been accustomed to regard him as the first sinner. Brigham Young was insistent upon another point in this connection: the Holy Ghost was *not* the father of Jesus Christ, for the Holy Ghost, he said, was the Spirit of the Lord, and as such he was in no position to beget children, while Adam was the Lord in the flesh and was fully capable of fatherhood. "Now, remember," Brigham Young said, "from this time forth, and for ever, that Jesus Christ was not begotten by the Holy Ghost. I will repeat a little anecdote. I was in conversation with a certain learned professor upon this subject, when I replied, to this idea—'if the Son was begotten by the Holy Ghost, it would be very dangerous to baptize and confirm females, and give the Holy Ghost to them, lest he should beget children, to be palmed upon the Elders by the people, bringing the Elders into great difficulties."[13]

These theological nuances which Brigham Young and his associates developed in connection with their defense of polygamy shocked their generation, and merely served to confirm in the minds of their contemporaries that these men were wicked and theoretically blasphemous as well as practically lecherous; whereas, the Mormons were honestly giving free rein to the simplicity of their own minds.

II

When polygamy was proclaimed openly by Brigham Young, some of the Saints refused to accept it, and believed that its proclamation meant that their elders had fallen from grace. The leader of this party was Gladden Bishop, and those who were of his opinion soon came to be known as Gladdenites. Gladden Bishop had been excommunicated and received back into the Church thirteen times. This opposition from within the fold

[13] *Journal of Discourses,* vol. 1, pp. 50-51.

infuriated Brigham Young, and he dealt with it in a sermon in these words:

"When I went from meeting, last Sabbath, my ears were saluted with an apostate crying in the streets here. I want to know if any of you who has got the spirit of 'Mormonism' in you, the spirit that Joseph and Hyrum had, or that we have here, would say, Let us hear both sides of the question, let us listen, and prove all things? What do you want to prove that an old apostate, who has been cut off from the Church thirteen times for lying, is anything worthy of notice?

"I heard that a certain gentleman, a picture maker in this city, when the boys would have moved away the waggon in which this apostate was standing, become violent with them, saying, Let this man alone, these are Saints that are persecuting (sneeringly). We want such a man to go to California, or anywhere they choose. I say to those persons, you must not court persecution here, lest you get so much of it you will not know what to do with it. DO NOT court persecution.

"We have known Gladden Bishop for more than twenty years, and know him to be a poor, dirty curse. Here is sister Vilate Kimball, brother Heber's wife, has borne more from that man than any other woman on earth could bear; but she won't bear it again. . . . I say to you Bishops, do not allow them to preach in your wards. Who broke the roads to these valleys? Did this little nasty Smith, and his wife? No, they stayed in St. Louis while we did it, peddling ribbons, and kissing Gentiles. I know what they have done here— they have asked exorbitant prices for their nasty stinking ribbons. (Voices, 'That's true.') We broke the roads to this country. Now, you Gladdenites, keep your tongues still, lest sudden destruction come upon you.

"I will tell you a dream that I had last night. I dreamed that I was in the midst of a people who were dressed in rags and tatters, they had turbans upon their heads, and these were also hanging in tatters. The rags were of many colors, and, when the people moved, they were all in motion. Their object in this appeared to be, to attract attention. Said they to me, 'We are Mormons, brother Brigham.' 'No, you are not,' I replied. 'But we *have been,*' said they, and they began to jump, and caper about, and dance, and their rags of many colors were all in motion, to attract the attention of the people. I said, 'You are no Saints, you are a disgrace to them.' Said they, *'We have been Mormons.'* By and bye along came some mobocrats, and they greeted them with, 'How do you do, sir, I am happy to see you.' I felt ashamed of them, for they were in my eyes a disgrace to 'Mormonism.' Then I saw two ruffians, whom

I knew to be mobbers and murderers, and they crept into a bed, where one of my wives and children were. I said, 'You that call yourselves brethren, tell me, is this the fashion among you?' They said, 'O, they are good men, they are gentlemen.' With that, I took my large bowie knife, that I used to wear as a bosom pin in Nauvoo, and cut one of their throats from ear to ear, saying, 'Go to hell across lots.' The other one said, 'You dare not serve me so.' I instantly sprang at him, seized him by the hair of the head, and, bringing him down, cut his throat, and sent him after his comrade; then told them both, if they would behave themselves, they should yet live, but if they did not, I would unjoint their necks. At this I awoke.

"I say, rather than that apostates should flourish here, I will unsheath my bowie knife, and conquer or die. (Great commotion in the congregation, and a simultaneous burst of feeling, assenting to the declaration.) Now, you nasty apostates, clear out, or judgment will be put to the line—and righteousness to the plummet. (Voices generally, 'Go it, go it.') If you say it is right, raise your hands. (All hands up.) Let us call upon the Lord to assist us in this, and every good work." [14]

The meetings of the Gladdenites were arbitrarily broken up, but they themselves, in spite of all threats, were allowed to live in the city uninjured. Soon, however, most of them disappeared, some going to California and some rejoining the Church.

The publication of the revelation on polygamy, and the open acknowledgment of its practice started a long period of vehement hostility to the Mormons. Dr. Bernhisel, the Mormon delegate to Congress, remarked that when the doctrine of plural wives was preached openly, the cat was let out of the bag, to which Brigham Young and Heber Kimball remarked that the cat had many kittens, which would always be a source of antagonism, for "Christ and Satan never can be friends; light and darkness will always remain opposites." It became the general opinion in the eastern states that polygamists were some species of beast, not at all resembling other forms of humanity, except in general, deceptive appearance. We find this attitude applied even to the offspring of polygamists: "Mr. Hart was the son of polygamous parents," wrote Charles W. Hemmenway in his *Memoirs of My Day,* "and yet he was a most exemplary, intelligent, and companionable young gentleman." The doctrine of plural marriage has always been called by the more picturesque and less polished of its

[14] *Journal of Discourses,* vol. i, pp. 82-83.

enemies the doctrine of "spiritual wifery." Those who opposed it could see in polygamy only a violent form of adultery, which was all the more reprehensible because it was practised openly and defended brazenly.

The Mormon point of view was entirely the reverse, for adultery to the Mormons was the worst crime a man could commit except murder. They distinguished between polygamy and adultery by reference to the life of King David. All David's wives, they said, were sacred and legal, but when he appropriated the wife of Uriah, he committed adultery, and God punished him for it. The Mormons believed that the penalty for adultery should be death. Howard Egan shot and killed his wife's seducer, James Monroe. In his speech defending Egan, George A. Smith said that the principle of the Mormon community was, "The man who seduces his neighbor's wife must die, and her nearest relative must kill him." Brigham Young agreed with this principle and promulgated it in a sermon, but he offered a mitigation of it to the consideration of his people:

"Let me suppose a case. Suppose you found your brother in bed with your wife, and put a javelin through both of them, you would be justified, and they would atone for their sins, and be received into the kingdom of God. I would at once do so in such a case; and under such circumstances, I have no wife I love so well that I would not put a javelin through her heart, and I would do it with clean hands. But you who trifle with your covenants, be careful lest in judging you will be judged.

"Every man and woman has got to have clean hands and a pure heart to execute judgment, else they had better let the matter alone.

"Again, suppose the parties are not caught in their iniquity, and it passes along unnoticed, shall I have compassion on them? Yes, I will have compassion on them, for transgressions of the nature already named, or for those of any other description. If the Lord so order it that they are not caught in the act of their iniquity, it is pretty good proof that He is willing for them to live; and I say let them live and suffer in the flesh for their sins, for they will have it to do.

"There is not a man or woman, who violates the covenants made with their God, that will not be required to pay the debt. The blood of Christ will never wipe that out, your own blood must atone for it, and the judgments of the Almighty will come, sooner or later, and every man and woman will have to atone for breaking their covenants. To what degree? Will they have to go to hell? They are in hell enough now. I do not wish them in a greater hell, when their consciences condemn them all the time. Let compassion reign in our bosoms. Try to comprehend how weak we are, how we are organized, how the spirit and the flesh are continually at war." [15]

The Mormons never tired of crying out against the hypocrisy of the Gentiles, who could tolerate prostitution and persecute polygamy. Orson Pratt wrote that they "strain at a gnat and swallow a camel," but the position was exactly the reverse. The Gentiles of the East could not possibly swallow such a large camel as polygamy, but promiscuous prostitutes, be they ever so numerous, were merely gnats to the righteous. They only came out at night, while polygamy stared people in the face brazenly. When Christian gentlemen traded with prostitutes, they did so in the knowledge that they had sinned, and afterwards rushed to their Father and asked Him to forgive them, for they knew not what they did, but the Mormons, in the minds of the Christian gentlemen, committed the unforgivable sin : they lived with more women than one and did not seem to realize that they were doing wrong, but, on the contrary, insisted that their way was the only righteous way. This was far from a gnat to the churchgoers of the eastern United States. The Mormons, on the other hand, maintained that the Gentile world practised in an ugly, immoral form what the Mormons preached as a beautiful, divine doctrine; they argued that the Bible forbids prostitution, but permits polygamy, while the modern world forbade polygamy, but tolerated prostitution. It was inconceivable to them that this could be just or righteous, for the Bible was the book of their law and the inspiration of their morality.

Two weeks before he publicly announced the principle of plural marriage Brigham Young expressed his opinion of the inconsistency of the Christian morality :

"Admit, for argument's sake, that the 'Mormon' Elders have more wives than one, yet our enemies never have proved it. If I had forty wives in the United States, they did not know it, and could not substantiate it, neither did I ask any lawyer, judge, or magistrate for them. I live above the law, and so do this people. Do the laws of the United States require us to crouch and bow down to the miserable wretches who violate them? No. The broad law of the whole earth is that every person has the right to enjoy every

[15] *Journal of Discourses*, vol. 3, p. 247.

mortal blessing, so far as he does not infringe upon the rights and privileges of others. It is also according to the acts of every legislative body throughout the Union, to enjoy all that you are capable of enjoying; but you are forbidden to infringe upon the rights, property, wife, or anything in the possession of your neighbor. I defy all the world to prove that we have infringed upon that law. You may circumscribe the whole earth, and pass through every Christian nation, so called, and what do you find? If you tell them a 'Mormon' has two wives, they are shocked, and call it dreadful blasphemy; if you whisper such a thing into the ears of a Gentile who takes a fresh woman every night, he is thunderstruck with the enormity of the crime. The vile practice of violating female virtue with impunity is customary among the professed Christian nations of the world; this is therefore no marvel to them, but they are struck with amazement when they are told a man may have more lawful wives than one! What do you think of a woman having more husbands than one? This is not known to the law, yet it is done in the night, and considered by the majority of mankind to be all right. There are certain governments in the world, that give women license to open their doors and windows to carry on this abominable practice, under the cover of night. Five years ago the census of New York gave 15,000 prostitutes in that city. Is that law? Is that good order? Look at your Constitution, look at the Federal law, look at every wholesome principle, and they tell you that death is at your doors, corruption in your streets, and hell is all open, and gaping wide to inclose you in its fiery vortex. To talk about law and good order while such things exist, makes me righteously angry. Talk not to me about law." [16]

According to Brigham Young, the sex contract between men and women outside the Mormon community was as short in duration as that entered into between a patron and a livery stable proprietor: "They are hired the same as you would hire a horse and chaise at a livery stable; you go out a few days for a ride, return again, put up your horse, pay down your money, and you are freed from all further responsibility." [17]

Visitors to Salt Lake City had to admit in their accounts of life among the Mormons that they met with no prostitutes and with very few women on the streets after dark. The town which they had expected to be startlingly immoral and enticingly free, they found to be a cold, orderly, regulated city, with all the social life concentrated in the institution of the family and the organiza-

[16] *Journal of Discourses,* vol. 1, p. 361.
[17] *Journal of Discourses,* vol. 12, p. 270.

tion of the Church. After visiting Salt Lake City, Justin Mc-Carthy wrote: "So I can well imagine one of these superseded and lonely wives in Salt Lake City, crying aloud in the bitterness of her heart, 'Give us polygamy as in Turkey.'" No two institutions could possibly be more dissimilar in their practical operation than Mormon plurality and Moslem polygamy. The urge of the Mormons' polygamy was based fundamentally upon the ordinary sex instinct. A man looked upon a woman and saw that she was good; he took her to wife, and she bore him children. The Mormons' consciences, however, never allowed them to admit to themselves the sensual origin of this propulsion. In order to assuage those consciences, which were of Puritan stock, they made a divine principle of their desires. They even took unto themselves as a matter of duty many wives they could not have desired. Brigham Young married some of the wives of Joseph Smith as part of his duty. It was also comforting for the Mormons to take a few elderly, homely wives, for their presence in the household was a constant reminder that, after all, polygamy was practised in obedience and for the sole purpose of salvation, and not by any chance for sensual gratification. The polygamous husbands showed little sentiment for their wives, and any favoritism was usually clandestine; to make love freely and frankly on a large scale would have been to the Mormons too much in the nature of an eastern seraglio, and most of them had been raised in New England farmhouses or Anglo-Saxon hovels—the very thought of a harem was enough to engender the fear of hell.

It is the natural tendency of a man to admire the freedom implied by the principle of polygamy, but, as the Mormons formulated and carried out that principle, it was more oppressive and destructive of liberty than monogamy, even to the male. Mormon men were expected to take wives, and unless a Mormon did so with celerity and with regularity, his standing in the community was lowered, and he was looked upon not only with disdain, but also with distrust. And it is just as conceivable that a man might not want more than two or three wives, as it is that he might become tired of one. Unfortunately, many Mormons had wives foisted upon them for the sake of their religion rather than for the exercise of their pleasure; and then they had to suffer the maddening accusation of their Gentile visitors that they were lascivious beasts. As a matter of fact, when the Mormons practised polygamy, they merely carried conventional morality to an

extreme. While polygamy had its origin in the sensuality of
Joseph Smith, its natural development was along the lines of the
most conventional morality, somewhat multiplied. Back of this
morality was the natural, sexual desire, and during the nineteenth
century in the United States the Mormons were not the only
people to clothe their natural impulses in the robes of divine sanction. Cults and sects arose, thoroughly religious in their nature,
whose fundamental purposes were to give one man many wives,
or one woman many husbands; sometimes complete promiscuity
among the members of a select community was the tenet of the
faith, and occasionally, as in the case of the Shakers, the object
was celibacy.

Brigham Young insisted in his sermons that polygamy was
never synonymous with lust. God, he said, commanded, and man
had nothing to do but obey. "I would rather take my valise in
my hand to-day," he told his congregation, "and never see a wife
or a child again, and preach the Gospel until I go into the grave,
than to live as I do, unless God commands it. I never entered
into the order of plurality of wives to gratify passion. And were
I now asked whether I desired and wanted another wife, my
reply would be, It should be one by whom the Spirit will bring
forth noble children. I am almost sixty years old; and if I now
live for passion, I pray the Lord Almighty to take my life from
the earth." The irreverent might be led to believe that perhaps
it was because he was sixty years old that he was no longer governed by passion, but further along in this sermon he made clear
that for sixty years his life had been pure: "Ask these sisters
(many of them have known me for years) what my life has been
in private and in public. It has been like the angel Gabriel's, if
he had visited you; and I can live so still. But how are we to be
made happy? There is one course—love the Giver more than the
gift; love Him that has placed passion in me more than my
passions." [18]

It seemed to be necessary to emphasize often that the Giver of
wives and husbands was to be regarded more than the gift. Heber
Kimball said in a sermon: "Some men think if they can get a
woman that has a handsome face, that is all there is of it. But
it is that woman that has a head and sensibility—I do not care if
her head is three feet long,—it has nothing to do with the character that lives in the body." And Brigham Young once ad-

[18] *Journal of Discourses,* vol. 9, pp. 36-37.

dressed the sisters directly on the relative positions of duty and love, for some of them who were married to elderly Mormons forgot that relativity in their unhappiness:

"I am now almost daily sealing young girls to men of age and experience. Love your duties, sisters. Are you sealed to a good man? Yes, to a man of God. . . . Sisters, do you wish to make yourselves happy? Then what is your duty? It is for you to bear children, in the name of the Lord, that are full of faith and the power of God,—to receive, conceive, bear, and bring forth in the name of Israel's God, that you may have the honor of being the mothers of great and good men—of kings, princes, and potentates that shall yet live on the earth and govern and control the nations. Do you look forward to that? or are you tormenting yourselves by thinking that your husbands do not love you? I would not care whether they loved a particle or not; but I would cry out, like one of old, in the joy of my heart, 'I have got a man from the Lord!' 'Hallelujah! I am a mother—I have borne an image of God!' " [19]

Woman, according to Brigham Young, was a receptacle, and the main purpose of polygamy was the increased breeding facilities which it afforded. Therefore, anything in the nature of birth control was extremely repugnant to him and to his followers. Heber Kimball once delivered a picturesque and forceful sermon on that subject:

"Suffice it to say I have a good many wives and lots of young mustards that are growing, and they are a kind of fruitful seed. . . . It is so with 'Mormonism'; it will flourish and increase, and it will multiply in young 'Mormons.' 'To be plain about it, Mr. Kimball, what did you get these wives for?' The Lord told me to get them. 'What for?' To raise up young 'Mormons,'—not to have women to commit whoredoms with, to gratify the lusts of the flesh, but to raise up children.

"The priests of the day in the whole world keep women, just the same as the gentlemen of the Legislatures do. The great men of the earth keep from two to three, and perhaps half-a-dozen private women. They are not acknowledged openly, but are kept merely to gratify their lusts; and if they get in the family way, they call for the doctors, and also upon females who practise under the garb of midwives, to kill the children, and thus they are depopulating their own species. (Voice: 'And their names shall come to an end.') Yes, because they shed innocent blood.

[19] *Journal of Discourses,* vol. 9, p. 37.

"I knew that before I received 'Mormonism.' I have known of lots of women calling for a doctor to destroy their children; and there are many of the women in this enlightened age and in the most popular towns and cities in the Union that take a course to get rid of their children. The whole nation is guilty of it. I am telling the truth. I won't call it infanticide. You know I am famous for calling things by their names.

"I have been taught it, and my wife was taught it in our young days, when she got into the family way, to send for a doctor and get rid of the child, so as to live with me to gratify lust. It is God's truth, and the curse of God will come upon that man, and upon that woman, and upon those cursed doctors. There is scarcely one of them that is free from sin. It is just as common as it is for wheat to grow.

"Do we take that course here? No . . . and I have had altogether about fifty children; and one hundred years won't pass away before my posterity will out-number the present inhabitants of the State of New York, because I do not destroy my offspring. I am doing the works of Abraham, Isaac, and Jacob; and if I live and be a good man, and my wives are as good as they should be, I will raise up men yet, that will come through my loins, that will be as great men as ever came to this earth; and so will you.

"I will tell you that some of the most noble spirits are waiting with the Father to this day to come forth through the right channel and the right kind of men and women. That is what has to be yet; for there are thousands and millions of spirits waiting to obtain bodies upon this earth." [20]

One of the rules of Mormon polygamy enjoined continence for the wife during the period of gestation. The Mormons found in the advisability of continence during this period an indication of the divine economy of the system of plural marriage. Romania B. Penrose in a lecture on hygiene before the Female Relief Society of Salt Lake City said: "There is nothing in the economy or requirements of man's life which requires this abstinence beyond the temperate limit of his powers of vitality; and this to me is a proof unanswerable and *prima facie* on the spheres of manhood and womanhood, of the divinity,—and I believe it is a necessity for the salvation of the human race,—of the truth and divinity of plural marriage."

Occasionally Brigham Young forgot that wives were merely divine instruments for the population of the earth with the

[20] *Journal of Discourses,* vol. 5, pp. 89-90.

righteous, and he offered them as rewards and sources of pleasure, comfort, and rejuvenation. For example, he gave Bishop John D. Lee a seventeenth wife in 1858. "I was sealed to her," wrote Lee, "while a member of the Territorial Legislature. Brigham Young said that Isaac C. Haight, who was also in the Legislature, and I, needed some young women to renew our vitality, so he gave us both a dashing young bride." This was an interesting, if unusual, method of obtaining vital legislation. Heber Kimball gave the congregation one Sunday morning the benefit of his observations of the rejuvenating effect of plural wives:

"I would not be afraid to promise a man who is sixty years of age, if he will take the counsel of Brother Brigham and his brethren, that he will renew his age. I have noticed that a man who has but one wife, and is inclined to that doctrine, soon begins to wither and dry up, while a man who goes into plurality looks fresh, young, and sprightly. Why is this? Because God loves that man, and because he honors His work and word. Some of you may not believe this; but I not only believe it—I also know it. For a man of God to be confined to one woman is small business; for it is as much as we can do now to keep up under the burdens we have to carry; and I do not know what we should do if we had only one wife a piece." [21]

Brigham Young enjoyed great power as the arbiter who sealed or refused to seal women to men. He once warned the elders in a sermon to guard the privilege of polygamy carefully, lest it be taken from them:

"The Elders of Israel frequently call upon me—'Brother Brigham, a word in private, if you please.' Bless me, this is no secret to me, I know what you want, it is to get a wife! 'Yes, brother Brigham, if you are willing.'

"I tell you here, now, in the presence of the *Almighty God,* it is not the privilege of *any Elder* to have even ONE *wife,* before he has *honored* his *Priesthood,* before he has *magnified* his *calling.* If you *obtain one,* it is by *mere permission,* to see *what* you will *do, how* you will act, whether you will *conduct yourself* in *righteousness* in that *holy estate.* TAKE CARE! Elders of Israel, *be cautious!* or you will lose your wives and your children. If you abuse your wives, turn them out of doors, and treat them in a harsh and cruel manner, you will be left wifeless and childless; you will have no

[21] *Journal of Discourses,* vol. 5, p. 22.

increase in eternity. You will have bartered this blessing, this privilege away; you will have sold your birthright, as Esau did his blessing, and it can never come to you again, *never*, NO NEVER!

"Look to it, ye Elders! You will awake from your dream, alas! but too soon, and then you will realize the truth of the remarks I am making to-day. Whose privilege is it to have women sealed to him? It is his who has stood the *test*, whose *integrity* is unswerving, who *loves righteousness because it is right*, and the *truth because there is no error therein*, and *virtue because* it is a *principle* that *dwells* in the *bosom* of Him who sits *enthroned* in the *highest heavens;* for it is a principle which existed with God in all eternities, and is a *co-operator*, a *co-worker* betwixt *man* and his *Maker*, to *exalt* man, and *bring* him into his *presence*, and *make* him like unto *Himself!* It is such a man's privilege to have wives and children, and neighbors, and friends, who wish to be sealed to him. Who else? *No one.* I tell you *nobody else.* DO YOU HEAR IT?" [22]

Brigham Young was anxious to preserve his position as dispenser of wives. He and Heber Kimball frequently warned the missionaries who went forth every year to convert the Gentiles and returned from England with flocks of women, that woman was the most powerful temptation in the way of man. In a letter to his son William, who was a missionary in England, Heber Kimball wrote: "William, as to yourself, with all your brethren, we have no fears but that you will do right, and remember the parable of the sheep and good shepherd, and suffer not yourselves to be tempted to take any of the sheep until you come home, and get the consent of the good shepherd. We are aware that the English girls' cheeks look very red and rosy: where any of the Elders have stung them, it has been death to the stinger—that's all." [23] In a sermon Heber Kimball developed this metaphor of Mormon women and sheep, and he warned the shepherds again: "I have said that you have no business to make a selection of any of these sheep, or to make a choice of them, or make any covenant with them, until they are brought home and placed in the fold, and then if you want a sheep or two, ask the shepherd for them, and if you choose a sheep without taking this course you will get your fingers burnt. Why? Because they are his sheep—mark it. . . . I would rather have my head laid upon a

22 *Journal of Discourses*, vol. I, p. 119.
23 *Millennial Star*, vol. 17, p. 521.

block, and severed from my shoulders than ever make a proposal to any woman living upon the earth and marry her, unless I had permission from the chief shepherd. *That tells it.*" [24]

It is said that the missionaries did not always obey this injunction. One anti-Mormon writer and lecturer described his view of the Mormon missionary activities in these words: "These Libertines and habitual Lechers, are thrown upon the British public for three years, and we are expected to believe that during that time they live a life of Celibacy. You can believe it if you like; I don't; nor shall I, until fish live without water. Mormon fish are not long out of water in England, if at all: there is so much water around our little Island." This same author also accused the Mormon missionaries of not waiting for the marriage privileges until after the rites were celebrated in Salt Lake City. "To describe that journey," he wrote, "is impossible here; but, in passing, I must say, the Missionaries, who had been three years in England, seemed to have special regard for the Female Lambs of the flocks, and were I to tell what I saw during that six weeks' journey over the plains, camping out as we had to, night after night, and sleeping in waggons, under waggons, under trees, bushes, or any shelter we could find: I say, were I to tell all I then saw and heard this book could not be sent by mail, while I myself would be sent to jail. If I protested in any way I was kindly informed that I had better mind my own business, or I should be put where the dogs could not bite me." [25]

III

The effects of polygamy on the Mormon women are difficult to discover in detail, for the Mormon women kept both their home life and their mental struggles to themselves, and especially did they hide from prying Gentile eyes whatever troubles they may have had. The information which is available from Gentile sources is largely lurid in its implications, but dull and insignificant in its fact; it was impossible for a Gentile to live in the intimacy of a Mormon household, and he or she was therefore compelled to gather information at the back-stairs, under dramatic, but inaccurate, circumstances. The vehement anti-polygamy ladies and clergymen spoke and wrote against the institution not with

[24] *Journal of Discourses,* vol. I, p. 207.
[25] *Uncle Sam's Abscess,* by W. Jarman, p. 39; pp. 45-46.

reason, but with sentiment, as their weapon, and their works offer moral indignation instead of argument. They used such phrases as "degrading the womanhood of the nation," and "lowering the light of the world," but they rarely became specific. They had printed many pitiful tales with plots so similar that one is inclined to suspect their authenticity. In each case an innocent and trusting young English girl falls unwarily into the arms of a leering Mormon elder, who, before she recovers from her bliss, transports her several thousand miles across the ocean and the plains to Utah, where she discovers to her undying chagrin that he has half-a-dozen other wives. The girl, who is usually seventeen years old and frequently an orphan, spends the rest of her life languishing, and finally dies of a broken heart.

It seemed impossible for the contemporaries of Brigham Young to realize that the institution of polygamy, like that of marriage, worked differently with different temperaments, that for some women it was entirely satisfactory, and others resented its practical details. Naturally, there were family quarrels. Brigham Young's son, Brigham Young, Jr., wrote in his diary: "Had a family dinner at our house some little feeling was developed and Della went home with her children which caused us all to feel unpleasant, but an excellent dinner to which Della contributed a share, made us all very well content." [26] There were many women in Utah who accepted polygamy as a comforting principle, and were happy in its practice, and there were others who never became accustomed to the association of fellow wives, and, forced by their pride or their lack of courage to endure that association, lived unhappily ever afterwards. An example of the first class is found in the case of one of Brigham Young's wives, who fell in love with him and is said to have worked seven years in his household as a servant for the privilege of being married to him. She had a son and was happy. It did not worry her placid disposition that she enjoyed only one-twentieth, approximately, of her husband's time and attention. Her mind was occupied with that twentieth, and with the multiplicity of duties and opportunities afforded by Brigham Young's immense family household. For sensitive souls polygamy must have proved as unhappy as marriage to one man or woman frequently proves to be, but the majority of Mormon women were apparently satisfied with it, for

[26] Manuscript Diary of Brigham Young, Jr., p. 235. In the Manuscript Collection of the New York Public Library.

their sensibilities were not developed by their education and environment beyond their powers of satisfaction. To their well-meaning sisters who wished to emancipate them from a bondage which they did not feel, or at least did not acknowledge, the Mormon women answered that if a father can love six children, he can also love six wives.

There was, however, much real pathos as a result of polygamy, which it is impossible to present because of the lack of information from the women who suffered it. That there was considerable jealousy we know from the sermons of Brigham Young. Upon one occasion he remarked that the greatest curse God had placed upon women was when he told Eve, "Thy desire shall be to thy husband." "Continually wanting the husband," complained Brigham Young. " 'If you go to work, my eyes follow you; if you go away in the carriage, my eyes follow you, and I like you and I love you, I delight in you, and I desire you should have nobody else.' I do not know that the Lord could have put upon women anything worse than this; I do not blame them for having these feelings. I would be glad if it were otherwise." [27] He argued that the duty of a wife was to submit, for it was written in the Bible, "and he shall rule over you," but he was compelled to admit that the women frequently refused to accept their situation with complacency. In his own family he experienced what the whole community was experiencing, for he once said in a sermon: "A few years ago one of my wives, when talking about wives leaving their husbands, said, 'I wish my husband's wives would leave him, every soul of them except myself.' That is the way they all feel, more or less, at times, both old and young. The ladies of seventy, seventy-five, eighty, and eighty-five years of age are greeted here with the same cheerfulness as are the rest. All are greeted with kindness, respect, and gentleness, no matter whether they wear linsey or silks or satin, they are all alike respected and beloved according to their behavior; at least they are so far as I am concerned. . . . I love my wives, respect them, and honor them, but to make a queen of one and peasants of the rest I have no such disposition, neither do I expect to do it." [28] This sermon was delivered, however, before Brigham Young met Amelia Folsom, who, as we shall see, occupied the position of a queen in his domestic kingdom.

[27] *Journal of Discourses*, vol. 16, p. 167.
[28] *Journal of Discourses*, vol. 9, pp. 195-196.

In the opinion of Brigham Young women were created to submit to the will of their husbands, and the woman who bore her wrongs patiently would triumph in the other world. The responsibility for those wrongs would rest eventually with the husband, but it sometimes must have seemed as if heaven were a long way off. Brigham Young admired women personally and in the abstract, but in his mind they were primarily a spiritual chattel, whose duty it was to be taken care of by husbands whose duty it was to take care of them. In testifying to his respect for women, he once remarked that the greatest resource of Utah was its women, to which George D. Prentice, the humorist, added, "It is very evident that the prophet is disposed to husband his resources."

However much he admired them, Brigham Young felt that it was impossible for the comfort of his position to allow women to dictate to him, and he therefore felt that they were never meant by God to enjoy that privilege. "Where is the man," he said in the pulpit, "who has wives, and all of them think he is doing just right to them? I do not know such a man; I know it is not your humble servant. If I would only be dictated by women I should make a hell of it; but I cannot be, I can humor them and treat them kindly, but I tell them I shall do just what I know to be right, and they may help themselves the best they can. I do not say that in so many words, but that is what I mean, and I let them act it out." [29] Occasionally Brigham Young became impatient with the discontent of his own wives and those of the other members of the community. On Sunday, September 21, 1856, he delivered a sermon addressed particularly to whining wives in which he offered them their freedom:

"Now for my proposition; it is more particularly for my sisters, as it is frequently happening that women say they are unhappy. Men will say, 'My wife, though a most excellent woman, has not seen a happy day since I took my second wife'; 'No, not a happy day for a year,' says one; and another has not seen a happy day for five years. It is said that women are tied down and abused: that they are misused and have not the liberty they ought to have; that many of them are wading through a perfect flood of tears, because of the conduct of some men, together with their own folly.

"I wish my own women to understand that what I am going to say is for them as well as others, and I want those who are here to

[29] *Journal of Discourses,* vol. 17, p. 160.

tell their sisters, yes, all the women of this community, and then write it back to the States, and do as you please with it. I am going to give you from this time to the 6th day of October next, for reflection, that you may determine whether you wish to stay with your husbands or not, and then I am going to set every woman at liberty and say to them, Now go your way, my women with the rest, go your way. And my wives have got to do one of two things; either round up their shoulders to endure the afflictions of this world, and live their religion, or they may leave, for I will not have them about me. I will go into heaven alone, rather than have scratching and fighting around me. I will set all at liberty. 'What, first wife too?' Yes, I will liberate all.

"I know what my women will say; they will say, 'You can have as many women as you please, Brigham.' But I want to go somewhere and do something to get rid of the whiners; I do not want them to receive a part of the truth and spurn the rest out of doors.

"I wish my women, and brother Kimball's and brother Grant's to leave and every woman in this Territory, or else say in their hearts that they will embrace the Gospel—the whole of it. Tell the Gentiles that I will free every woman in this Territory at our next Conference. 'What, the first wife too?' Yes, there shall not be one held in bondage, all shall be set free. And then let the father be the head of the family, the master of his own household; and let him treat them as an angel would treat them; and let the wives and the children say amen to what he says, and be subject to his dictates, instead of their dictating to the man, instead of their trying to govern him.

"No doubt some are thinking, 'I wish brother Brigham would say what would become of the children.' I will tell you what my feelings are; I will let my wives take the children, and I have property enough to support them, and can educate them, and then give them a good fortune, and I can take a fresh start.

"I do not desire to keep a particle of my property, except enough to protect me from a state of nudity. And I would say, wives you are welcome to the children, only do not teach them iniquity; for if you do, I will send an Elder, or come myself, to teach them the Gospel. You teach them life and salvation, or I will send Elders to instruct them.

"Let every man thus treat his wives, keeping raiment enough to clothe his body; and say to your wives, 'Take all that I have and be set at liberty; but if you stay with me you shall comply with the law of God, and that too without any murmuring and whining. You must fulfil the law of God in every respect, and round up your shoulders to walk up to the mark without any grunting.'

"Now recollect that two weeks from to-morrow I am going to set you at liberty. But the first wife will say, 'It is hard, for I have lived with my husband twenty years, or thirty, and have raised a family of children for him, and it is a great trial to me for him to have more women'; then I say it is time that you gave him up to other women who will bear children. If my wife had borne me all the children that she ever would bear, the celestial law would teach me to take young women that would have children. . . .

"Sisters, I am not joking, I do not throw out my proposition to banter your feelings, to see whether you will leave your husbands, all or any of you. But I do know that there is no cessation to the everlasting whining of many of the women in this Territory; I am satisfied that this is the case. And if the women will turn from the commandments of God and continue to despise the order of heaven, I will pray that the curse of the Almighty may be close to their heels, and all the day long. And those that enter into it and are faithful, I will promise them that they shall be queens in heaven, and rulers to all eternity.

" 'But,' says one, 'I want to have my paradise now.' And says another, 'I did think that I should be in paradise if I was sealed to brother Brigham, and I thought I should be happy when I became his wife, or brother Heber's. I loved you so much, that I thought I was going to have a heaven right off, right here on the spot.'

"What a curious doctrine it is, that we are preparing to enjoy! The only heaven for you is that which you make yourselves. My heaven is here—(laying his hand upon his heart). I carry it with me. When did I expect it in its perfection? When I come up in the resurrection; then I shall have it, and not till then.

"But now we have got to fight the good fight of faith, sword in hand, as much so as men have when they go to battle; and it is one continual warfare from morning to evening, with sword in hand. This is my duty, and this is my life. . . .

"But how is it now? Your desire is to your husband, but you strive to rule over him, whereas the man should rule over you.

"Some may ask whether that is the case with me; go to my house and live, and then you will learn that I am very kind, but know how to rule.

"If I had only wise men to talk to, there would be no necessity for my saying what I am going to say. Many and many an Elder knows no better than to go home and abuse as good a woman as dwells upon this earth, because of what I have said this afternoon. Are you who act in that way, fit to have a family? No, you are not, and never will be, until you get good common sense. . . . If I were talking to a people that understood themselves and the doctrine of the holy Gospel, there would be no necessity for saying this, because you would understand. But many here have been (what shall I say? Pardon me, brethren,) hen-pecked so much, that they do not know the place of either man or woman; they abuse and rule a good woman with an iron hand. With them it is as Solomon said—'Bray a fool in a mortar among wheat, with a pestle, yet will not his foolishness depart from him.' You may talk to them about their duties, about what is required of them, and still they are fools, and will continue to be.

"Prepare yourselves for two weeks from to-morrow; and I will tell you now, that if you will tarry with your husbands, after I have set you free, you must bow down to it, and submit yourselves to the celestial law. You may go where you please, after two weeks from to-morrow; but, remember, that I will not hear any more of this whining." [30]

The wives decided to submit to their lot, for there was no exodus of Mormon women two weeks later. However, they did not cease their whining altogether, for there are other sermons indicating that the women were frequently discontented and continued to express themselves accordingly. Heber Kimball admitted that he had a few wives whom he could not control: "I would as soon try to control a rebellious mule," he said, "as to control them. . . . But when a woman begins to dispute me, about nine times out of ten I get up and say, 'Go it,' and then go off about my business; and if ever I am so foolish as to quarrel with a woman, I ought to be whipped; for you may always calculate that they will have the last word." [31]

When the authority of Brigham Young and the wish of a wife conflicted, Heber Kimball was certain of his path, and he told the congregation what he would do if a choice were necessary: "What!—sustain a woman, a wife, in preference to sustaining the Prophet Joseph, brother Brigham, and his brethren! Your religion is vain when you take that course. Well, my wife may say, 'If you will sustain Brigham in preference to me, I will leave you.' I should reply, 'Leave and be damned!' And that very quickly. That is a part of my religion—'Leave quickly, you poor snoop.' . . . I should lead her; and she should be led by me, if I am a good man; and if I am not a good man, I have no just right in this Church to a wife or wives, or to the power to propagate my species. What, then, should be done with me? Make a

[30] Journal of Discourses, vol. 4, pp. 55-57.
[31] Journal of Discourses, vol. 5, p. 276.

eunuch of me, and stop my propagation." [32] When Orson Hyde said in a sermon that no man could be saved who allowed a woman to rule over him, an anxious English emigrant spoke up in the audience and asked, "What, then, will become of Prince Albert and Queen Victoria?" Hyde answered, "General and eternal principles are too stubborn to yield to individual accommodation. They must see to their own affairs."

Brigham Young did not believe that woman's place was exclusively in the home. He urged those who did not have families to occupy all their time, to learn printing or to act as clerks in stores. Selling tape, he told his congregation, was not a man's job, and he asked the women to study bookkeeping and arithmetic so that they could take the places of men in stores. After the telegraph came to Utah, he suggested that the women act as telegraphers instead of men, who would then be free to dig and to cut down trees in the cañons. "See a great big six-footer working the telegraph," he said. "One of them will eat as much as three or four women, and they stuff themselves until they are almost too lazy to touch the wire. There they sit. What work is there about that that a woman cannot do? She can write as well as a man, and spell as well as a man, and better, and I leave it to every man and woman of learning if the girls are not quicker and more apt at learning in school than the boys." Brigham Young also believed it was the duty of wives to help on farms and to do all their own housework; he frequently instructed them in his sermons in this branch of their work, the main principle of his system of domestic science being that everything has its place and should be in it. He alone had no place, but felt that his influence extended even to the care and feeding of children, and the fashions of his wives and those of his brethren.

The subject of woman's dress was one which Brigham Young never tired of discussing with his people, in his effort to make them economize. He was particularly in favor of homespun garments of a modest, uniform cut, and he vehemently opposed following Gentiles in their styles of dress. The *Mormon Expositor,* a small newspaper edited by anti-Mormons in Salt Lake City, printed a sermon by Brigham Young on this subject, which was delivered on the first Sunday in September, 1861, but which it was thought advisable not to reprint in the church *Journal of Discourses:*

[32] *Journal of Discourses,* vol. 5, pp. 28-29.

"Give us a little Gentileism," said Brigham Young, "for Heaven's sake, you say. The women say, let us wear hoops, because the whores wear them.

"I believe if they were to come with a cob stuck in their behind, you would want to do the same. I despise their damnable fashions, their lying and whoring; and God being my helper, I'll live to see every one of those cussed fools off the earth, saint or sinner. I don't know that I have a wife but what would see me damned rather than that she should not get what she wanted, and that is what I think of all of them, and the men too.

"I would see a Gentile further in Hell than they ever got before I would follow their fashions, if it did not suit me. There is not a day I go out but I see the women's legs, and if the wind blows you see them up to their bodies.

"If you must wear their hoops, tie them down with weights, and don't let your petticoats be over your heads. It is ridiculous and should not be. It belongs to a set of whory congregations that love iniquity and to corrupt themselves one with another. It belongs there. It don't belong to this community.

"How do you think I feel about it? Who cares about these infernal Gentiles? If they were to wear a s—t pot on their head, must I do so? I know I ought to be ashamed, but when you show your tother end I have a right to talk about tother end. If you keep them hid, I'll be modest, and not talk about them.

"There are those fornication pantaloons, made on purpose for whores to button up in front. My pantaloons button up here (showing how) where they belong, that my secrets, that God has given me, should not be exposed.

"You follow the Gentiles and you will be partakers of their plagues if you don't look out. That is the work of the Lord.

"Break off from your sins by righteousness. Will you do it? This is the word of the Almighty to you, through his servant Brigham. Keep your secrets secret, and hide your bodies and preserve your bodies.

"Now, if a whore comes along and turns up her clothes, don't turn up yours and go through the streets." [33]

Brigham Young was frequently so outspoken in his sermons that it was considered wiser not to print some of them exactly as he delivered them, and he sometimes edited them himself before they were published for the edification of the Saints abroad. He once said in a sermon: "Brother Heber says that the music is taken out of his sermons when brother Carrington clips out

[33] *Mormon Expositor*, vol. i, no. i, Salt Lake City, 1875.

words here and there; and I have taken out the music from mine, for I know the traditions and false notions of the people. Our sermons are read by tens of thousands outside of Utah. Members of the British Parliament have those *Journals of Discourses,* published by brother Watt; they have them locked up, they secrete them, and go to their rooms to study them, and they know all about us. They may, perhaps, keep them from the Queen, for fear that she would believe and be converted. . . . In printing my remarks, I often omit the sharp words, though they are perfectly understood and applicable here; for I do not wish to spoil the good I desire to do. Let my remarks go to the world in a way the prejudices of the people can bear, that they may read them, and ponder them, and ask God whether they are true." [34] Unfortunately, therefore, we must supply with our imaginations some of the poignancy with which he spiced his sermons, and which was removed when they were canned for general consumption. Frequently, however, he did not take the music out of his discourses, and he once excused himself for his language in the pulpit, "where," he remarked, "I do all my swearing." He also said that he had a wheelbarrow full of letters from friends who urged him to be more cautious in his expressions of opinion and in the language he used to express them; he told of his feelings when he received such letters: "Do you know how I feel when I get such communications? I will tell you, I feel just like rubbing their noses with them. If I am not to have the privilege of speaking of Saint and sinner when I please, tie up my mouth and let me go to the grave, for my work would be done. . . . I feel as independent as an angel. . . . It is for me to pursue a course that will build up the kingdom of God on the earth, and you may take my character to be what you please, I care not what you do with it, so you but keep your hands off from me." [35]

When he was discussing women's fashions, Brigham Young did not spare his own family. "I asked some of my wives the other evening," he said, " 'What is the use of all this velvet ribbon —perhaps ten, fifteen, twenty, or thirty yards, on a linsey dress?' Said I, 'What is the use of it? Does it do any good?' I was asked, very spiritedly and promptly, in return, 'What good do those buttons do on the back of your coat?' Said I, 'How many have I got?' and turning round I showed that there were none

[34] *Journal of Discourses,* vol. 5, pp. 99-100.
[35] *Journal of Discourses,* vol. 3, pp. 48-49.

there." He then went on to say that he had offered frequently to give his wives bills of divorcement if they could not stop yielding to the foolish demands of fashion.[36] The Grecian Bend, with its yards of waste material, offended Brigham Young's sense of economy, and he remarked that if the size continued to increase at the current rate of fashion, "you will not be able for the life of you, to tell a lady, at a distance, from a camel." He warned the Mormon women that the Grecian Bend would result in deformed children, and he said that he preferred to see a "Mormon Bend." Another source of offense to Brigham Young's eyes was the length of women's dresses. "You know," he once said, "it is the custom of some here to have a long trail of cloth dragging after them through the dirt; others, again, will have their dresses so short that one must shut his eyes, or he cannot help seeing their garters. Excuse me for the expression; but this is true, and it is not right." [37] To illustrate the importance of using enough material in the waist as well as the skirt, Brigham Young told an anecdote in one of his sermons: "I will relate a circumstance which I heard, that took place in the metropolis of our country. A gentleman, a stranger, was invited to a grand dinner party there. The ladies of course were dressed in the height of fashion, their trails dragging behind them, and their—well, I suppose there was a band over the shoulder to the waist, but I do not recollect whether the gentleman said there was or not; but one gentleman present, who knew this gentleman was a stranger, said to him, with all the loveliness and elegance in his heart that one could imagine—'Is not this beautiful? Did you ever see the like of this?' 'No, sir,' said the party questioned, 'never since I was weaned.' Well, all this, you know, is custom and fashion." [38]

Brigham Young would have been strenuously opposed to bobbed hair, for on July 19, 1877, he remarked in a sermon, "You see a girl with her hair clipped off in the front of her head; she looks as though she had just come out of a lunatic asylum." His ideal of feminine beauty was a combination of simplicity and cleanliness, and he once expressed his preferences in an interesting sermon:

"My wives dress very plainly, but I sometimes ask them the utility of some of the stripes and puffs which I see on their dresses. I

[36] *Journal of Discourses*, vol. 14, pp. 18-19.
[37] *Journal of Discourses*, vol. 14, p. 103.
[38] *Journal of Discourses*, vol. 15, p. 39.

remember asking a lady this question once, and enquired if they kept the bed bugs and flies away. Well, if they do that they are very useful; but if they do not, what use are they? None whatever. Now some ladies will buy a cheap dress, say a cheap calico, and they will spend from five to fifteen dollars' worth of time in making it up, which is wasting so much of the substance which God has given them on the lust of the eye, and which should be devoted to a better purpose. I have had an observation made to me which I believe I will relate; I never have done it, but I believe I will now. It has been said to me—'Yes, brother Brigham, we have seen ladies go to parties in plain, home-made cloth dresses, but every man was after the girls who had on a hundred dollars' worth of foll-the-roll, and they would dance with every woman and girl except the one in a plain dress, and they would let her stay by the wall the whole evening.' It may be in some cases, but should not be. It adds no beauty to a lady, in my opinion, to adorn her with fine feathers. When I look at a woman, I look at her face, which is composed of her forehead, cheeks, nose, mouth and chin, and I like to see it clean, her hair combed neat and nice, and her eyes bright and sparkling; and if they are so, what do I care what she has on her head, or how or of what material her dress is made? Not the least in the world. If a woman is clean in person, and has on a nice clean dress, she looks a great deal better when washing her dishes, making her butter or cheese, or sweeping her house, than those who, as I told them in Provo, walked the streets with their spanker jib flying. . . . Do not fine feathers look well? Yes, they are very pretty, but they look just as well on these dolls, these fixed up machines which they have in the stores, as anywhere else; they certainly add nothing to the beauty of a lady or gentleman, so far as I ever saw." [39]

Whatever may have been Brigham Young's esthetic reasons for favoring simplicity in dress and home manufacture of it, the economics of his position is explained by the fact that during his long life he had twenty-seven wives and thirty-one daughters.

The Mormon women, Brigham Young said, should emulate the angels, and in one of his sermons he told them how a female angel did not dress:

"Suppose that a female angel were to come into your house and you had the privilege of seeing her, how would she be dressed? Do you think she would have a great, big peck measure of flax done up like hair on the back of the head? Nothing of the kind. Would she have a dress dragging two or three yards behind? Nothing of

[39] *Journal of Discourses*, vol. 18, pp. 74-75.

the kind. Would she have a great, big—what is it you call it? A Grecian or Dutch— Well, no matter what you call it, you know what I mean. Do you think she would have on anything of that kind? Not at all. No person in the world would expect to see an angel dressed in such a giddy, frivolous, nonsensical style. She would be neat and nice, her countenance full of glory, brilliant, bright, and perfectly beautiful, and in every act her gracefulness would charm the heart of every beholder. There is nothing needless about her. None of my sisters believe that these useless, foolish fashions are followed in heaven. Well, then, pattern after good and heavenly things, and let the beauty of your garments be the workmanship of your own hands, that which adorns your bodies." [40]

From Brigham Young's description one would conclude that a female angel was never much of an expense to her husband.

In the effort to standardize the dress of the Mormon women, and to prevent the extremes which he dwelt upon so often of a dress which was so long that it dragged dirt, or so short that it revealed the tops of the stockings, Brigham Young designed a costume for the Mormon women, which consisted of a modest sunbonnet and a simple cape, but only a few of them wore it for a short time, and he was compelled until the last years of his life to continue his propaganda against the extravagant absurdities of fashion. He had been successful in dictating to his people on almost every subject, but this was one on which he was destined to fail because of the force of personality arrayed against him.

Brigham Young did not omit references to the vanity and immodesty of men's clothes in his discussion of dress. He said often in the pulpit that he himself preferred homespun for his own use, but that he always appeared in black broadcloth because his wives and daughters insisted that he dress carefully and luxuriously: "If they were to say, 'Brother Brigham, wear your home-made, we like to see you in it, I would give away my broadcloth, but to please the dear creatures I wear almost anything." To the young men he once spoke his mind on the subject of their tight trousers:

"There is a style of pantaloons very generally worn, about which I would say something if there were no ladies here. When I first saw them I gave them a name. I never wore them; I consider them uncomely and indecent. But why is it that they are worn so generally by others? Because they are fashionable. If it were the fashion to go with them unbuttoned I expect you would see plenty of our Elders wearing them unbuttoned. This shows the power that fashion exerts over the majority of minds. You may see it in the theater; if you had attended ours recently you might have seen that that was not comely; you might have seen Mazeppa ride, with but a very small amount of clothing on. In New York I am told it is much worse. I heard a gentlemen say that a full dress for Mazeppa there was one Government stamp. I do not know whether it is so or not. Fashion has great influence everywhere, Salt Lake not excepted." [41]

Heber Kimball was more vehement in his denunciation of tight trousers for men when he discussed them one Sunday morning from a hygienic point of view:

"I am opposed to your nasty fashions and everything you wear for the sake of fashion. Did you ever see me with hermaphrodite pantaloons on? (Voice: 'Fornication pantaloons.') Our boys are weakening their backs and their kidneys by girting themselves up as they do; they are destroying the strength of their loins and taking a course to injure their posterity.

"Now, just look at me. I have no hips projecting out; they are straight down with my sides. I am serious myself, although I can smile and laugh when I am serious; but these ridiculous fashions I despise, and God knows I despise anything that will tend to destroy the lives of my sisters. What is your existence worth to you? It is worth everything to your posterity; and you ought to consider their interest as well as your own.

"There is not a woman in this congregation but would be as straight as I am, if she did not destroy her shape. . . .

"You may take all such dresses and new fashions, and inquire into their origin, and you will find, as a general thing, they are produced by the whores of the great cities of the world—London, New York, and from Paris, and from all the Gentile cities.

"Now, if you are determined to destroy yourselves, I am perfectly willing, providing you do not destroy the fruit of your loins; but many of you are taking a course to destroy that by your ridiculous fashions. . . . Do not desire your children or your children's children to stop their growth, and do not you take a course to render them impotent and imbecile. I am talking to you, ladies; and then, again, I am talking to you, gentlemen, that wear those hermaphrodite pantaloons." [42]

41 *Journal of Discourses,* vol. 14, p. 21.
42 *Journal of Discourses,* vol. 6, pp. 191-193.

It is easy to realize from the sermons of Brigham Young and his associates that the institution of polygamy was not permitted to engender in the Mormon community a tendency towards silken boudoirs and Moslem divans. Polygamy, as practised by Brigham Young's adherents and as preached by him, was a growth on the native Puritanism of the Mormon fathers and forefathers. They suppressed rigorously all the externals of its inherent sensuality. Neatness was preferred to beauty, and economy to adornment. A thing of beauty was never accepted as its own excuse for existence, because it interfered with the stern exigencies of a pioneer civilization. This, perhaps, was what led Mark Twain to conclude concerning polygamy:

"Our stay in Salt Lake City amounted to only two days, and therefore we had no time to make the customary inquisition into the workings of polygamy and get up the usual statistics and deductions preparatory to calling the attention of the nation at large once more to the matter. I had the will to do it. With the gushing self-sufficiency of youth I was feverish to plunge headlong and achieve a great reform here—until I saw the Mormon women. Then I was touched. My heart was wiser than my head. It warmed towards these poor, ungainly, and pathetically 'homely' creatures, and as I turned to hide the generous moisture in my eyes, I said, 'No—the man that marries one of them has done an act of Christian charity which entitles him to the kindly applause of mankind, not their harsh censure—and the man that marries sixty of them has done a deed of open-handed generosity so sublime that the nations should stand uncovered in his presence and worship in silence." [43]

[43] *Roughing It,* vol. i, pp. 121-122.

Chapter VIII

BRIGHAM YOUNG AND HIS WIVES

I

ONE of the subjects of popular speculation in the United States from 1852 until 1877 was the number and quality of Brigham Young's wives. Estimates in the newspapers ranged from forty to two hundred, and the editor of the London *Daily Telegraph* said, on what he considered good American authority, that some of Brigham Young's wives were old enough to be his grandmothers and the rest young enough to be his granddaughters. Artemus Ward told his audiences, "I undertook to count the long stockings, on the clothes-line, in his back yard one day, and I used up the multiplication table in less than half an hour." Artemus Ward had previously estimated the number of Brigham Young's wives as eighty, but he later said of this calculation: "I have somewhere stated that Brigham Young is said to have eighty wives. I hardly think he has so many. Mr. Hyde, the backslider, says in his book that 'Brigham always sleeps by himself, in a little chamber behind his office;' and if he has eighty wives I don't blame him. He must be bewildered. I know very well that if I had eighty wives of my bosom I should be confused, and shouldn't sleep anywhere." Inquisitive visitors to Salt Lake City were in the habit of counting the number of doors and windows in Brigham Young's houses in an attempt to estimate the exact number of his wives. One day he was seen riding in a large carriage with some of his children and some of his neighbors; the report was sent east that Brigham Young had sixteen wives and fourteen children, for some one had counted the occupants of the coach. Of this report Brigham Young remarked, "But this does not begin to be the extent of my possessions, for I am enlarging on the right hand and on the left, and shall soon be able, Abraham like, to muster the strength of my house, and take my rights, asking no favors of Judges or Secretaries." One lady visitor asked Brigham Young if she might see his wives, to which he replied, "They are not on exhibition, madam." The extent of Brigham Young's possessions in money and wives was the subject of rumor on the streets of Salt Lake City among the oracles of the curb. One of these told a writer from the East when asked whether Brigham was very rich, "Oh, yes, he has eight million in the Bank of England." The informer was unable to say whether the eight million were pounds, shillings, pence, or dollars, but he was certain that the amount was eight million something. "Wives!" he exclaimed, "do you know that he has them in every part of Utah? He has got more than a thousand scattered around."

Brigham Young usually refused either to affirm or to deny the rumors of the extent of his family. He rather enjoyed the speculation, and he whetted the curiosity of the public by saying nothing, but giving the impression that they really did not know the half of his prosperity. He once urged the people to take their wives and families for excursions in the country around Salt Lake City, and in his sermon stated his intention to do so himself. "Though," he said, "you know what they say about me in the east; should I take my ninety wives and their children, with carriages and waggons enough to convey them, it would make such a vacuum here, and so many others would wish to go, that there would be no Salt Lake City. I think I will take a few of them, but I dare not take the whole, for if I did they would then know how many wives I have got, and that would not do."

The subject of Brigham Young's wives was a great source of income to the professional wits of the day. Mark Twain, George D. Prentice, and Artemus Ward, besides innumerable anonymous newspaper humorists, commented, whenever the opportunity offered, on Brigham Young's family life. When Brigham Young said in a sermon that he supposed he had a great deal more influence in Utah than Moses had among the children of Israel, George D. Prentice commented: "Very likely. But not more than Moses might have had if the children had been his own instead of Israel's." Artemus Ward wrote an imaginary interview with Brigham Young, which was published in a magazine a few years before the humorist visited Salt Lake City to study the Mormons at first hand as a source of humor. Ward was very much worried when he finally arrived in Salt Lake City that his statements would prejudice Brigham Young and his associates and lead to difficulties. Brigham Young was somewhat annoyed by the article, which he had read, but he consented to meet Artemus Ward, and he did not mention the article. The humorist was treated with great courtesy, nursed by the Mormons when he was taken seriously ill with mountain fever, and given facilities for investigation. The only reference to the embarrassing article was a quiet remark by one of the elders to Artemus Ward that it was the opinion among the Mormons that he would have done better to have visited them before writing about them instead of afterwards. In the light of the following quotation, which comprises the main part of Artemus Ward's premature, imaginative article, this treatment was extremely liberal:

" 'You air a marrid man, Mister Yung, I bleeve?' sez I, preparin to rite him sum free parsis.

" 'I hev eighty wives, Mister Ward. I sertinly am marrid.'

" 'How do you like it as far as you hev got?' sed I.

"He sed 'middlin,' and axed me wouldn't I like to see his famerly, to which I replide that I wouldn't mind minglin with the fair Seck & Barskin in the winnin smiles of his interestin wives. He accordingly tuk me to his Scareum. The house is powerful big & in a exceedin large room was his wives & children, which larst was squawkin and hollerin enuff to take the roof rite orf the house. The wimin was of all sizes and ages. Sum was pretty & sum was plane— sum was helthy and sum was on the Wayne—which is verses, tho sich was not my intentions, as I don't prove of puttin verses in Proze rittins, tho ef occashun requires I can Jerk a Poim ekal to any of them Atlantic Munthly fellers.

" 'My wives, Mister Ward,' sed Yung.

" 'Your sarvant, marms,' sed I, as I sot down in a cheer which a red-headed female brawt me.

" 'Besides these wives you see here, Mister Ward,' sed Yung, 'I hav eighty wives more in varis parts of this consecrated land which air Sealed to me.'

" 'Which?' sez I, gittin up & starin at him.

" 'Sealed, Sir! sealed.'

" 'Whare bowts?' sez I.

" 'I sed, Sir, that they was sealed!' He spoke in a traggerdy voice.

" 'Will they probly continner on in that stile to any grate extent, Sir?' I axed.

" 'Sir,' sez he turnin red as a biled beet, 'don't you know that the rules of our Church is that I, the Profit, may hev as many wives as I wants?'

" 'Jes so,' I sed. 'You are old pie, ain't you?'

" 'Them as is Sealed to me—that is to say, to be mine when I wants um—air at present my speeretooul wives,' sed Mister Yung.
" 'Long may thay wave!' sez I, seein I shood git into a scrape ef I didn't look out.
"In a privit conversashun with Brigham I learnt the follerin fax: It takes him six weeks to kiss his wives. He don't do it only onct a yere & sez it is wuss nor cleanin house. He don't pretend to know his children, thare is so many of um, tho they all know him. He sez about every child he meats call him Par, & he takes it for grantid it is so. . . ."

Brigham Young did not object to, nor was he hurt by, much of this part of Artemus Ward's sketch. What offended him was the statement with which Artemus Ward ended his imaginary conversation, especially since it was the moral judgment of a man who had never visited those he described, and whose business, as we may gather from the above, was not primarily moral judgment: "I girded up my Lions & fled the Seen. I packt up my duds & left Salt Lake, which is a 2nd Soddum & Germorrer, inhabited by as theavin & onprincipled a set of retchis as ever drew Breth in eny spot on the Globe." Even the studied misspelling fails to relieve this statement of its harsh and angry invective. After he had enjoyed the opportunity of a visit to the Mormons, Artemus Ward was sorry he had ever written that hypercritical paragraph.

Artemus Ward, after he visited the Mormons, delivered a lecture upon them in the eastern states and in England. He could not resist commenting on the mother-in-law aspect of polygamy, and he said among other things concerning Brigham Young: "I saw his mother-in-law while I was there. I can't exactly tell you how many there is of her—but it's a good deal. It strikes me that one mother-in-law is about enough to have in a family—unless you're very fond of excitement." This subject of the mother-in-law in polygamy was once earnestly discussed by Joseph F. Smith, one of Brigham Young's successors to the Presidency, who said in the course of a lecture to the young men and young women of Utah: "Many people in this world joke about their mothers-in-law, as if to have a mother-in-law is one of the curses of humanity. I want to say now, to you all, that the best friends I ever had have been my mothers-in-law. I loved and honored them and shall ever hold their memory sacred. They were true women and worthy of their daughters."

II

The study of genealogy has become widespread in Utah, where its intricacies afford all the fascination of an ingenious puzzle. In addition to the labyrinthine enchantments of Mormon family trees, however, the accuracy of their genealogy has a religious significance for the Mormons because they believe in and practise baptism for the dead. They baptize for their remote ancestors, and the more ancestors they can find the more they can baptize for by proxy, and the richer they will eventually be in relatives in heaven. This has always seemed to them a boon worth striving for painstakingly. Fortunately for the historian and biographer there is a Utah Genealogical Society and a *Utah Genealogical and Historical Magazine,* which has compiled and published the complete family history of Brigham Young, so that it is possible to give exact information concerning the numbers of his wives and children, who were not so countless as the numbers of their stockings hanging on the line.

Brigham Young once expressed his attitude towards women: "I will acknowledge," he said in a sermon, "with brother Kimball, and I know it is the case with him, that I am a great lover of women. In what particular? I love to see them happy, to see them well fed and well clothed, and I love to see them cheerful. I love to see their faces and talk with them, when they talk in righteousness; but as for anything more, I do not care. There are probably but few men in the world who care about the private society of women less than I do. I also love children, and I delight to make them happy." It would seem that he also loved to marry women and beget children, unless we can believe that he only saw his duty before God and carried it out nobly when he married twenty-seven wives and helped bring into the world fifty-six children.

As we have seen, Brigham Young's first wife, Miriam Works, died soon after she and her husband were baptized into the Mormon Church. They were married when he was twenty-three years old and she was eighteen. A few years after her death he married at Kirtland Mary Ann Angel, who was then thirty years old, when he was thirty-two. Mary Ann Angel had always been more interested in religion than in marriage; she was of Puritan stock and a Free Will Baptist before she met Brigham Young. She spent her adolescence and early youth studying the Scriptures diligently, and she decided never to marry until she met a man of God. When Brigham Young arrived in Kirtland, she apparently recognized in him the ideal combination of husband and pastor which she so much desired. The editors of the *Utah Genealogical and Historical Magazine* wrote of her: "In looks she always suggested the portraits of Martha Washington the 'Mother' of our Country." But, unlike the Mother of her country, she was not childless, but bore Brigham Young six children, including a set of twins, one of whom died in infancy. In later years, when the wives began to multiply, Mary Ann Angel was known as "Mother Young."

Brigham Young married his first polygamous wife on June 15, 1842, at Nauvoo. She was Lucy Ann Decker, who was twenty years old when Brigham Young married her; he was then forty-one. She bore him seven children. A year and a half later, on November 2, 1843, he married Harriet Elizabeth Campbell Cook, who was then nineteen years old, when her husband was forty-two, and on the same day he married Augusta Adams, who was then forty-one years old. Harriet Elizabeth Campbell Cook bore one son, Oscar Brigham Young, but Augusta Adams bore no children. Six months later, on May 8, 1844, Brigham Young married Clara Decker, the sister of his first polygamous wife, Lucy Ann Decker. She was six years younger than her sister, being exactly sixteen years old on her marriage day, when Brigham Young was one month short of forty-three. Clara Decker was the wife who accompanied Brigham Young in the party of pioneers to Utah. She bore him five children.

In September of 1844 Brigham Young married two women. On the 10th of the month he married Clarissa Ross, who was then thirty years old. She bore him four children. At some other time during September he married Emily Dow Partridge, who was then twenty years old, and who had been married to Joseph Smith the year before her marriage to Brigham Young. In the meantime Joseph Smith had been assassinated, and Brigham Young began dutifully to take over some of his wives. Emily Dow Partridge, who had borne no children to the Prophet, bore seven to Brigham Young. In February of 1845 Brigham Young married another of Joseph Smith's widows, Olive Grey Frost, who died in the following October without bearing any children. On April 30, 1845, he married Emmeline Free, who was the mother of ten of his children. In the same year, 1845, he also married Margaret Pierce, who had been the wife of one Morris Whitesides; her first husband had died six months before she became the tenth wife of Brigham Young, and, considerately, they named their first child Brigham Morris Young. She was twenty-two years old at the time of the marriage, when Brigham Young was forty-four.

The year 1846 was a year of many marriages for Brigham Young. It was the last year of the residence of the Mormons in Nauvoo, and perhaps he felt that he did not know when he would have an opportunity to marry again, for during that year he took eight wives. The hurry was so great, for the Mormons were preparing to leave Nauvoo, that Brigham Young married two women at a time on several days. On January 14, 1846, he married Louisa Beman, who had been one of Joseph Smith's wives. She was thirty-one years old when Brigham Young married her, and she bore two sets of twins, the first set being named appropriately Joseph and Hyrum, after their mother's first husband and his brother, and their father's Prophet and friend. The second set was named Alva and Alma respectively. They all died in infancy. On that same 14th of January, 1846, Brigham Young also married Margaret Maria Alley, who was then twenty years old, when her husband was forty-four. She bore him two children.

One week later, on January 21, 1846, Brigham Young spent an exciting day. He married four women. The first of these was Susan Snively, thirty years old, who bore no children, but who adopted a daughter, Julia, and she was raised as a member of the already large family. Then Brigham Young married Ellen Rockwood, a seventeen-year-old girl, who bore no children. Brigham Young then rested for lunch, and married in the afternoon Maria Lawrence, who had been one of the wives of Joseph Smith, and Martha Bowker, who was a Quakeress by birth. Neither of these women bore children. It will be observed that this eventful day, January 21, 1846, while it was a busy one, was not prolific of offspring, for none of the wives Brigham Young married on that day became a mother.

Twelve days after this quadruple marriage Brigham Young married Zina Diantha Huntington. She had one child by Brigham Young, and added to the family two children by another marriage. She was twenty-five years old at the time of her marriage to Brigham Young, and had been married to Henry Jacobs, from whom she was separated. Joseph Smith, the Prophet, married her in 1841, and after Smith's death she became the wife of Brigham Young and did not change thereafter. On the day after this marriage, February 3, 1846, Brigham Young married Naamah Kendel Jenkins Carter. About six months before he married her himself, Brigham Young had married her to John Saunders Twiss, who died a few months later. After her marriage to Brigham Young at the age of twenty-five, she always signed her name, Naamah Kendel Jenkins Carter Twiss Young. That was the last of Brigham Young's marriages in Nauvoo, for about one week later he left with the first group of Mormon refugees. Thus far he had married, including those wives who had died, nineteen women, and was living with seventeen of them.

While he was traveling across Iowa, Brigham Young married twice, both times on the same day, March 20, 1847. He married that day Mary Jane Bigelow, who was then twenty years old, and her sister, Lucy Bigelow, who was then sixteen years old. Brigham Young was then forty-five. Mary Jane bore no children, but her sister Lucy was the mother of three.

Brigham Young did not marry again until he was settled comfortably in Utah. On June 29, 1849, he married Eliza Roxey Snow, the Mormon poetess, whom we have quoted frequently. She had been the wife of Joseph Smith and was the sister of one of Brigham Young's main associates, Lorenzo Snow. She was then forty-five years old, when he was forty-eight; she had no children. Two years before he married her Brigham Young had given her a home in his family.

On October 3, 1852, soon after polygamy was publicly proclaimed, Brigham Young married Eliza Burgess, who was then twenty-four years old. He was fifty-one at the time. Eliza Burgess was an English girl of a poor family. She saw Brigham Young soon after her emigration and fell in love with him, but apparently she did not dare aspire to be his wife. She read, however, in the Old Testament that Jacob served seven years for a wife, and she read in the New Testament that "old things shall pass away and all things shall become new." She interpreted this to mean that a reversal of Jacob's servitude was permissible in the latter days, and she offered herself to Mother Young as a servant for seven years, demanding as her only reward that at the end of that time she be permitted to become one of Brigham Young's wives. Brigham Young was consulted on this novel

plan, and he had no objections to offer to Eliza's literal interpretation of select passages from the Bible. Perhaps he was even a
little flattered. Eliza served faithfully for seven years, receiving
nothing but her food, her board, and the sight of Brigham Young
with the privilege of working for him, however indirectly. At
the end of her time she was married to Brigham Young. She
was made very happy by the birth of a son, and she enjoyed the
satisfaction of seeing Brigham Young fondle her child and call
him his "English boy."

Brigham Young now began to grow into middle age, and his
marriages became fewer and farther between. Four years
elapsed after his marriage to Eliza Burgess before he married
Harriet Barney, who was then twenty-five years old. He was
fifty-four. She had been married young and divorced her first
husband. She brought three children by her first husband into
Brigham Young's enormous household and bore him one child.
They were married on March 14, 1856.

Brigham Young did not marry again for seven years, and then,
at the age of sixty-one, he fell passionately in love. Harriet
Amelia Folsom, who dropped the Harriet after her marriage to
Brigham Young, for there were already several by that name in
the family, was a tall, fair woman of twenty-five, who came to
Utah with her parents in 1862; they had all been Mormons, however, for many years. Amelia could play the piano, and she
could sing "Fair Bingen on the Rhine." Brigham Young was
captivated both by her appearance and by her accomplishments;
none of his other wives was so tall, so handsome, and so refined,
and none of his other wives could sing "Fair Bingen on the
Rhine." For hours every day Brigham Young's carriage was seen
outside Mrs. Folsom's door, the horses stamping with boredom
and swishing the flies with their tails, while their master never
seemed to tire of the company inside the house. It is said too
that at this time Brigham Young began to pay some attention to
his full beard and his thin brown hair, which suddenly began to
curl carefully. He also changed his homespun for broadcloth on
week-days. Those who watched the progress of this romance
with the careful attention of eager gossips also said that there
were rivals, and that the President, Prophet, Seer, and Revelator discouraged at least one of these rivals by patting him sig-
nificantly on the shoulder, thereby indicating with an additional
meaning gesture that it would be well for him to retire from the

chase. Another of the rivals, it is said, was sent suddenly on a mission to convert the heathen in far-away lands.

But, in spite of, or perhaps because of, all these precautions and all this solicitude, Amelia remained reluctant. She would not walk, she would not talk with the Prophet-President, and she was not thrilled by his offer of the keys of heaven. Twice, it is said, the Endowment House was warmed for the ceremony of marriage, and twice Brigham Young was disappointed. Finally, it was made clear to Amelia that her marriage to Brigham Young was the will of the Lord. Her parents, devout Mormons, pointed out that Brigham Young said so himself, and he was the only successor as Prophet, Seer, and Revelator in these latter days to the original Joseph Smith.

On January 24, 1863, Amelia Folsom became the bride of Brigham Young. And after all this trouble in getting her consent to the marriage, Brigham Young was arrested soon after it took place on a charge under the new anti-polygamy law, which had been passed by Congress the year before. However, he was not long in jail in the state where he was the most important personage.

Before she finally consented to marry Brigham Young, Amelia Folsom exacted many promises, which she proceeded to enforce as soon as they were married. She refused, for one thing, to live with the other wives in the two large buildings with their many quaint dormer windows, which Brigham Young had built to house his families. He built Amelia a house of her own, which was known throughout Utah for many years as "Amelia's Palace." She immediately took the position of head of the harem, which had at various times been occupied by other favorites, for, however divine the institution and impartial the intention, even Brigham Young could not avoid preferences in personalities. By virtue of her temper and determination Amelia held both Brigham Young and the other wives in a position subordinate to her will. She had fine clothes, which were not at all influenced by the ideas of fashion and economy which her husband expressed so vehemently in the pulpit; she had jewelry, and she had plenty of money to spend, as well as a carriage of her own. Whenever they went to the theater which Brigham Young had built in Salt Lake City, Amelia occupied the seat of honor next to her distinguished husband in his box, while the other wives occupied the special row of chairs reserved for them in the parquet. Whenever

Brigham Young went south for the winter on tours of inspection and for his health, Amelia now accompanied him, and she was soon generally recognized by the Mormons as the favorite. As such she was both feared and envied. In the dining-room where the whole family always ate together, Brigham Young and Amelia sat at a small table at the head of the room, while all the rest of the large family occupied a large table extending from the throne seats. Ann Eliza Young, who was somewhat biased and somewhat spiteful, as we shall see, wrote in her book of revelation concerning the household of her husband that the small table received many delicacies which were not served to the general multitude. Ann Eliza wrote bitterly, "Polygamist, as he professes to be, he is under the influence of Amelia, rapidly becoming a monogamist, in all except the name." [1] Amelia Folsom had no children.

Although Amelia Folsom exercised a great influence on her husband, that influence did not prevent subsequent marriages. Two years after they were married, Brigham Young married Mary Van Cott, on January 8, 1865. She was twenty-one, and he was sixty-three. She had been married before, and one of her daughters by that marriage later married one of Brigham Young's sons, John W. Young. She bore Brigham Young one child.

On April 6, 1868, when he was sixty-six years old, Brigham Young had his last, and his only disastrous, marital experience. He married Ann Eliza Webb, who was then twenty-four years old. She had been married five years before to James L. Dee. When Brigham Young and she had been married for seven years, and when Brigham Young was seventy-four years old, Ann Eliza sued him for divorce. She alleged neglect, cruelty, and desertion, and she demanded huge alimony. Her brief stated that Brigham Young was worth $8,000,000 and had an income of $40,000 a month. She asked for $1,000 a month during the period of the trial and $6,000 for preliminary counsel fees, with an award of $14,000 on the granting of her final decree of divorce and $200,000 for her maintenance thereafter. Brigham Young's answer denied the neglect, the cruelty, and the desertion. He also stated that his fortune, so far as he knew, did not exceed $600,000, and that his income was only $6,000 per month from all its sources. He offered to pay Ann Eliza $100 per month, if he was

[1] *Wife No. 19*, by Ann Eliza Young, p. 531.

obligated to pay her anything. Brigham Young pleaded that the marriage to Ann Eliza was not a legal marriage for two reasons; first, at the time of the marriage, she was not divorced from James L. Dee, and secondly because he, Brigham Young, was in the eyes of the law the husband only of Mary Ann Angel, the wife he married in Kirtland, Ohio. Brigham Young's brief stated that his marriage to Ann Eliza Young was regarded as sacred by the Church of Jesus Christ of Latter-day Saints, but that it could not be considered legal by the statutes of the United States, which did not recognize polygamous wives as wives, but merely tolerated them as concubines. He contended that unless the court was willing to recognize the legality of plural marriage, which recognition he had been clamoring for during many years, the marriage to Ann Eliza could not be regarded as legal.

The purpose of Ann Eliza Young was extortion, and Brigham Young, realizing this, took advantage of the technicalities of the law in his brief. He refused to pay the $3,000 counsel fees and the $500 per month alimony ordered by the court before the trial, and he was accordingly fined twenty-five dollars for contempt of court and commanded to spend one day in jail. At the time he was in feeble health and advanced age; he went to jail accompanied by his physician and nephew, Dr. Seymour B. Young. He spent the day and night in a comfortable room attached to the warden's quarters, while his friends and associates kept guard outside to prevent a repetition of the tragedy of Joseph Smith. This was on March 11, 1875. Five days later Judge McKean, who had sentenced Brigham Young, was removed from his position, and the Mormons claim that this was a direct result of the storm of protest in the press of the country for tyrannical treatment of an aged and distinguished man. The treatment Brigham Young received, however, was not very tyrannical, and Judge McKean was really removed because he had exceeded his authority in many other cases. He felt that he had a God-given mission to perform instead of duties to carry out, and his particular God-given mission was the extirpation of polygamy.

Judge McKean's successor, Judge David B. Lowe, decided that there had been no legal marriage between Brigham Young and Ann Eliza Young, and that therefore there could be no divorce and no alimony. But his successor decided that Brigham Young must pay alimony in arrears to the amount of $9,500 and be imprisoned until it was paid. The United States marshal considerately imprisoned Brigham Young in Brigham Young's own house, with his wives. He steadfastly refused to pay the alimony, and he was finally released from this residential imprisonment by Judge White. Still another judge reduced the accumulated alimony to $100 per month, which was the amount Brigham Young had originally offered, and he paid that sum after the court had threatened to attach his property. In April, 1877, the case came up for final trial, and the marriage was declared illegal. Brigham Young was compelled to pay no more alimony, but the costs of the trials were charged to him.

Ann Eliza Young, though she was unsuccessful in her effort to win some of Brigham Young's fortune, became by virtue of her divorce suit something of an ephemeral national figure. The publicity gained by her divorce suit won her lecture engagements throughout the United States, under the auspices of women's clubs, whose members were almost as interested in the Mormon women's husbands as they were in their own. After the possibilities of lecture tours were exhausted, Ann Eliza wrote her book, *Wife No. 19.* When she called her book by that title, she was flattering herself, for she was actually Wife Number Twenty-seven, including those who had died. The title of her book sounds enticing, but the book itself does not fulfil the promise of the title, for she told very little that was significant about Brigham Young and his wives, although she was intimately associated with that extraordinary household for seven years. Her book is made up largely of sentimental indignation against polygamy as an institution with very little supporting evidence for the horrors which she claimed resulted from its practice. One turns from its pages disappointed with the authoress, who did not make nearly the most of her opportunities, bored with her attempts to make of herself a martyr, and more than ever sympathetic with the trials of Brigham Young.

To sum up: Brigham Young had twenty-seven wives, although that many were never alive at the same time. Nine wives died before he died, and, if we exclude Ann Eliza Young, who left him, he was survived by seventeen. Brigham Young married twice before he was thirty-five years old, and in the period of five years, 1842-1847, when polygamy was first practised secretly, he married nineteen women. The other six wives he married from the time of his residence in Utah until his death. Two of Brigham Young's wives were sixteen years old when he married them, one was eighteen years old, one was nineteen, five were twenty, one was twenty-one, one was twenty-two, four were twenty-four, three were twenty-five, three were thirty, one was thirty-one, and two were forty-one and forty-five respectively, but these last two were widows of Joseph Smith, who were married because Brigham Young felt it an obligation to support them in their old age. These widows of Joseph Smith were married by Brigham Young for time only, for they already had engagements with the Prophet for eternity. The other wives who had been divorced or whose previous husbands had died, were married by Brigham Young for both time and eternity, for they preferred his company in the other world to that of their former husbands. It is said that Mary Ann Angel, who was married to Brigham Young at Kirtland before polygamy was established and after the death of his first wife, was worried about her position in heaven. She did not know, and apparently Brigham Young could not make it clear, whether she would be the queen in heaven, or whether Miriam Works, Brigham Young's ante-Mormon wife, would occupy that position. There was much to be said on both sides; Brigham Young had not been active in Mormonism during his association with Miriam Works, and Mary Ann Angel had been his first partner in polygamy, she having consented to the marriages with all the other wives, but, on the other hand, it would not be possible to repudiate Miriam Works, who had been faithful, and who was baptized a Mormon before she died. Frankly, Brigham Young and Mary Ann Angel were puzzled; it is to be hoped that this matter has now been straightened out to the satisfaction of all the parties concerned.

Brigham Young was always proud of the interest which Mormon women showed in him. He said to the congregation one Sunday morning, when he was fifty-six years old: "Do you think that I am an old man? I could prove to this congregation that I am young; for I could find more girls who would choose me for a husband than can any of the young men." He must have been conscious, however, of the possibility that the girls chose him for his distinction and position rather than for his manly vigor. Brigham Young was also sure that all women wanted to be married. When he was discussing polygamy with Schuyler Colfax, who was then Vice-President of the United States, Mr. Colfax argued, with some concern, that if one man had five or twenty wives, this abundance would cause others to be deprived of any

SOME OF BRIGHAM YOUNG'S WIVES

wives, for it was his opinion that men and women were practically equal in numbers throughout the world. Brigham Young answered that there were always some men who would never marry from choice, and Colfax asked if this did not also apply to the women. "There is not one woman in a million," answered Brigham Young, "who will not marry if she gets a chance."

In spite of the number of his wives, Brigham Young, if we can believe Ann Eliza Young, never lost his interest in new female faces and features. Ann Eliza wrote that Brigham Young fell passionately in love with Julia Deane Hayne, the actress, who played at the Salt Lake Theater. "He bestowed every attention upon the lady," wrote Wife No. 19, "had her portrait painted on his sleigh, and made her an actual offer of marriage, which she refused on the spot, without even taking time for consideration." Some one told Ann Eliza, and she repeated it to the world, that Brigham Young had ordered one of his wives to be baptized for Julia Dean Hayne when he heard that she had died, for he was determined that if he could not possess her in time, he would at least have her in eternity. Dr. Wyl in his *Mormon Portraits* quoted Heber Kimball on Brigham Young's interest in beautiful Gentile actresses. On one occasion Kimball is said to have assembled his own large family for prayers and was about to pray for Brigham Young. He sprang to his feet suddenly and said excitedly, "I can't pray for him, but he needs it badly enough, for the greater the strumpet, the more Brother Brigham is after her." Dr. Wyl wrote that he had this anecdote from a "perfectly responsible source," but he did not give that source.

According to Ann Eliza Young, Brigham Young and his son, Brigham, Jr., who was known throughout Utah as "Briggy," both became interested in a new and beautiful convert, one Lizzie Fenton. She was courted by both father and son, and there was intense interest in the community to see whether youth or experience would win. It is said that Brigham would arrive in his fine carriage to drive Miss Lizzie Fenton out into the country, and that as soon as he had left her, "Briggy" would hurry to the house and spend the rest of the day in her company. This continued for several months, and finally, Ann Eliza wrote, "Briggy" won the lady. Apparently Brigham Young, Jr., was satisfied with Lizzie Fenton, for many years later he composed this epitaph for her gravestone, and he recorded it in his diary:

"Tried in the furnace of this troubled life
Faithful as Daughter, Mother, Woman, Wife." [2]

In the choice of his wives, Brigham Young maintained, he was never guided by the desire for a dowry. He said to the congregation one Sunday: "Some want to marry a woman because she has got property; some want a rich wife; but I never saw the day when I would not rather have a poor woman. I never saw the day that I wanted to be henpecked to death, for I should have been, if I had married a rich wife. I asked one of my family, when in conversation upon this very point, what did you bring, when you came to me? 'I brought a shirt, and a dress, and a pair of slippers, and a sun-bonnet,' and she is as high a prize as ever I got in my life, and a great deal higher than many would have been with cart loads of silver and gold." [3]

III

Brigham Young preached to his people that cohabitation was solely for the purpose of procreation, and that all sexual intercourse should cease with pregnancy and should not be resumed until after the weaning of the child. "This rule," wrote John Hyde, an apostate Mormon leader, "he endeavors to keep, although the birth of children proves him to have violated his own law, certainly in one woman's exception." Hyde did not give statistics for his statement, but one would think that even anti-Mormons would be willing to forgive as only human the one lapse which Hyde claimed to have discovered by the use of mathematics. Hyde also wrote: "As cohabitation is merely for the purpose of procreation, therefore after his wives get past childbearing, they are entirely discarded. They live in his house and eat at his table, but all attention from him, as a husband, ceases." [4]

Whatever may have been his habits of cohabitation or his theories of procreation, Brigham Young's marriages resulted in a numerous progeny. When a Utah school teacher asked her geography class, "What are the principal means of transportation in Utah?" a small boy is said to have answered promptly, "Baby

[2] Manuscript Diary of Brigham Young, Jr., p. 53. In the Manuscript Collection of the New York Public Library.
[3] *Journal of Discourses*, vol. 4, p. 204.
[4] *Mormonism, Its Leaders and Designs*, by John Hyde, Jr., p. 156.

carriages." There must have been a full garage of baby carriages in the Brigham Young establishment, for he had a total of fifty-six children, thirty-one daughters and twenty-five sons, not including those who were adopted by childless wives or brought into the family from former marriages. The names of Brigham Young's children in the order of their appearance are:

Elizabeth Young	Marinda Hyde Young	Phebe Louisa Young
Vilate Young	Clarissa Maria Young	Brigham Morris Young
Joseph Angell Young	Jeannette Richards Young	Arta de Christa Young
Brigham Young, II.	Alva Young (twin)	Joseph Don Carlos Young
(twin)	Alma Young (twin)	Susa Young
Mary Ann Young (twin)	Zina Young	Lorenzo Dow Young
Alice Young	Evelyn Louisa Young	Miriam Young
Luna Young	Hyrum Smith Young	Albert Jeddie Young
John Willard Young	Caroline Young	Feramorz Little Young
Brigham Heber Young	Ernest I. Young	Alonzo Young
Edward Partridge Young	Nabbie Howe Young	Josephine Young
Oscar Brigham Young	Willard Young	Clarissa Hamilton Young
Mary Eliza Young	Dora M. Young	Charlotte Talula Young
Ella Elizabeth Young	Emmeline A. Young	Ruth Young
Mahonri Moriancumer	Shemira Young (a	Lura Young
Young	daughter)	Daniel Wells Young
Joseph Young (twin)	Alfales Young (a son)	Phineas Howe Young
Hyrum Young (twin)	Jedediah Grant Young	Rhoda Mabel Young
Fanny Young	Louisa Young	Ardelle Young
Emily Augusta Young		Fannie Van Cott Young

It will be noticed that except for the name of their father, few of the children bear the same name. There were several Josephs, namesakes of the Prophet and of Brigham Young's brother of that name, but one of them died before the others were born. There were two Clarissas, one Fanny and one Fannie, but they were born so many years apart from each other that there was little chance of getting them confused. Often at least one of Brigham Young's children bore the name of her mother. Some of the names, such as Alva and Alma and Mahonri Moriancumer, were taken from the Book of Mormon. Several of the children were named for Brigham Young's four brothers.

The wife who bore the largest number of children in the Young family was Emmeline Free Young, who, according to John Hyde, was Brigham's favorite before the advent of Amelia Folsom. Emmeline is said to have coaxed Brigham to curl his hair and used to put it up for him in curl papers and hairpins every night, but this is difficult to picture in view of the Mormon leader's determined character and dominating personality, unless we also remember his sense of humor. Emmeline Free Young bore ten children. Lucy Ann Decker, Brigham's first wife in polygamy, and Emily Dow Partridge were tied for second place with seven children each to their credit. Brigham Young had no children by eleven of his wives, so that the fifty-six were borne by sixteen of the wives.

During one period of his practice of polygamy the Brigham Young household was visited by a rapid succession of births, and it is said that Brigham Young asked Zina, one of his wives, to become a midwife, so that there might be some one always in the house who could assist at these functions. In 1825 Brigham Young's first child, a daughter, was born, and his second was not born until almost five years later. This was before he had heard of Mormonism and the principle of cohabitation for procreation only. Children were born in his houses about every four months during the first years after Brigham Young began to practise polygamy in earnest. 1849 was one of Brigham Young's most prolific years; five children were born into his family that year. A daughter was born on January 25, on March 1 another daughter, on July 30 another daughter, and on December 10th a daughter was born, and another daughter came four days later. Five children were also born in 1850, but some of them died at birth. Brigham Young became a father in January, February, March, and April of 1851, and in 1852 children were born in March, April, and May. In 1857 only one child was born, a daughter, in October, but that was the year, as we shall see, of the difficulties with the United States government, and the temporary exodus of the Mormons to southern Utah; Brigham Young was both busy and worried during that year. In 1859 no children were born, and the reason is impossible to discover, for there is no record of illness of Brigham Young during 1858. During the sixties, when he had arrived beyond the age of threescore, only two children were born each year during the first years of the decade. On March 4, 1861, two daughters were born to different wives. In February, 1863, three children were born, one on February 9, one on February 15, and one on February 22. In 1865, 1867, 1868, and 1869 Brigham Young's wives bore no children, but in January, 1870, when he was sixty-eight and a half years old, his last child, a daughter, was born.

After his visit to Utah, William Hepworth Dixon wrote: "Every house seems full; wherever we see a woman, she is nursing; and in every house we enter two or three infants in arms

BRIGHAM YOUNG'S TEN TALLEST DAUGHTERS

Lorenzo   Brigham   Phineas   Joseph   John

THE YOUNG BROTHERS

are shown to us. This valley is, indeed, the true baby land. For a man to have twenty boys and girls in his house is a common fact. A merchant, with whom we were dining yesterday, could not tell us the number of his children until he had consulted a book then lying on his desk. One of his wives, a nice English lady, with the usual baby at her breast, smiled sweet reproof on his ignorance; but the fact was so; and it was only after counting and consulting that he could give us the exact return of his descendants. This patriarch is thirty-three years old." The confusion created in a polygamous father's mind by the multiplicity of offspring is well illustrated by the testimony of Joseph F. Smith, then President of the Mormon Church, before the Smoot investigating committee of the Senate:

"MR. TAYLER: 'How many children have you had by Mary since 1890?'

"MR. SMITH: 'I have had Silas, Rachel, and James.'

"MR. TAYLER: 'Whose child is Agnes?'

"MR. SMITH: 'I meant to have said Agnes. It was a slip of the tongue. Silas, Agnes, and James.'

'MR. TAYLER: 'Whose child is Samuel?'

"MR. SMITH: 'He is her child.'

"MR. TAYLER: 'How old is he?'

"MR. SMITH: 'I could not tell you from memory.'

"MR. TAYLER: 'He is only 10 or 11 years old, is he not?'

"MR. SMITH: 'Well, I do not know exactly what his age is.'

"MR. TAYLER: 'How old is Calvin?'

"MR. SMITH: 'Calvin is about 14—or 15.'

"MR. TAYLER: 'That is, do you say 15 because—'

"MR. SMITH: '14 or 15, along there. I could not tell you from memory. . . .'

"MR. SMITH: 'I can furnish the committee a correct statement of exactly the ages and dates of my children, if I have the time to do it. . . .'

"MR. SMITH: 'I am not in the habit of carrying the dates of the births of my children in my mind. . . .'

"THE CHAIRMAN (SENATOR BURROWS): 'Mr. Smith, I will not press it, but I will ask you if you have any objection to stating how many children you have in all.'

"MR. SMITH: 'I have had born to me, sir, 42 children, 21 boys and 21 girls, and I am proud of every one of them.' " [5]

[5] Smoot Proceedings, vol. 1, p. 377.

Heber Kimball once boasted in the pulpit of the size of his posterity and how rapidly it would increase as the years passed. He asked the congregation how long they supposed it would take "a little man like me" to number over a million of posterity, and he gave them the answer: "A hundred years will not pass away before I will become millions myself. You may go to work and reckon it up, and twenty-five years will not pass away before brother Brigham and I will number more than this Territory"; and the population of the Territory at the time was estimated at 60,000. He pointed the moral: "Why do you not be profitable to yourselves, and put out your lives at usury?" At the time of his death, June 22, 1868, Heber Kimball had been the father of sixty-five children, and in 1882, twenty-five years after he delivered this sermon, his direct descendants numbered 172. He had been the husband of forty-five wives, almost twice the number Brigham Young married. At the funeral of his first wife, Vilate Kimball, Heber, pointing to the coffin, said touchingly: "There lies a woman who has given me forty-four wives." Kimball's biographer, Orson Whitney, wrote that he often heard Heber Kimball calling in his "stentorian tones: 'Abraham! Isaac! Jacob! Come in to prayers!' For these names, with many others of Scriptural origin, were all included in his family nomenclature." [6]

The immense advantage that polygamy had over monogamy in the numbers of offspring produced was often dwelt upon by the Mormons. In their English propaganda periodical, the *Millennial Star,* there appeared this fascinating problem in the mathematics of progeny:

"Monogamic Problem—A Monogamist married one wife. At the age of twenty there was born to him a son; at twenty-two a daughter was born; at twenty-four, another son; and so on, alternately, a son and a daughter every two years, until his wife had borne him ten children. Each of his male descendants, when about nineteen years of age, married a wife. At the age of twenty, each, like his father, was blessed with a son; at twenty-two, with a daughter; the increase, thereafter, being the same, in all respects, as in the family of the father. The female descendants remained unmarried. When this Monogamist became seventy-eight years old, what did his family number, including himself?

"Polygamic Problem.—Mr. Fruitful, a Polygamist, married forty

[6] *Life of Heber C. Kimball,* by Orson F. Whitney, pp. 433, 436.

wives. At the age of twenty, he had ten sons and ten daughters born; and each following year he had ten sons and ten daughters born, until each wife had borne him ten children. His male descendants, shortly after becoming nineteen years of age, married forty wives each. And at the age of twenty, each began to increase in children, the same, in all respects, as in the family of the father. The female descendants remained unmarried. When this Polygamist became seventy-eight years old, what did his family number, including himself?"

The good Mormon families in England who subscribed to the *Millennial Star* gathered round the fire and figured out this intensely human problem, and awaited anxiously the answers, which were printed two weeks later in their favorite periodical:

"Answers to the Monogamic and Polygamic Problems, Published in the 24th Number of the 'Star.'—The family of the Monogamist, when he was seventy-eight years old would number *one hundred and fifty-two.*

"The family of the Polygamist, when he was seventy-eight years old, would number, *Three millions, five hundred and eight thousand, four hundred and forty-one.*

"The answers to these interesting problems, show the immense superiority of Polygamy over Monogamy in the multiplication of the human species. With a knowledge of these mathematical facts, no one has any cause to wonder why the Almighty instituted Polygamy among the righteous in ancient times. It was the most effectual means of rapidly multiplying a righteous seed upon the earth. The restoration of the same divine law among the righteous of the nineteenth century, will produce the same important effects. Under the salutary influence of the heavenly and divine institution of Polygamy, the righteous, in the peaceful vales of Utah, can, with Isaiah, joyfully exclaim, '*A little one shall become a thousand, and a small one a strong nation.*' '*Who hath heard such a thing? Who hath seen such things? Shall the earth be made to bring forth in one day? or shall a nation be born at once? for as soon as Zion travailed she brought forth her children.*'"[7]

From reading their ideas on the subject of polygamy one gets the impression that the Mormons, acting under direct instructions from God, were in a fearful hurry to build up an enterprising earth, and that their sentiments were those of a wholesaler inter-

[7] *Millennial Star,* vol. 19, p. 384; p. 432.

ested in quantity production, rather than those of an individualist with a passion for quality.

The large numbers of children made birthdays and gifts matters of great practical importance in Mormon families. Parley P. Pratt wrote in his journal for April 12, 1855: "April 12th— This is my birthday. I am forty-eight years old. I wrote letters for home to-day and sent a set of books, viz., Book of Mormon, *Doctrine and Covenants, Hymn Book, Voice of Warning, Harp of Zion,* etc., to each of my wives, and to Parley, Olivia, and Moroni, my elder children; also books to my younger children, Alma, Nephi, Heleman, Julia, Lucy, Agatha, Belinda and Abinadi, Cornelia and Malona, and small presents and candies for the little ones, Phebe, Hannahette, Mary, Lehi, and Moroni W., all as a birthday present or memorial." [8]

Another aspect of this phase of polygamy was imagined by Mark Twain when in *Roughing It* he wrote of the interview of a mythical friend with Brigham Young:

"Sir," said Mark Twain's Brigham Young, "you probably did not know it, but all the time you were present with my children your every movement was watched by vigilant servitors of mine. If you had offered to give a child a dime, or a stick of candy, or any trifle of the kind, you would have been snatched out of the house instantly, provided it could be done before your gift left your hand. Otherwise it would be absolutely necessary for you to make an exactly similar gift to all my children—and knowing by experience the importance of the thing, I would have stood by and seen to it myself that you did it, and did it thoroughly. Once a gentleman gave one of my children a tin whistle—a veritable invention of Satan, sir, and one which I have an unspeakable horror of, and so would you if you had eighty or ninety children in your house. But the deed was done—the man escaped. I knew what the result was going to be, and I thirsted for vengeance. I ordered out a flock of Destroying Angels, and they hunted the man far into the fastnesses of the Nevada mountains. But they never caught him. I am not cruel, sir—I am not vindictive except when sorely outraged—but if I had caught him, sir, so help me Joseph Smith, I would have locked him into the nursery till the brats whistled him to death. . . ."

Although these may have been some of the trials of a father of fifty-six, the children sometimes profited by their numbers. In

[8] *Autobiography of Parley P. Pratt,* p. 474.

his eulogy of Heber C. Kimball, Orson F. Whitney revealed an aspect of polygamy overlooked by those men and women who described only its shame and its cruelties. "Woe betide the luckless wight," wrote Whitney, "who, even in childhood's days, imposed upon a 'Kimball boy.' The whole family of urchins would resent the insult, and that, too, with pluckiness surpassing even their numbers." One of Orson Whitney's wives was a Kimball.

In the practical operation of plural marriage there were unusual combinations of wives. Frequently two sisters were mar-

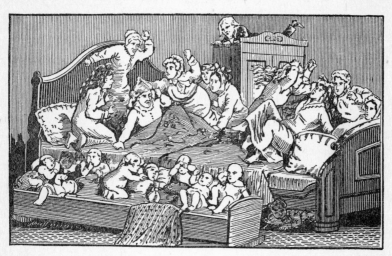

"THE BISHOP'S FAMILY AT TWO A.M."
A CONTEMPORARY CONCEPTION OF POLYGAMY
From "Uncle Sam's Abscess" by W. Jarman

ried to the same man, as we have seen in the case of Brigham Young's wives, and occasionally both a mother and a daughter were married to the same man on the same day. Artemus Ward commented on this kind of marriage: "I had a man pointed out to me who married an entire family. He had originally intended to marry Jane, but Jane did not want to leave her widowed mother. The other three sisters were not in the matrimonial market for the same reason; so this gallant man married the whole crowd, including the girl's grandmother, who had lost all her teeth, and had to be fed with a spoon. The family were in indigent circumstances, and they could not but congratulate themselves on securing a wealthy husband. It seemed to affect the grandmother deeply, for the first words she said on reaching her new home were: 'Now, thank God! I shall have my gruel reg'lar!' "

Phil Robinson, the English journalist, noted in *Sinners and Saints,* his account of his visit to Salt Lake City, several cases of strange marriages he had heard of in the city. They read like the elongated titles of Boccaccio's stories: "A young couple were engaged, but quarreled, and the lover out of pique married another lady. Two years later his first love, having refused other offers in the meantime, married him as his second wife. A man having married a second wife to please himself, married a third to please his first. 'She was getting old, she said, and wanted a younger woman to help her about the house.' A couple about to be married made an agreement between themselves that the husband should not marry again unless it was one of the relatives of the first wife. The ladies selected have refused, and the husband remains true to his promise. A girl, distracted between her love for her suitor and her love for her mother, compromised in her affections by stipulating that he should marry both her mother and herself, which he did. Two girls were great friends, and one of them, getting engaged to a man (by no means of prepossessing appearance), persuaded her friend to get engaged to him too, and he married them both on the same day."

That this custom of marrying both mother and daughter was not the imaginary fiction of visiting journalists is attested by John D. Lee, the Mormon bishop, in his book of confessions: "In the spring of 1845 Rachel Andora was sealed to me—the woman who has stood by me in all my troubles. A truer woman was never born. She has been by me true, as I was to Brigham, and has always tried to make my will her pleasure. I raised her in my family from five years of age. She was a sister of my first wife. Her mother, Abigail Sheffer, was sealed to me for an eternal state. The old lady has long since passed away, and entered into eternal rest and joy." Usually the mothers were sealed for eternity and not married for time.

John D. Lee also told an interesting tale of competition for wives between himself and Brigham Young, which illustrates well the advantage of Brigham Young's position in the community in the eyes of Mormon mothers who were seeking distinction for their daughters:

"My third wife, Louisa," wrote Lee, "is now the first wife of D. H. Wells. She was then a young lady, gentle and beautiful, and we never had an angry word while she lived with me. She and her sister Emeline were both under promise to be sealed to me. One day Brigham Young saw Emeline and fell in love with her. He asked me to resign my claims in his favor, which I did, though it caused me a great struggle in my mind to do so, for I loved her dearly. I made known to Emeline Brigham's wish, and even went to her father's house several times and used my influence with her to induce her to become a member of Brigham's family. The two girls did not want to separate from each other; however, they both met at my house at an appointed time and Emeline was sealed to Brigham, and Louisa was sealed to me. . . . By Louisa I had one son born, who died at the age of twelve. She lived with me about one year after her babe was born. She then told me that her parents were never satisfied to have one daughter sealed to the man highest in authority and the other below her. Their constant teasing caused us to separate, not as enemies, however. Our friendship was never broken. After we got into Salt Lake Valley she offered to come back to me, but Brigham would not consent to her so doing. Her sister became a favorite with Brigham, and remained so until he met Miss Folsom, who captivated him to a degree that he neglected Emeline, and she died broken-hearted." [9]

Greater love than this hath no man for his friend and pastor. But John D. Lee could afford to be generous, for he had received from the sealing hands of Brigham Young nineteen wives, by whom sixty-four children were born.

IV

An enterprising Mormon publisher once issued a picture book with short biographies and photographs of Brigham Young and his wives. In the introduction the anonymous author remarked of Brigham Young: "In none of his relations did his grandeur of character more strikingly manifest itself than in his home. His well executed plans commanded the admiration of his family; his kindness and indulgence challenged their deepest gratitude and affection. His hopes and purposes, joys and sorrows, were generally shared by his family, and with them, he enjoyed the most cordial relationship. His provident management secured for them comfortable homes, and ample provision for future needs, and to

[9] *Mormonism Unveiled*, by John D. Lee, p. 166.

his happy domestic relations is ascribed much of his success in life." This writer would have us believe that Brigham Young owed all that he was to his wives. But if Brigham Young shared his joys and his sorrows with his family the celebration must have unintentionally taken on the nature of a mass meeting and the condolence that of a large and impressive funeral.

Brigham Young once said concerning the relation between his wives and his business: "If I did not consider myself competent to transact business without asking my wife, or any other woman's counsel, I think I ought to let that business alone." Many husbands have said this, but there is reason to believe that Brigham Young practised it. He listened to his wives on matters of domestic detail, and he tried hard to give them what they wanted. He believed that he understood women, and it must be admitted that he had more experience than most men who claim that Utopian belief. Once he gave his more inexperienced brethren the benefit of his counsel on their relations with their wives:

"I am a great lover of good women," said Brigham Young. "I understand their nature, the design of their being, and their worth. I have been acquainted with hundreds of men, before I came into this Church, who believed that, if they did not dictate every five dollars or fifty cents that they had in their pockets, their wives were ruling over them. On this point I shall differ with all who differ with me. If I have five dollars and I can spare it, and my wife wants it, I tell her she is welcome to it. What do you want to get with it, wife? 'Oh, something that pleases me.' I do not believe in making my authority as a husband or a father known by brute force; but by a superior intelligence—by showing them that I am capable of teaching them. If I have a wife that wants to be humored with five dollars, yes, take it; I would humor her. If I commit wrong towards my family, it is because I let them use what they should not, or that which I might bestow upon the poor. I may humor them too much. I will humor a child with everything I consistently can. Does not God, in his providences, bear and forbear with us in our weaknesses and sins? . . .

"When I was first married, I was told that my wife would rule over me, because I was too indulgent; I do not think that she did. Wife, when you spin you may set the wheel where you please; and when I come in to sleep if you have moved the bed from the northeast corner of the room to the southeast corner it is all right, if you are pleased. This course is much more manly than to quarrel with her because she has moved the bed without your permission, or has put the shovel and tongs on the left instead of on the right hand side of the fire place, at the same time giving her to understand that you are the master of the house. But wife, I have made you a good water bench, and a sink, and under the sink have made a place for the swill pail, and I would like to have you to keep the pails in their respective places. If you will put the swill pail where the water pail should be, I must go somewhere else to drink water, and not run the risk of drinking out of the swill pail in the night. I can show you wife, where to put everything in your house. If she wants so many tucks in her dress, put in as many as you want, for you have to spin and weave the cloth; make the dress as you please, that is your business; and if I have five dollars that is not otherwise appropriated you are welcome to it. But if I have five dollars in my pocket I owe and have promised to pay to-morrow morning, it must be paid.

"If a woman can rule a man and he not know it, praise to that woman. They are very few who know well the office of a woman from that of a man. Imbecility is marked upon the people of the present age. All who have their eyes open to see and their minds enlightened to understand things as they are, will subscribe readily to this declaration. When the servants of God in any age have consented to follow a woman for a leader, either in a public or a family capacity, they have sunk beneath the standard their organization has fitted them for; when a people of God submit to that, their Priesthood is taken from them, and they become as any other people.

"I shall humor the wife as far as I can consistently; and if you have any crying to do, wife, you can do that along with the children, for I have none of that kind of business to do. Let our wives be the weaker vessels, and the men be men, and show the women by their superior ability that God gives husbands wisdom and ability to lead their wives into his presence." [10]

Ann Eliza Young found to her great disappointment that Brigham Young did not humor his wives much. She wrote that the chief topic of conversation with Brigham was economy in dress, and that "he practises the most rigid parsimony at home with his wives." "Except by Amelia," wrote Ann Eliza bitterly, "a request for any article of wearing apparel is the signal for all sorts of grumbling." Once Clara Decker, if we can believe Ann Eliza, turned on her husband:

"Clara Decker, one of his numerous wives, was sadly in want of some furs, and she did not hesitate to ask Brother Young to supply

[10] *Journal of Discourses,* vol. 9, pp. 307-308.

her needs. He became positively furious, and declared that her extravagance was beyond all endurance; she wanted to ruin him; she was determined to ruin him; all his wives were banded together for his financial downfall; and so on, with endless abuse. She listened to him patiently for a few minutes; then getting tired of all this abuse, she interrupted him:—

"'If you think, Brigham Young, that I care anything for you except for your money and what little I can get from you, you are mistaken. I might have cared more once; but that was a long time ago.'

"She then turned and left the room, leaving him petrified with amazement. A few hours after a set of furs was sent to her room. She quietly took them, and the subject was never referred to again." [11]

Ann Eliza asked for a set of furs the winter after her marriage to Brigham Young, and she wrote that Brigham Young flew into a rage at the request, mortifying her so much that she wept. The next time he visited her, however, he brought with him a set of furs, and they did not have another quarrel until she wanted a piece of silk to line the muff of the set of furs.

Whatever may have been his attitude at home, confronted with tears and the other practical aspects of the problem, Brigham Young's attitude in the pulpit was a stern one. He once said: ". . . ; and when a wife says, 'O, no, my dear, I think I understand this matter as well as you do, and perhaps a little better; I am conversant with all the whys and wherefores, and am acquainted with this little circumstance better than you are, and I think in this case, my dear, that I know better than you;' reply, 'Get out of my path, for I am going yonder, and you may whistle at my coat-tail until you are tired of it.' That is the way I would talk to my wives and children, if they intermeddled with my duties. And I say to them, If you cannot reverence me, tell me where the man is you can reverence, and I would speedily make a beeline with my carriage and servants and place you under his care." [12]

Although he was firm in the belief that wives must not meddle in their husband's business, he favored the right of a husband to interfere sometimes in the domestic affairs of the establishment. "If a man is a good husband," Brigham Young once told the con-

[11] *Wife No. 19*, pp. 132-133.
[12] *Journal of Discourses*, vol. 6, p. 45.

gregation, "and knows how to live, let him teach his wife how to cook the food he provides, as I have some of my wives, more or less, notwithstanding I have some excellent cooks; but I do not think that I have one but what I can teach in the art of cooking some particular varieties of food, for I have at times been obliged to pay considerable attention to this matter. . . . The man then has to buy the bonnets, the linings, the dress patterns, &c., and also hire them made; and he has to buy aprons, shoes, and stockings, and even the garters that are worn on the stockings. There is not judgment, economy, and force enough in some women to knit their own garters. . . . Let me tell you one thing, husbands; determine this year that you will stop buying these things, and say to your wife, 'Here is some wool; knit your own stockings, or you will not have any. . . .'" [13] Brigham Young maintained, however, that a husband had no right to ransack his wives' belongings. He said once in the pulpit: "Wives, let your husband's stores alone, if they have not committed them to your charge. Husbands, commit that to your wives that belongs to them, and never search their boxes without their consent. I can boast of this. I have lived in the marriage relation nearly thirty years, and I never was the man to open my wife's chest, without her consent, except once, and that was to get out a likeness that I wanted on the instant, and she was not at home to get it for me. That was the first time I ever opened a trunk in my life that belonged to my wife, or to my child." [14] The relationship of husband and wives under polygamy was such a difficult one that the people needed these simple discourses of instruction from their leader.

In Brigham Young's own household his wives did all the cooking, washing, cleaning, and waiting on table. All of them sewed, knit, and made homespun clothes and even carpets, and their accomplishments were one of the boasts of the community. One of the wives taught all the children, until Brigham Young finally established a private school for his own progeny. He hired a stenographer to teach them shorthand reporting, and he promised a black silk dress to the first of his daughters who learned to report one of his sermons. Sir Richard Burton described a conversation he had with Brigham Young: "On one occasion when standing with him on the belvidere, my eye fell upon a new erec-

[13] *Journal of Discourses*, vol. 4, pp. 313-319.
[14] *Journal of Discourses*, vol. 1, p. 316.

tion; it could be compared externally to nothing but an English gentleman's hunting stables with their little clock tower, and I asked him what it was intended for. 'A private school for my children,' he replied, 'directed by Brother E. B. Kelsey.' "

The word polygamy suggests among other things the luxury, ease, and languor of the Arabian Nights, but polygamy in Utah, and especially in Brigham Young's household, was quite another thing. Brigham Young had never been accustomed to luxury and had always been too busy for ease; he was constitutionally, and by habit, incapable of languor. His wives did not lie around in silks waiting for his embraces, for his conscience would not have permitted him to enjoy such a situation, and they were hardly formed for it; although some of them were quite beautiful in a striking rather than a wistful way, most of the wives were sharp-featured women, and not very decorative or ornamental. They were provided with comfortable rooms and adequate food. The entire establishment, although its quiet suggested a Moslem air of retirement to Sir Richard Burton, more closely resembled a New England household on a larger scale. Instead of one superficially forbidding lady in blacks or grays, there were nineteen of them. Most of Brigham Young's wives lived together in two large houses, the Lion House and the Bee-Hive. The emblem of the Lion House was a lion couchant, which had been formed for Brigham Young by a visiting sculptor. An anti-Mormon writer pointed out that this emblem was not appropriate for Brigham Young's house, because the lion takes only one mate, and he suggested as a fitting substitute the figure of a bull, but he remarked, correctly, that this was a matter of taste.

Ann Eliza Young had refused to join the rest of the wives in the Lion House and the Bee-Hive House, after she was married to Brigham Young. She described the cottage he furnished for her:

"He had wanted me to go to the Lion House to live; but on that point I was decided. I would stay at my father's house, but I would not go there; so he had made a home for me in the city. Such a home as it was! A little house, the rent of which would have been extremely moderate had it been a hired house, furnished plainly, even meanly, when the position of the man whose wife was to occupy it was considered. It was the very cheapest pine furniture which could be bought in the city, and the crockery was dishes that Brigham had left when he sold the Glove bakery. There were very

Lion House and Bee-Hive House

"Amelia's Palace"

few of these, and they were in various stages of dilapidation. My carpet was an old one, taken from the Lion House parlor, all worn out in the center, and, it being a large room, I took the outer edges and pieced out enough to cover two rooms, and the other floors were bare. I had no window curtains of any sort, and there being no blinds to the house, I had to hang up sheets to keep people from looking in." [15]

Once a month Ann Eliza drew rations from Brigham Young's steward's stores: five pounds of sugar, a pound of candles, a bar of soap, and a box of matches. The daily necessities were drawn as they were needed. The bread all came from the President's own bakery. Sometimes he issued a few yards of calico or bleached and unbleached muslin to each of his miniature army.

Brigham Young saw all his wives together at dinner. He usually rose in the morning at seven o'clock and went to his office before nine. The private room where he often slept adjoined his office. The barber came to his office at ten and shaved in the vicinity of his large brown beard or trimmed his hair while he continued to discuss church business with his associates. From ten until eleven he was accessible to Mormons who wished to see him for any reason. Dinner was served in the Lion House at two o'clock in the afternoon, and all the wives and children were usually present at this meal. This was the first meeting of the whole family during the day. Occasionally Brigham Young paid the wives individual visits in their rooms during the day. At night the entire family assembled again for prayers. At this function in the parlor attendance was compulsory. Brigham Young once advised his congregation: "Get your wives and children together, lock the door so that none of them will get out, and get down on your knees; and if you feel as though you want to swear and fight, keep on your knees until they are pretty well wearied, saying, 'Here I am; I will not abuse my Creator nor my religion, though I feel like hell inside, but I will stay on my knees until I overcome these devils around me.'" Upon another occasion, when he was discussing prayers, he said: "Let me tell you how you should do. If you feel that you are tempted not to open your mouth to the Lord, and as though the heavens are brass over your heads, and the earth iron beneath your feet, and that every thing is closed up, and you feel that it would be a sin for you to

[15] *Wife No. 19*, p. 458.

pray, then walk up to the devil and say, Mr. Devil, get out of my way; and if you feel that you cannot get down on your knees for fear you will swear, say, get down knees; and if they don't feel right when they are down, put something under them, some sharp sticks, for instance, and say, knees come to it. 'But I dare not open my mouth,' says one, 'for fear that I shall swear.' Then say, open, mouth, and now tongue, begin." After prayers the family usually went to bed. The story went about Salt Lake City that one of Brigham Young's wives erased the chalk mark on the door of another and enjoyed her husband's company during the night when it rightfully belonged to her sister wife, but there is no other evidence that chalk marks existed.

One of Brigham Young's daughters, Susa Young Gates, wrote a description of the home life of the family. She said that when young men visited the thirty-one daughters, they were all received together in the parlor, with a brilliantly lighted lamp on a center table. It was thus impossible to become affectionate without attracting the ridicule of sisters, and sisters are notoriously cruel. One night the lamp was turned low—no one knew exactly how it happened—and books were piled in front of it. Something— perhaps the silence—told Brigham Young that the parlor was not as usual, and he suddenly entered with a candle, went up to each couple, and shoved his candle near their faces, the better to see and to startle them. Without speaking he made the rounds, causing by his impressive promenade fearful embarrassment. Then he silently walked up to the lamp, knocked over the barricade of books, and turned the light to its full brilliance. If the young men who visited his daughters did not leave the parlor at ten o'clock Brigham Young appeared with an armful of hats and asked each to identify his own.[16]

Brigham Young had very definite ideas concerning the care and feeding of children, which he tried to carry out in the laboratory with which nature had provided him. He delivered a sermon one Sunday at Ogden, illustrating his own method of correcting very young children:

"If you find that children are cruel, do not contend with them, soothe them, and invite those who through accident have injured a little sister to pity her. 'You have accidentally hurt your little sister, go and kiss her.' By taking this course you will have good children,

[16] *North American Review*, vol. 150.

and they will not contend with each other. I am talking to you of that which I know. I have had an experience in these matters.

"I will relate a little incident that occurred in my own family. A little boy about three and a half years old was very ill. His mother would feed him bread and milk, or whatever he wished. As soon as he could stand by her, every day he wanted his bread and milk. Just as soon as he had got what he wanted, he would throw up his hand, and away went the basin to the floor. His mother did not know what to do. Said I, 'If you will do just as I tell you, I will tell you what to do. The next time you sit down to feed this little boy, when he has got through he will knock the dish out of your hand.' Said I, 'Lean him against the chair, do not say one word to him, go to your work, pay no attention to him whatever.' She did so. The little fellow stood there, looked at her, watched her; then he would look at the basin and spoon, watch his mother, and look at the basin and spoon again. By and by he got down and crept along the floor and climbed up to the chair, and then set the basin on the table, and crept until he got the spoon and put it on the table. He never tried to knock that dish out of her hand again. Now she might have whipped him and injured him, as a great many others would have done; but if they know what to do, they can correct the child without violence." [17]

Upon another occasion Brigham Young suggested to the women that they wash their children with warm water and soft flannel instead of hard cold water and rough cloth, "and," he added, "instead of giving them pork for their breakfast, give them good wholesome bread and sweet milk, baked potatoes, and also buttermilk if they like it, and a little fruit, and I would have no objections to their eating a little rice." He also urged fathers and mothers not to talk baby talk to their children, although he admitted he did so himself, but was trying hard to break himself of the habit. "I differ," Brigham Young once said, "with Solomon's recorded saying as to spoiling the child by sparing the rod. True it is written in the New Testament that 'whom the Lord loveth he chasteneth.' It is necessary to try the faith of children as well as of grown people, but there are ways of doing so besides taking a club and knocking them down with it." There were no lame, deformed, or blind children among Brigham Young's fifty-six.

In public Brigham Young paid careful, almost methodical, attention to his wives. At the frequent balls held in the Social Hall he sat on a sofa, in later years, with Amelia on one side of

[17] *Journal of Discourses*, vol. 19, p. 70.

him and Mother Young on the other. The rest of his wives grouped themselves about the trio to the best of their ability. During the period of Amelia's ascendancy Brigham usually danced the first cotillion with her, and in the course of the evening he took care to dance at least once with all of his wives who might be present. His dancing was lively and active, and one of his former followers recorded that he took great pleasure in being absolutely correct and enjoyed thoroughly the "brakedown" step at the end. It was said that a Mormon invented a double cotillion, so that two ladies were attached to each gentleman, which was hailed as a great device of genius, for there were often three times the number of women in the ballroom as there were partners for them. Anti-Mormons invented many wild rumors of the attendant circumstances of the eminently respectable Mormon social functions, but the prize for imagination should have been offered to a certain Mrs. M. J. Gildersleeve, of the International Council of Women, who stated confidently in one of her speeches on Mormons, "At their dances they give wine to the young to rouse their passions."

It was ever a source of wonder to inquisitive Gentiles that Brigham Young and his associates could live in amity and peace with so many wives. Erastus Snow once explained in a sermon: "They cannot understand it, because they are governed by their passions, and not by principles; and it is the hardest thing in the world for them to be convinced that this people are governed by principle. This is the doctrine we have been preaching abroad, and it is the very thing the Gentiles will not receive; and they marvel and wonder that we do not tear each other's eyes out. They say this would be the case with them: in a little while they would be bald and blind and full of wounds, bruises, and putrifying sores; or, like the Kilkenny cats, use each other up all but the tails, and then the tails would jump at each other. So it would be among them indeed; for there is no law of the Lord that would keep the people together a minute in the peace and order that exist here." On the whole, it would seem, the Mormons were governed by principles to such an extent, that their life was dull and hampered, but they had accustomed themselves so thoroughly to the bonds of principle rather than the license of passion that they did not feel their chains. Orson Pratt, their indefatigable philosopher, devised for the benefit of the community a set of rules for polygamists, which he published soon after polygamy was publicly proclaimed. Among them was this significant advice: "Rule 4th—Betray not the confidence of your wives. There are many ideas in an affectionate, confiding wife which she would wish to communicate to her husband, and yet she would be very unwilling to have them communicated to others. Keep each of your wives' secrets from all the others, and from any one else, unless in cases where good will result by doing otherwise." The other rules urged impartiality towards the various wives and their children, and advised a husband never to reprove one wife in the presence of the others. There were also rules for the wives against tattling and slander. Orson Pratt particularly asked them not to correct the faults of another wife's children without express permission from the mother.

Chapter IX

POLYGAMY AND THE LAW

THE existence of unusual sexual conditions in Utah was a convenient outlet for the moral indignation of the rest of the country. The same intense missionary spirit of a part of the United States population which leads this country to support so many enterprises among the non-Christian nations of the earth soon discovered in Mormonism, and particularly in polygamy, an ideal beast to convert or to kill. The startling fact that this beast was present within our own borders led those people who interested themselves in its actions to wish more passionately to kill it as soon as they began to lose hope of its conversion. "From the time of the prehistoric sex-worship of primitive peoples," wrote Theodore Schroeder, the psychologist, "to this very hour, the desire to regulate other people's sexual affairs has been the most zealously pursued of all the ambitions of religious societies."

Polygamy was known to the zealous clergymen and hostile editors of the eastern United States as that "peculiar institution," and it was often referred to by that description instead of by its name. Whether this was from delicacy or malice, one does not know, but the newspapers and clergymen seemed to feel that they had accomplished an argument when they had established a nickname. But they did not rest with nicknames. For thirty years clergymen, women's societies, and editors kept up a steady barrage of propaganda against the horrors of Mormon polygamy, and the clergymen especially seemed to forget some of their Christianity in the heat of the battle, for there is no other way of explaining the statement one Sunday morning of the Rev. Mr. DeWitt Talmage to his fashionable congregation, "that polygamy will never be driven out of Utah except at the point of the bayonet." Another Christian minister, the Rev. Dr. Crosby, of Chicago, remarked at the same time that "Mormonism ought to be dynamited." The Rev. Dr. Parkhurst, a popular preacher of New York, pointed out one Sunday in a sermon the dangers of insidious Mormon propaganda: "Mormon literature is being circulated in our streets and distributed in our schools. I am credibly informed that a little boy of eight surprised his mother by coming home from one of our schools a while ago and saying to her: 'Mother, when I get to be a man, I am going to have five wives. Teacher says I may.'" Dr. Parkhurst seemed to imply that Teacher was a Mormon spy, but he offered no evidence for his accusation; she may have been merely a pagan.

Besides those Gentiles who had never visited Utah and observed the practical operation of a household with many wives and one husband, there were hundreds of anti-polygamists who did visit there, and who invariably returned filled with what they had set out to find. The extraordinary quality of the domestic arrangement entered into by a Mormon annoyed these people frightfully. Schuyler Colfax, Vice-President of the United States, wrote to his cousin Carrie from Salt Lake City: "We saw one house where a man, quite poor, had three wives and but two rooms in the house, one to cook and eat in, and the other with two beds in. You can imagine, without my enlarging on it, what a man who has no wife at all thinks of such a system." There appeared to be an element of bachelor's envy mixed with the Vice-Presidential indignation. For a moment his mind may have harbored the sad reflection of Sir Richard Burton, who was also a Gentile in Utah, and who, when he noted in his book the surrounding abundance and his own appetite, was moved to quote:

> "Water, water every where,
> And not a drop to drink!"

Paper-covered fictions with frontispieces of semi-naked women being bathed in the Salt Lake City Endowment House by men with leering eyes came in a constant stream from the presses of the cheap publishing houses of the moral states. The writers and publishers, under the pretense of moral outrage, were enabled to print with impunity enticing pictures of Mormon life in all its delectable horror, and they found a ready market for their literature throughout the country.

With the exception of the indignant clergymen the women were the most virulent on the subject of plural marriage. Sir Richard Burton wrote that "when the fair sex enters upon the subject of polygamy, it apparently loses all self-control, not to say its senses." It is noteworthy that the ranks of anti-polygamy had few women who had been Mormons before they became lecturers. The conspicuous exception is the case of Ann Eliza Young, who went throughout the country under the auspices of Major J. B. Pond. The anti-Mormon women writers and speakers felt that they were leaders in a great cause; they were "striking the fetters of plurality off their suffering sisters." And they were amazed and deeply hurt when the sisters denied the suffering and resented the word "fetters." The Mormon women retorted sharply that women who busied themselves so much about polygamy were jealous because they did not have even portions of husbands themselves. The Mormon women felt that by the very practice of polygamy they were elevating American womanhood, and they hoped sincerely to convert those anti-polygamists who wished to raise them from degradation. Mormon wives also considered themselves artists in marriage, and they thought of the Gentile women as uninitiated lay critics, whose opinions were only worthy of condescending pity. Apropos of this similarity of purpose on both sides, the English journalist, Phil Robinson, remarked: "When Stanley was in Central Africa, he was often amused and sometimes not a little disgusted to find that instead of *his* discovering the Central Africans, the Central Africans insisted on discovering *him*. . . . Something very like this will be the fate of those who come to Utah thinking they will be received as shining lights from a better world. They will not find the women of Utah waiting with outstretched arms to grasp the hand that saves them. There will be no stampede of downtrodden females. On the contrary, the clarion of woman's rights will be sounded, and the intruding 'champions' of that cause will find themselves attacked with their own weapons, and hoisted with their own petards."

Among the foremost of the women agitators against polygamy was Kate Field, the journalist, who was more capable than the others, but no less unreasonably bitter. She lectured and wrote on the subject of polygamy after an extensive tour of Utah, and she tried to enlist Mark Twain in the cause, for in *Kate Field A Record* by Lilian Whiting there is this letter to her from Samuel L. Clemens, publisher:

"Your notion and mine about polygamy is without doubt exactly the same; but you probably think we have some cause of quarrel with those people for putting it into their religion, whereas I think the opposite. Considering our complacent cant about this country of ours being the home of liberty of conscience, it seems to me that the attitude of our Congress and people toward the Mormon Church is matter for limitless laughter and derision. The Mormon religion *is* a religion: the negative vote of all the rest of the globe could not break down that fact; and so I shall probably always go on thinking that the attitude of our Congress and nation toward it is merely good trivial stuff to make fun of.

"Am I a friend to the Mormon religion? No. I would like to see it extirpated, but always by fair means, not these Congressional rascalities. If you can destroy it with a book,—by arguments and facts, not brute force,—you will do a good and wholesome work. And I should be very far from unwilling to publish such a book in case my business decks were clear. They are not clear now, however, and it is hard to tell when they will be. . . .

"Hartford, March 8, 1886.

"SAMUEL L. CLEMENS."

It was not long before the constant hammering at its doors of women, clergymen, editors, and religious associations produced a semblance of action from Congress. First a bill was passed making marriage with more than one woman in the territories of the United States a crime punishable by imprisonment and a fine. But this was successfully evaded by the Mormons, who claimed that they did not legally marry their wives according to the United States law, and were therefore the husbands of no more than one woman each. The Mormons also maintained that Congress had no constitutional right to legislate on marriage, even in the territories over which it had almost supreme jurisdiction. When Senator Lyman Trumbull said to Brigham Young, "I have no doubt that Congress has a right to legislate upon the subject of the marriage relation, and to regulate it," Brigham Young asked: "Then why not legislate about the intercourse of the sexes?" Once in a sermon Brigham Young asked rhetorically: "Why does not our government make a law to say how many children a man shall have? They might as well do so as to make a law to say how many wives a man shall have."

Those same people who were insisting upon the right of popular sovereignty as a principle in the matter of slavery, found it exceedingly repugnant when applied to polygamy. The United States Supreme Court finally settled the practical aspects of the question by its decision against George Reynolds, Brigham

Young's secretary, whose case was brought up as a test case. "In our opinion," said the Court, "the statute immediately under consideration is within the legislative power of Congress. . . . Laws are made for the government of actions, and, while they cannot interfere with mere religious belief and opinions, they may with practices. Suppose one believed that human sacrifices were a necessary part of religious worship, would it be seriously contended that the civil government under which he lived could not interfere to prevent a sacrifice? Or, if a wife religiously believed it was her duty to burn herself on the funeral pile of her dead husband, would it be beyond the power of the civil government to prevent her carrying her belief into practice?" By this decision the Mormons were told, in effect, that they might preach what they pleased, but that they must be very careful what they practised. They would have maintained that logically, on the principles of individual liberty, wives had as much right to burn themselves on the funeral pyres of their husbands as men once had to buy a glass of beer.

The Civil War intervened to save the Mormons from immediate action on the question of their right to polygamy. Brigham Young steadfastly maintained that they would never abandon that right. He once asked in a sermon: "How will they get rid of this awful evil in Utah? They will have to expend about three hundred millions of dollars for building a prison, for we must all go into prison. And after they have expended that amount for a prison, and roofed it over from the summit of the Rocky Mountains to the summit of the Sierra Nevada, we will dig out and go preaching through the world. (Voice on the stand: 'What will become of the women, will they go to prison with us?') Brother Heber seems concerned about the women's going with us; they will be with us, for we shall be here together. This is a little amusing." [1]

In the spring of 1862 a company of volunteers from California under General Connor encamped in Salt Lake City. Their guns were trained on Brigham Young's residence, and it was rumored that they intended to seize Brigham Young and to take him to Washington for trial under the law which prohibited marriage with more than one woman. The Mormons became nervous and guarded the house of their President carefully. At the sounding of a signal all the male citizens of Salt Lake City could be sum-

[1] *Journal of Discourses*, vol. 4, p. 39.

moned in a few minutes to his residence. But the purpose of this expedition was not to capture Brigham Young, but to keep him loyal to the Washington government during the Civil War, although he had from the first showed no signs of disloyalty, but had pledged his support to President Lincoln. Brigham Young had recently been married again, and in order to prevent conviction under the new anti-bigamy law of 1862, he had himself arrested and brought before a friendly federal judge. The witnesses were all Brigham Young's clerks or friends, and the case was dismissed on the grounds that there was no evidence of his recent marriage, although the whole town knew about it. When Senator Trumbull visited Salt Lake City in 1869, he asked Brigham Young: "Mr. Young, may I say to the President that you intend to observe the laws under the constitution?" "Well— yes—we intend to," Brigham Young answered. "But may I say to him that you will do so?" insisted Senator Trumbull. "Yes, yes; so far as the laws are just, certainly," was Brigham Young's noncommittal answer.

But the President, who was then Ulysses S. Grant, was determined that something more than that promise was needed, and especially did he feel that more laws might be effective. In his third annual message to Congress, sent on December 5, 1871, Grant suggested that polygamy must be abolished, and in his succeeding messages he kept urging Congress to do something about making it a crime, but Congress never seemed to be able to make up its political mind on the subject. It seemed to Grant that it was preposterous that polygamy should exist in a Christian nation, though why it was preposterous, he never said. He contented himself with branding it in his annual messages as "licensed immorality," and coupling it with the importation of Chinese women for immoral purposes, which seemed to be a flourishing trade on the Pacific Coast at the time. General Grant's appointee as territorial governor of Utah, J. Wilson Shaffer, consulted an apostate Mormon on the expediency of attacking polygamy. This man, who was no longer associated with the Mormon Church, is reported to have answered: "I married my wives in good faith. We have lived together for years, believing it was the will of God. The same is true of the Mormon people generally. Before I will abandon my wives as concubines, and cast off my children as bastards, I will fight the United States Government down to my boots. What would you do, Governor, in the like case?" And the Governor is reported to have answered with feeling, "By God, I would do the same!"

This aspect of the problem presented a dilemma to both Mormons and anti-polygamists. Concubine was a term a good Christian only accepted without a blush in eastern romances, and bastard was a popular oath for the expression of the utmost contempt. The United States Government and anti-polygamous orators asked pious Mormons to make their wives the one, and their children the latter. President Grant had this phase of the problem presented to his attention, for in his message to Congress he urged that something be done about the "innocent children" who were the by-products of polygamy, and he suggested, without definitely recommending it, that Congress pass an act authorizing the territorial legislature of Utah to legitimize all children born prior to a fixed date.

Meanwhile, the people of Utah were making desperate efforts to turn their territory into a state. Its population was large enough, and the Mormons knew that once they had a state government, they could pass whatever marriage laws they pleased for their own government. The anti-polygamists also realized this, and in spite of all its petitions and its population, Utah was continued as a territory. The threat was held over the Mormons that unless they promised to be good men and abandon their wives, they never would be admitted into the Union as a sovereign state. Thomas Fitch, a senator-elect, called upon President Grant to talk about the affairs of the Mormon community, and fortunately the interview was reported by the Washington correspondent of the *Cincinnati Commercial*. Colonel Fitch found President Grant enjoying a cigar:

"'Mr. President,' said Colonel Fitch, 'I want to try and convince you of the advisability of admitting Utah into the sisterhood of States.'

"'I am unalterably opposed to the admission of Utah,' answered the President.

"'Yes, but you have been prejudiced against the people out there by unfair advisers,' said Fitch.

"'I am unalterably opposed to the admission of Utah,' was the reply.

"'But our population is sufficient; we have made a fair constitution, and it would be a great relief to the people out there to get into the Union.'

" 'I am unalterably opposed to the admission of Utah,' again replied the firm man.

" 'Under any terms?'

" 'Yes, under any terms. At least they should not come in until they learn how to behave themselves.'

" 'If you refer to polygamy, they will no doubt surrender that for the sake of admission and peace, although it is one of the doctrines of their church.'

" 'And murder is one of the doctrines of the church, ain't it?'

" 'No, indeed, there are less murders committed there than in any of the surrounding Territories. As I said before, you have been very much misinformed about the true condition of affairs. You surely don't believe everything you hear against the Mormons?'

" 'Where there is so much smoke there must be fire,' answered the President.

" 'Suppose we should say the same about all the lies told about you.'

"Silence and smoke.

" 'By admitting us the troubles out there would be at an end.'

"Silence and smoke.

" 'It is of the highest importance to the welfare of her people and the development of the rich resources of the Territory that Utah be admitted.'

"Silence and smoke.

" 'Is your mind, Mr. President, so firmly made up, that whatever arguments might be addressed to you would be useless?'

" 'I am unalterably opposed to the admission of Utah,' replied our firm President, and the charming interview ended." [2]

Brigham Young once told his congregation: "Do you think that we shall ever be admitted as a State into the Union without denying the principle of polygamy? If we are not admitted until then, we shall never be admitted. These things will be just as the Lord will." But even in Brigham Young's lifetime there was a tendency to compromise for the benefit of statehood. In the School of the Prophets, which was established by Brigham Young in Salt Lake City for the education of himself and his associates, Daniel Wells spoke on December 9, 1871. He was reported as follows: "President Wells talked on polygamy—would not think it strange if God would take that principle back to himself for a season, through the wickedness of his people." But God did not take action while Brigham Young was still alive.

[2] *Americana,* vol. 9, p. 1039, footnote 21.

A few years after the death of Brigham Young, the Edmunds Act was passed by Congress. Previously Congress had passed another law, depriving those Mormons who had more than one wife of the right to vote. The Mormons accepted this deprivation and went on living with more than one wife instead of voting. In 1869 another futile attempt to break down polygamy was made. Some one in Congress had the idea, which was considered brilliant, of abolishing polygamy by granting the vote to the women of Utah, and a bill was presented giving the vote to women in all the territories, for general legislation could not be passed for Utah alone. It was assumed, of course, that the women of Utah would rise up, and by the use of their ballots would destroy their most sacred institution. To this end, the bill was called, "A Bill to Discourage Polygamy in Utah." But Congressmen were surprised when William H. Hooper, the Mormon delegate to Congress from Utah, spoke in favor of the bill, and they were amazed when the official Church newspaper, the *Deseret News,* printed editorials approving the measure strenuously. The bill never came to a vote in either house of Congress. The following year the territorial legislature of Utah granted the vote to women in the territory, and they promptly voted as their husbands did, thus forming a powerful political advantage to the Mormon Church in Utah.

The Edmunds Act of 1882 provided that any person in the territories of the United States who had a wife and married another should be fined not more than $500 and imprisoned for not more than five years. It also provided that any male person in the territories who cohabited with more than one woman was guilty of a misdemeanor and was thereby subject to a fine of $300 or six months' imprisonment, or both. This act also legitimated those marriages performed before January 1, 1883, and deprived any polygamist of the right to vote or to hold office under the United States Government. An amendment passed five years later provided that a husband or a wife might testify against each other concerning polygamy, and it also abolished female suffrage in the territories. Any man who could not swear that he was obeying the laws of the United States, and particularly the Edmunds Act, was deprived of the right to serve on any jury, and the United States Government was granted the right to escheat the property of any corporation whose members were violating the first anti-bigamy law of 1862. In addition it was provided

THE MORMON PROBLEM SOLVED

BRIGHAM—"I must submit to your laws—but what shall I do with all these?"

U. S. GRANT—"Do as I do—give them offices."

From a contemporary cartoon

that immigration for the purpose of adding to the polygamous population of Utah should be prohibited, and the Perpetual Emigration Fund of the Mormon Church was declared dissolved as a corporation. The corporation known as the Church of Jesus Christ of Latter-day Saints was also dissolved.

The United States Government began to enforce this act vigorously. One of the first results of the Edmunds Act came after the election of Brigham H. Roberts as delegate to Congress from Utah. Shortly before Mr. Roberts was to take his seat in Congress one of his wives bore him twins. This was an unfortunate coincidence, for it accentuated the fact that he practised polygamy. The *Salt Lake Tribune,* an anti-Mormon newspaper, printed a cartoon of the Roberts twins holding hands, dancing and chanting:

"Oh, ho, there goes pa
Down to Washington,
But he won't take ma."

Congress denied Mr. Roberts the right to hold a seat, and when he returned to Utah, the *Tribune* printed the twins again, and again they were holding hands and dancing. This time they chanted:

"Oh, ho, here comes pa
Back from Washington,
Too much ma!"

The Church determined to fight the Edmunds Act, and in an epistle the First Presidency, which was no longer headed by Brigham Young, for he had died five years before the Edmunds Act was passed, declared:

"We did not reveal celestial marriage. We cannot withdraw or renounce it. God revealed it, and he has promised to maintain it and to bless those who obey it. Whatever fate, then, may threaten us, there is but one course for men of God to take; that is, to keep inviolate the holy covenants they have made in the presence of God and angels. For the remainder, whether it be life or death, freedom or imprisonment, prosperity or adversity, we must trust in God. We may say, however, if any man or woman expects to enter into the celestial kingdom of our God without making sacrifices and without being tested to the very uttermost, they have not understood the Gospel. . . . Who would suppose that any man, in this land of religious liberty, would presume to say to his fellow-man that he had no right to take such steps as he thought necessary to escape damnation? Or that Congress would enact a law which would present the alternative to religious believers of being consigned to a penitentiary if they should attempt to obey a law of God which would deliver them from damnation?"

This statement was issued on October 5, 1885. During the next five years 1,100 Mormons were put in jail, and all the leaders of the Church were either in jail or fugitives from justice. The United States had determined to extirpate polygamy. All the Mormon Church property was confiscated by the United States Government except those buildings used for religious purposes. Immigration of converts was stopped. The Supreme Court of the United States had meanwhile declared the Edmunds Act constitutional, and its provisions were being carried out to the letter. The Mormons once more found themselves in grave difficulties. Wilford Woodruff, who was then the President of the Church, issued a proclamation in which he declared that while polygamy was divine, it was inexpedient. This was not considered satisfactory by the federal authorities, and on September 25, 1890, Wilford Woodruff issued a manifesto to the Saints, which read:

"To Whom It May Concern.
"Inasmuch as laws have been enacted by Congress, which laws have been pronounced constitutional by the court of last resort, I hereby declare my intention to submit to these laws, and to use my influence with the members of the church over which I preside to have them do likewise.
"There is nothing in my teachings to the church, or in those of my associates, during the time specified, which can be reasonably construed to inculcate or encourage polygamy, and when any elder of the church has used language which appeared to convey any such teachings he has been promptly reproved.
"And now I publicly declare that my advice to the Latter-Day Saints is to refrain from contracting any marriage forbidden by the law of the land."

This proclamation was ratified unanimously by the next general conference of the Church at Salt Lake City, on October 6, 1890. But it was somewhat difficult, in view of the Church's previously defiant attitude, to explain the part God had played in this latest pronouncement. President Woodruff told his flock: "It is not wisdom for us to make war upon 65,000,000 people. The prophet organized the church; and all that he has promised in this code of revelations has been fulfilled as fast as time would permit. That which is not fulfilled will be." President Woodruff also said that both Joseph Smith and Brigham Young had visited him in dreams, and that he was given to understand by them that this sudden about-face on the subject of polygamy was approved by them, and by God. But it was still somewhat difficult to make many of the obstinately faithful believe that it was necessary to abandon a divine institution because the United States Government, which they had always had reason to believe more infernal than divine, insisted upon it. Woodruff said in answer to this strong argument that he was an old man, that he was soon to face not only his maker, but also Joseph Smith, his prophet, Brigham Young, his adored leader, and John Taylor, his immediate predecessor as President, and that he would not willingly do anything rash with the certain knowledge that he must soon answer for his action before that formidable quartet. He said that he knew it to be the will of God that the persecuted Mormons should yield, and he quoted to them the revelation of Joseph Smith which said that God would excuse them from carrying out anything which their enemies hindered them from carrying out. They had tried their best, said President Woodruff, to do their duty by marrying as many wives as possible for as many years as possible, but the wicked United States Government and its Gentiles opposed them furiously, and God would forgive the Mormons the lapse of their duty, whatever He might do to the wicked Gentiles. But there were still annoying skeptics who wanted to know why, if this were the case, it had been necessary for more than a thousand Mormons to go to jail for practising polygamy before it was abandoned. The answer was: "We have waited for the Lord to move in the matter."

The Woodruff Manifesto officially ended polygamy, and in a few years Utah was officially received as a state of the United States. Phil Robinson wrote concerning this attempt to force Mormons out of polygamy: "In the same way the monogamist reformers, having twice failed to persuade the wives of Utah to abandon their husbands by giving them facilities for doing so, are now going to take their husbands from them by the force of the law . . . and, like the old Inquisitors who burnt their victims to save them from heresy, they are going to make women wretched in order to make them happy." But it was one thing to pass laws and issue manifestoes forbidding the practice of polygamy, and it was quite another to prevent men from living with their wives. The federal government, at the instance of women anti-polygamists, established a huge home, of the proportions and aspect of an army barracks, for the wives of Mormons, whom they expected the Edmunds Act to deprive of homes. But no wife of a Mormon ever entered this bleak institution, for their former husbands continued to support them, and also quietly to live with them.

The Church was placed in a peculiar theoretical position and also in an embarrassing practical position by the Woodruff Manifesto. It was impossible to deny the divinity of plural marriage without also denying the divine authenticity of Joseph Smith. But the United States Government had said angrily that polygamy, far from being divine, was vulgar, and that government passed laws making it a serious crime. The only possible position for Saints, therefore, was to cling tenaciously to the divinity of their principle, and at the same time to disclaim vehemently that they ever practised any longer what they had preached for so many years. And they were forced thereby to acknowledge, reluctantly, that Congress was mightier than God.

The President of the Church and all his followers, however, did not consider that a Congressional decree was retroactive, and their wives therefore continued to enjoy their society and to clothe with earthly tabernacles the souls who were wandering about the celestial kingdom anxiously awaiting their turns to become children of this disheartening world. Joseph F. Smith, who succeeded Wilford Woodruff as President of the Church, explained his position to the Smoot Investigating Committee with great feeling:

"MR. SMITH: '. . . But I was placed in this position. I had a plural family, if you please; that is, my first wife was married to me over thirty-eight years ago, my last wife was married to me over twenty years ago, and with these wives I had children, and I simply took my chances, preferring to meet the consequences of the law rather than to abandon my children and their mothers; and I have cohabited with my wives—not openly, that is, not in a manner that I thought would be offensive to my neighbors—but I have acknowledged them; I have visited them. They have borne me children since 1890, and I have done it, knowing the responsibility and knowing that I was amenable to the law.'

" 'Since the admission of the State there has been a sentiment existing and prevalent in Utah that these old marriages would be in a measure condoned. They were not looked upon as offensive, as really violative of law; they were, in other words, regarded as an existing fact, and if they saw any wrong in it, they simply winked at it. In other words, Mr. Chairman, the people of Utah, as a rule, as well as the people of this nation, are broad-minded and liberal-minded people, and they have rather condoned than otherwise, I presume, my offense against the law. I have never been disturbed. Nobody has ever called me in question that I know of, and if I had, I was there to answer to the charges or any charge that might have been made against me, and I would have been willing to submit to the penalty of the law, whatever it might have been.'

"Mr. Tayler (cross-examining counsel) : 'So that obedience to the law is perfectly satisfied, according to your view of it, if one is ready to pay the penalty for its violation?'

"Mr. Smith : 'Not at all. I should like to draw a distinction between unlawful cohabitation and polygamy. There is a law prohibiting polygamy, plural marriages. . . . That law, gentlemen, has been complied with by the church; that law has been kept by the church; and there never has been a plural marriage by the consent or sanction or knowledge or approval of the church since the manifesto.

" 'The law of unlawful cohabitation is another law entirely, and relates to the cohabitation of a man with more than one wife. That is the law which I have presumed to face in preference to disgracing myself and degrading my family by turning them off and ceasing to acknowledge them and to administer to their wants—not the law in relation to plural marriage. That I have not broken. Neither has any man broken it by the sanction or approval of the church.'

"Mr. Tayler : 'You say that there is a State law forbidding unlawful cohabitation?'

"Mr. Smith : 'That is my understanding.'

"Mr. Tayler : 'And ever since that law was passed you have been violating it?'

"Mr. Smith : 'I think likely I have been practicing the same thing even before that law was passed.'

"Mr. Tayler : 'Yes.'

"Mr. Smith : 'Long years before the law was passed.'

"Mr. Tayler : 'You have not in any respect changed your relations to these wives since the manifesto or since the passage of this law of the State of Utah. I am not meaning to be unfair in the question, but only to understand you. What I mean is, you have been holding your several wives out as wives, not offensively, as you say. You have furnished them homes. You have given them your society. You have taken care of the children they bore you, and you have caused them to bear you new children—all of them.'

"Mr. Smith : 'That is correct, sir.'

"Mr. Tayler : 'That is correct?'

"Mr. Smith : 'Yes, sir.'

"Mr. Tayler : 'Now, since that was a violation of the law, why have you done it?'

"Mr. Smith : 'For the reason I have stated. I preferred to face the penalties of the law to abandoning my family.'

"Mr. Tayler : 'Do you consider it an abandonment of your family to maintain relations with your wives except that of occupying their beds?'

"Mr. Smith : 'I do not wish to be impertinent, but I should like the gentleman to ask any woman, who is a wife, that question.'

"Mr. Tayler : 'Unfortunately, or fortunately, that is not the status of this examination at this point.'

"Mr. Smith : 'All the same; it is my sentiment.' "

Here Senator Foraker intervened with the objection that, "What we want are facts." Then the attorney for the prosecution, Mr. Tayler, proceeded to extract facts, and President Smith admitted frankly that his wives had borne eleven children since the manifesto prohibiting polygamy, and that each of his five wives had given birth to at least one of these children. Senator Burrows, the Chairman, then asked:

"The Chairman : 'I wish to ask a question right here. You speak of your unwillingness to abandon your children.'

"Mr. Smith : 'Yes, sir.'

"The Chairman : 'Why is it necessary, in order to support your children, educate, and clothe them, that you should continue to have children by a multiplicity of wives?'

"Mr. Smith : 'Because my wives are like everybody else's wife.'

"The Chairman : 'I am not speaking of them.'

"Mr. Smith : 'I understand.'

"The Chairman : 'I am speaking of the children now in existence born to you.'

"Mr. Smith : 'Yes.'

"The Chairman : 'Why is it necessary to continue to have issue by five wives in order to support and educate the children already in existence? Why is it necessary?'

"MR. SMITH: 'It is only to the peace and harmony and good will of myself and my wives; that is all.'

"THE CHAIRMAN: 'Then you could educate your children and clothe them and feed them without having new issue?'

"MR. SMITH: 'Well, yes; I possibly could, but that is just exactly the kernel in the nut.'

"THE CHAIRMAN: 'Yes.'

"MR. SMITH: 'I have chosen not to do that, Mr. Chairman.'" [3]

It is rumored to-day that polygamy is still practised among the Mormons, and that men still live with more than one wife; it would be unnatural if there were not some sporadic cases of the latter, for the habits of a lifetime are difficult to throw off, and those few who are old enough to have had many wives before it was against the law to have them, are likely to visit them occasionally. Brigham Young's son, Brigham Young, Jr., was interviewed at Los Angeles on October 31, 1900. He recorded in his diary: "Reporter . . . sought to gain some information about me & my companion: Polygamy came in for a share of attention. She was horrified to think that I still treated my three wives as usual." [4] But, on the whole, polygamy has disappeared, for economic reasons as well as because of legal enactments. The young men find it difficult to support huge families now that Utah is no longer an exclusively agricultural community. As soon as the pioneers began to die the force within the Mormon Church against polygamy became stronger, for the pioneers were neither self-conscious nor sentimental. Their descendants went to colleges in the East, or associated more with Gentiles as more Gentiles came to Utah, and the result was that they became a bit ashamed of their grandmothers, and especially of the fact that they had so many of them. It came to be considered bad form among young Mormons to have more than one wife. Brigham Young was never disconcerted by the grins which polygamy invariably brought forth from those monogamists who were not self-righteous enough to groan at it, but the smiles of the Gentiles were too much for those who came after Brigham Young, and they have been as anxious to live like all other good Americans as their fathers were complacent in their differences.

[3] Proceedings of Reed Smoot Investigation, vol. 1, pp. 129-131; p. 334.

[4] Manuscript Diary of Brigham Young, Jr., p. 10. In the Manuscript Collection of the New York Public Library.

Brigham Young's son wrote in his diary on Monday, September 30, 1901 : "Met with some of my sons on street. Had lunch with them. They are good boys but don't work at religion much. I pray they may mend their ways." [5]

Even during Brigham Young's lifetime it was sometimes difficult to persuade young men to marry extensively. Heber Kimball once said in the pulpit: "I wish more of our young men would take to themselves wives of the daughters of Zion, and not wait for us old men to take them all; go ahead upon the right principle, young gentlemen, and God bless you for ever and ever, and make you fruitful, that we may fill the mountains and then the earth with righteous inhabitants." Brigham Young once addressed the girls directly in a sermon, and he advised them to invite the men to marry them: "Tell the young men," he said, "that you will sustain yourselves, and teach them how to sustain themselves if they do not know how, if they will only come and marry you. Now, girls, court up the boys, it is leap year. Give them to understand in some way that it is all right. . . . Tell the boys what to do, and you sisters of experience, ye mothers in Israel, go to and get up your societies, and teach these girls what to do, and how to get the boys to come and marry them. The neglect and lazy habits which our boys are falling into are a disgrace to us, to say nothing about the sin of such conduct. They produce nothing, and consider themselves unable to take care of a family, and they will not marry." [6]

From a somewhat different point of view Artemus Ward imagined leap year among the Mormons:

"I regret to say that efforts were made to make a Mormon of me while I was in Utah.

"It was leap-year when I was there—and seventeen young widows —the wives of a deceased Mormon—offered me their hearts and hands. I called on them one day—and taking their soft white hands in mine—which made eighteen hands altogether—I found them in tears.

"And I said—'Why is this thus? What is the reason of this thusness?'

" 'Oh—soon thou wilt be gonested away!'

"I told them that when I got ready to leave a place I wentested.

"They said—'Doth not like us?'

[5] Manuscript Diary of Brigham Young, Jr., p. 153.
[6] Journal of Discourses, vol. 12, pp. 203-204. Delivered April 8, 1868.

"I said—'I doth—I doth!'

"I also said—'I hope your intentions are honorable—as I am a lone child—my parents being far—far away.'

"They then said—'Wilt not marry us?'

"I said—'Oh—no—it cannot was.'

"Again they asked me to marry them—and again I declined. When they cried—

" 'Oh—cruel man! This is too much—oh! too much!'

"I told them that it was on account of the muchness that I declined."

Chapter X

SHAM BATTLE

I

THERE were other causes of dissension between the Mormons and the rest of the population of the United States besides polygamy, and these led first to conflicts by individuals, and finally to battle between the Mormons and the government. Polygamy caught the attention of the country and focused it upon Utah, and once in focus through those glasses non-Mormons saw much there to irritate them. "Among the fastnesses of the Rocky Mountains," wrote a writer for the benefit of the readers of the *Atlantic Monthly,* "there is a community which blends the voluptuousness of Bagdad with the economy of Cape Cod. . . . In the Endowment House at Salt Lake City, secret rites are practised of a character similar to the mysteries of the Nile, and presided over by Young and Kimball, two Vermont Yankees, with all the solemnity of priests of Isis and Osiris." Whatever else they might be, a people who could be described in such terms were interesting to newspaper readers. Brigham Young wrote to his associate, George Q. Cannon, who was then in charge of the missionary work in England: "The only thing interesting, however, that comes from Utah, is awful disclosures about polygamy, and a general hostility to the Government. I do not know that the world will ever tire upon these *interesting* subjects, they seem so pleased with them that they continually serve them up, dish after dish, course after course, and like the Indian at the feast, who had taken sucketash every time, when asked the fifth, and last time, what he would have, replied that he would take a little more sucketash. So with the world, they have great delight in false and calumnious statements made about 'Mormons,' and polygamy appears to form their chief attraction."

The same causes which had operated against the Mormons in Missouri and Illinois once more became effective soon after they were settled comfortably in Utah. As soon as their isolation was broken by the flow of emigration westward, Salt Lake City was visited by Gentiles, some of whom remained there, while others wrote home about the Mormons to their favorite newspapers. The chief cause of complaints, besides polygamy, was that the Mormons were ruled autocratically and acted politically as a group. They had formed a theocracy in a country which had always boasted of its democracy, and especially of its complete freedom from religious domination. By their power over their own courts the Mormons controlled justice, and men who did not agree faithfully with Brigham Young came to feel a desperate sense of grievance, which was justified by their situation. A Mormon juror would not convict a Mormon, if it could be avoided, when a Gentile or an apostate was the plaintiff, and the chances of conviction were abnormally great when the Gentile or an apostate was the defendant. The essence of the Mormon ecclesiastical polity was that the brethren were naturally opposed to the rest of the world, for the rest of the world had been opposed to the brethren for so long. A man who felt that he was right would experience an impotent frenzy in the face of such a force of unanimity and prejudice. There were only two ways out: an appeal to the federal government and violence. In their appeals to the federal government some of the Gentiles threatened violence, which they were too powerless to carry out without the aid of the federal government.

Vague rumors also reached the East that Brigham Young and his Mormons were guilty of personal deeds of murder and crime. "According to their version," Brigham Young once said, "I am guilty of the death of every man, woman, and child that has died between the Missouri river and the California gold mines; and they are coming here to chastise me. The idea makes me laugh; and when do you think they will get a chance? Catching is always before hanging."

Another cry against the Mormons was that at heart they were disloyal to the United States Government. In their expression of contempt the Mormons were frequently outspoken; they dwelt feelingly on the wrongs which several state governments had subjected them to, and which the federal government had permitted to be executed without interference. But the Mormons were quite willing to be loyal so long as they were unmolested, and they were sincerely grateful to those Presidents and politicians who helped them or showed any confidence in their honesty of purpose.

The relation of the Mormon territory of Utah to the federal government and the various states was likened by Brigham Young to that of Joseph and his brethren and their father Jacob:

"They," said Brigham Young, referring to Joseph's brethren, "persecuted him, and lied to their father about him, and tried to alienate the feelings of the old man from him, and succeeded in a measure in estranging the feelings of the father from the young child. So it is with the General Government and us. We have plead time and time again, and we will plead, saying, 'Spare us, love us; we mean to be one of the best boys you have got; be kind to us, and if you chasten us, it may be said that we have kissed the rod and reverenced the hand that gave it, and tried again: but be merciful to us, for do you not see that we are a dutiful child?' But no, Tom, Bill, Dick, Harry, and the rest of the boys are eternally running to the old man with lies in their mouths, and he will chastise little Joseph. And though the old fellow has not come out in open war upon him, and arrayed the force and arms of the Government to kill the boy, yet he sleeps in his chair, and dreams it over, and talks in his sleep, saying, 'Go it, boys; go it, boys; we will not say anything here.' And Tom, Bill, Dick, &c., commence pounding on to little Joseph; and the old man is dozing in his chair, saying, 'Go it, boys.' What will become of little Joseph? I will tell you. We are a child of the Government, one of the youngest children, and we cling to our parent, and desire to be reckoned in the family, and to hail our brethren as brethren, and be numbered among them either in a Territorial or State capacity. What next? The cry is raised by the older boys that 'it never will do to admit this younger child into the Union, he is an alien, and we must exclude him.' I will tell you what this will amount to, they will pound and abuse little Joseph until his affections are entirely weaned from his parent, and from his brethren, and he becomes an independent boy. Who will cause this, the 'Mormons'? No, the elder brethren will do it. They will urge on their hostility against little Joseph until he is driven into Egypt for succor. Well, if this is not Egypt enough, where will you find it?"[1]

Those who took the most active part in the opposition to the Mormons were the federal officers who were sent to Utah to occupy the positions of United States judges. Appointments in the far-away territory were not considered either profitable or pleasurable, and only the lowliest hangers-on of the political administration accepted them or asked for them. In exaggerated

[1] *Journal of Discourses*, vol. 2, p. 185.

terms, but with a sentiment that was on the whole true, John Taylor once described in a sermon the process by which federal officers were selected for Utah:

"When a President is elected, a crowd of men press around him, like so many hungry dogs, for a division of the spoils, saying, 'Mr. President, what are you going to do for our town? Remember, here is Mr. So-and-so, who took a prominent position. We want such a one in such an office.' And, finally, after worryings and teasings, and whining and begging, some of those little men, mean, contemptible pups, doggery men, broken-down lawyers, or common, dirty, political hacks, bring up the rear, swelled up like swill barrels; they come to the table for the fragments, and, with a hungry maw and not very delicate stomach, whine out, 'Won't you give me a place, if it is only in Utah?' In order to stop the howling, the President says, 'Throw a bone to that dog, and let him go out'; and he comes out a great big 'United States' officer, dressed in a lion's garb, it is true, but with the bray of an ass. He comes here, carrying out his groggery and whoring operations, and seeking to introduce among us eastern civilization.

"The people here, however, feel a little astonished, some of them, although they are not very much astonished at anything that transpires; and when they look at him, they say in their simplicity, 'Why, that man is acting like a beast.' His majesty, however, swells up, struts and puffs, and blows, and says, 'You must not insult me: I am a United States' officer; you are disloyal. I am a United States' officer; don't speak to me.' Of course, you are, and a glorious representative you are." [2]

The public pronouncements and personal habits of the early federal officers who were sent to preside over them annoyed the Mormons more than any of their official acts. Particularly did they resent the characters and actions of Judge Brocchus and Judge Drummond. In September, 1851, a meeting was called at the Bowery in Salt Lake City to decide upon sending a block of marble as Utah's contribution to the Washington Monument. Judge Perry E. Brocchus, who had arrived in Utah two months before, asked for permission to speak at the meeting, which was granted to him. He cautioned the Mormons against expressions of disloyalty to the Government, and in particular he referred to a fiery speech made on the occasion of the last Pioneer Day by Daniel H. Wells, in the course of which the Mormon leader had

[2] *Journal of Discourses*, vol. 5, p. 120.

declared that "the United States were a stink in our nostrils." The Judge also referred to a sermon of Brigham Young's concerning Zachary Taylor, late President of the United States, who had died in 1850, and whose death was announced to the people by Brigham Young in the following words: "Zachary Taylor is dead and gone to hell, and I am glad of it! I prophesy, in the name of Jesus Christ, and by the power of the priesthood that is upon me, that any other President of the United States who shall lift his finger against this people, will die an untimely death, and go to hell." Judge Brocchus remarked that unless the Mormons could send their block of marble with sincerity and loyalty behind it, they should not send it at all. The Judge had begun his speech in a friendly tone, thanking the Mormons for their kindness to him during a recent illness: "He had been sick among them," said a report of the speech, "and been kindly treated; the flies had been brushed from his face by a lady, and he was thankful." Then he gave his advice concerning loyalty; which was received in silence, and followed this by addressing himself to the ladies and advising them "to become virtuous," the implication being that to do so they must abandon polygamy. Immediately the congregation was in an uproar, for if there was one thing a lady living in polygamy could not endure it was the implication that she was doing so for pleasure rather than out of duty. Several Mormons clamored to answer Judge Brocchus, but Brigham Young arose and calmed the turbulence.

Brigham Young remarked that Judge Brocchus had insulted them, and reiterated his earnest opinion that Zachary Taylor was at that moment in hell. When the Judge objected again, Heber Kimball rose, tapped him on the shoulder, and assured him that he need not doubt it, for he would see General Taylor when he himself got there. This assurance took on the nature of an ominous threat, when Brigham Young said later concerning the incident: "If I had but crooked my little finger, he would have been used up; but I did not bend it. If I had, the sisters alone felt indignant enough to have chopped him in pieces." This statement when carried to the eastern states, impressed the people more with the power of Brigham Young's little finger than with his restraint.

Judge Brocchus left Utah with his associate judges soon after this incident, and they wrote a statement of conditions there, by which they intended to arouse sympathy for their position and opposition to the Mormons, but, unfortunately for their cause, they included in their exposé the statement: "Polygamy monopolized all the women, which made it very inconvenient for the Federal officers there." That sentence was seized upon by the Mormons to indicate their character, and accepted by the Gentiles as proof of their immorality.

After the hurried departure of Judge Brocchus and his associates the next United States officials with whom Brigham Young had to deal were Colonel E. J. Steptoe and Judge J. T. Kinney. The Mormons received these officials courteously, and they liked the Mormons. At the time there was opposition to the reappointment of Brigham Young as Governor of the Territory of Utah, and the new officials endeared themselves to the Mormons by sending a petition to President Franklin Pierce, urging him to reappoint Brigham Young, and praising highly the Mormon President's ability, honesty, and loyalty to the Constitution. President Pierce reappointed Brigham Young as Governor, and on the celebration of the following Fourth of July, 1855, this toast was offered by the Mormons in gratitude: "President Franklin Pierce—may he live till his popularity is equal to his virtues; and may no future President of the United States do any more harm or less good."

The Mormons gave a grand ball in honor of Colonel Steptoe and Judge Kinney. They were introduced to the leading ladies of the community, but, according to the Mormons, these officers returned the hospitality, of their hosts by attempts upon the virtue of their wives. Heber Kimball, with the vigor and frankness for which he was famous in the community, denounced Colonel Steptoe and Judge Kinney in the pulpit as seducers, and openly accused them of what he called "breaking through the bulwarks with women," and taking "unhallowed liberties with the females." It was soon after revealed by the Mormons that the United States military officers and their soldiers had seduced Indian squaws. The officers left the Territory and denounced the Mormons as much as they had previously praised them.

It was Judge W. W. Drummond, however, who shocked the Mormons more than any other federal official because of his personal habits, and irritated them more than any other Gentile by his reports of their own conduct. The Judge came to Utah with a woman who was not his wife, after abandoning the woman who was, together with their children. When he heard cases against the Mormons, the lady friend with whom he was traveling sat on the bench beside him and wrote *billets doux* to the judge while he was supposed to be listening to the evidence. This loving exchange of affection between the Judge and his lady took place at a murder trial once, and when Bill Hickman heard of it, he was very angry: "I heard this," he wrote in his confessions, "in Salt Lake City a few days before leaving for Filmore and made an assertion on the street that if I had a murder case before him, and he had that woman on the bench, I would kick them both out of the house. He heard this before I got to Filmore, and issued a bench warrant for my arrest for contempt of court. I heard of it when I got to town, and said if he served such a writ on me I would horsewhip him. It was not served." Judge Drummond was highly contemptuous of public opinion, for besides his public acknowledgment of his mistress, he told Remy, the French naturalist and author who was visiting Salt Lake City at the time, that money was his god, "and he added, without shame, that we might note this profession of his faith in our journal." Heber Kimball said of Judge Drummond in a sermon: "There is a poor curse who has written the bigger part of those lies which have been printed in the States; and I curse him, in the name of Israel's God, and by the Priesthood and authority of Jesus Christ; and the disease that is in him shall sap and dry up the fountain of life and eat him up. Some of you may think that he has not the disease I allude to; but he is full of pox from the crown of his head to the point of its beginning. That is the curse of that man; it shall be so, and all Israel shall say, Amen. (The vast congregation of Saints said, 'Amen.')" [3]

In an angry sermon which he delivered on Sunday morning, February 18, 1855, Brigham Young told his objections to the United States judges and soldiers who were sent from Washington to help him govern Utah:

"Now I will tell you one thing that I am opposed to, and that this people are opposed to; it is to a man's coming here as an officer, with a bit of sheep's skin in his pocket having some great man's name to it, and saying, 'I am a gentleman, I am a high-minded gentleman; can you tell me where I can find a woman to sleep with me to-night?' and setting up gambling shops, and drinking, and carousing, and stirring up strife, and hatching up law-suits; hunting

[3] *Journal of Discourses,* vol. 5, p. 32.

out disaffected spirits, and then lecturing the people on morality, wishing them to become like other communities, and saying to Mrs. Such-a-one or Miss Such-a-one, 'Won't you ride with me—won't you take a sleigh ride to-night with me? I am a high-minded gentleman.' A prudent father, or husband, says, 'Come home here; this is your place; you have no business with strangers.' What is the result of this? Why, from most of the high-minded gentlemen, you can hear, 'God damn the Mormons, they are opposed to the Federal Government, because they will not let us sleep with their wives and daughters.' I am opposed to such men, and am after them with the barbed arrows of the Almighty. To what extent? Let them intrude upon the chastity of my family, and, so help me God, I will use them up. (All the congregation said, 'Amen.') Such characters may cry, 'Aliens, aliens; the Mormons are all hostile to the government,' and they may cry it until they are in hell." [4]

The United States officials did cry, "Aliens, Aliens!" and they were listened to with consideration in Washington. They spread rumors that the Mormons not only lacked respect and loyalty for the United States Government, but that Brigham Young had threatened them with personal danger in his sermons, and they forgot to mention that the only threats he made against them were directed against their personal conduct rather than their official acts. The result was an agitation in Washington to remove Brigham Young as Governor of Utah, to which he replied in a sermon: "We have got a Territorial Government, and I am and will be Governor, *and no power can hinder it, until the Lord Almighty says, 'Brigham, you need not be Governor any longer'*; and then I am willing to yield to another Governor." [5] This attitude of defiance occasioned much newspaper comment in the East, and soon men in Washington and newspapers elsewhere began to advocate sending an army to Utah for the purpose of placing in power a new governor and of protecting the United States judges who were sent there.

II

In 1857 President Franklin Pierce, who had been negatively friendly to the Mormons, was no longer in office, and James Buchanan was President of the United States. In his first annual

[4] *Journal of Discourses*, vol. 2, pp. 182-183.
[5] *Journal of Discourses*, vol. 1, p. 187.

message to Congress on December 8, 1857, Buchanan pointed out that Brigham Young was Governor of Utah, Superintendent of Indian Affairs of the Territory, and President of the Church of Jesus Christ of Latter-day Saints.

"His power has been, therefore," wrote Buchanan, "absolute over both church and State. The people of Utah, almost exclusively, belong to this church, and believing with a fanatical spirit that he is governor of the Territory by divine appointment, they obey his commands as if these were direct revelations from Heaven. If, therefore, he chooses that his government shall come into collision with the government of the United States, the members of the Mormon church will yield implicit obedience to his will. Unfortunately, existing facts leave but little doubt that such is his determination. Without entering upon a minute history of occurrences, it is sufficient to say that all the officers of the United States, judicial and executive, with the single exception of two Indian agents, have found it necessary for their personal safety to withdraw from the Territory, and there no longer remains any government in Utah but the despotism of Brigham Young. This being the condition of affairs in the Territory, I could not mistake the path of duty. As Chief Executive Magistrate, I was bound to restore the supremacy of the Constitution and laws within its limits. In order to effect this purpose, I appointed a new governor and other federal officers for Utah, and sent with them a military force for their protection, and to aid as a *posse comitatus,* in case of need, in the execution of the laws." [6]

President Buchanan went on to say that with the religious opinions of the Mormons he had no quarrel, "as long as they remained mere opinion." He then accused Brigham Young of gathering arms and munitions and of tampering with the Indians for the purpose of making them hostile towards the United States Government. "This is the first rebellion," Buchanan added, "which has existed in our Territories; and humanity itself requires that we should put it down in such a manner that it shall be the last. To trifle with it would be to encourage it and to render it formidable. We ought to go there with such an imposing force as to convince these deluded people that resistance would be vain, and thus spare the effusion of blood. We can in this manner best convince them that we are their friends, not their enemies." And to convince the Mormons more fully that the United States were

[6] *Works of James Buchanan,* vol. 10, pp. 152-154.

their friends and not their enemies, Mr. Buchanan asked for the right to raise four additional regiments, besides the 2,500 troops he had already despatched to Utah.

Mr. Seth Pecksniff would have shouted "Bravo" to Mr. James Buchanan's message, and that is exactly what a Pecksniffian Congress did when it voted the additional regiments and the money necessary for this military expedition. The explanation of President Buchanan's action does not lie, however, in his message to Congress. He had read the reports of federal officers in Utah, it is true, and he felt sincerely that the Mormons were in a state of mild rebellion, but he himself was suffering from a great fear of secession. Almost as soon as Buchanan became President, the conflict over slavery began to assume dangerous proportions, and throughout his administration he was in terror of being forced into a civil war. By sending troops to Utah, Buchanan wished to demonstrate to the southern states that the federal government would not countenance rebellion. There was also a more immediate reason for the expedition. John B. Floyd was Buchanan's Secretary of War. General Scott, who was Chief of Staff, wrote later in his Memoirs: "The expedition set on foot by Mr. Secretary Floyd, in 1857, against the Mormons and Indians about Salt Lake was, beyond a doubt, to give occasion for large contracts and expenditures, that is, to open a wide field for frauds and peculation. This purpose was not comprehended nor scarcely suspected in, perhaps, a year; but, observing the desperate characters who frequented the Secretary, some of whom had desks near him, suspicion was at length excited." [7] It is said also that Floyd planned this expedition of the best part of the trained standing army to far-away Utah, because he was a southerner and wished, if the prevalent threats of war should result in a conflict, to have as much of the northern army as possible where they could not return in a hurry. Several millions of dollars were spent on supplies for the army, and the man who furnished it with flour made a profit of $170,000. "Who has made the money in what is called the 'Utah War'?" asked Brigham Young in the pulpit. "Mr. Floyd, Secretary of War, expected to make a large amount. When he started his crusade, I considered that he would make some five millions of dollars. He has probably done so, and he will lose the whole of it, and will become a stink and a

[7] *Memoirs of Lieut. General Winfield Scott, Written by Himself,* vol. 2, p. 604.

by-word among his friends, and will rot; and very many of you will see it come to pass." [8] This prediction came true. In 1860 Buchanan asked for Floyd's resignation because of scandal over army contracts. In the following year he was indicted for frauds in connection with the Department of Interior, but there was not enough evidence to warrant a trial. When the Civil War finally broke out, Floyd joined the Confederate States Army as a high officer, and when the army with which he was stationed was forced to surrender, he fled with his troops and was relieved of his command. In 1863 he died.

There was also a political reason for Buchanan's expedition against Brigham Young. The new Republican Party, with John C. Frémont as its candidate, had adopted in its platform at the last election a plank signifying that the party was opposed to "those twin relics of barbarism—polygamy and slavery." They also had adopted that phrase as their campaign slogan, and this placed their rivals the Democrats under the necessity of doing something, or at least, appearing to do something, about the Mormons, since they did not dare alienate their stronghold of power, the South, by even appearing to do something about slavery. Buchanan was a Democrat, and it was up to him to act so that his party could go into the next campaign with something to its credit against polygamous Utah. Stephen Douglas, the most popular Democrat of the time, had done his share by his speech which we have already quoted, in which he called Mormonism an ulcer in the body politic that must be cut out if it could be removed in no other way. To which statement Heber Kimball replied in a sermon: "They [the U. S. troops] are out there: they have been sitting on Ham's Fork so long, it has begun to ulcerate, as that nasty fop Douglas, uses the term,—that little nasty snot-nose: you cannot call him anything half so mean as he is—the nastiest of all nasties that God could suffer on the earth." The well-known policy of the Democrats was complete freedom for the territories to decide whether they wished slaves. It might be argued with logic that the territories should also have enjoyed freedom to decide whether they were to have wives, but north and south were able to unite against polygamy, for the south had many slaves and did not have many wives. The results were Douglas's speech and Buchanan's expedition.

General Harney was appointed by the War Department to lead

[8] *Journal of Discourses*, vol. 8, p. 357.

the expedition against Utah. He was known throughout the West by the unenviable and contemptuous addition to his name of "the Squaw Killer," because of the nature of his activities in some of the Indian wars which had made him famous in the East, where they were talked about, and notorious in the West, where they were fought. General Harney did not wish the appointment, however, and he managed to get his orders changed, so that Brigadier-General Albert Sidney Johnston was appointed in his stead.

Brigham Young planned a large camping party to Cottonwood Canyon to celebrate Pioneer Day, July 24, 1857. He had issued two thousand invitations to his friends and followers, and while they were enjoying themselves with games and songs, commemorating the day of arrival in Utah, messengers came from Salt Lake City with news for Brigham Young that 2,500 United States soldiers had left the eastern states with a new governor for Utah and new judges for its courts.

The Mormons began to prepare for defiance and for defense. Their sentiments were expressed in a song called "Du dah," which was popular among them at the time:

"Old Uncle Sam has sent, I understand,
                    Du dah,
A Missouri ass to rule our land,
                    Du dah! Du dah day.
But if he comes we'll have some fun,
                    Du dah,
To see him and his juries run,
                    Du dah! Du dah day.

"Chorus: Then let us be on hand,
        By Brigham Young to stand,
        And if our enemies do appear,
        We'll sweep them from the land."

In his sermons Brigham Young denounced the army as nothing but another illegal mob set upon the Mormons by the government. "They say," he said, "that their army is legal, and I say that such a statement is as false as hell, and that they are as rotten as an old pumpkin that has been frozen seven times and then melted in a harvest sun. Come on with your thousands of illegally-ordered troops, and I will promise you, in the name of Israel's

God, that you shall melt away as the snow before a July sun." [9]
Brigham Young refused to acknowledge the soldiers as part of
the army of the United States until he, as Governor of Utah,
should be officially notified that they were such, and he promised
to treat them as he would an armed mob of Missourians bent on
destroying the Mormons. As Governor of Utah he issued a
proclamation of martial law, in the course of which he wrote:
"We are condemned unheard, and forced to an issue with an
armed mercenary mob, which has been sent against us at the
instigation of anonymous letter-writers, ashamed to father the
base, slanderous falsehoods which they have given to the public;
of corrupt officials who have brought false accusations against us
to screen themselves in their own infamy; of hireling priests and
howling editors, who prostitute the truth for filthy lucre's sake."

Heber Kimball was as defiant as his leader. "Send 2,500
troops here, our brethren," he said one Sunday morning in a
sermon, "to make a desolation of this people! God Almighty
helping me, I will fight until there is not a drop of blood in my
veins. Good God! I have wives enough to whip out the United
States; for they will whip themselves. Amen." He also advised
the men of the congregation to go to sleep each night with bowie
knives and loaded revolvers under their pillows, and he described
Buchanan's aims in these words: "Then came President Pierce,
and he did not strive to injure us. We hoped that the next after
him would do us justice; but he has issued orders to send troops
to kill brother Brigham and me, and to take the young women
to the States. The woman will be damned that will go: she shall
dry up in the fountain of life, and be as though she never was.
But there ain't any a-going, (Voices: 'There are none that want
to go!') unless they are whores. If the soldiers come here, those
creatures will have the privilege of showing themselves and of
becoming debauched." [10]

In spite of the boldness of their leaders, many of the Mormons
were frightened at the prospect of an invading army. John Taylor offered them this comfort in one of his sermons: " 'But,' says
one, 'I have got a son, who has gone out upon the Plains, and
perhaps the soldiers will kill him.' Let them kill him. (President
Kimball, 'There can be more made.') I suppose there can. . . .
I have seen the time I could have died as easily as to have turned

[9] *Journal of Discourses*, vol. 5, p. 230.
[10] *Journal of Discourses*, vol. 5, pp. 88-89; p. 132.

my hand over; but I did not feel like it. (President H. C. Kimball: 'You did not have time.') Supposing I live, I have got a work to do; and if I die, I shall still be engaged in the cause of Zion. Why, great conscience! what difference does it make? They can only kill the body. And do not we know that we have an interest beyond the grave?—that we have drunk of that fountain which springs up into eternal lives? Then what difference does it make?" Although the Mormons knew that they had an interest beyond the grave, and felt that the soldiers could only kill the body, it did seem to make some difference, for many of them remained frightened even after this reassurance. Even Brigham Young, although he never showed signs of fear or anxiety, was determined to take care of this mortal coil. "And if the wicked should succeed in taking my life," he said, "the keys of the kingdom will remain with the Church. But my faith is that they will not succeed in taking my life just yet. They have not as good a man to deal with as they had when they had Joseph Smith. I do not profess to be very good. I will try to take care of number one, and if it is wicked for me to try to preserve myself, I shall persist in it; for I am intending to take care of myself." [11] To that end he is said to have carried a large bone-handled bowie knife with him every day, and to have placed a loaded rifle on the wall behind his desk.

Brigham Young also used the impending arrival of troops as an argument in favor of his pet policy, home manufacture of goods. Every Sunday in the pulpit he or one of his associates urged the people to make their own clothes instead of wasting money by purchasing them from Gentile traders, for soon they would be cut off from the channels of trade by an invading army.

The plan of defense which Brigham Young formulated was bold, daring, and spectacular. He planned sincerely to burn Salt Lake City and move his entire people into the desert settlements of the south. As part of the preparation for this plan Brigham Young warned his people:

"I have told you that if this people will live their religion, all will be well; and I have told you that if there is any man or woman that is not willing to destroy anything and everything of their property that would be of use to an enemy, if left, I wanted them to go out of the Territory; and I again say so to-day; for when the time comes

[11] *Journal of Discourses*, vol. 5, pp. 76-77; p. 191.

to burn and lay waste our improvements, if any man undertakes to
shield his, he will be sheared down; for 'judgment will be laid to
the line and righteousness to the plummet.' Now the faint-hearted
can go in peace; but should that time come, they must not interfere. Before I will suffer what I have in times gone by, there
shall not be one building, nor one foot of lumber, nor a stick, nor
a tree, nor a particle of grass and hay, that will burn, left in reach
of our enemies. I am sworn, if driven to extremity, to utterly lay
waste, in the name of Israel's God." [12]

Then all those who were willing to set fire to their property rather
than to submit to military rule, were asked to raise their hands,
and all the hands in the congregation were raised. This was
neither braggadocio nor an insincere threat. In preparation for
the execution of this plan, people began to move from the land
and houses which it had cost them ten years of toil to develop and
to build. The *Deseret News* press was moved to Fillmore, where
the paper was published for eighteen weeks. The grain in the
Church tithing house was sent to the southern settlements, and all
the Church records were packed in cases and taken to Provo,
where a temporary Church office was established. The Mormons
were particularly anxious to leave no grain and provisions for the
advancing troops. Meanwhile, thirty thousand Mormons got into
their waggons with all their movable possessions and started
south. Brigham Young said of this exodus: "It has been asked,
'Have you counted the cost?' Yes, for ourselves; but I cannot
begin to count it for our enemies. It will cost them all they have
in this world, and will land them in hell in the world to come,
while the only trouble with us is that we have two or three times
more men than we need for using up all who can come here to
deprive us of our rights. . . . 'Will you ask any odds of them?'
No; in the name of Israel's God we will not; for as soon as we
ask odds, we get ends—of bayonets." [13]

Meanwhile, Captain Van Vliet, who had been sent ahead to
purchase forage and lumber for the United States troops, arrived
in Salt Lake City on September 8, 1857. He had been told that
he would not be allowed to enter the Territory, but he was
received cordially by Brigham Young. He assured the Mormons
that the troops would not molest them if they did not molest the
troops and received their new governor and judges without oppo-

[12] *Journal of Discourses*, vol. 5, p. 232.
[13] *Journal of Discourses*, vol. 5, p. 232.

sition. One of the accusations against Brigham Young was that he detained in Utah those who wished to leave the Territory. In a discourse before Captain Van Vliet and the assembled congregation Brigham Young said: "If it were any use, I would ask whether there is ONE person in this congregation who wants to go to the United States; but I know that I should not find any. But I will pledge myself that if there is a man, woman, or child that wants to go back to the States, if they will pay their debts, and not steal anything, they can go; and if they are poor and honest, we will help them to go. That has been my well-known position all the time." [14] Brigham Young once made this offer to the government: "I will make this proposition to Uncle Sam. I will furnish carriages, horses, the best of drivers, and the best food I have, to transport to the States every man, woman, and child that wishes to leave this place, if he will send on at his own expense all those who want to come to Utah; and we will gain a thousand to their one, as all who understand the matter very well know." Later, Governor Alfred Cumming posted a notice that he would furnish protection to any people to go where they pleased. Of the entire community fifty-six men, thirty-three women, and seventy-one children were registered in his office as desirous of leaving Utah with federal aid, and these were, according to the Governor, people who "desire to improve their circumstances and realize elsewhere more money by their labor."

While the troops were on the way, and the Mormons were moving out, Colonel Thomas L. Kane arrived in Salt Lake City. He had been friendly with the Mormons eleven years before during their exodus from Nauvoo, and he had been their unofficial defender at Washington ever since. Colonel Kane persuaded Brigham Young, who valued his opinion and trusted his sincerity, to receive and to recognize the new governor, without any escort of troops. When he had received Brigham Young's promise to compromise to this extent, Colonel Kane started east to join the army, and he persuaded Alfred Cumming, the new governor, to proceed to Salt Lake City without troops.

As Governor Cumming proceeded to Salt Lake City, he was escorted by Mormon militia and was greeted by the Mormon band, which played The Star-Spangled Banner, Yankee Doodle, and Hail, Columbia, as a testimonial of Mormon loyalty. The Governor said later that such enthusiasm for the national airs

[14] Journal of Discourses, vol. 5, p. 230.

could not possibly be feigned. In order to impress the new governor with their military strength, the Mormon militia stopped his convoy every few miles. This was done at night, and the password was demanded. Then the same company of militia dashed a few miles ahead of the Governor's escort, and a different voice asked for the password. The Governor thus received the impression that the mountains were filled with Brigham Young's troops.

After Brigham Young received Governor Cumming, the war was not ended, for he had not yet consented to receive the advancing troops. He still insisted that if the troops camped in Salt Lake City, he would burn the city, and the exodus of its Mormon inhabitants continued. Meanwhile, the Mormon militia were doing everything possible to make the journey of the troops difficult. They burned the grass in advance of the army, so that their animals were weak from lack of fodder; they caused stampedes among the army's cattle and set fire to several trains of its provisions. The Mormon men were ordered not to shed blood if it was possible to avoid it, but to do their utmost to annoy the expedition. Brigham Young gave ironically the reason for burning the grass, "That we may have a better crop next year, which, you are aware, is customary in prairie regions."

Brigham Young, as the troops were coming closer, declared that he would make "a Moscow of Utah, and a Potter's Field of every canyon" if the soldiers fought the Mormons. The exodus and this determination to burn what they had spent ten years in building were of great sentimental value to the Mormons, for their daring was reported in the eastern newspapers and captured the imagination of the public, who did not bother about the political issues involved. And those people who had been in the minds of newspaper readers lascivious, bearded villains who dared to live openly with more wives than one, became sturdy martyrs who boldly and bravely sacrificed everything for the sentiment of religious freedom. Once more, and for the fourth time in their history, persecution had worked to the great advantage of the Mormons, in spite of the material losses which it entailed. Before long Buchanan was blamed for a blunderer, and Brigham Young praised as a statesman by the newspapers of the eastern states.

Meanwhile, the 2,500 United States soldiers were slowly, and with difficulty, making their way across the country. General Albert Sidney Johnston discovered after unpacking the supplies furnished to him that, in spite of the several millions of dollars which they had cost the government, nothing was right. For the 2,500 men there were 3,150 bedsacks, useful for pleasure parties picnicking in summer, but useless for soldiers wintering 7,000 feet above sea level in mountains where the temperature was always below zero during the night. The supplies unfortunately contained only 723 blankets for the 2,500 men. More than 1,500 pairs of epaulets and metallic ornaments for collars and caps were carefully packed, but there were only 938 coats and 676 great coats. There were 307 cap-covers, but only 190 caps. There were only 823 pairs of boots and 600 pairs of stockings, but there were 1,190 military stocks.

The Quartermaster's Department had neglected to provide any salt for the soldiers' food, believing that carrying salt to Salt Lake was comparable to carrying coals to Newcastle, but in the practical action on this principle, the officials neglected to take into consideration that it was a long journey to Salt Lake. Brigham Young heard of the lack of salt and the inconvenience it was causing the troops. He sent some of his men to the army with several mule teams loaded with salt, "enough," he wrote to General Johnston, "to last until spring, when the army should retrace its steps to the United States, as enter the Mormon settlement it should not." But General Johnston refused the salt because he felt that he could not recognize Brigham Young by accepting a present from him. "Your salt," he told the Mormon messengers, "you will take back with you; not, as I tell you, because I suspect its purity, but I will not accept a present from an enemy of my Government." Brigham Young had suggested testing the purity on the Mormon messengers.

General Johnston, with the tactics of a soldier rather than the tact of a diplomat, wished to give the Mormons an opportunity to join issue with the troops and thereby settle their obedience once for all by a spanking. But President Buchanan took more seriously their threat to burn their homes, and he also did not wish to incur the expense of a long guerilla war in the mountains, for the United States treasury was low.

The only acts of hostility committed by the Mormons were the burning of Fort Bridger and Fort Supply, where the troops had planned to spend the winter, and the capture and burning of seventy-five waggons loaded with provisions and tents. General Johnston sent ahead an advance expedition under Colonel Alexander while the main body of troops spent the winter at Fort Bridger. Colonel Alexander and his command encamped a short distance from Salt Lake City, and Brigham Young started a correspondence with the Colonel by sending him two copies of the latest numbers of the *Deseret News* to "enliven the monotonous routine of camp life." The relations of the enemies were most cordial. Brigham Young invited Colonel Alexander and his troops to visit the city and promised them an escort there and back to their camp. He also allowed those residents of the city who had friends in the camp to visit it. In one of his letters to Colonel Alexander Brigham Young wrote: "If you persist in your attempt to permanently locate an army in this Territory, contrary to the wishes and constitutional rights of the people therein, and with a view to aid the administration in their unhallowed efforts to palm their corrupt officials upon us, and to protect them and blacklegs, black-hearted scoundrels, whoremasters, and murderers, as was the sole intention in sending you and your troops here, you will have to meet a mode of warfare against which your tactics furnish you no information." When Colonel Alexander answered by complaining against the Mormon mode of warfare—burning and running away—Brigham Young answered him in a sermon: "Colonel Alexander complains of our mode of warfare. They have two or more field-batteries of artillery with them, and they want us to form a line of battle in an open plain and give them a fair chance to shoot us. I did not tell the Colonel what I thought; but if he had a spark of sense, he must be a fool to think that we will ever do any such thing. I am going to observe the old maxim—

> " 'He that fights and runs away
> Lives to fight another day.' "

In another sermon Brigham Young told his people what he might do if he were a United States army officer sent to Utah to fight Mormons:

"Were I an officer sent to Utah for the purpose of aiding the unhallowed oppression of the innocent, (and in this connection I disclaim all personalities) I would know the facts in the case before I would make any hostile move; and sooner than side with tyranny and murder, I would resign my commission, and say, 'Take it and stick it in your boot, and go to hell, and I will go my way.' And

I would rather go and raise my own potatoes for my wives and children than to hold office under such a set of administrators and bow down to their wicked designs; though, if I were of the world, I should probably do as the rest do." [15]

President Buchanan sent to Utah in addition to the army two peace commissioners, Powell and McCulloch, and they bore a proclamation from the President telling the inhabitants of Utah that they were in a state of rebellion, but offering them pardon for all their sins and crimes if they would receive Governor Cumming and his escort of soldiers. Governor Cumming had already been received in the empty city, but the reception must have been very formal, for Brigham Young told his people in the pulpit that he hoped when the Governor came, "the feeling of the people would be cold enough to freeze peaches." Brigham Young finally consented to meet the peace commissioners, and he expressed his willingness to compromise in these words: "I have no character—no pride to gratify—no vanity to please. If a man comes from the moon and says he will pardon me for kicking him in the moon yesterday, I don't care about it, I'll accept his pardon, it don't affect me one way or the other." Some of the more belligerent Mormons wished Brigham Young to throw Buchanan's pardon in his face, but he himself was convinced that he could agree with the new governor, who was patient and conciliatory, and perhaps he also realized that he could not fight the United States Government indefinitely without great damage to his people's prosperity. It was arranged between Brigham Young and the peace commissioners that the troops should be allowed to march through Salt Lake City, but that they must not camp within the city. The spot selected for their camp was Cedar Valley, forty-four miles away.

By this time the only Mormons left in Salt Lake City were those who had been stationed there with straw and kindling, ready to start the fire on instructions from their leaders. The final entry of Johnston and his troops into deserted Salt Lake City was described by an army correspondent:

"All day long, from dawn until sunset, the troops and trains poured through the city, the utter silence of the streets being broken only by the music of the military bands, the monotonous tramp of

[15] *Journal of Discourses*, vol. 5, p. 235.

the regiments, and the rattle of the baggage waggons. Early in the morning the Mormon guards had forced all their fellow-religionists into the houses, and ordered them not to make their appearance during the day. The numerous flags that had been flying from staffs on the public buildings during the previous weeks were all struck. The only visible groups of spectators were on the corners near Brigham Young's residence, and consisted almost entirely of gentile civilians. The stillness was so profound that during the intervals between the passage of the columns, the monotonous gurgle of the city creek struck on every ear."

Soon afterwards Brigham Young brought his people back to Salt Lake City from the settlements in the south, and the war between the Mormons and the government was ostensibly finished. It has always been a source of ironic interest to the Mormons that General Albert Sidney Johnston, who was vehement in his opinions against the rebels of Utah, several years later became a hero of the Confederate States Army, and died fighting against the United States at the Battle of Shiloh.

The Utah Expedition cost the United States Government $15,000,000, and accomplished nothing that could not have been accomplished by tactful negotiations with Brigham Young. It was known in the United States as "Buchanan's blunder," and caused considerable ridicule in Europe, where the dramatic exodus of the Mormons from their city and the threat to burn it were compared with the daring of the Dutch when they submerged Holland to save it from France. Brigham Young was referred to as a new Prince of Orange.

During the occupation of Utah by the United States troops there was much disorder. The army had been accompanied by the usual quantity and quality of camp-followers, whose occupations were gambling, drinking, and private quarrels. Their influence on the young Mormons was strong, and at one time there was, it is said, a murder every week on the streets of Salt Lake City. Coupled with these were murders said to have been authorized and stimulated by the Church and by Brigham Young, in the effort to persuade the undesirable element to kill each other off.

Civil War soon broke out in the East, and the army was recalled from Utah. Then Mormons could be seen on the streets in the blue uniforms of the United States Army, which they had purchased very cheaply at the sales of army material. Brigham Young bought up most of the army supplies, and he made a large profit by selling them to his people and to the Gentiles. It was not considered wise to sell munitions to Mormons, and therefore all that could not be carried back to the East were piled in pyramids and exploded to the delight of Mormon children and the chagrin of their economical fathers.

Difficulties with governors and judges continued after the Utah Expedition. There was Judge Sinclair, who loved whiskey, and, according to the Church newspaper, was often found "lying in the street in a helpless condition." He and one of the Indian agents, C. L. Craig, drew pistol and knife against each other, but both "were too drunk to do any hurt." Judge Sinclair was remembered by the Mormons not only for his love of whiskey, but also as the judge who sentenced a man to be hanged on a Sunday. The day was changed, but the Mormons never forgot the Judge's sacrilegious *faux pas*. President Lincoln's appointee as territorial governor, John W. Dawson, arrived in Salt Lake City in December, 1861. His first official act was a speech on disloyalty. He had been in Utah two weeks when he made proposals to a woman which she did not take kindly, and the threats which her male relatives visited upon the Governor caused him to seek the seclusion of his lodgings. Some Mormons followed him there and beat him strenuously. Those who were guilty of this rash assault were tried and punished by the Mormons, for Brigham Young was very angry with them for their tactless conduct; one of the guilty was shot while trying to escape to California.

Other governors succeeded, and there was perpetual wrangling and accusation. The governors accused the Mormons of murder, treason, and polygamy, and the Mormons accused the governors of personal immorality and political ambition. It was unfortunate for their moral position that most of the men who held federal offices in Utah and spoke angrily against polygamy as a principle, were addicted in private to the acts which they so strenuously deplored as vices in public. They were far away from home and from neighbors whose opinions they considered it advisable to respect, and their position resembled that of soldiers in foreign wars, with the usual result in that situation of a complete exercise of the freedom of their natural impulses. To the Mormons, who coated their impulses with sanctity, the personal acts of the federal officials seemed outrageous and degenerate.

Though he was no longer officially Governor of Utah, Brigham

Young's influence with his people made him the supreme authority. "Though I may not be Governor here," he said once, "my power will not be diminished. No man they can send here will have much influence with this community, unless he be the man of their choice. Let them send whom they will, and it does not diminish my influence one particle. As I said, the first time I spoke on the stand, my Governorship and every other ship under my control, are aided and derive direct advantage from my position in the Priesthood."

Brigham Young believed that a good man should rule as long as he showed himself capable of ruling, and he was in favor of this not only in his own position, but in that of the President of the United States. "Can the Constitution be altered?" he once asked. "It can; and when we get a President that answers our wishes to occupy the executive chair, there let him sit to the day of his death, and pray that he may live as long as Methuselah; and, whenever we have good officers, strive to retain them, and to fill up vacancies with good men, until there are none who would let the nation sink for a can of oysters and a lewd woman." His whole political philosophy favored a benevolent, paternal despotism, which would force people to do what their righteous and religious leaders thought was best for them.

During the Civil War Brigham Young sided with the North, but the Mormon part in that war consisted in keeping the Indians quiet. Lincoln had said, when asked what his policy towards the Mormons was, that he would let them alone if they would let him alone, and this unwritten agreement was kept. The outbreak of the Civil War was considered in Utah one of the crowning events of Mormon prophecy. Joseph Smith, as we have seen, predicted many years before that civil war would break out, and when it did the people were more than ever satisfied with their prophet. Brigham Young, however, urged his people not to boast about this triumph, for he was both sensitive enough and keen enough to realize that such an attitude would arouse the resentment of those who were fighting, and would outrage the religious sensibility of those who were watching. He desired neither the unnecessary opposition of Americans, nor the contempt of Europeans, for he needed them both in his business of building up a Mormon theocracy.

Chapter XI

MOUNTAIN MEADOWS MASSACRE

I

WHILE the United States troops were still on their way to Utah to enforce submission to the government and to protect any who might need protection, there occurred the most terrible incident in Mormon history, and the one event which gave the color of truth to the stories of murder and oppression which had been circulated concerning the Mormons for so long. The massacre of California emigrants which took place in the autumn of 1857 at Mountain Meadows is an indelible Mormon crime, but it is possible to understand its causes and its circumstances, for it was not, as anti-Mormons have claimed for so many years, a case of Sadistic joy in murder for its own sake, or the sudden outcrop of a long stimulated hatred for Gentiles.

In order to understand the Mountain Meadows Massacre, it is first necessary to realize the state of mind of the Mormons during 1856 and 1857. During the year 1856 there took place, under the leadership of Brigham Young and his fiery associate, Jedediah M. Grant, what is known in the Mormon Church as the Reformation. There had been during 1854 and 1855 a period of dangerous famine and intense hard times. This led some of the people to leave the valley of the Great Salt Lake and its crickets, grasshoppers, and drought, for California, where there were gold, warm days, and rich soil. Many Mormons were induced by the contrast with their own lot, however temporary their leaders insisted it was, and what seemed to be the eternal golden prosperity of nearby California, to abandon their religion for the ease and comfort of this world. The religious community was thereby threatened with partial disintegration, and the leaders were thereby led to use exhortation, persuasion, and, finally, compulsion, to keep their people in what they sternly and sincerely believed were the paths of righteousness. Famine and hard times had also led to quarrels among the Saints about property and about wives.

398

Obedience to Brigham Young's will was not so general as he wished and as he had been in the habit of expecting. Therefore, he and his associates, Jedediah Grant and Heber Kimball, decided to bring the people to a realization of the value of virtue by vigorous action against vice.

For one thing, the Saints had begun to ignore the Sabbath. The wars against grasshoppers and crickets had made it necessary to work sometimes on Sunday, and this led quickly to a habit of mind that regarded Sunday as the same as every other day. Then, too, the strong community spirit had inculcated in some men the habit of regarding their neighbor's ox or his ass as their own, especially if they happened at the moment to be in great need of an ox or an ass. This soon developed into the same attitude toward a neighbor's wife. It is said that at a meeting of the principal members of the priesthood, Brigham Young said in the course of a harangue: "All you who have been guilty of committing adultery, stand up." To his amazement and chagrin three-fourths of the brethren present promptly stood up. It was explained that Brother Brigham had meant, of course, that only those who had committed adultery since they became Mormons need stand. All the guilty brethren remained standing. Brigham Young was overwhelmed, and he prescribed immediate baptism for the remission of sins, and it was made clear that after this batch of sins had been washed away, they could be forgotten and need never again be acknowledged so publicly.

Brigham H. Roberts, assistant historian of the Church, in discussing what he termed the "sex sins" of the community, wrote: "The unsettled life of the ten years between the exodus from Nauvoo and the beginning of 'the Reformation' was crowded with circumstances that lent themselves to continuous temptations in this kind of evil. There were the long weeks of ocean travel by mixed companies in slow-sailing vessels; followed by long journeys of the same mixed companies up the American rivers, in crowded steamboats; or day and night travel in more crowded railway trains to the western terminal of the railroads. Then there was the longer overland journeying by hand cart or ox train means of travel, all classes being thrown into constant and closest contact, which not all the care of the organized camp, nor the watchfulness of faithful pastors could rob of insidious and sometimes ruinous temptations." [1]

[1] *Americana,* vol. 8, pp. 459-462.

Brigham Young, with Yankee enthusiasm, declared in a sermon one Sunday that not only were the Mormons "the best looking and finest set of people on the face of the earth," not only could they "pray the best, preach the best, sing the best," but also that they had among them "the greatest and smoothest liars in the world, the cunningest and most adroit thieves, and any other shade of character that you can mention." He said that the Gospel net dragged in all kinds of fish, and that many of them proved, upon closer inspection, to be rotten.

Several times Brigham Young had said in the pulpit that those who wished to leave the Saints were free to do so if they paid their debts. What Brigham Young resented, however, was the action of apostates after they had left the Church. Apostates had done the Mormons so much harm with their enemies in Missouri and Illinois that Brigham Young had come to fear and to hate them for the tales they now told in California and in the East. It was determined during the Reformation to exercise as much intimidating control over the dissatisfied as possible, and this control in the last extremity extended sometimes to murder. There was, for example, the case of William Parrish, who had been one of the trusted members of the Church in Nauvoo. He became dissatisfied in Utah and made secret plans to leave for California. At the suggestion of Brigham Young, who knew everybody's plans before they were consummated, Bishop Johnson looked into Parrish's intentions. The Bishop visited Parrish with two other agents of the Church, Durfee and Potter, and they gained his confidence by professions of their own dissatisfaction and by promises of aid. A week later Parrish's horses were stolen. Finally, Durfee and Potter planned to aid Parrish to leave Utah. They arranged with him to meet him outside the city, and when they had met, Durfee returned to Salt Lake City to get Parrish's two sons, Orrin and Beason. While Parrish and Potter were waiting for Durfee and the young boys, William Bird, who was lying in hiding, fired a shot, which by mistake hit Potter instead of Parrish. Potter died. Bird came into the open, and when Parrish asked him if he had killed Potter, he drew a bowie knife and stabbed Parrish fifteen times in the back, sides, and arms. Bird returned to his hiding-place, and when Durfee returned with Parrish's two sons, William Bird from his ambush shot Beason dead and tried to kill Orrin, who escaped after the first shot hit his cartridge box.

There were other cases of murder, not so well substantiated as the Parrish case, which was fully investigated by the federal official, Judge Cradlebaugh. It is clear that Brigham Young and his associates had aroused themselves to the point of fanaticism in their determination to keep men righteous by any means, and to prevent them from telling tales if they could not be kept faithful. It is claimed that during this wave of fanaticism men were not only murdered, but were sometimes flogged, and often castrated. How much of this was true, it is impossible to determine, but that some of it was true is easily discerned from the sermons of the time and the confessions of former Mormons. John D. Lee wrote: "In Utah it has been the custom of the Priesthood to make eunuchs of such men as were obnoxious to the leaders. This was done for a double purpose: first, it gave a perfect revenge, and next, it left the poor victim a living example to others of the dangers of disobeying counsel and not living as ordered by the Priesthood." Lee also maintained that, "In Utah it was the favorite revenge of old, worn-out members of the Priesthood, who wanted young women sealed to them, and found that the girl preferred some handsome young man. The old priests generally got the girls, and many a young man was unsexed for refusing to give up his sweetheart at the request of an old and failing, but still sensual apostle or member of the Priesthood." [2]

Another of Brigham Young's henchmen, who wrote his confessions, was Bill Hickman. He was a man who never objected to killing another man, if he felt that the man deserved to be dead, or if he was convinced that the act was necessary to preserve either himself or his Church from danger or inconvenience. When a man he was about to hang for murder told Hickman he would come back and haunt him for the rest of his life, Hickman calmly replied, "I am not much afraid of live men, and much less of dead ones." Bill Hickman was known for many years as Brigham Young's Destroying Angel. In his book Hickman recorded his murders and his scalpings with a charming lack of bravado, shame, or sentimentality. He rarely implicates Brigham Young directly, but he intimates that in some instances the Presi-

[2] *Mormonism Unveiled,* by John D. Lee, p. 284. It is necessary to note that Lee's book was touched up by his lawyer, W. W. Bishop, who claimed that he only altered a word or straightened a sentence here and there. But it is possible that in the process he heightened an effect.

dent of the Church let it be known that a man was undesirable, and then allowed Hickman to use his own violent judgment on the case. Hickman was capable of beating a man to death with the butt end of his rifle, literally without thinking about it afterwards, and he was at one time firmly convinced that anything Brigham Young ordered was just, and that in return for obedience he would receive eternal spiritual salvation.

Hickman was only one of the executioners of the Reformation, but Jedediah Grant was its firebrand. "As for you miserable, sleepy 'Mormons,'" Grant said in a sermon, "who say to those wretches, [the Gentiles] 'Give us your dimes, and you shall have our wheat, and our daughters, only give us your dimes and you shall have this, that, and the other,' I not only wish but pray, in the name of Israel's God, that the time was come in which to unsheathe the sword, like Moroni of old, and to cleanse the inside of the platter, and we would not wait for the decision of grand or traverse juries, but we would walk into you and completely use up every curse who will not do right." [3]

Brigham Young had decided that the time had come to unsheathe the sword, and for "judgment to be laid to the line and righteousness to the plummet." For this purpose he brought forth the most appalling theory of Mormon theology, the doctrine of blood atonement for sins. According to this theory, there exist certain sins for which atonement can only be had by shedding the blood of the sinners. Among these sins were apostasy, unfaithfulness to the marriage obligations on the part of the wife, and the shedding of innocent blood. In a sermon Brigham Young once explained the theory to the congregation, whom he hoped to reform:

"There are sins that men commit for which they cannot receive forgiveness in this world, or in that which is to come, and if they had their eyes open to see their true condition, they would be perfectly willing to have their blood spilt upon the ground, that the smoke thereof might ascend to heaven as an offering for their sins; and the smoking incense would atone for their sins, whereas, if such is not the case, they will stick to them and remain upon them in the spirit world.

"I know, when you hear my brethren telling about cutting people off from the earth, that you consider it is strong doctrine; but it is to save them, not to destroy them. . . .

[3] *Journal of Discourses,* vol. 3, p. 235.

"I do know that there are sins committed, of such a nature that if the people did understand the doctrine of salvation, they would tremble because of their situation. And furthermore, I know that there are transgressors, who, if they knew themselves, and the only condition upon which they can obtain forgiveness, would beg of their brethren to shed their blood, that the smoke thereof might ascend to God as an offering to appease the wrath that is kindled against them, and that the law might have its course. I will say further; I have had men come to me and offer their lives to atone for their sins.

· "It is true that the blood of the Son of God was shed for sins through the fall and those committed by men, yet men can commit sins which it can never remit. As it was in ancient days, so it is in our day; and though the principles are taught publicly from this stand, the people do not understand them; yet the law is precisely the same. There are sins that can be atoned for by an offering upon an altar, as in ancient days; and there are sins that the blood of a lamb or a calf, or of turtle doves, cannot remit, but they must be atoned for by the blood of the man." [4]

And in another sermon Brigham Young emphasized that true love was a love that would shed blood in order to insure for the loved one eternal salvation:

"All mankind," he said, "love themselves, and let these principles be known by an individual, and he would be glad to have his blood shed. That would be loving themselves, even unto an eternal exaltation. Will you love your brothers or sisters likewise, when they have committed a sin that cannot be atoned for without the shedding of their blood? Will you love that man or woman well enough to shed their blood? That is what Jesus Christ meant. He never told a man or woman to love their enemies in their wickedness, never. . . .

"I have seen scores and hundreds of people for whom there would have been a chance (in the last resurrection there will be) if their lives had been taken and their blood spilled on the ground as a smoking incense to the Almighty, but who are now angels to the devil, until our elder brother Jesus Christ raises them up—conquers death, hell, and the grave. I have known a great many men who have left this Church for whom there is no chance whatever for exaltation, but if their blood had been spilled, it would have been better for them. The wickedness and ignorance of the nations forbid this principle's being in full force, but the time will come when the law of God will be in full force.

[4] *Journal of Discourses,* vol. 4, pp. 53-54.

"This is loving our neighbor as ourselves; if he needs help, help him; and if he wants salvation and it is necessary to spill his blood on the earth in order that he may be saved, spill it. Any of you who understand the principles of eternity, if you have sinned a sin requiring the shedding of blood, except the sin unto death, would not be satisfied nor rest until your blood should be spilled, that you might even gain that salvation you desire. That is the way to love mankind." [5]

This was the height of fanatical Puritanism. The world to come, with its promise of eternal salvation and unsurpassable glory, was everything, and this world with its joys and amusements was correspondingly insignificant. The doctrine of blood atonement was a terrible doctrine, and the fact that there are few instances of its actual practice, does not detract from its philosophical terror. Brigham Young was now beginning to lose patience with mankind because it just would not be saved, according to his plans, and he therefore gave free rein to his implicit and sincere belief that some men and women should be killed for their own good. The doctrine of blood atonement is illustrated by a joke Brigham Young told in one of his sermons:

"And I some expect that many will be brought into close places, as the Jew was by the Catholic priest. The Jew fell through the ice, and was about to drown, and implored the Catholic priest to pull him out. 'I cannot,' said the priest, 'except you repent, and become a Christian.' Said the Jew, 'Pull me out this once.' 'Do you believe in the Lord Jesus Christ, and the Holy Catholic Church?' asked the priest. The Jew answered, 'No, I do not.' 'Then you must stay there,' and the priest held him under the water awhile. 'Do you believe in Jesus Christ now?' 'O yes, take me out.' 'Well,' remarked the priest, 'thank God that another sinner has repented; you are safe now, and while you are safe I will send you right to heaven's gate,' and he gave the Jew a push under the ice."

It was one of the limitations of Brigham Young's mind that he himself always preferred a dead saint to a living sinner.

That this doctrine of blood atonement created terror of conscience among the Saints and led to self-slaughter in the cause of righteousness, is illustrated by one story told by a former Mormon leader. One of the wives of a Mormon of Salt Lake City was unfaithful to him while he was on a mission in foreign lands.

[5] *Journal of Discourses*, vol. 4, pp. 219-220.

When he returned, the Church was in the throes of the Reformation, and his wife believed that she was doomed to lose the right to those children she had borne her husband in lawful wedlock, and that she would be separated from him and from them in eternity. She told her husband of her fears and of her sin, and he agreed with her that the fears were justified and the sin awful. She sat on her husband's knee and embraced him as she had never done before, while, as he returned her kisses, he cut her throat and thereby sent her spirit to the gods in all its former purity.[6]

The Reformation caused Mormons to confess all the sins they could think of, but Brigham Young was forced to admit in a sermon that "there has been more confessing than forsaking." Another effect of the Reformation was the death of its author. Jedediah M. Grant, who had suggested the Reformation to Brigham Young, was so busy baptizing Saints for the remission of their sins and therefore had to be in the water so much, that he contracted pneumonia and died in 1856, lamented by all the faithful.

But the worst effect of the Reformation was its influence on the state of mind of the community. Murder became a righteous duty at times, and against sinners and enemies it was no longer regarded as a sin. Obedience to the leaders of the Church was considered a supreme duty, and the entire Mormon population was keyed up to a pitch of fiery faith by the psychological effect of the terrifying doctrine of blood atonement, and by the excitement which a renewal of righteousness caused in their minds.

II

Parley P. Pratt, one of the leading members of the Church, and its most active missionary, was accused early in 1857 of seducing the wife of H. H. McLean, a merchant of San Francisco. Pratt, according to McLean, wished to make Mrs. McLean the seventh Mrs. Pratt, and Mrs. McLean was willing. But Mr. McLean was not, and in order to prevent his wife from joining the Mormons, her husband had adopted the course which was most likely to throw her into their arms. He sent their children to her father's house in New Orleans, where she quickly

[6] *The Rocky Mountain Saints*, by T. B. H. Stenhouse, pp. 469-470.

followed, and by pretending to repent of her Mormon tendencies, succeeded in getting her children back again. As soon as she had possession of them, she started for Utah. McLean pursued her. Meanwhile, Mrs. McLean had been corresponding with Parley Pratt, and Mr. McLean was looking for Mr. Pratt as well as for his wife and children. He intercepted a letter from Pratt to his wife, by which he discovered that they had an appointment to meet near Fort Gibson in the Cherokee Indian reservation. McLean followed and caught up with them. He brought legal action in Arkansas against Pratt, and great excitement was caused by the trial, in the course of which McLean introduced numerous cipher letters written by his wife and by Pratt. It was with difficulty that the judge kept the mob from lynching Pratt. McLean became so enraged that he drew his pistol in the court room and threatened to shoot Pratt there. Pratt was declared innocent of McLean's charges against him and left town early in the morning. McLean followed, and near Van Buren, Arkansas, on May 14, 1857, he stabbed Pratt and killed him. A year before he was killed Parley Pratt had written an address which was delivered before the territorial legislature of Utah on "Marriage and Morals in Utah," in the course of which he approved with fervor the Bible penalties for adultery, which, he pointed out, consisted of stabbing or stoning the guilty party to death.

This murder of one of their leaders enraged the Mormons, and they were disposed to have vengeance if possible. In September of 1857 a party of one hundred and thirty-six emigrants on their way from Arkansas to California passed through Utah. Those of the party who had not come from Arkansas were said to be from Missouri and Illinois, and the rumor was spread among the Mormons that these last were members of the mob that had murdered the Prophet Joseph Smith. As the emigrants passed through Utah, the Mormons were instructed to give them no aid, to sell them no provisions, and to adopt a negative hostility towards them in every way. At the time the army of the United States was on its way to Utah, and the Mormons were adopting an attitude of suspicious hostility towards all emigrants, but these who came directly from the state where Parley Pratt had just been killed, were regarded with special enmity, for the Mormons have never hesitated to attribute the sins of the fathers not only to the children, but also to the grandfathers, and even to the sisters, the cousins, and the aunts.

PARLEY P. PRATT

HEBER C. KIMBALL

JEDEDIAH M. GRANT

ORSON PRATT

The Mormons claimed that as these Arkansas emigrants made their way through Utah to the south they fought with Indians and poisoned wells with arsenic and cattle with strychnine. It has been established that some oxen died while these emigrants were in the neighborhood, but it was likely that they died of the poisonous weeds which were prevalent in the deserts of southern Utah. There was no evidence that the emigrants had either arsenic or strychnine in their baggage. On September 3, 1857, the emigrants arrived at Mountain Meadows. Mountain Meadows lay in a long valley. It was a level stretch of green seven miles long, entirely surrounded by hills and mountains, with a small gap at either end, leading out into the desert on one side and towards Jake Hamblin's ranch on the other. A small stream ran through the meadows, and near this the emigrants camped.

At daybreak on Monday, September 7, as they were lighting their camp fires for breakfast, the emigrants were fired upon by Indians and white men dressed as Indians. More than twenty were killed and wounded, and the cattle were driven off by their assailants. The surviving emigrants barricaded themselves behind their waggons and prepared to withstand a siege. The attacking party retired to the hills and shot down on the emigrants who showed their heads outside their entrenchment. Soon the Arkansas people began to suffer from lack of water, for it was impossible to get any from the near-by stream until after dark, and then the risk of being shot in the attempt was great.

After four days of siege, a waggon with a flag of truce approached the emigrants' corral. John D. Lee came to offer them protection if they would surrender their arms and ammunition. They consented to do this, after he had informed them that he was a Mormon and would take them to the nearest Mormon settlement, Cedar City, where they would be safe from the "Indians" who had attacked them. All the weapons were then placed in one waggon, and the wounded and children were placed in special waggons. The Mormon troops whom Lee had brought with him then opened order, and the emigrants marched with Mormons on either side of them, first the women, and then the men. As soon as they had marched a short distance, the Mormon guards turned on the emigrants and shot every one of them dead. Meanwhile, Lee, with several assistants, had taken charge of the waggons with the wounded and the children. When they heard the guns of their companions, Lee and his assistants shot into the waggons of wounded and children. McCurdy, one of Lee's assistants, approached a waggon containing sick and wounded, raised his rifle and said, "O Lord, my God, receive their spirits, it is for thy Kingdom that I do this." Thereupon he shot a man whose head was lying on another's breast and killed both with one ball. Indians and Mormons joined Lee and killed the rest of the sick and wounded, after they had finished with those capable of resistance. All except seventeen small children, who were too young to be able to describe the massacre, were killed.

After the sick, the wounded, and the children had been killed, the Mormons took breakfast, and, having finished their meal, returned to bury the dead. But while the white men had been eating, the Indians had been stripping the bodies of men and women of their clothes and their valuables. The skulls of the emigrants had been battered in, and their scalps removed along with their clothes, so that naked and mutilated bodies lay strewn about the meadows in horrible disorder. Lee and his associates then told the Mormons under their command that they must tell no one, not even their wives, what had happened, and that if they were ever questioned concerning this massacre, they must attribute everything to the Indians. The bodies were then piled in heaps and covered with dirt, which the rain and the wolves soon removed.

A few days before this massacre at Mountain Meadows a messenger had been sent to Brigham Young asking what the policy towards the emigrants should be. The messenger arrived in Cedar City again a few days after the massacre with an order from Brigham Young to allow the emigrants to pass through unmolested. The Mormon leaders of the southern district who had issued the orders for the massacre and carried out their execution, Isaac C. Haight, John M. Higbee, John D. Lee, and William C. Dame, were then worried about the righteousness of their action and its possible consequences. They sent Lee to report the massacre to Brigham Young, and to ask for his advice. Lee acted throughout, he claimed later in his confession, on the orders of Isaac C. Haight, who was his superior in the Church hierarchy, and who had promised him both celestial reward and temporal benefit if the emigrants were properly killed. Lee started on his ten days' journey from Cedar City to Brigham Young's office. He said later that as soon as he could see Brigham Young, he gave him all the details of the massacre, and that, "when he heard my story he wept like a child, walked the floor, and wrung his hands in bitter anguish. . . ." [7] When Lee had finished his story, he wrote later, Brigham Young said:

"This is the most unfortunate affair that ever befell the Church. I am afraid of treachery among the brethren that were there. If any one tells this thing so that it will become public, it will work us great injury. I want you to understand now, that you are *never* to tell this again, not even to Heber C. Kimball. *It must* be kept a secret among ourselves. When you get home, I want you to sit down and write a long letter, and give me an account of the affair, charging it to the Indians. You sign the letter as Farmer to the Indians, and direct it to me as Indian Agent. I can then make use of such a letter to keep off all damaging and troublesome enquiries." [8]

Brigham Young then added: "If only men had been killed, I would not have cared so much; but the killing of the women and children is the sin of it. I suppose the men were a hard set, but it is hard to kill women and children for the sins of the men. This whole thing stands before me like a horrid vision." The next morning when Lee called on Brigham Young again, the Prophet and President said:

"I have made that matter a subject of prayer. I went right to God with it, and asked Him to take the horrid vision from my sight, if it was a righteous thing that my people had done in killing those people at the Mountain Meadows. God answered me, and at once the vision was removed. I have evidence from God that He has overruled it all for good, and the action was a righteous one and well intended. The brethren acted from pure motives. The only trouble is they acted a little prematurely; they were a little ahead of time. I sustain you and all the brethren for what they did. All that I fear is treachery on the part of some one who took a part with you, but we will look to that."

For many years after the Mountain Meadows Massacre Brigham Young and John D. Lee were on terms of friendship. In his testimony before the Third District Court of Utah James

[7] *The Lee Trial! An Exposé of the Mountain Meadows Massacre,* by the Salt Lake *Daily Tribune* Reporter, p. 9.
[8] Lee's *Mormonism Unveiled,* pp. 252-253.

McGuffie, a faithful Mormon, was asked: "What I want to get at is whether you know, of your own knowledge, that after that massacre John D. Lee continued to be on terms of friendship with the President of the Church?" "Oh, yes," he answered, "and got two more women after that: got two at a lick—an English girl; she died."

Brigham Young sent his report as Superintendent of Indian Affairs for Utah Territory to the Commissioner of Indian Affairs at Washington on January 6, 1858, and in it he summed up the Mountain Meadows Massacre with this explanatory statement:

"On or about the middle of last September a company of emigrants traveling the southern route to California, poisoned the meat of an ox that died, and gave it to the Indians to eat, causing the immediate death of four of their tribe, and poisoning several others. This company also poisoned the water where they were encamped. This occurred at Corn Creek, fifteen miles south of Fillmore City. This conduct so enraged the Indians, that they immediately took measures for revenge. . . . Lamentable as this case truly is, it is only the natural consequence of that fatal policy which treats the Indians like the wolves, or other ferocious beasts. I have vainly remonstrated for years with travelers against pursuing so suicidal a policy, and repeatedly advised the Government of its fatal tendency. It is not always upon the heads of the individuals who commit such crimes that such condign punishment is visited, but more frequently the next company that follows in their fatal path become the unsuspecting victims, though peradventure perfectly innocent."

Perhaps this explanation of the Mountain Meadows Massacre would have been accepted as the truth, but, unfortunately for the Mormon position, there existed those seventeen small children, who were believed to be living with the Indians who had massacred their parents. Relatives and friends in Arkansas urged the federal government to search for these children, and in the course of the search it was found that the children were living with Mormons, and not with Indians. Further investigation led to the suspicion that the Mormons were involved in the massacre. Dr. J. Forney, successor to Brigham Young as Superintendent of Indian Affairs, gathered the children together, and he found that they ranged from three to seven years of age. They remembered only their first names, and that their fathers, mothers, brothers, and sisters had been killed. They were returned to relatives in Arkansas in June, 1859.

Several years after the massacre a military detachment was sent to Mountain Meadows to bury the bones of the emigrants. Major Carlton, commander of this expedition, found the bones uncovered by wolves. After his men had buried them, they erected a monument, and on one of the rocks they cut the words, "Here lie the bones of 120 men, women, and children, from Arkansas, murdered on the 10th day of September, 1857." And upon a cross bar, they painted: "Vengeance is mine, saith the Lord, and I will repay it." This monument was destroyed soon after the next visit of Brigham Young to that section of Utah.

Meanwhile, John D. Lee and Brigham Young continued to be friends. Whenever Brigham Young and his large retinue visited Cedar City, Lee entertained them. Then, seventeen years after the massacre, Lee was suddenly cut off from the Church, and no explanation was offered for the action. Soon afterwards, on November 9, 1874, Lee was arrested and taken to Fort Cameron, Beaver County, Utah. When Lee was excommunicated, Brigham Young had informed his wives that they were at liberty to leave him, and eleven of them promptly did so. Judge Cradlebaugh, federal judge for Utah Territory, had held an investigation into the massacre two years after it was committed, but he was not able to get information sufficient to warrant indictments. It was not until a bill was passed authorizing federal officers in Utah to impanel jurors that any indictments could be returned by non-Mormon grand jurors.

John D. Lee was tried for murder in July, 1875. The jury was made up of a majority of Mormons, and finally they failed to agree. In September, 1876, Lee was tried again, and this time the Church, which had supported him at the first trial, withdrew its support. The facts brought out at the first trial had aroused resentment throughout the country, and news and comment on the trial were printed in newspapers everywhere. Many editorial writers suggested that if Lee were acquitted, he should be lynched. The disagreement of the Mormon jury at the first trial also led newspapers to suggest that justice was impossible in Brigham Young's stronghold. Brigham Young and the Church leaders came to the conclusion that it would be wise for the Church to withdraw any influence on the jurors at the second trial, and they offered up Lee as a sacrifice to justice. At his second trial Lee was convicted of murder in the first degree and sentenced to be shot at the scene of the massacre.

While he was in prison awaiting execution, John D. Lee wrote his confessions, which he entrusted to his lawyer, W. W. Bishop, who published them some years after Lee's death under the title, *Mormonism Unveiled.* "I once thought," wrote Lee, "that I never could be induced to occupy the position that I now do, to expose the wickedness and corruption of the man whom I once looked upon as my spiritual guide, as I then considered Brigham Young to be. Nothing could have compelled me to this course save an honest sense of the duty I owe myself, my God, the people at large, and my brethren and sisters who are treading the downward path that will lead them to irretrievable ruin, unless they retrace their steps and throw off the yoke of the tyrant, who has long usurped the right of rule that justly belongs to the son of Joseph, the Prophet." This was a great change from Lee's former attitude, which was described by one who knew him: "Lee is a good, kind-hearted fellow, who would share his last biscuit with a fellow-traveler on the plains, but at the next instant, if Brigham Young said so, he would cut that fellow-traveler's throat." John D. Lee had decided to betray Brigham Young, because Brigham Young had betrayed John D. Lee by delivering him as a sacrifice to save the name of the Church. This sudden thrust into the dungeons to await the lions of the law opened Lee's eyes to past incidents. He now saw without the eye of faith, but with the eye of reason, and the change in the point of view made him realize the significance of many events which he had previously accepted with unquestioning confidence.

In September, 1857, according to Lee's own story, he was sent for by the Mormon military commander of southern Utah, Isaac C. Haight. The two men met at Haight's house and went from there to the Old Iron Works near Cedar City, where they spent the night under the stars talking.

"After we got to the Iron Works," wrote Lee, "Haight told me all about the train of emigrants. He said (and I then believed every word that he spoke, for I believed it was an impossible thing for one so high in the Priesthood as he was, to be guilty of falsehood) that the emigrants were a rough and abusive set of men. That they had, while traveling through Utah, been very abusive to all the Mormons they met. That they had insulted, outraged, and ravished many of the Mormon women. That the abuses heaped upon the people by the emigrants during their trip from Provo to Cedar City, had been constant and shameful; that they had burned fences and destroyed growing crops; that at many points on the road they had poisoned the water, so that all people and stock that drank of the water became sick, and many had died from the effects of poison. These vile Gentiles publicly proclaimed that they had the very pistol with which the Prophet Joseph was murdered, and had threatened to kill Brigham Young and all of the Apostles. That when in Cedar City they said they would have friends in Utah who would hang Brigham Young by the neck until he was dead, before snow fell again in the Territory! They also said that Johnston was coming, with his army, from the East, and they were going to return from California with soldiers, as soon as possible, and would then desolate the land, and kill every damned Mormon man, woman and child that they could find in Utah."

Haight told Lee that it had been decided to arm the Indians, to give them food and ammunition, and to set them upon the party of wicked emigrants. He did not say who had decided this, but he pointed out that Brigham Young had declared martial law in the Territory because of the advancing expedition of United States troops, and that therefore these emigrants had no right to travel through the Territory without a pass from Brigham Young. Haight then said that it was Lee's job to round up the Indians, and to tell them that the Mormons were at war with the "Mericats," which was the Indian nickname for Americans. "I asked him," wrote Lee, "if it would not have been better to first send to Brigham Young for instructions, and find out what he thought about the matter." "No," answered Haight, "that is unnecessary, we are acting by orders."

After he had received these instructions from Haight, Lee joined the Indians, and he found that they had already attacked the emigrants. He camped with them, and he wrote of his experience the first night: "I spent one of the most miserable nights there that I ever passed in my life. I spent much of the night in tears and at prayer. I wrestled with God for wisdom to guide me. I asked for some sign, some evidence that would satisfy me that my mission was of Heaven, but I got no satisfaction from God." On the following day Lee and a detachment of Mormons and Indians made the truce with the emigrants, and killed them. The night before the final deception and murder of the emigrants Lee and his Mormon companions knelt in a circle, with elbows touching, and prayed for divine aid and guidance. When they arose, Major Higbee said, "I have the evidence of God's approval of our mission. It is God's will that we carry out our instructions to the letter." "It helps a man a great deal in a fight," Lee wrote in his confession, "to know that God is on his side."

It is probable that the direction of this massacre was the work of Isaac C. Haight, who was the leader of the Church in the district where it took place, and who used John D. Lee to carry it out. The men and women of this southern district of Utah had been aroused to fear and antagonism by the impending arrival of United States troops, whose purpose they did not know, and by the rumors circulated concerning the depredations of the emigrants. The state of mind in the neighborhood of Mountain Meadows is illustrated admirably in a sermon which George A. Smith delivered a few days after the massacre took place, but before news of it had reached Salt Lake City. Smith had just returned from a trip to Cedar City and the Mountain Meadows district. Later it was said that he bore orders from Brigham Young for the massacre, but there was no evidence for this accusation. Smith visited Parowan, Iron County, where he found the militia preparing for active operations. "They had assembled together," he said, "under the impression that their country was about to be invaded by an army from the United States, and that it was necessary to make preparation by examining each other's arms, and to make everything ready by preparing to strike in any direction and march to such places as might be necessary in the defense of their homes. . . . They were willing at any moment to touch fire to their homes, and hide themselves in the mountains, and to defend their country to the very last extremity." Wherever he went, George A. Smith found the same preparations. "They had heard," he said of the people of Penter, "they were going to have an army of 600 dragoons come down from the East on to the town. The Major seemed very sanguine about the matter. I asked him, if this rumor should prove true, if he was not going to wait for instructions. He replied, There was no time to wait for any instructions; and he was going to take his battalion and use them up before they could get down through the kanyons; for, said he, if they are coming here, they are coming for no good." This spirit led George A. Smith to conclude: "There was only one thing that I dreaded, and that was a spirit

in the breasts of some to wish that their enemies might come and
give them a chance to fight and take vengeance for the cruelties
that had been inflicted upon us in the States. . . . But I am perfectly aware that in all the settlements I visited in the south,
Fillmore included, one single sentence is enough to put every man
in motion.   In fact, a word is enough to set in motion every man,
or set a torch to every building, where the safety of this people
is jeopardized." [9]

The emigrants from Arkansas and Missouri had the misfortune
to pass through these settlements at the worst possible moment
for their safety.   It required only the rumor that some of them
were the murderers of Joseph Smith and that all of them were
the enemies of the Mormons and friends of the oncoming United
States forces, to work up into a frenzy of recrimination those
Mormons who were thirsting for revenge and anxious to protect
themselves from dangers which they were anticipating.

Brigham Young was never accused, even by John D. Lee, of
direct responsibility for the massacre at Mountain Meadows.   For
Lee's second trial Brigham Young sent a written deposition of
his testimony and examination by a lawyer, for he claimed that
his health and his age—he was then seventy-five years old—prevented him from traveling to Beaver County, where the trial was
held.   In this examination, which was not admitted for the defense at the first trial, but which was introduced and admitted for
the prosecution at the second, Brigham Young was asked: "Did
John D. Lee report to you at any time after this massacre what
had been done at that massacre, and if so, what did you reply to
him in reference thereto?"   He answered: "Within some two or
three months after the massacre he called at my office and had
much to say with regard to the Indians, their being stirred up to
anger and threatening the settlements of the whites, and then
commenced giving an account of the massacre.   I told him to
stop, as from what I had already heard by rumor, I did not wish
my feelings harrowed up with a recital of detail."   But Brigham
Young's feelings were not easily "harrowed up," and it was
usually his desire to know the details of everything that happened in his demesne.

Brigham Young shares in the responsibility for this massacre
indirectly.   He had frequently talked against Gentiles in the
pulpit, and particularly against California emigrants.   He had

[9] *Journal of Discourses,* vol. 5, pp. 221-225.

also caused his people to believe that a man who killed a Gentile or an apostate Mormon was no more than the instrument of God, and that his responsibility was no greater than the knife which was used to slit the throat or the bullet that was fired at the victim. In the excitement of the time of stress Brigham Young's assistants interpreted his general philosophy literally, and their assistants, the common people, were subject to pressure that kept them obedient to their leaders. Nephi Johnson, who was in the party of Mormons who executed the Mountain Meadows Massacre, testified at Lee's trial:

"What do you mean by your evidence, where you were asked by Mr. Howard a question, and you answered that you would not have gone to the Meadows if you had known what was to be done? Answer: That is, not if I could help it.

"State whether you were under any compulsion. Answer: I didn't consider it was safe for me to object.

"Explain what you mean, that is what I want. Where was the danger—who was the danger to come from if you objected—from Haight or those around him—from Indians, or from the emigrants? Answer: From the military officers.

"Where? Answer: At Cedar City.

"Was Haight one of those military officers? Answer: Yes, sir.

"You thought it would not be safe for you to refuse, had you any reasons to fear danger—had any persons ever been injured for not obeying, or anything of that kind? Answer: I don't want to answer.

"It is necessary to the safety of the man I am defending, and I therefore insist upon an answer. Had any person ever been injured for not obeying, or anything of that kind? Answer: Yes, sir; they had." [10]

When John D. Lee was finally arrested for the Mountain Meadows Massacre, he was found hiding in a chicken pen on his farm at Panguitch, Utah. He was forced out of his hiding-place by the marshal with some difficulty. He was calm, and asked to see the pistol that had been pointed at his head, remarking that it was the queerest-looking pistol he ever did see. His wives, however, were frantic with excitement, and William Stokes, the deputy marshal who arrested Lee, sent for a pitcher of wine to calm the women and refresh the soldiers. They all drank, and one of Lee's

[10] *Mormonism Unveiled,* p. 349.

daughters, as she raised the pitcher, said: "Here's hoping that father will get away from you, and that if he does, you will not catch him again till hell freezes over." "Drink hearty, Miss," answered Stokes. The rumor was circulated that an attempt would be made by some of Lee's army of sixty-four children to rescue him from the law, and he was guarded with extraordinary precautions.

Lee was led to his execution by a strong guard of soldiers and a cortège of newspaper correspondents and lawyers. In the twenty years since the massacre the green valley of Mountain Meadows had changed to an arid plain. The pine boards for Lee's coffin were transported with the execution party, and the carpenters began hammering them into a coffin, while Lee sat a short distance away watching them with intense interest. A photographer took some pictures of the scene. Lee asked to talk to the photographer and said to him: "I want to ask a favor of you; I want you to furnish my three wives each a copy. Send them to Rachel A., Sarah C., and Emma B." Those were the only faithful wives left of the nineteen. The photographer promised to carry out this request, and then Lee posed for the photographs. He addressed the group of people about him, assuring them that he was innocent in intent, and that he had only obeyed the orders of his superiors and was the victim at a sacrifice. He said that he still believed in the divinity of Joseph Smith, but that he no longer believed in the virtue of Brigham Young. Then his eyes were blindfolded, and he sat on his own coffin. A Methodist minister delivered a fervent prayer, to which Lee listened attentively. "I ask one favor of the guards," he said, as soon as the prayer was finished, "spare my limbs and center my heart." He then straightened up, still sitting on his coffin, and said: "Let them shoot the balls through my heart. Don't let them mangle my body." The marshal assured him that the aim would be accurate. The command was given, "Ready, aim, fire." Five soldiers fired, and Lee fell back on the top of his own coffin without a moan, as the echo of the shots reverberated through the surrounding hills.

Chapter XII

A COOPERATIVE ZION

I

AFTER the Mormons had spent the first ten critical years of their existence in Utah without conquest by the elements or extirpation by their opponents, the next twenty years of Brigham Young's life and the life of the Church were spent in keeping the community a community. Brigham Young reiterated in the pulpit the promise which veiled a threat, that only by clinging together in a righteous community could the people hope to be saved when the Son of Man should reappear and the Saints inherit the earth. If they believed in their religion at all, Mormons believed that they were the last chosen people, and that this time God meant to adhere to His choice. They would inherit the earth and turn it into a golden, glorious kingdom of God. Believing this, it was impossible for Mormons to leave for California and Oregon without first losing all their faith.

In his later years one of Brigham Young's favorite verses of the Bible was from the revelation received by John on the Isle of Patmos: "Come out of her, O my people, be not partakers of her sins, lest ye receive her plagues, for her sins have reached unto heaven." He continually urged his people to forsake Babylon and her ways, and especially not to import either her manners or her merchandise. And as he grew older his insistence upon home industry and thrift grew greater, until it assumed the proportions of a mania. In his opinion the most wicked of all evils was idleness and the most stultifying of all indulgences was leisure. He favored pleasure in the form of recreation, because he realized that it was necessary in order that men's minds might be capable of good work, but the cornerstone of Mormonism was work, and the diversions were merely ornaments. With such a temperament it was inevitable that he should succeed in the management of a community knit together by a compelling religious

418

fervor. There was no place in his economy for the artistic temperament, which thrives on leisure and is actuated by whim, but the character of his communicants and the nature of their problems had very little need for the artistic temperament.

The impression that one gathers from reading Brigham Young's extempore sermons is that he was preoccupied with the financial, economic, civic, and commercial needs of his flock to a much greater extent than he was with their spiritual welfare. He always placed the latter far above temporal needs and desires, but the spiritual details, such as dogmas, doctrine, and revelations he left to the memory of Joseph Smith, the Seer and Prophet, and to less busy elders whose minds were inclined that way. His sermons, it is true, are filled with gospel exhortations and with scriptural illustrations, but these he used mainly to serve his arguments for confidence in his administration and as propaganda for converts, of which the undeveloped territory was always in great need. The subjects of most of the sermons are practical problems which even Saints cannot ignore. He eloquently rebuked the Saints for not paying their tithes to the Church; he told them how to protect themselves and their farms from the Indians; he urged them not to be wasteful of the things God had given them, for, "If a man is worth millions of bushels of wheat and corn, he is not wealthy enough to suffer his servant girl to sweep a single kernel of it into the fire, let it be eaten by something, and pass again into the earth, and thus fulfil the purpose for which it grew."

Brigham Young's problem was to maintain enough public spirit in a communistic order of society to make every man willing to help another. The Mormon community was not communistic in the modern sense of the term, for every man was allowed to get and to keep as much as he could, but at the same time it was necessary to provide for the needs of the whole, and it was Brigham Young's job to make his Saints see the value of contributing to the community. That was the most difficult job in the community.

It was frequently assumed during his lifetime that Brigham Young profited tremendously himself by the wealth of the Church which he did so much to increase, and the implication was that he was therefore a fraud. It is true that when he died he left to his seventeen surviving wives and forty-four surviving children a fortune of about $2,000,000. During the last years of his life he lived in comfort, without extravagance, and in ease, without luxury. His policies were profitable to him personally, but they were proportionately profitable to every man in the community, and since he formulated and carried out those policies, he was, according to the capitalistic standards by which he was judged, entitled to an even greater personal reward than he accumulated. He gathered his own wealth by personally dealing in cattle and agriculture. He gave himself concessions in lumber from the cañons, and he worked those concessions. He drew no salary from the wealth of the community, like an ordinary king, and it must always be remembered that in the eyes of his followers he was not only a king, but a prophet and a priest as well. His genius for economic organization was worth to his community in dollars and cents whatever he wished to ask for it, but he preferred to exercise it for himself as well as for the Church, and he earned his own living while aiding his people to earn theirs.

Brigham Young not only made his people prosperous, but he forced them to conserve their prosperity. He insisted that in a community which was entirely dependent upon its own resources for food and sustenance waste was intolerable; but even in the kingdom of heaven waste would have been intolerable to Brigham Young, for he was the kind of man who, when he saw a pin, invariably picked it up. This habit of mind occasionally degenerated into stinginess, as when, in the pulpit, he complained bitterly that the carpenters he employed robbed him by taking home with them in the pockets of their working clothes a few of his nails.

When Brigham Young organized charity, he preferred to do so by means of work. He explained his aim once in a sermon:

"Some have wished me to explain why we built an adobe wall around this city. Are there any Saints who stumble at such things? Oh, slow of heart to understand and believe. I build walls, dig ditches, make bridges, and do a great amount and variety of labor that is of little consequence only to provide ways and means for sustaining and preserving the destitute. I annually expend hundreds and thousands of dollars almost solely to furnish employment to those in want of labor. Why? I have potatoes, flour, beef, and other articles of food, which I wish my brethren to have; and it is better for them to labor for those articles, so far as they are able and have opportunity, than to have them given to them. They work, and I deal out provisions, often when the work does not profit me.

"I say to all grunters, grumblers, whiners, hypocrites, and syco-phants, who snivel, crouch, and crawl around the most contemptible of all creatures for a slight favor, Should it enter my mind to dig down the Twin Peaks, and I set men to work to do so, it is none of your business, neither is it the business of all earth and hell, provided I pay the laborers their wages. I am not to be called in question as to what I do with my funds, whether I build high walls or low walls, garden walls or city walls; and if I please, it is my right to pull down my walls to-morrow. If any one wishes to apostatize upon such grounds, the quicker he does so the better; and if he wishes to leave the Territory, but is too poor to do so, I will assist him to go. We are much better off without such characters." [1]

Brigham Young did not ask for this authority, however, with-out the knowledge that his people knew he deserved it. "You know my life;" he once told them, "there is not a person in this Church and kingdom but what must acknowledge that gold and silver, houses and lands, &c., do multiply in my hands. There is not an individual but what must acknowledge that I am as good a financier as they ever knew, in all things that I put my hands to." But he took very little credit for all this to himself. "What do you suppose," he once asked the congregation, "I think when I hear people say, 'Oh, see what the Mormons have done in the mountains. It is Brigham Young. What a head he has got! What power he has got! How well he controls the people!' The people are ignorant of our true character. It is the Lord that has done this. It is not any one man or set of men; only as we are led and guided by the spirit of truth. It is the oneness, wisdom, power, knowledge, and providences of God; and all that we can say is, we are his servants and handmaids, and let us serve him with an undivided heart." But it must be admitted that Brigham Young gave the Lord a very powerful helping hand.

It was wise of Brigham Young to disclaim modestly the credit for the Mormon achievement, not only because the disclaimer took away some of the responsibility for mishaps, but also because it enabled him to insist, as he always did, that things spiritual and things temporal were one and indissoluble; thus he was able to control the most minute temporal affairs of his people by insist-ing that they were interwoven with the spiritual dominion of which he was placed in charge. The Church was organized com-

[1] *Journal of Discourses,* vol. 8, p. 11.

pactly under the control of the President. The Territory was divided into stakes of Zion, over which there was a president, appointed by Brigham Young, and approved by the people over whom he was to exercise supervision. This stake usually corresponded to a county, except where the county was too populous, when several stakes were formed. Each stake was divided into wards, and over each ward there was a bishop, who was also selected by Brigham Young. In that way Brigham Young had control of every district of his domain, because he had his own major-domo in each district. This bishop was in charge of all the families of his ward, and through him Brigham Young was able to know the exact social, political, economic, and spiritual condition of every member of every Mormon family, if he so desired. The extent of this control is admirably illustrated by the report of a ward teacher to his ward bishop:

"Brother Brown and I visited Block Number Seven, spending two evenings in making the round. We found Sister Hagreen first-rate. She has had a bad cold, but is gradually improving. Brother and Sister Johnson we found in good health. Brother Sorenson's boy has a broken leg and he has been laid off work for two weeks. Brother Sorenson had a letter from his son Henry, who is on a mission in Australia, asking for $10 to assist in building a meeting house. I think we should furnish the money. Sister Knowles is getting very feeble. She is nearly ninety years old, and needs a sack of potatoes and flour. A lady living in the middle of the block—recently moved in—has a baby, a little boy. He should be named. Everything on our block is in good shape and the Saints in fine spirit, though inclined to shirk meetings." [2]

Sir Richard Burton wrote that the Mormon polity was based upon "the fact that liberty is to mankind in mass, a burden far heavier than slavery." The Mormons had each an oral vote, that is, they were asked at the semi-annual conferences to sustain their leaders by raising their hands, and to oppose them just as publicly. "His poor single vote," wrote Burton, "from which even the sting of the ballot has been withdrawn, gratifies the dignity of the man, and satisfies him with the autocracy which directs him in the way he should go. He has thus all the harmless pleasure of voting, without the danger of injuring himself by his vote."

[2] *World's Work*, vol. 5, p. 2893, Dec. 1902.

This Sir Richard Burton found superior to the democratic method of freeing "mankind from king and kaiser," and subjecting them "to snobs and mobs." "I know no form of rule superior to that of Great Salt Lake City," concluded Burton; but, perhaps, he would have found Brigham Young's domination oppressive at times if he had been born a Mormon and forced thereby to live under its minute dictates.

Such a system of government placed enormous responsibility upon Brigham Young, who was its first autocrat. His position was complicated still further, for besides being a Moses to his people, he was also a self-appointed Solomon, and he sat in judgment on the cases of their petty quarrels, which he insisted they should bring before the Church tribunals rather than the state courts. The plaintiff and the defendant appeared with their witnesses before the president of their stake and his twelve councilors. Prayer was offered up, and God's aid was asked in favor of justice. The case was stated by the parties to it, the witnesses were heard, and the councilors decided. Then prayer was offered up again, the adversaries shook hands, and there were no costs.

Brigham Young hated lawyers, and tried to do everything possible to make their trade negligible in Utah. He made his people afraid of lawyers by insisting upon the dishonesty and trouble fomenting characteristics of men of that profession. The dignity of the law appeared to him an amusing sham:

"Some men will go into court and spend five hundred dollars and feel as nicely about it as possible, even when their case has not been adjudicated as justly as a sensible 'Mormon' boy, ten years old, would do it. And yet, when they know this fact full well, they will spend their time, day after day, and their means with seeming contentment, saying to themselves, 'Oh, if we can only go into the court, and address the court, and say, may it please the court, may it please your honor, may it please you, gentlemen of the jury, O, how joyous we shall be—we shall feel as though we were men of some importance, if we can only get up and strut and splutter before a court.' Even when merely a judge is sitting there, like a bean on the end of a pipe stem, who would be flipped off should a grain of good sense happen to strike him, how big he feels while sitting there for days to adjudicate a case that should not require five minutes." [3]

[3] *Journal of Discourses,* vol. 3, p. 326.

For those who loved the processes of justice in themselves rather than the ends which they were designed to serve, Brigham Young had the greatest contempt. While court was being held in February, 1856, Brigham Young noticed a large number of Mormons lounging about the court house, waiting for they knew not what. He sent one of his clerks to take all their names, and he sent them on missions, some to grow cotton in Los Vegas, others to make settlements in unoccupied territory, and others to convert the heathen in the Sandwich Islands.

Brigham Young's conception of his own divine authority is illustrated by a comparison he made between the latter days and those of Moses: "The Ark, containing the covenant—or the Ark of the Covenant in the days of Moses, containing the sacred records, was moved from place to place in a cart. And so sacred was that Ark, if a man stretched forth his hand to steady it, when the cart jostled, he was smitten, and died. And would to God that all who attempt to do the same in this day, figuratively speaking, might share the same fate. And they will share it sooner or later, if they do not keep their hands and tongues, too, in their proper places, and stop dictating the order of the Gods of the Eternal Worlds."

Brigham Young maintained that nothing should be done without his advice and permission. When a man decided to enter a certain business, he was expected to consult Brigham Young before he took action. When a ball was planned, his permission was necessary, and before the invitations were issued the list of guests was submitted for his approval. Before the married men courted additional wives, they were supposed to consult him on their choice, and the young men were taught that before they made love to specific young women, it was their duty to get the permission of Brother Brigham. The symbol of the Church was a lugubrious and ominous All-Seeing Eye, with the motto beneath, "Holiness to the Lord." That eye was, for all practical purposes, the eye of Brigham Young; he was familiarly known to some of the Mormons as "the Old Boss." Heber Kimball once said in a sermon, "If brother Brigham tells me to do a thing, it is the same as though the Lord told me to do it."

Brigham Young's word with Heber Kimball was the final word on all subjects, and he was not by any means the meekest of the Mormons. Thomas Bullock, Leo Hawkins, and a few others were talking one day with Heber Kimball in the church offices about the Resurrection. One of the brethren wanted to know whether, when the body came forth from the grave, any hole would be left in the ground. "No," said Heber Kimball, "not at all, the atoms will be reunited, and they won't leave no hole." He began to elaborate on this theory, when Brigham Young walked in. The question was referred to him, and he said: "Why, yes, certainly it will. Christ is the pattern, you know; and he had to have the stone rolled away from the sepulcher, and that left the hole visible, for did not the soldiers see it?" "Brother Brigham," said Heber Kimball, "that is just my opinion." When science or art conflicted with the views of Brigham Young, it was the earnest opinion of the leaders of the Church that the theories of science or art must be altered or abandoned.

Brigham Young felt no sense of responsibility to anybody but God. "No man need judge me," he once told the people. "You know nothing about it, whether I am sent or not; furthermore, it is none of your business, only to listen with open ears to what is taught you, and serve God with an undivided heart." And he justified this unbounded confidence in himself and in God by references to the past achievements of the partnership. It was also Brigham Young's contention that the Saints' money was not their own, but that, in the last analysis, it belonged to God, for had not God by his bounteous blessings contributed the means for its accumulation? Therefore, when God needed money, through the agency of the Church of Jesus Christ of Latter-day Saints, it was the duty of the faithful to give back to Him what He had given to them. In this way Brigham Young made taxes a tenet of the faith. Not only was the Lord entitled to a tenth of the possessions of the Saints, but He was also entitled to their personal services on public works, when His representative, Brigham Young, issued the order.

But in spite of all his sermons it was sometimes difficult for Brigham Young to collect the Lord's money. The Saints regarded their tithing obligations much as the average man regards his income tax, as something to submit to only under the strictest compulsion. As there was no law compelling them to give one-tenth of their income to the Church, but merely a church doctrine, it was sometimes difficult to collect in full. Brigham Young, by the threat of damnation, was able to collect a large part of the tithes.

There was practically no one in Utah who realized fully what

Brigham Young was trying to do. For his own people he had
to couch all his ideas in a religious mold, which he was able to
do with sincerity, because he believed in God, and he believed in
Joseph Smith. It was impossible, however, to convert the Gentiles, and especially the federal officials, to the idea of a benevolent
despotism, because for them it was not benevolent, and they therefore saw no reason why it should be despotic. By ruthless and
vigorous measures of control Brigham Young was successful in
operating his coöperative community. For a time it looked as if
he would be defeated, but he countered every attack with one
more powerful of his own. When isolation was broken and
business expanded, changing the community from purely agricultural to industrial as well, more powerful forces, those of
economics, threatened Brigham Young's control.

II

Isaiah had once said, "A great highway shall be cast up," and,
upon another occasion, "They shall come with speed swiftly."
When the Union Pacific Railway was nearing completion, the
Mormons recalled these sayings and looked with satisfaction on
their approaching fulfilment. The Mormons, in spite of their
desire for isolation, had realized that sooner or later there would
be a railroad across the continent, and they also had realized
the great commercial advantage such an enterprise would be to
them. As early as 1852 they had sent a petition to Congress
urging the construction of a railroad to the shores of the Pacific,
but Congress was busy with slavery, and later with the Civil
War. As soon as the gold rush caused him to realize that the
Mormons would not be the only inhabitants of the western quarter of the United States, Brigham Young planned to take financial
advantage of the presence of their neighbors. When he found
that compact, self-sufficient isolation was impossible, Brigham
Young decided upon a course of economic conquest, for he knew
well that the way to political salvation in the United States was
through economic strength, and he therefore concentrated upon
making Utah a prosperous part of the country in which the
Mormons were forced by fate to live. Had he maintained a
fanatic desire for isolation in the face of natural developments,
the Mormons, like the Indians, would have been swept into disintegration and death. But Brigham Young was a Yankee him-

self, and he began to fight the oncoming horde with their own weapons.

Statesmen in Washington who could think of no other way of solving the annoying problem of polygamy relied on the Pacific railroad, by its penetration of the Mormon isolation and the permeation of the community with Gentiles, to solve the problem for them. The railroad, however, had run enough trains to go around the world several times before polygamy was finally abolished. Brigham Young had once remarked concerning these Congressional hopes that he would not give much for a religion that could not stand the advent of a railroad.

Brigham Young set about getting contracts for the construction of the part of the railroad in and near Utah, and he made a great profit from the construction of the few hundred miles of railroad which were built by laborers under his control. On January 10, 1870, a grand celebration was held in Utah to commemorate the completion of the railway as far as that Territory. The last spike was hammered in with due ceremony, and the railroad was dedicated to God. A song immortalized the construction of the Utah portion of the Union Pacific in these words:

"At the head of great Echo, the railway's begun,
The Mormons are cutting and grading like fun;
They say they'll stick to it until it's complete—
When friends and relations they're hoping to meet.

"Hurrah, hurrah, the railroad's begun,
Three cheers for the contractor; his name's Brigham Young.
Hurrah, hurrah, we're honest and true,
And if we stick to it, it's bound to go through.

"Now there's Mr. Reed, he's a gentleman too—
He knows very well what the Mormons can do.
He knows they will earn every cent of their pay,
And are just the right boys to construct a railway."

Soon after the railroad was completed, parties of senators began to pour into Salt Lake City to see what Mormonism was like. Lady lecturers followed the senators, and they spent a week in Utah gathering information for anti-polygamous lectures, which they delivered with success in their home towns. Editors, clergymen, and English writers followed, and then came bank presidents and railroad officials, who investigated the resources of the Territory and found them to be great. For many years Salt Lake City became a Palace of the Freaks, and many visitors on their way to the climate of California from that of the East stopped over to look at the strange people. And the strangest of all was Brigham Young, the number of whose wives and the extent of whose possessions were so grossly exaggerated. People boasted that they had seen him in his tall black "stove-pipe" hat, and his quaint black cape. A legend of his personality gradually grew up from passing glimpses of his physical person, and he became a national figure of monstrous proportions, which still exists in the imaginations of most people to whom his name is mentioned. When Barnum visited Salt Lake City soon after the completion of the railroad, Brigham Young asked him how much he would give to exhibit him in New York and the eastern cities. "Well, Mr. President," Barnum said, "I'll give you half the receipts, which I will guarantee shall be $200,000 per year, for I consider you the best show in America." "Why didn't you secure me years ago when I was of no consequence?" asked Brigham Young. "Because you would not have 'drawn' at that time," Barnum answered.

The telegraph had already been constructed in Utah, and Brigham Young organized the Deseret Telegraph Company, with himself as president. He also organized and constructed the Utah Railroad for intrastate communication. He was not always successful, however, in his commercial enterprises. The first attempt he made to set up a beet sugar factory is said to have cost the Church $60,000, and the Cottonwood Canal was an unsuccessful and costly attempt to make water run uphill.

This change in the economic aspect of the community life made Brigham Young cling more desperately than ever to his economic theory. He was still insistent upon the principle of home manufacture in preference to importation, and he urged its practice even when a rule of living laid down by the Church was thereby violated. The Saints were not supposed to chew or to smoke tobacco, but they did so. "We, the Latter-day Saints," Brigham Young once said in a sermon, "care but little about tobacco; but as 'Mormons,' we use a great deal." He then estimated that $60,000 went out of the Territory annually to supply the people with tobacco. "Tobacco can be raised here as well as it can be raised in any other place," he said. "It wants attention and care.

If we use it, let us raise it here. I recommend for some man to go to raising tobacco." Although he used tobacco himself both for chewing and smoking in violation of the church rule, Brigham Young always maintained that its use in any form was a loathsome habit. "A doctor told an old lady in New York," he once said, "when she insisted upon his telling her whether snuff would injure her brain, 'It will not hurt the brain: there is no fear of snuff's hurting the brain of any one, for no person that has brains will take snuff.'"

It was anticipated that the railroad would bring to Utah a flood of Gentile merchants who would take the Saints' money from the Church and the community to the East. In order to prevent this, Brigham Young organized a boycott of Gentile merchants, and he kept insisting in his sermons that his Saints should deal only with each other. When the Gentile merchants found the Mormon boycott was costing them too much, they organized and offered to sell out to Brigham Young and the Mormon merchants, and to leave Utah. As much as he wanted them to go, Brigham Young was too shrewd to accept this offer. Had he accepted, another excuse would have been offered for interference by the federal government, for an exodus in a body of all the Gentile merchants would have been proof to the rest of the country that no non-Mormon could live and do business in Utah. Brigham Young answered the Gentiles that any merchant, Jew, Mohammedan, or Christian, who was not a rogue, was welcome to do business in Utah. He also added that he had not asked the merchants to come, and he had no reason to ask them to leave. But he used all his efforts to make their business unprofitable while they remained. The larger merchants could withstand the force of his propaganda, for there were always many Mormons who, in spite of the advice and the anger of their leader, considered that they should be allowed to buy where, when, and what they pleased. In order to distinguish his shop from that of a Gentile, every Mormon merchant had a sign over his door with the symbol of the All-Seeing Eye and beneath it the motto, "Holiness to the Lord."

After the Civil War, however, Brigham Young began to lose some of his control of the Mormon merchants. The first dissenters were the Walker brothers, four enterprising Englishmen, who had settled in Utah and were regular members of the Mormon Church. They had made money by dealing with the United

States soldiers stationed at Camp Douglas during the Civil War, and after the war their enterprises increased steadily in scope and in value. When they were called upon by the Church authorities for their tithes of ten per cent. of their annual income, one of the brothers replied by sending his check for $500 to the bishop of his ward with instructions that it be used for charity. When this check was brought to Brigham Young, he refused to accept it in lieu of the tithe, and Walker replied by tearing it up. That was the signal for war between Brigham Young and the Walker brothers. Brigham Young did his utmost to keep his brethren from buying at their stores, but he was not altogether successful, for the Walkers were the largest and most enterprising merchants in the Territory, and Mormons continued to trade with them in secret, for they carried the best goods and the most varied assortments. However, their sales were said to have decreased from $60,000 a month to $5,000 a month during Brigham Young's campaign against them. After the Walker brothers were excommunicated, they gave $1,000 to the Perpetual Immigration Fund to help bring some of their poor fellow countrymen to Utah. Brigham Young announced in the pulpit that they would be blest for their generosity, but that Mormons must not trade with them.

W. S. Godbe, another prosperous merchant of Utah, was also an elder in the Mormon Church. He, with E. L. T. Harrison, published a literary magazine in Salt Lake City, known as *The Utah Magazine*. The demand for literature, however, proved slight, and the magazine was soon discontinued. Godbe, with Harrison, who was his editor, took a trip to New York as recreation after their unsuccessful attempt to make literature in Utah. Both of them were beginning to find the literary crudities of the Book of Mormon too much for their credulity and their faith. During the long days and nights in the stage-coaches and the railroad cars they spoke to each other frankly of their doubts, and they began to admit to themselves that they were on the way to apostasy. But they had made Utah their home for many years, all their friends and associations were there, Godbe's large and profitable business was there, and they did not wish to abandon all these ties and move to another part of the country. In their New York hotel they decided one evening to pray for guidance. While they knelt in prayer, they heard a voice which spoke words of consolation. What those words were they never said, but during the next three weeks, while Godbe went about the streets purchasing goods for his store in Salt Lake City, Harrison sat in the hotel room writing out a series of questions on religion and philosophy. In the evenings both men remained in their room to receive the "bands of spirits" who visited them nightly. Mr. Harrison asked the spirits his questions, one by one, and the two men carefully wrote down the answers. These sessions lasted for two hours every evening, and at the end of three weeks Godbe and Harrison had accumulated considerable spiritual information. Mr. Harrison later told some friends in Salt Lake City that he had received a communication from Humboldt's spirit that, when he revealed it, would some day upset the Darwinian theory, but Mr. Darwin's spirit did not seem to think it worth while to reply. The spirits also told the two men much about Mormonism and its origins in the spirit power of Joseph Smith, and they indicated to Godbe and Harrison how much was true and how much was false in Smith's doctrines.

When Godbe and Harrison returned to Salt Lake City, they formed a little group of men who were discontented with the rule of Brigham Young. They began to publish another magazine, in which they exposed the ignorance and superstition of the age, and, by implication, that of Brigham Young. Harrison, the editor of the magazine, was promptly ordered to go on a mission to England, and some of his associates were listed for missions elsewhere, but all refused to obey Brigham Young's commands.

One of the things which the spirits of New York told Harrison and Godbe was that the mineral wealth of Utah should be developed. Brigham Young had for many years refused to allow his Mormons to engage in mining, in spite of the wealth of silver and gold which was being unearthed in nearby Nevada and California, and in spite of indications that there was mineral wealth in Utah. The mining propaganda of the Godbeites, as they soon were called, was in direct opposition to the anti-mining ideas of Brigham Young. All the followers of Godbe and Harrison were excommunicated and delivered over to the buffetings of Satan. In the course of the hearing on their excommunication the Godbeites asked a significant question. "We inquired," wrote Harrison, "whether it was not possible for us to honestly differ from the presiding priesthood, and were answered that such a thing was impossible. 'We might as well ask whether we could honestly differ from the Almighty.' Against this excess of authority we solemnly protested." After their excommunication the Godbeites published, besides their magazine, a dissenting newspaper, the *Salt Lake Tribune,* in which they advocated their own brand of spiritualistic salvation.

The Godbeite schism was nothing more than the inevitable struggle between Brigham Young's ideas and individualistic big business. Brigham Young wished to keep his territory as free from Gentiles as possible, and the mining schemes of the Godbeites, which they advocated even more strenuously than they did their religious ideas, would have brought to Utah hordes of unruly men from the rest of the country. In the struggle Godbe's mercantile business was ruined, but he organized in London the Chicago Silver Mining Company, which proved one of the most successful mining enterprises in Utah.

Brigham Young opposed the introduction of mining into Utah, not because his economics were reactionary, but because he was far-sighted from the point of view of his own coöperative community. He believed firmly in hard work and thrift, which had thus far proved so eminently successful in Utah. But the whole aim of a miner was to strike luck and make money fast. It was therefore natural that Brigham Young should struggle with all his powerful influence against the development of parts of his Territory into a mess of small huts and temporary structures, whose occupants were interested in digging gold and silver from the ground rather than planting crops in it.

Brigham Young's early trade of carpenter had its effect on the orderly disposition of his mind. It impressed him with the necessity of making two joints meet and fit perfectly, and in the process he was quite willing to saw a little from one or the other, or both; men to him were like boards, except that they frequently proved harder to manage. He was building a mansion, and if he found knots in his lumber which could not be removed or varnished, he threw the boards away and hoped that some one or something would burn them up. He was apt to regard any expression of personality and individuality as an act of disobedience, and it seemed impossible for him to realize that a man might regard himself with justice as more important than the aggregation to which he belonged. To him the all-important thing was the aggregation, and no man had a right to interfere with its prosperity. The spirit of coöperation had become a mania with him, and he used the whole force of his own personality in its interests. He himself was never eccentric; he had worked with Joseph Smith during the lifetime of the Prophet in a subordinate capacity, and, so far as we know, he was content to do so forever, providing his work afforded opportunities for the capacities which he knew he possessed. He never betrayed cravings for personal glory, but his vanity was likely to be more than satisfied by the realization that he was the state and the church too; he could afford to merge his own personality in his organization, for his organization was his personality to a greater extent than any organization was ever the expression of one man in the history of the United States.

A few years before the Godbeite rebellion Brigham Young was confronted with another schism, which was of a more religious nature. Joseph Morris was a Welsh emigrant Mormon who lived in an obscure settlement in Weber County. In November, 1860, he was suddenly inspired by God to reform the Mormon Church. He walked forty miles from his home to Salt Lake City to offer Brigham Young two letters which he said he had received from God. The purport of these letters was that Brigham Young must reform if he wished to be saved. In spite of the distance Morris had come, and in spite of the awful contents of the divine letters, Brigham Young is said to have answered them "with a brief and filthy response." Morris's neighbors, however, believed in him, and when he returned home, he formed them into a new branch of the Mormon Church. His main difference with Brigham Young's church was one of opinion concerning the exact time of Christ's coming. Joseph Morris maintained that Christ would be with them any day, and that preparations must be made speedily to receive him in righteousness. As early as 1859 Morris had written Brigham Young to say that he did not believe that Young was a prophet. In the letter to Brigham Young in which he announced his own divinity he wrote: "And I saw an angel come down from heaven, having the key of the bottomless pit, and a great chain in his hand. And he laid hold on the dragon, that old serpent, which is the Devil, and Satan, and bound him a thousand years. Who is that angel? It is your humble servant." Morris also pretended to be a latter-day Moses. The Mormons claimed that Morris had been excommunicated from the Church twice for immorality, and that at the very time when he was pretending to be a prophet, he was living in adultery, or as Wilford Woodruff expressed it: "I told Morris that he was not a Prophet of God, neither the 7th Angel; that when the 7th Angel came to earth he would not spend the first year of his mission with a woman whose husband was crazy, and commit adultery with her."

Joseph Morris soon had five hundred followers. He received more numerous and more detailed revelations than Joseph Smith had received. Three English clerks and three Danish clerks were employed daily in writing his heavenly communications. The only extant revelation of Joseph Morris's is even more crude than any received by Joseph Smith. It began: "Behold, I am He that shuts, and no one opens, and that opens and no one shuts, even Jesus Christ; and I am about to speak unto you again, concerning my servant John Parsons, according to your request." [4] In his own neighborhood Morris wore a royal robe and a crown, and carried a regal scepter. The Mormons have gone to some pains to show that Joseph Morris was mentally deranged as a result of severe burns he received before his arrival in Utah and of a severe illness he contracted en route from Wales. But this was taking dangerous ground, for the only form his alleged insanity ever took was a fertility in the reception of divine revelations, and their own prophet had been rather good at that sort of thing himself. They also wrote of Joseph Morris as if it were incredible that a man should get revelations from God in the latter half of the nineteenth century, and the scorn they heaped upon him is the same variety that was inflicted upon Joseph Smith by the Gentiles during the first half of the century.

Brigham Young sent John Taylor and Wilford Woodruff to investigate Morris's colony, and all its members were summarily excommunicated. Brigham Young had learned nothing practical from the psychology of the Mormon persecutions, and the result of this wholesale excommunication was to increase the numbers of the colony by many previously faithful members of Brigham Young's community.

Since, according to Joseph Morris, Christ would be along any day, it was not necessary for the true believers to have much property in the future, and he urged with success that they consecrate all their possessions to the new church, to be used by the individuals who owned them only as they needed them. But Christ did not come, and the enthusiasm of Morris's believers

[4] *A Voice from the West to the Scattered People of Weber and All the Seed of Abraham.* San Francisco, 1879.

began to cool. Some of them decided to leave the colony, and to take their former possessions with them. Then the quarrels began. Some of those who left took better cattle from the common compound than they had brought, or refused to share the proportion of expenses they had helped to incur. The dissenters from Morris's judgments on these matters appealed to the courts at Salt Lake City, and writs were issued, but they were not honored by the Morrisites. Then the anti-Morrisites began to seize the wheat of their former brethren as it was sent to the mill, and in this act some of them were taken prisoners and shut up in a calaboose improvised for the occasion at Kington Fort.

Meanwhile, Joseph Morris had assured his faithful followers that the second advent of Christ was nearer than ever, and that there was no longer any need to plow or to sow, because they already had sufficient cattle and grain to sustain them until his arrival. But Morris and his associates had provided themselves with rifles and ammunition for use until Christ should appear to defend them. The Mormon courts sent a posse against them with orders to liberate the prisoners held at Kington Fort. From a mountain overlooking the Morrisite community the posse sent a message that unless the leaders surrendered themselves and their prisoners within thirty minutes, forcible measures would be taken. When he received this message, and his followers asked him what he was going to do about it, Joseph Morris replied that he would "go and inquire of the Lord." He was heard throughout the settlement praying earnestly. When he finally came from his house, the women and children and most of the men were gathered together waiting for him. He carried in his hand a piece of paper which proved to be a revelation, and he began to read it to his privy council. In it God said that their enemies were about to be destroyed, and that not a hair of the head of one Morrisite would be damaged. Everybody prayed, and the revelation was then read to the assembled people. Richard Cook, a Morrisite leader, arose to ask the congregation which they preferred to obey, a temporal demand for surrender, or a divine revelation from God. Just as they were about to vote on this question, a cannon boomed, and two women in the front rows of the Bowery fell dead. The thirty minutes of the demand for the surrender were up, and the posse from Salt Lake City began to triumph over the revelation from God. The next moment the lower jaw of a young girl of thirteen was shot off, and her screams put an end to the meeting. The people were advised to hurry to their homes and defend themselves. They hardly needed the advice, for they had already begun to make for cellars and potato-pits. The firing continued with terrifying regularity.

For three days firing on both sides continued, and then the Morrisites raised a white flag. Colonel Burton, in charge of the Mormon posse, rode towards them on horseback. He was excited, for he did not trust either Morris or his followers. "Where is the man?" he asked one of his party. Joseph Morris was pointed out to him, and Burton rode up to the new prophet and demanded in the name of the Lord that he surrender. "No, never, never!" answered Morris. He expressed a desire to speak to his people, and began to say, "Brethren, I've taught you true principles—" when Colonel Burton drew his revolver and shot him through the neck and shoulder, remarking, "There's your prophet." Firing again, he asked the frightened people, "What do you think of your prophet now?" He then shot Joseph Banks, Morris's leading associate, and killed a Mrs. Bowman, who had just shrieked at him, "Blood-thirsty wretch!" He is also credited with the death of another woman. The rest of the Morrisites were then marched to Salt Lake City, where some of the men were tried and convicted of murder, but all were pardoned by Governor S. S. Harding.[5] A crop of Messiahs arose from among Morris's followers after the death of their prophet. Among these was Goodmund Goodmundson, who offered a few revelations in Sacramento, California, but his divinity died from lack of support.

III

His quarrels with rival merchants and rival prophets made Brigham Young more determined than ever to knit his Zion closer. In 1860 several Mormons asked Brigham Young for permission to organize a large Mormon coöperative business, which would sell general merchandise to Mormons throughout the Territory, and would get its capital from them. At the time Brigham Young was still advocating home manufactures in preference to importation, and he refused to sanction the scheme. It was only after the railroad reached Utah and the scale of business changed com-

[5] This account of the Morrisite episode is based on the information in Bancroft's *History of Utah* and Stenhouse's *Rocky Mountain Saints*.

pletely, that Brigham Young realized that he could no longer confine his people to home consumption of home industry. In order to combat the activities of the large Gentile and apostate merchants, Brigham Young organized Zion's Coöperative Mercantile Institution. This was a great blow to the Gentile merchants, and after its organization Brigham Young was known among them as The Profit.

Zion's Coöperative Mercantile Institution was a great weapon in the hands of Brigham Young. The Church as a corporation and Brigham Young personally were both large investors in the enterprise, and the magnitude which the coöperative institution soon attained increased Brigham Young's power in the community and also enabled him to find employment for his numerous sons and their large families. The coöperative soon established its own factories and workshops, and before long it became the largest organization of its kind in the West. No Mormon who had not paid his tithing was allowed to invest in the coöperative store, and this was a bludgeon in the hands of the Church tax collectors, for investment in the institution soon proved both profitable and advisable. No Mormon merchant could afford to remain outside the organization. The small merchant was swallowed up unless he joined, and the large merchant could not withstand the overwhelming competition. The coöperative institution also prevented individual Mormons from becoming too wealthy at the same time that it increased the corporate wealth of the Church. It was the great solution to Brigham Young's last problem, the problem of keeping his people progressive and at the same time preventing them from becoming rebellious. By means of Zion's Coöperative Mercantile Institution the Mormons were enabled to take part in the big business activities of the period, and the leaders of the Church became the leaders of big business in Utah.

But Brigham Young knew that one coöperative mercantile institution, however large, could not absorb the fortunes of individuals forever. Besides, there were many branches of industry and agriculture which were not touched by the institution. In his last years he tried to establish a form of communism which would bind his people together inseparably. In the hearing on the excommunication of the Godbeites Brigham Young said: "These men complain because they are called upon to submit their financial affairs to the control of the servants of God. But I tell them that the day is coming, and is near at hand, when the Latter-day Saints will give their wages to the bishop of the Church, and they will give them back what they think is right for the support of their families." It was exactly this system which Brigham Young introduced in 1870.

Joseph Smith, it will be remembered, had advocated what he called the United Order of Enoch, which required each Saint to consecrate all his property to the Church, and he received back what he needed as he needed it. When he was advocating a revival of this system in 1870, Brigham Young told his people: "Will there be any rich or poor then? No. How was it in the time of Enoch? Had they some rich and some poor? Did some ride in their silver carriages, as I do? No. If I had my way, we would foot or ride together, and we shall see the day when we shall do it." He elaborated in detail this great dream ‘of his last years at the semi-annual conference of the Church in October, 1872:

"Now suppose we had a little society organized on the plan I mentioned at the commencement of my remarks—after the Order of Enoch—would we build our houses all alike? No. How should we live? I will tell you how I would arrange for a little family, say about a thousand persons. I would build houses expressly for their convenience in cooking, washing and every department of their domestic arrangements. Instead of having every woman getting up in the morning and fussing around a cook-stove or over the fire, cooking a little food for two or three or half a dozen persons, or a dozen, as the case may be, she would have nothing to do but go to her work. Let me have my arrangement here, a hall in which I can seat five hundred persons to eat; and I have my cooking apparatus—ranges and ovens—all prepared. And suppose we had a hall a hundred feet long with our cooking room attached to this hall; and there is a person at the further end of the table and he should telegraph that he wanted a warm beafsteak; and this is conveyed to him by a little railway, perhaps under the table, and he or she may take her beafsteak . . . and we can seat five hundred at once and serve them all in a very few minutes. And when they have all eaten the dishes are piled together, slipped under the table, and run back to the ones who wash them. We could have a few Chinamen to do that if we did not want to do it ourselves. Under such a system the women could go to work making their bonnets, hats and clothing, or in the factories. I have not time to map it out before you as I wish to. But here is our dining room, and adjoining this is our prayer room, where we would assemble perhaps five hundred persons at one time, and have our prayers in the evening and in the morning. When we had our prayers and our breakfast, then each and every one to his business. But the inquiry is, in a moment, How are you going to get them together? Build your houses just the size you want them, whether a hundred feet, fifty feet or five, and you have them so arranged that you can walk directly from work to dinner. 'Would you build the houses all alike?' Oh no, if there is any person who has better taste in building than others, and can get up more tasteful houses, make your plans and we will put them up, and have the greatest variety we can imagine.

"What will we do through the day? Each one go to his work. . . . Work through the day, and when it comes evening, instead of going to a theater, walking the streets, riding, or reading novels— these falsehoods got up expressly to excite the minds of youth— repair to our room, and have our historians, and our different teachers to teach classes of old and young, to read the Scriptures to them; to teach them history, arithmetic, reading, writing, and painting; and have the best teachers that can be got to teach our day schools. Half the labor necessary to make a people moderately comfortable now, would make them independently rich under such a system. . . . And when Sunday morning came every child would be required to go to the school room, and parents to go to meeting or Sunday school, and not get into their waggons or carriages, or on the railroads, or lounge around reading novels; they would be required to go to meeting, to read the Scriptures, to pray and cultivate their minds. . . .

"A society like this would never have to buy anything; they would make and raise all they would eat, drink and wear, and always have something to sell and bring money, to help to increase their comfort and independence.

" 'Well, but,' one would say, 'I shall never have the privilege of riding again in a carriage in my life.' Oh what a pity! Did you ever ride in one when you had your own way? No, you never thought of such a thing. Thousands and thousands of Latter-day Saints never expect to own a carriage or to ride in one. Would we ride in carriages? Yes, we would; we would have them suitable for the community, and give them their proper exercise; and if I were with you, I would be willing to give others just as much as I have myself. And if we have sick, would they want a carriage to ride in? Yes, and they would have it too, we would have nice ones to carry out the sick, aged and infirm, and give them exercise, and give them a good place to sleep in, good food to eat, good company to be with them and take care of them. . . .

"If I had charge of such a society as this to which I refer, I would not allow novel reading; yet it is in my house, in the houses of my counsellors, in the houses of these Apostles, these Seventies and High Priests, in the houses of the High Council in this city, and in other cities, and in the houses of the Bishops, and we permit it; yet it is ten thousand times worse than it is for men to come here and teach our children the a b c, good morals, and how to behave themselves, ten thousand times worse! You let your children read novels until they run away, until they get so that they do not care— they are reckless, and if you do not break their backs and tie them up they will go to hell. That is rough, is it not? Well, it is a comparison. You have got to check them some way or other, or they will go to destruction. They are perfectly crazy. Their actions say, 'I want Babylon stuck on to me; I want to revel in Babylon; I want everything I can think of or desire.' If I had the power to do so, I would not take such people to heaven. God will not take them there, that I am sure of. He will try the faith and patience of this people. I would not like to get into a society where there were no trials; but I would like to see a society organized to show the Latter-day Saints how to build up the kingdom of God.

"Do you think we shall want any lawyers in our society? No, I think not. . . . I feel about them as Peter of Russia is said to have felt when he was in England. He saw and heard the lawyers pleading at a great trial there, and he was asked his opinion concerning them. He replied that he had two lawyers in his empire, and when he got home he intended to hang one of them. That is about the love I have for some lawyers who are always stirring up strife. Not but that lawyers are good in their place; but where is their place? I cannot find it. . . .

"Would you want doctors? Yes, to set bones. We should want a good surgeon for that, or to cut off a limb. But do you want doctors? For not much of anything else, let me tell you. Only the traditions of the people lead them to think so; and here is a growing evil in our midst. It will be so in a little time that not a woman in all Israel will dare to have a baby unless she can have a doctor by her. I will tell you what to do, you ladies, when you find you are going to have an increase, go off into some country where you cannot call for a doctor, and see if you can keep it. I guess you will have it, and I guess it will be all right, too. . . . I say that unless a man or woman who administers medicine to assist the human system to overcome disease, understands, and has that intuitive knowledge, by the Spirit, that such an article is good for that individual at that very time, they had better let him alone. Let the sick do without eating, take a little something to cleanse the stomach,

bowels and blood, and wait patiently, and let Nature have time to
gain the advantage over the disease. . . .

"If this could be done I want to say to the Latter-day Saints,
that I have a splendid place, large enough for about five hundred
or a thousand persons to settle upon, and I would like to be the
one to make a donation of it, with a good deal more, to start
the business, to see if we can actually accomplish the affair, and
show the Latter-day Saints how to build up Zion." [6]

The Saints would have had to be saints in deed as well as in
name to carry out Brigham Young's ideal of a huge orphan
asylum, where all mature men and women were to be instructed in
what they must do and prevented from doing what they preferred.   He himself realized the difficulty of imposing an ideal
on another person, for in the course of the above sermon, he
interpolated this statement: "But I would not form a society, nor
ask an individual to go to heaven by breaking all the bones in his
body, and putting him in a silver basket, and then, hitching him to
a kite, send him up there.   I would not do it if I had the power,
for if his bones were not broken he would jump out of the basket,
that is the idea.   I see a great many who profess to be Latter-day
Saints, who would not be contented in heaven unless their feelings
undergo a great change, and if they were there, you would have
to break their backs, or they would get out.   But we want to see
nothing of this in this little society."

A community along the lines laid down by Brigham Young
was organized at a place in southern Utah appropriately named
Orderville.   Brigham Young gave it aid, advice, and encourage-
ment, and it survived until a few years after his death, when it
was discontinued because it was found impracticable.   Brigham
Young's ideas on the United Order were then ignored, but some
Mormons still believe it to be a divine institution.

IV

Even without the regimen proposed by Brigham Young in his
plans for the United Order of Enoch, there were complaints that
life in Utah lacked spice and variety.   "It is frequently remarked," Brigham Young once said, "that there is too much

[6] *Journal of Discourses,* vol. 15, pp. 220-227.

sameness in this community. True, we do not have the variety they do in the world, drinking, carousing, quarreling, litigation, etc. But if you want a change of this kind, you can get up a dog fight. I think that would be about the extent of the quarreling you want to see. It would be as much as I would desire to witness. I have seen enough of the world, without ever desiring to behold another drunken man. I never wish to see another lawsuit. I feel perfectly satisfied without it."

Although he refused to countenance drinking, carousing, or quarreling for pleasure, Brigham Young favored other more innocent diversions. He loved dancing and the theater, and he frequently attacked the state of mind which could regard those pleasures as sins.

"You are well aware," Brigham Young once said in the pulpit, "that the wickedness of the world, or the apostasy of the Church is so great, that those who now profess religion cannot enjoy their own natural privileges in the world. In many places their folly and superstition are so great that they would consider they had committed the sin of blasphemy if they happened to hear a violin. The world could not hire a good, honest, sound Presbyterian, of the old fashion and cut, to look into a room where a company of young men and women were dancing, lest they should sin against the Holy Ghost. This over-righteous notion is imbibed by the generality of professors of religion, but it is because they themselves have made it a sin. Let us look at the root of the matter. In the first place, some wise being organized my system, and gave me my capacity, put into my heart and brain something that delights, charms, and fills me with rapture at the sound of sweet music. *I* did not put it there; it was some other being. As one of the modern writers has said, 'Music hath charms to soothe the savage breast.' It has been proved that sweet music will actually tame the most malicious and venomous beasts, even when they have been stirred up to violent wrath, and make them docile and harmless as lambs. Who gave the lower animals a love for those sweet sounds, which with magic power fill the air with harmony, and cheer and comfort the hearts of men, and so wonderfully affect the brute creation? It was the Lord, our heavenly Father, who gave the capacity to enjoy these sounds, and which *we* ought to do in His name, and to His glory. But the greater portion of the sectarian world consider it sacrilege to give way to any such pleasure as even to listen to sweet music, much more to dance to its delightful strains." [7]

[7] *Journal of Discourses,* vol. 1, p. 48.

Brigham Young also said that he got very little time for exercise, and that he took it in the form of dancing, and thereby he killed two birds with one stone, for he was enabled also to exercise and to amuse his wives. Dances were highly important in a polygamous community, where wives did not see much of their husbands who were busy supporting and entertaining multiple households. Some kinds of dancing, however, did not meet with Brigham Young's approval. He refused to allow the polka at Mormon dances, and he once said in a sermon: "But a man or woman that intends, when they go into a room prepared for music and dancing, to serve the Devil a little while, I would to God they would go to California, where they may serve the Devil all they desire to. . . . Those who cannot serve God with a pure heart in the dance should not dance."

The balls organized under the supervision of Brigham Young at the Social Hall which he built for that purpose were sumptuous and exclusive. Tickets were sold at ten dollars each, and the ticket entitled the bearer to bring with him one wife. For any other wives he might care to bring the husband paid two dollars each. The hall was decorated with evergreens and paper ornaments, and in the center was a large evergreen floral decoration reading "Our Mountain Home." The festivities began as early as four o'clock in the afternoon, when Brigham Young entered, called the assembly to order, and prayer was offered and the congregation blessed by its President. Brigham Young then led off in the first cotillion with one of his wives. At eight o'clock supper was announced, and it was usually an enormous meal, without wine, but with many varieties of meats, including bear and beaver, and with various native vegetables. After the meal, the dancing began again, and songs were sung or duets played between dances. Prayer closed the party at about five o'clock in the morning.

During their first years in Utah dramatic performances were frequently given by the Mormons in the Social Hall. The Deseret Dramatic Association was formed in 1860 by energetic members of the community. The manager called on Brigham Young and offered to reserve the house for him and his family any night he named. Brigham Young accepted the offer, and the manager sent ninety tickets, which were used by Brigham Young, his wives, and children. The few spare tickets were used by Heber Kimball and some of his family. Brigham Young enjoyed this performance so much that he decided that he must have a regular professional theater, and he set about building one.

The Salt Lake Theater was the largest theater in the United States west of Chicago when it was completed. It seated 3,000 persons, and its interior was, according to Artemus Ward, "quite as brilliant as that of any theater in London." On March 6, 1862, the Salt Lake Theater was opened, and formally dedicated to the Lord by Daniel H. Wells, who prayed that He would allow therein no "disorder, drunkenness, debauchery, or licentiousness of any sort or kind." Then Brigham Young delivered an address on "The Capacity of the Human Body and Mind for Development." A choir sang The Star-Spangled Banner and the Marseillaise, for the Civil War was still in progress. Then the comic drama *The Pride of the Market* by J. R. Planché was performed by the members of the Deseret Dramatic Association. At the second performance, given on the following Saturday night, this popular play was repeated, and a farce, *Stage Secrets,* was also performed.

The success of the theater was immediate, and Brigham Young, through his manager, who was also his son-in-law, Hiram B. Clawson, sent east for Thomas A. Lynne, a popular tragedian of the time, to act as instructor to the Mormon actors and actresses. Lynne was the first star of the Salt Lake Theater, and he appeared there in *Virginius*. In November, 1863, Mr. and Mrs. Selden Irwin appeared in *The Lady of Lyons,* which was the most popular play produced at the theater, and it continued twice a week until the following April. Maude Adams's mother, who was born near Salt Lake City, made her début at the Salt Lake Theater. She played there in *The Two Orphans*. The plays of Shakespeare and Molière were produced; Lawrence Barrett appeared in *Henry V,* and E. A. Sothern played in *Lord Dundreary* and *David Garrick*. During the last years of his life Brigham Young saw the best actors and actresses in the country perform at the theater he had started. Adelaide Neilson played there in *Romeo and Juliet* and in *As You Like It*. Tony Pastor's vaudeville company appeared at the theater during August, 1877, and E. L. Davenport played there in *Hamlet* and *Richelieu*.

During the season of 1864 George Pauncefort, the English actor, who was superior in ability to any actor who had previously played at Salt Lake City, appeared there for a short engagement. Brigham Young went to see his first performance, but, suddenly, in spite of the glowing reports of his friends, he refused to occupy his usual box. Pauncefort had brought with him as his leading lady Mrs. Florence Bell, who, it is recorded, was more beautiful than she was talented. Brigham Young soon learned that Mr. Pauncefort and Mrs. Bell were for all practical purposes Mr. and Mrs. Pauncefort, but that they had neglected the formality of a marriage license. He immediately absented himself and his harem from the theater during the remainder of Pauncefort's engagement, remarking that he "would not come into the theater while that man Pauncefort was there."

An incident which caused as much comment in Salt Lake City as the Pauncefort scandal was Brigham Young's own infatuation for Julia Dean Hayne. He gave several parties for this attractive actress during her long engagement at the Salt Lake Theater, where she played in the rôles of Camille, Lady Macbeth, Lucretia Borgia, Medea, and Aladdin in *The Wonderful Lamp*. Brigham Young is said to have named his sleigh The Julia Dean, and he also wished to make her first a Mormon and then a Mrs. Young, but Mrs. Hayne, who was divorced from Mr. Hayne, found a younger admirer in the Gentile Secretary of Utah Territory, James G. Cooper, whom she married.

Brigham Young interfered with the drama again in 1869, when Lucille Western and James A. Herne played Nancy and Bill Sykes in *Oliver Twist*. In the scene where Bill Sykes beats Nancy to death with his stick Lucille Western came on the stage after the beating in the adjoining room, with her hair disheveled and hiding her face. Suddenly she turned towards the audience, and, throwing back her hair, disclosed a face covered with stage gore. "On this occasion," wrote John S. Lindsay, the historian of the Mormon theater, who was an eyewitness, "the picture was so revolting that several women in the audience fainted—everybody was shocked. . . . President Young was very angry over it. The picture was very abhorrent; there is no knowing what the physiological results were; it was rumored afterwards that a number of children were birthmarked as the result of it." Brigham Young gave orders that the play was not to be repeated, and he sent messengers all over the city to tell the people not to go to see it, if it should be produced again. The managers withdrew the play, but Lindsay wrote that Brigham Young's orders only aroused the curiosity of the people.

Brigham Young hated tragedies, and in the speech with which he opened the Salt Lake Theater he remarked, "If I had my way, I would never have a tragedy played on these boards. There is enough of tragedy in everyday life, and we ought to have amusement when we come here." In that same speech he laid down these rules of morality:

"When the Saints come into this building, and look on this stage, to see our brethren and sisters perform to satisfy the sight, to satisfy the ear, and the desires and mind of the people, I want you to pray for them that the Lord Almighty may preserve them from ever having one wicked thought in their bosoms, that our actors may be just as virtuous, truthful, and humble before God and each other as though they were on a Mission to preach the Gospel.

"I say to those who perform, if anything is discovered contrary to the strictest virtue and decorum, the offenders must leave this building. I intend this remark to apply also to the musicians. I wish the dramatic company to seek diligently and in all kindness to promote the happiness of all concerned.

"Unless by my order I do not wish a drop of intoxicating liquor brought into this house; I want the actors behind the curtain, the musicians in the orchestra, and the audience to hear and observe this.

"When this house is finished, there will be places in the passages where cakes, pies, fruits, &c., can be bought; but no intoxicating liquor will be allowed in these saloons. No drunken person will be permitted to enter this house; I will not have it polluted and disgraced by the presence of the drunken, nor my brethren and sisters, who strive continually to do right, annoyed by the filthy breath of a poor, miserable filthy loafer.

"We intend to preserve the strictest order here; we do expect the people to come to this house praying, and their whole souls devoted to God, and to their religion.

"Tragedy is favored by the outside world; I am not in favor of it. I do not wish murder and all its horrors and the villainy leading to it portrayed before our women and children; I want no child to carry home with it the fear of the fagot, the sword, the pistol, or the dagger, and suffer in the night from frightful dreams. I want such plays performed as will make the spectators feel well; and I wish those who perform to select a class of plays that will improve the public mind, and exalt the literary taste of the community." [8]

[8] *Journal of Discourses,* vol. 9, pp. 243-245.

At the theater Brigham Young often sat in a rocking chair in the middle of the parquet, surrounded by his wives. When the play dragged, Artemus Ward reported, Brigham Young fell into a doze or rose and left the theater. Brigham Young believed so firmly in home industry that he was in favor of making the Salt Lake Theater exclusively Mormon in its acting personnel as well as its management, except for a few visiting stars. He persuaded several of his own daughters to act in the theater. Alice, Emily, and Zina appeared regularly in the plays. Alice told Hepworth Dixon at dinner one day, "I am not myself very fond of playing, but my father desires that my sister and myself should act sometimes, as he does not think it right to ask any poor man's child to do anything which his own children would object to do."

Admission to the Salt Lake Theater was sometimes paid for in merchandise, and Artemus Ward gave in his book of travels this list of his receipts at the box office when he lectured there:

"Among my receipts at the box-office this night were—
20 bushels of wheat.
5   "   " corn.
4   "   " potatoes.
2   "   " oats.
4   "   " salt.
2 hams.
1 live pig (Dr. Hingston chained him in the box-office).
1 wolf-skin.
5 pounds of honey in the comb.
16 strings of sausages—2 pounds to the string.
1 cat-skin.
1 churn (two families went in on this; it is an ingenious churn, and fetches butter in five minutes by rapid grinding).
1 set of children's under-garments, embroidered.
1 keg of apple-sauce.
One man undertook to pass a dog (a cross between a Scotch terrier and a Welsh rabbit) at the box-office, and another presented a German-silver coffin plate, but the Doctor very justly repulsed them both."

V

While he was building places of recreation for his community, Brigham Young did not neglect the places of worship. At first when the Saints settled in Utah, they gathered for worship and instruction in a small tabernacle in winter and in a large, open-air bowery in summer. Finally, Brigham Young built an enormous, oval-domed Tabernacle on Temple Square, which was so constructed that it required no posts to hold up its egg-shaped roof. The new Tabernacle seated about 8,000 persons, and the acoustics were so good that every sound was heard in every part of the building, unless the speaker rumbled too loudly. A large organ was built by Mormon mechanics, which was the pride of the community for many years, both because of its size and its tone.

The greatest work of Mormon construction, however, was the Temple, which took exactly forty years to complete, and which was not finished until many years after Brigham Young's death. The corner stone of the Temple was laid in 1853, but work was discontinued from time to time because of lack of funds or lack of coöperation. The huge granite blocks of which the building is constructed were dragged slowly by ox-teams from the cañons some miles away. This part of the labor alone required years for its completion. The Temple was supposed to be constructed by revelation, but Truman O. Angell was its temporal architect. Brigham Young wished the Temple built on such a solid foundation that it would last until the millennium, and in order to insure this, he ordered the foundation taken out and relaid, when he discovered that it had been laid "on chinky, small stones," instead of solid rock. The Temple is said to have cost $4,000,000 to construct. It was finally finished in 1893, and dedicated by President Wilford Woodruff.

According to a pamphlet of lavish praise published soon after the Temple was completed, the Salt Lake Temple has many things that Solomon's Temple, in all its simple grandeur, lacked: "Four engines and dynamos, with a capacity of two thousand electric lights, as well as the pumps, boilers, etc., and the motive power for the two handsome elevators that operate in the central west tower directly in front of us." It also has a central heating plant and a perfect system of ventilation, with "sixteen fans, each of one-half horse power," which are miraculously started by merely pressing an electric button. The baptismal font is a triumph of modern science, according to the anonymous writer of this pamphlet entitled *House of the Lord, Historical and Descriptive Sketch of the Salt Lake Temple:* "It is of cast iron; is reached by a short flight of iron steps at either end, and rests

MORMON TEMPLE IN SALT LAKE CITY

SALT LAKE THEATER

upon the backs of twelve life-sized bronzed oxen, which stand within a railed enclosure sunk some three feet below the main floor. A genuine masterpiece of the artificer is this font, viewing it from whatsoever standpoint we may, for it is large without being oppressive and pleases not less with the massiveness of its construction than with the chaste elegance of his design. By the simplest sort of a contrivance it can be filled with water, or, the water being in, it can be emptied—the entire proceeding requiring but sixteen minutes." This device made it very convenient for baptizing large numbers of people for their fathers and grandfathers. This Mormon writer also praises highly the magnificent bath tubs, with hot and cold water, and the onyx wash basins, fifteen of them, and "each is of rare beauty, and conveys the impression of an immense gem." "The sanitary arrangements throughout are faultless," and this could hardly be said for Solomon's Temple, with which the Salt Lake Temple invited comparison.

On the walls in some of the rooms of the Temple are oil paintings of "The Crucifixion," and the "Descent from the Cross," by new masters. A painting of "Christ Preaching to the Nephites," was proudly proclaimed to be 12 x 18 feet in dimension. Vast, dazzling chandeliers of glass hang from the ceilings, giving promise of blinding brilliance when they are illuminated. In one of the rooms of the western wing "is a mammoth mirror," and there are "colossal triple mirrors" in another vast room, which has twenty Grecian columns. Frescoes depicting scenes from the Book of Mormon adorn the walls. In the ascent to one of the towers "every floor is supplied with fire hose conveniently disposed, so that in case the unexpected, we might almost say the impossible, should happen, adequate remedy and protection would be at hand. In the top of the opposite tower beyond the elevator is a permanent reserve tank with a capacity of seven thousand gallons of water."

The Mormons have aroused curiosity among Gentiles concerning the interior of their Temple by permitting none but Mormons to enter it. The exterior view of it is stern, and stolidly impressive. The massive building with its six rugged spires is, like the Mormon character, plain to a fault. No building was ever more typical of the dogged determination of the people who built it than the Mormon Temple.

The prayer dedicating the Temple to the Lord, delivered on

April 6, 1893, by President Wilford Woodruff, contained this passage:

"We pray thee to bless, that they decay not, all the walls, partitions, floors, ceilings, roofs and bridging, the elevators, stairways, railings and steps, the frames, doors, windows, and other openings, all things connected with the lighting, heating, and sanitary apparatus, the boilers, engines, dynamos, the connecting pipes and wires, the lamps and burners, and all utensils, furniture and articles used in or connected with the holy ordinances administered in this house, the veils and the altars, the baptismal font and the oxen on which it rests, and all that pertains thereto, the baths, washstands and basins. Also the safes and vaults in which the records are preserved, with the records themselves, and all books, documents, and papers pertaining to the office of the recorder, likewise the library, with all the books, maps, instruments, etc., that may belong thereto. We also present before thee, for thine acceptance, all the additions and buildings not forming a part of the main edifice, but being appendages thereto; and we pray thee to bless all the furniture, seats, cushions, curtains, hangings, locks, and fastenings, and multitudinous other appliances and appurtenances found in and belonging to this Temple and its annexes, with all the work of ornamentation thereon, the painting and plastering, the gilding and bronzing, the fine work in wood and metal of every kind, the embroidery and needlework, the pictures and statuary, the carved work and canopies. Also the materials of which the buildings and their contents are made or composed—the rock, lime, mortar and plaster, the timbers and lath, the wood of various trees, the gold and silver, the brass and iron, and all other metals, the silk, wool, and cotton, the skins and furs, the glass, china, and precious stones, all these and all else herein we humbly present for thine acceptance and sanctifying blessing." [9]

Obviously, the President was determined to leave nothing to the Imagination.

[9] *House of the Lord, Historical and Descriptive Sketch*, p. 27.

Chapter XIII

THE END

I

As he felt himself growing old and feeble, Brigham Young became more than ever anxious to knit his organization closer and closer. He continued to urge coöperation, home manufactures, the United Order, and coördination of the Stakes of Zion. With his last public breath, which was a "Circular of the First Presidency," issued at Salt Lake City on July 11, 1877, he advocated these things, and also education for the children; but he insisted that the school books should be published in Utah, and written there if possible, rather than imported at unnecessary expense from the East. The teachers, too, he wrote, should be Latter-day Saints, so that the children might learn only what they ought to know.

Once every year Brigham Young visited the settlements in the north and in the south, and during his last winters he spent much time in the milder southern settlements. A long train of coaches, carrying him and some of his wives, his Apostles, elders, and parts of their families traveled over the dusty roads, sometimes accompanied by a guard of Piute Indian warriors and armed Mormon militia. Before Brigham Young reached a settlement of his people a detachment of cavalry met his cavalcade, and nearer the settlement all the school children, in stiff white dresses and blouses, holding small flags, were lined up to greet him. In the larger settlements there was always a brass band, and the people were frequently grouped together along the roadway with banners describing their condition. For the aged men there was the banner, "Fathers in Israel," and for the elderly women, "Mothers in Israel." The young men bore a banner with the device, "Defenders of Zion," and the young women stood under the ensign, "Daughters of Zion, Virtue." The small children were designated in large letters, "The Hope of Israel." Other banners pro-

451

claimed sentiments of welcome, some reading, "Hail to Zion's Chief," and others, "God Bless Brigham Young." Occasionally a disagreeable incident marred the welcome. A visitor to Utah witnessed the last impressive procession in which Brigham Young took part during 1877. As the long line of carriages passed through the town of Ephraim, Ole Petersen, a Scandinavian convert who claimed that he had been cheated of his land by Brigham Young and sent on a mission that he might be robbed the more easily, waited for Brigham Young's carriage, shook his fist at the Prophet, and shouted in a strident voice: "Oh, you Cheat! Oh, Church Fraud! You coward to forsake your tools! You are the man that they should have hung instead of Lee!" The carriages rolled by, but it was observed that Brigham Young's hard, thin mouth tightened, and his hands clenched the seat of his coach.

When he was seventy years old, Brigham Young was arrested, as we have already noted, for "lascivious cohabitation," a crime which was punishable under the new laws by ten years' imprisonment and a fine of $1,000. At about the same time he was also indicted for murder, a charge based on the confessions of Bill Hickman, who wrote that he had killed men at the suggestion of Brigham Young. On this charge Brigham Young was not admitted to bail, but out of consideration for his feeble health and his age, he was confined in one of his own houses for more than five months. A New York *Tribune* correspondent visited Brigham Young during this period of arrest. "I found the Mormon chief," he wrote, "reclining in his easy chair, with a shawl spread over him. He said he was better, but weak from a severe attack of diarrhea, and too feeble to talk much. When asked how he felt in regard to the indictment and arrest, he said, 'It is as easy as an old shoe.' He had no fears of the result. All attempts to destroy him and his people had failed heretofore."

At this critical time for Brigham Young the United States courts in Utah found themselves without money. The territorial legislature, which was controlled by the Mormons, refused to appropriate any money for the federal courts, and the Department of Justice held that the federal courts were not federal courts when they were trying territorial cases. This brought about a deadlock, and the consequent postponement of Brigham Young's trial for murder. Judge McKean, who had been a Methodist minister before he was a judge, and who considered that he was a crusader in a glorious fight against theocracy, refused to admit Brigham Young to bail, and he remained in his rocker with his shawl spread about his shoulders for several months longer. Finally, the United States Supreme Court handed down its decision in the Engelbrecht case, by which the whole course of Judge McKean's action in impaneling special non-Mormon juries to try cases involving Mormons was declared illegal, and all Judge McKean's indictments were dismissed.

During Brigham Young's confinement the semi-annual conference of the Church was due to be held, but it was postponed until he could be present. It was finally held on April 28, 1871, and the *Deseret News* reported the scene: Brigham Young said, "A word to the Latter-day Saints: Good morning." The congregation responded, "Good morning." "How do you do?" asked Brigham Young. "Very well," answered the whole congregation. "How is your faith this morning?" he inquired. "Strong in the Lord," they answered. "How do you think I look after my long confinement?" he asked. "First rate," the congregation answered. Brigham Young then told them that everything was always in the hands of the Lord, and that he had enjoyed a fine rest during his five months' confinement to his house.

The stream of distinguished visitors continued to pour into Salt Lake City. In October, 1875, President Grant stopped there. Brigham Young met him in his private car, and both presidents uncovered. "President Grant," said President Young, "this is the first time I have ever seen a President of my country." It is said that as Grant was driven through lines of smiling Sunday school children, he asked whose children they were. "Mormon children," answered Governor Emery. "For several moments the President was silent," recorded a Mormon writer, "and then he murmured, in a tone of self-reproach, 'I have been deceived!'" Perhaps President Grant had expected that polygamy bred monsters, and perhaps he said no such thing.

Those visitors who called on Brigham Young and wrote their impressions of him always liked him. He was affable and courteous to strangers, and he did not object to their curiosity concerning him, so long as it did not enter too personally into his relations with his wives. He was about five feet ten inches in height, broad and thick-set, giving the impression of stolidity and vigor. His head was large and covered with soft auburn hair, which reached to the ear lobes in a half curl. His eyes were a cold gray, and they gazed at a stranger with a calm, but reserved, almost suspicious expression. The left eyelid drooped slightly from the effects of neuralgia, which he suffered from frequently, and which was the reason he kept his head covered except in his own house. His nose was sharp, somewhat pointed, and bent slightly towards the left. His mouth was long, with tightly compressed, thin lips, which hid the imperfect teeth of his lower jaw, except when he was talking. He wore no moustache, but a beard about six inches long covered his chin. When he stood, his heavy, broad shoulders stooped slightly. In the face there was an unmistakable expression of ironic humor, which illuminated somewhat the forbidding determination and self-assurance. In his pictures there is no trace of the kindliness which it is said he exhibited in the privacy of his family and in his relations with his associates.

The Prophet-President looked to Sir Richard Burton like a gentleman farmer of New England, and the fine state of preservation Burton attributed "to his habit of sleeping, as the Citizen Proudhon so strongly advises, in solitude." Brigham Young's lack of pretension, and the power expressed in his appearance, impressed Burton favorably, for his personality contrasted strikingly with the "semi-maniacal self-esteem" of the Eastern religious prophets whom Burton had met in the course of his travels. When Burton asked Brigham Young if he might become a Mormon, Brigham Young answered, "I think you have done that sort of thing before, Captain," for he was familiar with Burton's liberal habit of joining every religion with which he came into contact.

A man who met Brigham Young on the street or in his office was not likely to notice anything remarkable in the appearance of one who was acclaimed as an inspired genius by his friends and followers and denounced as a criminal fiend by his enemies and competitors. In the pulpit he was apt to show to the greatest advantage. He was no orator, and he was not eloquent; his grammar was sometimes irregular, and his pronunciation was often faulty; but there was no public character in the country at the time who used such vigorous and honest language to express his blunt, sincere ideas. He refused to believe that a spade by any other name would be nearly so effective. As a statesman Brigham Young is one of the few Americans deserving of the adjective great. In a situation of precariousness and importance

BRIGHAM YOUNG IN HIS LAST YEARS
From a contemporary photograph

he showed himself a man of resourcefulness and sturdiness, and his personality contributed as much as that of any one man to the development of the western half of the United States. He indicated to Americans of the eastern states what could be done with their unexploited frontier, and by successfully dominating his band of faithful disciples in the wilderness, he demonstrated that a wilderness could become paradise enough. Beset by the opposition of the government, competing creeds of Christianity, the force of ridicule, and the power of intolerant prejudice, he built his scattered and insecure community into a compact body of self-supporting people, who were soon able to dominate their section of the world by their industry and their faith, as well as by their egotism and their intolerance.

In one of his letters to the New York *Herald* Jedediah M. Grant, who, like all his associates, obeyed and worshiped Brigham Young, wrote: "I can't undertake to explain Brigham Young to your Atlantic citizens, or expect you to put him at his value. Your great men Eastward are to me like your ivory and pearl-handled table knives, balance handles, more shining than the inside of my watch case, but, with only edge enough to slice bread and cheese or help spoon victuals, and all alike by the dozen one with another. Brigham is the article sells out West with us, between a Roman cutlass and a beef butcher knife, the thing to cut up a deer or cut down an enemy, and that will save your life or carve your dinner every bit as well, though the handpiece is buckhorn and the case a hogskin hanging in the breech of your pantaloons. You, that judge of men by the handle and sheath, how can I make you know a good *Blade?*"

II

Almost every year during the last ten years of his life Brigham Young watched one of his pioneers and his friends disappear. Heber Kimball died in 1868, and Jedediah Grant more than ten years before. Brigham Young lived on in almost complete possession of his vigorous faculties. These personal deaths neither dismayed nor disheartened him, for he lived in the perfect faith that he would see all these men and women again. In his unique funeral oration over the body of his best friend, Heber Kimball, Brigham Young said: "I will say to his wives and his children that I have not felt one particle of death in his house nor about it, and through this scene we are now passing I have not felt one particle of the spirit of death. He has fallen asleep for a certain purpose—to be prepared for a glorious resurrection; and the same Heber C. Kimball, every component part of his body, from the crown of his head to the soles of his feet, will be resurrected, and he, in the flesh, will see God and converse with Him; and see his brethren and associate with them and they will enjoy a happy eternity." With this firm conviction, which he considered ought to be shared by all the faithful, there was no room for sentimentality in his mind, and no time for it in his life. "It would be a pleasure to us," he added in this funeral sermon, "if it would be prudent and we had the time, for you to see the corpse; but it would not be prudent and we have not the time. This, perhaps, will be a matter of regret to many of you; but you must put up with it. I want to say to every one who wishes to see Brother Heber again, live so that you will secure to yourselves a part in the first resurrection, and I promise you that you will meet him and shake hands with him. But if you do not live so, I can give you no such promise."

Death to Brigham Young was a solemn ritual, the forerunner of great benefits, but it was not the occasion for sorrow or sentimentality. John Baptiste, a resident of Salt Lake City, was discovered robbing the graves in the Mormon cemetery, and the people became excited and demanded vengeance. Brigham Young took up the problem in a sermon, in which he expressed his views of death and the responsibility of relatives and friends towards those who had partaken of it:

"It appears that a man named John Baptiste has practised robbing the dead of their clothing in our grave yard during some five years past. If you wish to know what I think about it, I answer, I am unable to think so low as to fully get at such a mean, contemptible, damnable trick. To hang a man for such a deed would not begin to satisfy my feelings. What shall we do with him? Shoot him? No, that would do no good to anybody but himself. Would you imprison him during life? That would do nobody any good. What I would do with him came to me quickly, after I heard of the circumstance; this I will mention, before I make other remarks. If it was left to me, I would make him a fugitive and a vagabond upon the earth. This would be my sentence, but probably the people will not want this done.

"Many are anxious to know what effect it will have upon their dead who have been robbed. I have three sisters in the grave yard in this city, and two wives, and several children, besides other connections and near relatives. I have not been to open any of their graves to see whether they were robbed, and do not mean to do so. I gave them as good a burial as I could; and in burying our dead, we all have made everything as agreeable and comfortable as we could to the eye and taste of the people in their various capacities, according to the best of our judgments; we have done our duty in this particular, and I for one am satisfied. I defy any thief there is on earth or in hell to rob a Saint of one blessing. A thief may dig up dead bodies and sell them for the dissecting knife, or may take their raiment from them, but when the resurrection takes place, the Saints will come forth with all the glory, beauty, and excellency of resurrected Saints clothed as they were when they were laid away.

"Some may inquire whether it is necessary to put fresh linen into the coffins of those who have been robbed of their clothing. As to this you can pursue the course that will give you the most contentment and satisfaction; but if the dead are laid away as well as they can be, I will promise you that they will be well clothed in the resurrection, for the earth and the elements around it are full of these things. . . .

"Some I have been informed, can now remember having had singular dreams, and others have heard rappings on the floor, on the bedstead, on the door, on the table, &c., and have imagined that they might have proceeded from the spirits of the dead calling on their friends to give them clothing, for they were naked. My dear friends have not been to me to tell me that they were naked, cold, &c.; and if any such rappings should come to me, I should tell them to go to their own place. I have little faith in those rappings. If I felt that I ought to pay attention to such things, I would not, so to speak, let my right hand know what my left did; and it would require a greater power than John Baptiste to make me believe either a truth or a lie. . . .

"If any wish to open the graves of their dead and put clothing on the coffins to satisfy their feelings, all right; I am satisfied. I am also satisfied that had we been brought up and traditionated to burn a wife upon the funeral pile, we should not be satisfied unless this practice was followed out; we would have the same grief and sorrow that we now have when we find that our dead have been robbed of their clothing. . . . The power and influence of tradition has a great deal to do with the way we feel about this matter of our dead being robbed.

"We are here in circumstances to bury our dead according to the order of the Priesthood. But some of our brethren die upon the ocean; they cannot be buried in a burying ground, but they are sewed up in canvas and cast into the sea, and perhaps in two minutes after they are in the bowels of the shark, yet those persons will come forth in the resurrection, and receive all the glory of which they are worthy, and be clothed upon with all the beauty of resurrected Saints, as much so as if they had been laid away in a gold or silver coffin, and in a place expressly for burying the dead. . . . I am aware of the excited state of the feelings of the community; I have little to say about the cause of it. The meanness of the act is so far beneath my comprehension that I have not ventured to think much about it." [1]

When he was delivering a funeral oration for his friend Jedediah M. Grant, Brigham Young recalled to the people the funeral of Jesus. After speaking of the uselessness of mourning, he remarked: "I have often reflected with regard to paying particular respect to that which is useless, to that which is nothing at all to us. And while waiting in the vestry, I was pondering upon how many bands of music attended Jesus to the tomb, upon what the procession was, how many wore crape, who mourned, and the situation of the mourners." Then he went on to say that he hoped that when his time came to die none would cry over his body, "nor make any parade, but give me a good place where my bones can rest, that have been weary for many years, and have delighted to labor until nearly worn out; and then go home about your business, and think no more about me, except you think of me in the spirit world, as I do about Jedediah."

Brigham Young once told the people that he personally preferred spiritual resurrection to temporal immortality, and he expressed his feelings in these familiar terms: "If the Lord Almighty proffered to revoke the decree, 'Dust thou art, and to dust thou shalt return,' and say to me, 'You can live for ever as you are;' I should say, 'Father, I want to ask a few questions upon this point. Shall I still be subject to the toothache, to the headache, to the chills and fever, and to all the diseases incident to the mortal body?' 'Oh, yes, but you can live, and never die.' 'Then I would have you, Father, to let the old decree stand good; I find no fault with your offer, it may be a good one; but I have the promise of receiving my body again—of this body coming up in

[1] *Journal of Discourses*, vol. 9, pp. 192-194.

the morning of the resurrection, and being re-united with the spirit, and being filled with the principles of immortality and eternal life. Thank you, Father, I would rather take a new body, and then I shall get a good set of new teeth. My sight, too, is failing; if I want to read, I cannot do it without using glasses; and if I wish to walk a few miles, I cannot do it without making myself sick; if I wish to go out on a journey, I am under the necessity of taking the utmost care of myself for fear of injuring my health; but when I get a new body, this will not be so; I shall be out of the reach of him that hath the power of death in his hands, for Jesus Christ will conquer that foe, and I shall receive a new body, which will be filled with eternal life, health, and beauty." [2]

On Thursday, August 23, 1877, when he was seventy-six years old, Brigham Young suffered from an attack of cholera morbus, which is said to have been the result of eating green corn and peaches. On Friday the doctors, whom he had been willing to consult, in spite of his general opinions concerning the profession, said that he was convalescent, but he grew worse, and the next day, Saturday, his severe pain was relieved with morphine. Sunday he fell into a coma and remained practically unconscious until Tuesday. Besides the four physicians who attended him, the leading brethren of the Church came to his bedside, lay hands upon him, and prayed for his recovery, but inflammation of the bowels had set in, and more reliance was placed on artificial respiration than on prayer. On Tuesday he remained unconscious, and many at the bedside thought he had died, but artificial respiration was used for more than nine hours. John W. Young gave his father the ordinance for the sick. Tuesday night the physicians abandoned hope for his recovery; they tried injections of stimulants through the bowels, but the pain was so great that the patient cried out continually, and the treatment had to be discontinued. At four o'clock in the afternoon of Wednesday, August 29, 1877, he died. It is said that he murmured, "Joseph, Joseph, Joseph, Joseph," and added something else which was inaudible. But it is also said that his last words were, "I feel better."

The body was taken from the Lion House to the Tabernacle on Saturday morning, September 1, and until noon the following

[2] *Journal of Discourses*, vol. 1, p. 271.

day long lines of people came to take a last look at their leader. People came in special trains to look at the corpse, and it was estimated that more than 25,000 Mormons visited the Tabernacle during the day.

Four years before his death Brigham Young wrote out the following directions for his own funeral:

"I, Brigham Young, wish my funeral services to be conducted in the following manner: When I breathe my last, I wish my friends to put my body in as clean and wholesome a state as can conveniently be done, and preserve the same for one, two, three or four days, or as long as my body can be preserved in good condition.

"I want my coffin made of plain one-and-a-quarter redwood boards, not scrimped in length, but two inches longer than I would measure, and from two to three inches wider than is commonly made for a person of my breadth and size, and deep enough to place me on a little comfortable cotton bed, with a good suitable pillow in size and quality. My body dressed in my Temple clothing, and laid nicely into my coffin, and the coffin to have the appearance that if I wanted to turn a little to the right or left I should have plenty of room to do so; the lid can be made crowning.

"At my interment I wish all my family present that can be conveniently, and the male members to wear no crape on their hats or coats; the females to buy no black bonnets or dresses nor black veils, but if they have them they are at liberty to wear them.

"And services may be permitted, as singing and a prayer offered, and if any of my friends wish to say a few words they are desired to do so.

"And when they close their services, to take my remains on a bier and repair to the little burying ground which I have reserved on my lot east of the White House on the hill. On the southeast corner of this lot I have a vault built of mason work large enough to receive my coffin, and that they may place in a box, if they choose, the same as the coffin—redwood—then place rocks over the vault sufficiently large to cover it, that the earth may be placed over it— as fine dry earth as can be had—to cover it until the walls of the little cemetery are hid, which will leave me in the southeast corner.

"This vault ought to be roofed over with some kind of temporary roof. There let my earthly tabernacle rest in peace and comfort and have a good sleep until the morning of the first resurrection—no crying world mourning with any one.

"I have done my work faithfully and in good faith. I wish this to be read at the funeral, provided that if I should die anywhere in the mountains I desire the above directions respecting my place of burial should be observed. But if I should live to get back to the church in Jackson County, Mo., I wish to be buried there.

"BRIGHAM YOUNG,
"President of the Church of Jesus Christ
of Latter-Day Saints." [3]

At 11:30 on Sunday morning, September 2, the funeral services began. Most of Brigham Young's seventeen surviving wives and forty-four surviving children were present, together with the rest of his family, numbering several hundred. The great Tabernacle organ played the Dead March from Saul and Mendelssohn's Funeral March, as well as special hymns and a Mormon funeral march composed for the occasion. After the ceremonies four thousand people marched eight abreast to the grave. It is said that Mary Ann Angel, Brigham Young's first wife, leaned on the arm of Amelia Folsom, his favorite.

Brigham Young's will was a complicated document. It established a trust fund for "the mothers of my children," as he phrased it legally. Mary Ann Angel and Amelia Folsom received together the residence he had built for Amelia, called the Guardo House, and known more familiarly as "Amelia's Palace." The other wives remained in the Lion House. The mothers received proportionate shares of the estate, which is said to have amounted to $2,000,000, and they were charged with the duty of contributing to the support of their children. As the mothers died the estate was to be revalued, and the children were to receive their final shares. The administration of the estate was difficult. Besides their income from the mills and factories, the wives and their children also received individually parcels of real estate in Utah. The will also provided for a cemetery for the family, and the place of burial of each wife and her children was apportioned.

Two years after Brigham Young's death some of the wives and children sued the executors of the estate, charging fraud. They claimed that the executors had turned over to the Church some of Brigham Young's personal property. The Church proved that the property had been held in trust for it by Brigham Young, but the contesting heirs received as a compromise $75,000. This compromise was arranged, because it was found impossible to determine exactly what was Brigham Young's and what was the Church's property. The charge was made that Brigham Young

[3] *Death of President Young.* Deseret News Publishing Co., 1877.

had balanced his account with the Church in 1852 by telling the clerk to put the sum of $200,000 to his credit "for services rendered," and that he had done the same in 1867 with the sum of $967,000. But he himself maintained in his sermons that his money and the Church's money were kept separately, and that the accounts borrowed from each other but always paid back what was owed.

After the death of Brigham Young there was much speculation concerning its effect on the future of Mormonism. His sons, Brigham, Jr., and John W. Young, were anxious to succeed him, but the succession went to the President of the Twelve Apostles, according to the principle laid down by Brigham Young after the death of Joseph Smith, and which has been followed ever since. John Taylor automatically became President.

One Sunday morning in October, 1877, the Rev. DeWitt Talmage paused in the interpretation of the Gospel of Christ long enough to offer this suggestion to the national government: "Now, my friends, now at the death of the Mormon chieftain, is the time for the United States Government to strike. Let as much of their rich lands be confiscated as will pay for their subjugation. If the Government of the United States cannot stand the expense, let Salt Lake pay for it. Set Phil Sheridan after them. Give him enough troops, and he will teach all Utah that 40 wives is 39 too many. Now is the time when they are less organized than they have been." [4] But Brooklyn's belligerent preacher was destined to be disappointed. The Church did not die with Brigham Young, as he and so many others hoped it would, and the hated polygamy was practised for almost fifteen years after the death of the Mormon Chieftain.

[4] *New York Times,* October 28, 1877.

the Trial of Lieutenant-Colonel Frémont. Exec. Document 33, 30th Congress, 1st Session.

GILLILAN, JAMES DAVID. *Thomas Corwin Iliff.* New York, 1919.

Gospel Herald. Voree, Wisconsin, 1848.

Governors' Letter-Books 1840-1853. Illinois State Hist. Library. Springfield, 1911.

GRANT, J. M. *Three Letters to the New York Herald.* Pamphlet published from articles in New York *Herald* of March 9, April 8, April 25, 1852.

GREELEY, HORACE. *An Overland Journey.* New York, 1860.

GREENE, JOHN P. *Facts Relative to the Expulsion of the Mormons from the State of Missouri.* 1839.

GREGG, THOMAS. *The Prophet of Palmyra.* New York, 1890.

GUNNISON, LIEUT. J. W. *The Mormons.* Philadelphia, 1852.

HAVEN, CHARLOTTE. "A Girl's Letters from Nauvoo." *Overland Monthly,* Dec., 1890.

HICKMAN, BILL. *Brigham's Destroying Angel.* New York, 1872.

HOWE, E. D. *Mormonism Unveiled.* Painesville, Ohio, 1834.

HYDE, JOHN, JR. *Mormonism: Its Leaders and Designs.* New York, 1857.

Illinois, The History of Adams County, Chicago, 1879.

Inside of Mormonism, The. S. L. City, 1903.

JAMES, WILLIAM. *The Varieties of Religious Experience.* New York, 1902.

JARMAN, W. *Uncle Sam's Abscess, or Hell upon Earth for U. S.* Exeter, England, 1884.

JENSON, ANDREW. *The Historical Record,* vols. 5-8. S. L. City, 1886.

JILLSON, CLARK. *Green Leaves from Whitingham, Vermont.* 1894.

JOHNSTON, WILLIAM PRESTON. *The Life of Gen. Albert Sidney Johnston.* New York, 1878.

Journal of Discourses by Brigham Young, President of the Church of Jesus Christ of Latter-day Saints, His Two Counsellors, The Twelve Apostles and Others, vols. 1-19. Liverpool, 1854-1878.

KANE, THOMAS L. *The Mormons.* Philadelphia, 1850.

KAUFFMAN, RUTH and REGINALD WRIGHT. *The Latter Day Saints.* London, 1912.

KENNEDY, J. H. *Early Days of Mormonism.* New York, 1888.

KENNEDY, J. H. "The Three Witnesses of the Book of Mormon." *Magazine of Western History,* March, 1890.

KNIGHT, LYDIA. *Lydia Knight's History.* S. L. City, 1883.

Latter Day Saints' Messenger and Advocate, vols. 1-3. Kirtland, Ohio, 1834-1837.

LEAVITT, M. B. *Fifty Years in Theatrical Management.* New York, 1912.

LEE, JOHN DOYLE. *Mormonism Unveiled.* St. Louis, 1891.

Lee Trial!, The. S. L. City, 1875.

LEGLER, HENRY E. *A Moses of the Mormons.* [James J. Strang.] Michigan Pioneer and Hist. Society, vol. 32. Lansing, Mich., 1903.

LINDSAY, JOHN S. *The Mormons and the Theatre.* S. L. City, 1905.

LINFORTH, JAMES. *Route from Liverpool to Great Salt Lake Valley.* Liverpool and London, 1855.

LINN, WILLIAM ALEXANDER. *The Story of the Mormons.* New York, 1902.

LITTLE, JAMES A. *From Kirtland to Salt Lake City.* S. L. City, 1890.

LITTLEFIELD, LYMAN OMER. *Reminiscences of Latter-Day Saints.* Logan, Utah, 1888.

MCCARTHY, JUSTIN. "Brigham Young." *The Galaxy,* Feb., 1870.

MACK, SOLOMON. *A Narrative of the Life of Solomon Mack.* (n.d. About 1810.)

MARRYAT, CAPT. FREDERICK. *The Travels and Adventures of Monsieur Violet.* London, 1874.

MATHER, FREDERIC G. "The Early Days of Mormonism." *Lippincott's Mag.,* Aug., 1880.

Millennial Star. Vols. 1-40. Liverpool and London.

Missouri, The Commonwealth of. St. Louis, 1877.

Missouri, Copy of a Memorial to the Legislature of.

Mormon, Book of. First edition. Palmyra, New York, 1830.

Mountain Meadows Massacre. Senate Exec. Document 42, 36th Congress, 1st session.

Nauvoo Expositor. Only issue published, June 7, 1844, Nauvoo, Illinois.

Nauvoo Neighbor. Dec. 27, 1843 to Oct. 1, 1845. Nauvoo, Illinois.

Nauvoo Rustler. July 1, 1890-April 21, 1891. Nauvoo, Illinois.

Niles' National Register. Various numbers from 1840-1880.

Pioneers, The Utah. S. L. City, 1880.

Polk, James K., The Diary of. Chicago, 1910.

POOLEY, WILLIAM VIPOND. *The Settlement of Illinois.* Bull. of the Univ. of Wisconsin, No. 220, History Series, vol. 1, no. 4. Madison, Wis., May, 1908.

PRATT, ORSON. *A Series of Pamphlets.* Liverpool, 1851.

PRATT, PARLEY P. *The Autobiography of Parley Parker Pratt.* Chicago, 1888.

PRINCE, WALTER FRANKLIN. "Psychological Tests for the Authorship of the Book of Mormon." *American Journal of Psychology,* vol. 28, no. 3, July, 1917.

QUINCY, JOSIAH. *Figures of the Past.* Boston, 1883.

REMY, JULES. *A Journey to Great Salt Lake City*. London, 1861.

REYNOLDS, JOHN. *My Own Times*. Illinois, 1855.

RICHARDSON, JAMES D. *A Compilation of the Papers and Messages of the Presidents*. Vols. 5, 7, 8, 9. Washington, 1898.

RILEY, I. WOODBRIDGE. *The Founder of Mormonism*. New York, 1902.

ROBERTS, BRIGHAM H. "History of the Mormon Church." *American Historical Magazine* and *Americana*, 1901-1906.

ROBERTS, BRIGHAM H. *The Mormon Battalion*. S. L. City, 1919.

ROBERTS, BRIGHAM H. "The Origin of the Book of Mormon." *American Historical Magazine*, vols. 3 and 4, New York, 1908 and 1909.

ROBERTS, BRIGHAM H. *The Rise and Fall of Nauvoo*. S. L. City, 1900.

ROBERTS, BRIGHAM H. *Succession in the Presidency*. S. L. City, 1900.

ROBINSON, PHIL. *Sinners and Saints*. Boston, 1883.

SALISBURY, HERBERT SPENCER. "The Mormon War in Hancock County." *Illinois State Hist. Society Journal*, vol. 8, no. 2, 1915.

SCHROEDER, THEODORE. *The Sex-Determinant in Mormon Theology*. New York, 1908.

SCOTT, WINFIELD. *Memoirs*. New York, 1864.

Scrapbook of Newspaper Clippings Relating to Mormons. N. Y. Public Library.

Scraps of Biography. Juvenile Instructor Office, S. L. City, 1883.

Seer, The. Vols. 1 and 2. Washington, D. C., 1853 and 1854.

SLATER, N. *Fruits of Mormonism*. Coloma, California, 1851.

SMITH, JOSEPH. *Correspondence Between Joseph Smith, the Prophet, and Col. John Wentworth, James Arlington Bennet, and John C. Calhoun*. New York, 1844.

SMITH, JOSEPH. *History of the Church of Jesus Christ of Latter-Day Saints. Period I. History of Joseph Smith, the Prophet, By Himself*. Vols. 1-6. S. L. City, 1902 ff.

SMITH, JOSEPH. *Views of the Powers and Policy of the Government of the United States*. Pittsburgh, 1844.

SMITH, JOSEPH. *The Voice of Truth*. Nauvoo, Ill., 1844.

SMITH, LUCY. *Biographical Sketches of Joseph Smith, the Prophet, and His Progenitors for Many Generations*. Liverpool, 1853.

SMOOT, REED. *Proceedings before the Committee on Privileges and Elections of the United States Senate*, four volumes. Washington, 1904.

SNOW, ERASTUS. *Discourse on the Utah Pioneers*. S. L. City, 1880.

SNOW, ELIZA R. *Biography and Family Record of Lorenzo Snow*. S. L. City, 1884.

SNOW, ELIZA R. *Poems*, two volumes. S. L. City.

SNYDER, DR. J. F. "Governor Ford and His Family." *Journal of the Illinois State Hist. Society*, July, 1910, vol. 3, no. 2. Springfield.

STANTON, Rev. W. A. *Three Important Movements*. Philadelphia, 1907.

STENHOUSE, T. B. H. *The Rocky Mountain Saints*. New York, 1873.

STENHOUSE, MRS. T. B. H. *An Englishwoman Among the Mormons*. London, 1882.

STEVENSON, ELDER EDWARD. *Reminiscences of Joseph, the Prophet*. S. L. City, 1893.

STRANG, JAMES JESSE. *The Diamond: Being the Law of Prophetic Succession*. Voree, Wisconsin, 1848.

STRANG, JAMES JESSE. *The Prophetic Controversy*. 1854.

TEMPLE, SALT LAKE. *House of the Lord, Historical and Descriptive Sketch*. S. L. City, 1897.

THOMPSON, CHARLES. *Evidences in Proof of the Book of Mormon*. Batavia, N. Y., 1841.

Times and Seasons. Vols. 1-6. Nauvoo, Ill., 1840-1846.

TOWLE, NANCY. *Vicissitudes Illustrated*. Portsmouth, 1833.

TUCKER, POMEROY. *Origin, Rise and Progress of Mormonism*. New York, 1867.

TULLIDGE, EDWARD W. *Life of Brigham Young*. New York, 1876.

TULLIDGE, EDWARD W. "The Reformation in Utah." *Harper's Magazine*, 1871, vol. 43.

TYLER, DANIEL. *A Concise History of the Mormon Battalion in the Mexican War*. S. L. City, 1881.

Utah Genealogical and Historical Magazine, vol. 11. 1920.

Voice from the West, A. San Francisco, 1879.

Voree Herald, vol. 1, no. 9, Voree, Wisconsin. 1846.

WARD, ARTEMUS. *Artemus Ward, His Book*. New York, 1862.

WARD, ARTEMUS. *Artemus Ward's Lecture*. London, 1869.

WARD, ARTEMUS. *Artemus Ward; His Travels*. New York, 1865.

Warsaw Signal. Warsaw, Illinois, 1844-1845.

WEBB, ROBERT C. *The Real Mormonism*. New York, 1916.

WHITE, STEWART EDWARD. *The Forty-Niners*. Yale University Press. 1920.

WHITING, LILIAN. *Kate Field A Record*. Boston, 1899.

WITMER, ELDER DAVID. *An Address to All Believers in Christ*. Richmond, Missouri, 1887.

WHITNEY, ORSON F. *Life of Heber C. Kimball*. S. L. City.

WHITNEY, ORSON F. *The Mormon Prophet's Tragedy*. S. L. City, 1905.

WHITNEY, ORSON F. *History of Utah*, four volumes. S. L. City.

WOODRUFF, WILFORD. *Leaves from My Journal*. S. L. City, 1909.

WRIGHT, THOMAS. *The Life of Sir Richard Burton*. London, 1906.

WYL, DR. W. *Mormon Portraits*. S. L. City, 1886.

YOUNG, ANN ELIZA. *Wife No. 19*. Hartford, Conn., 1875.

YOUNG, BRIGHAM. *Death of President Brigham Young*. S. L. City, 1877.

YOUNG, BRIGHAM. *Fraud on the Will*. S. L. City.

YOUNG, BRIGHAM. *Pictures and Biographies of Brigham Young and His Wives*. S. L. City.

YOUNG, BRIGHAM. *Brigham Young's Will*. S. L. City.

YOUNG, BRIGHAM. *Life of, Anonymous*. S. L. City, 1893.

YOUNG, LEVI EDGAR. *The Founding of Utah*. New York, 1923.

Zion's Reveille. Voree, Wisconsin, 1847.

INDEX

471